HISTORY OF BALLARAT

and

SOME BALLARAT REMINISCENCES

William Bramwell Withers

History of Ballarat and Some Ballarat Reminiscences,
Facsimile Edition
Published by Ballarat Heritage Services, 1999
From the original Edition W. B. Withers, History of Ballarat,
First published 1870
And W. B. Withers, Some Ballarat Reminiscences,
First published 1895/96

ISBN   1 876478 78 0

This publication is presented on paper containing archival properties. The original lithograph, hand-folded and inserted in the front of this publication, has been reproduced from the 1870 Special Edition History of Ballarat, of which only 100 copies were produced.

Printed in Ballarat by F.R.P. Printing Pty. Ltd. Wendouree
Bound by Ristori Bookbindery, Allendale

CONTENTS

View of Ballarat, 1870

Introduction

Contents

William Withers, Ballarat Historian

Photographs of Ballarat Pioneers

Preface   v-ix

List of Illustrations, Plans, &c   xi

Appendices   xiii-xv

Table of Contents

History of Ballarat by W. B. Withers   1-216

Peter Lalor (photograph)   125

Charles Joseph La Trobe (photograph)   216a

Charles Hotham (photograph)   216b

Some Ballarat Reminiscences by
W. B. Withers   217-275

Index   276-290

WILLIAM B. WITHERS Esq

WILLIAM WITHERS
BALLARAT HISTORIAN

The first significant chronicle of Ballarat's history was the publication of William Bramwell Withers' *History of Ballarat* in 1870. W.B. Withers arrived in Ballarat in 1855, and lived in this city for almost fifty years. He was therefore uniquely placed to chronicle Ballarat's history.

Withers was born on the twenty-seventh of July 1823, at Whitchurch, Hampshire, England, and was the youngest son of a tenant farmer and Methodist lay preacher, Jason Withers.

William Withers was educated at a grammar school until the age of thirteen when he was apprenticed to his uncle, who was a general storekeeper at Winchester. His penchant for writing showed early and in 1846 he wrote articles for temperance and vegetarian journals.

He migrated to Natal, South Africa in 1849, after purchasing three hundred acres with a legacy. But the solitude did not suit him so he became a writer, and eventually migrated to Australia on the *Hannah* in November 1852.

Like so many prospectors he walked to Ballarat, but failed in his attempt to strike it rich, and returned to Melbourne. Withers worked as a journalist in Melbourne, in 1854 on the *Argus* and *Herald*, before moving to Ballarat in July 1855. He worked as a reporter and part time compositor on the *Ballarat Times*, and was employed on the twenty-second of September 1855, by the editor of the newly founded Ballarat *Star*, quickly establishing a solid reputation with the newspaper.

He was described as a 'fluent and scholarly journalist' who often spiced his reporting with appealing humour and, as a mining correspondent, he documented business and investment in the booming township of Ballarat for both the *Star* and *Miner & Weekly Star* newspapers. In 1859 he was elected to the first committee of the Ballarat Mechanics' Institute. Domestically he shared a comfortable home with Mrs. Mary Dusatoy in Lyons Street, Ballarat.

Withers decided to write a history of Ballarat, and corresponded with early pioneers of the goldfields, and participants and witnesses of the Eureka Stockade, as well as surviving early squatters. His *History of Ballarat* was published as a twelve part series in 1870, and was so popular that a bound book was printed and immediately sold out.

He became part owner of the Ballarat *Star*, wrote several novels, and then transferred his talents to *The Courier*. His best book, *History of Ballarat*, was reprinted in 1887.

In the late 1800s Victoria was enjoying heady days; economic, political and cultural affairs were going through many changes, and the proposed Commonwealth of Australia was moving into view. The Mechanics' Institute, Art Gallery, School of Mines, and various debating societies were all well established Ballarat institutions, which provided avenues for self advancement and education.

Withers and the Ballarat-based Australian Historical Records Society, which later became known as the Ballarat Historical Society, were both interested in similar things, and in many ways led Australia in Australian History.

In the latter half of the nineteenth century no self-respecting school taught Australian history, and indeed there was a widely held view that the colonies of Australia did not have a history. Many people still regarded England as "home". This situation continued to prevail long after the local born population outnumbered immigrants.

Thus, Ballarat's first historian broke new ground in 1870 with the publication of his book. Several other cities, including Warrnambool, subsequently had their early history written by journalists.

A century ago Ballarat had the benefit of William Bramwell Withers' keen insight, and the enthusiasm of several local organisations, which actively promoted the importance of Ballarat.

In 1901 Withers left his beloved Ballarat and removed to Sydney where he was living with Mrs. Dusatoy and her son, William Leslie Withers Dusatoy, but he continued to write for the Ballarat *Courier*.

He returned to England in 1903 and enjoyed a nostalgic return visit to Winchester, which he chronicled in the Ballarat *Star*. Withers died of a cerebral haemorrhage at Dulwich Hill, Sydney, on the fourteenth of July 1913 and was buried in the Anglican section of Rookwood cemetery.

Peter Butters
Peter Mansfield

W. H. Bacchus.   Thos. Waldie.   John Winter.

Thos. L. Learmonth.   Dr. A. Thompson.   S. L. Learmonth.

Archd. Ficken.   W. H. Pettett.   Rev. Thos. Hastie.

PORTRAITS OF SOME OF THE EARLY PASTORAL SETTLERS

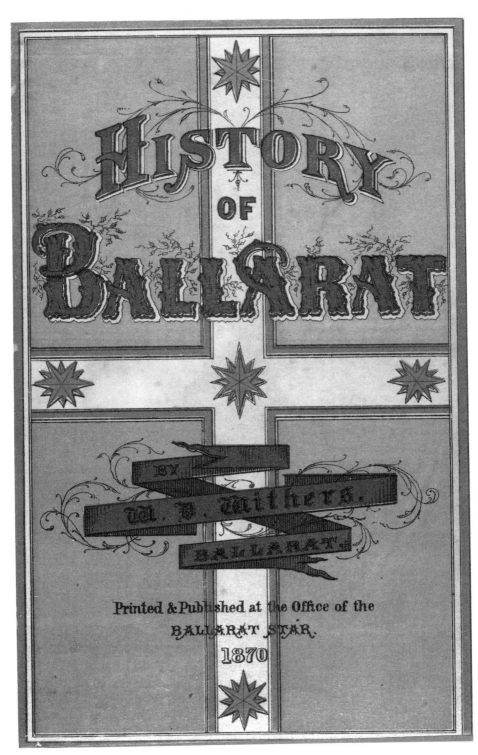

HISTORY

OF

BALLARAT

BY
W. B. Withers.

BALLARAT

Printed & Published at the Office of the
BALLARAT STAR.
1870

L. N.

TO YOUR MEMORY,

WHOSE

FRAGRANCE

"NO TIME CAN CHANGE,'

I REVERENTLY DEDICATE

THIS RECORD

OF

CHANGE.

PREFACE.

THIS little History, in eight chapters, only touches a few of the more prominent incidents connected with pastoral settlement and the gold discovery in the Ballarat district. The compiler has seen the growth of the town from a mere collection of canvas tents among the trees and on the grassy slopes and flats of the wild bush to its present condition. Less than twenty years ago there was not a house where now stands this wealthy mine and farm-girdled city, whose population is nearly equal to the united populations of Oxford and Cambridge, and exceeding by several thousands the united populations of the cities of Winchester, Canterbury, Salisbury, and Lichfield at the time of the gold discovery. This is one of the truths which are magnificently stranger than fiction.

Some of the first workers in this mighty creation are still here. Of the pastoral pioneers there are still with us the Messrs. Learmonth, Pettett, Waldie, Winter, Fisken, Coghill, and Bacchus; and the Rev. Thomas Hastie is still living at the Manse at Buninyong.

Down the valley of the Leigh, where the Sebastopol streets and fences run over the eastern escarpment of the table land, may still be seen the sandstone foundations of a station begun by the Messrs. Yuille, whom the coming of the first hosts of gold-hunters scared away from a place no longer fit, in their opinion, for pastoral occupation. Those unfinished walls are in a paddock overlooking a little carse of some four or five acres by the creek side, owned by an Italian farmer, and close to the junction of the Woolshed Creek with the main stream in the valley. On the other side of the larger stream rise basaltic mounds, marked with the pits and banks of the earlier miners. Like the trenches of an old battle-field, these works of the digging armies of the past are now grass-grown and spotted with wild flowers. All around, the open lands of fifteen years ago are turned into streets and fields and gardens. A little way lower down the valley, where the ground has a broad slope up from the left bank of the Leigh to the foot of the ranges, was the Magpie rush of 1855-6. For a mile nearly every inch of frontage was fought for then, and a town of over four thousand inhabitants sprang up. Gold was found plentifully, and warehouse, hotel, and saloon crowded close with dwelling and church along the thoroughfare. A summer flood surprised the dwellers on the lowland and carried off lives as well as property, mingling a tragic sorrow with the losses of the unsuccessful. Time, less sudden than the midsummer freshet, but more sweeping, has cleared the ground of almost every vestige of the busy but fragile life of fifteen years ago. But the eternal sense of the Infinite survives "our little lives" and all their fitful pulsations of varying passion. Yonder, where, by the bush track side, the rounding slope swells upon the south, stands a church, sombre, lonely, and silent as the Roman sentinel at Pompeii when all around him had fled or fallen. This is all, save here and there heaps of broken bottles and sardine tins half hidden by the grass, and a few faint trench and building lines, softened by the rains, and bright at this time with the young verdure of the turning season. The most curious eye could now discover no other traces of the rush if it were not for the broader and 'deeper marks left where the first miners fought their industrial way, and where, for years, their followers retraced the golden trail. On going up the Yarrowee banks northward a space, as one looks up the valley he sees, beyond the city, the bare top, the white artificial chasms and banks and mounds, where Black Hill raised its dark dense head of forest trees before the digger rent the hill in twain, and half disembowelled the swelling headland.

Besides the pastoral settlers already mentioned, there are yet with us some of the first discoverers. Esmond is still here. Woodward and Turner, of the Golden Point discoverers, are still here in Ballarat, and Merrick and some others of that band remain in the district. Others who followed them within the first week or two are also amongst our busy townsfolk of to-day.

While these remained it was thought desirable to gather some of the honey of fact from fugitive opportunity, that it might be garnered for the historian of the future. Nearly all the persons whose names have been mentioned above have assisted in the preparation of this narrative by furnishing valuable contributions from their own recollections, and the compiler takes this occasion to thank them and others, including legal managers of mines, whose ready courtesy has enabled him to do what he has done to rescue from forgetfulness the brief details here chronicled touching the history of this gold-field. He has borrowed some facts and figures, too, from Mr. Harrie Wood's ably compiled notes, published in Mr. Brough Smyth's "Gold-fields and Mineral Districts of Victoria." To the officers of most of the public institutions referred to he also owes the acknowledgment of much courtesy; and to Mr. Huyghue, a gentleman still holding office in Ballarat, and who was in the public service here at the time of the Eureka Stockade, thanks are due, both by the publisher and compiler, for notes of that period, and for the extremely interesting illustrations of the Stockade, the Camp, and other spots, copied from original drawings. The publisher also acknowledges the courtesy of Mr. Ferres, the Government printer, in supplying original documents, and of Mr. Noone in giving valuable assistance in connection with their re-production by the photo-lithographic process. The contributions of newspaper correspondents during the Eureka Stockade troubles have also assisted the compiler, and notably the letters of the correspondent of the *Geelong Advertiser* in 1854-5. But to Mr. John Noble Wilson, the commercial manager of the *Ballarat Star*, is due, on the part of all concerned, the recognition of his suggesting the narrative, of his constant cordial co-operation, and his untiring ingenuity in making suggestions and collecting materials both for the text and the illustrations. The re-produced proclamations by the Government, which the reader will find at intervals, as well as many of the original documents, are the fruit of that gentleman's assiduity in collecting materials of interest and pertinence.

It has been necessary to record the fact that the tragic issue of the license agitation was mainly due to the mistakes of the governing authorities, even as the unrighteous rigors of the digger-hunting processes were made more poignant by the haughty indiscretions and brutal excesses of commissioners and troopers. But it is equally incumbent on the recorder to recognise the more agreeable fact that there were officers in both grades who did their harsh duties differently. Some of these are still in the service, and retain the respect they won in the more troublous times by their judicious and humane administration of an obnoxious law, for the existence of which they were in no way responsible.

In the matter of gold statistics there has been found great difficulty, for the early records were imperfect, and the later ones are little, if in anywise, superior; while searches for the first newspaper accounts of the gold discovery have shown that, both in Melbourne and Geelong, the public files have been rifled of invaluable portions by the miserable meanness of some unknown thieves.

The future we have not essayed to divine. What the past and the present of our local history may do to enable the reader to speculate upon the future, each one must for himself determine, though the faith of the Ballarat of to-day in the Ballarat of the future may, we think, be more accurately inferred from the stable monuments of civic enterprise, and the many signs of mining, manufacturing, and rural industry around, than from the occasional forebodings of fear in seasons of depression. In less than two decades we have created a large city, built up great fortunes, laid the foundations of many commercial successes, and sown the seeds of yet undeveloped industries; and those who have seen so much should not readily think that we are near the exhaustion of our resources, either in the precious minerals, or the still more precious spirit of enterprise and industry necessary for the development of the wealth of nature around us. For the good done, and for the doers of the good, we may all be thankful, if not proud; and, in proportion as we are thus moved, we may look with confident hope towards the future, whose uncertain years are lit up with the radiance of the past, and shaped to our vision by the promise of the present.

Among modest writers it is the fashion not only to write prefaces, but to excite attention to wonderful merit by apologies for defects. The present writer burns to be in the fashion. He craves the indulgence of the reader in informing that important personage that the ordinary duties of a reporter on a daily morning paper are not luxuriously light, and that the compilation of the following narrative has been a refreshing appendage to the daily discharge of such ordinary duties, *plus* a bracing exercise of sub-editorial function. He has, no doubt, amply vindicated Bolingbroke's accurate apothegm, and especially in this preface. Both preface and narrative may be regarded as a verbose exaggeration of the importance of the subject. The answer to that is, that the writer has written mainly for those who know the place, and, knowing it, are proud of it; for those who believe in the future in reserve for it, for the colony to which it belongs to-day, and for the empire of which it some day may be a not altogether unimportant portion.

In the City of York, where memory and fancy, busy with the records and the remains of the past, make of the softened lights and shadows and many-colored figures of mediæval English history an inexpressible charm, the glorious Minster rises over all supreme in its solemn and saintly beauty. Whatever pilgrim there has studiously perused that marvellous "poem in stone" may have seen over one of the doorways the work of some loving and pious egotist in the following inscription :—" Ut rosa flos florum, sic tu es domus domorum." Let us be permitted, with similar egotism, if not with equal piety, to inscribe here, as over one of the portals of approach to one of the golden fields and cities of Victoria :—Ut aurum metallorum pretiosissimum, sic tu es camporum aureorum princeps, urbiumque opulentissima.

W. B. W.

Ballarat, 22nd June, 1870.

LIST OF ILLUSTRATIONS, PLAN, &C.

Ballarat : Looking East from Lyons Street. — General View from
        Black Hill to Mount Buninyong, embracing all the sources of
        the early gold discoveries. (*Frontispiece*)

Withers Portrait

Ballarat Pioneers Portraits

The Gravel Pits, 1854

Verns "Plan of Organisation for the Diggers"

The Government Camp, 1854 — Troops arriving from Melbourne

The Governor's Proclamation of the 2nd December, 1854

The French Consul's Notice to French residents

Plan of Attack on the Eureka Stockade, 1854

Plan Showing the Site of the Eureka Stockade, 1870

Proclamation issued by "Robert Rede" on the morning of Sunday,
        after the attack

Proclamation of Martial Law

Lalor Photographic Portrait

Requisition to the Mayor of Melbourne to call a public meeting " for
        taking measures for the better protection of the city, &c."

Section of the Shaft of an Alluvial mine (The Nelson and Wellington
        Company, Frenchman's Lead)

Section of Quartz Reef workings, Old Post Office Hill

"View of Ballarat, 1858, "showing what at that time was a tolerably
        correct representation of the western part of the town —
        fac simile of an old Lithograph

La Trobe Photographic Portrait

Hotham Photographic Portrait

APPENDICES.

Appendix A. REWARDS TO GOLD DISCOVERERS.

Appendix B. ELECTIONS FOR THE LEGISLATIVE ASSEMBLY.

Appendix C. JOURNALISM UNDER DIFFICULTIES.

Appendix D. FIRST SALES OF BALLARAT LAND.

Appendix E. THE INSURGENT FLAG AND SOME OTHER EUREKA
STOCKADE MATTERS.

Appendix F. AGRICULTURAL AND PASTORAL STATISTICS.

Appendix G. ESMOND STILL A WORKING MAN.

Appendix H. FLOODS IN BALLARAT EAST.

Appendix I. MAGPIE RUSH.

Appendix J. LOCAL COURT OBITUARY.

Appendix K. LETTERS BY VERN.

Appendix L. OLD AND NEW GRAVEYARDS.

Appendix M. MINING TIMBER, GUTTER FOSSILS, EARLY FACTS.

Appendix N. POPULATION RETURNS.

Appendix O. MURDER OF MR. FRANCIS.

Appendix P. CHARACTER OF THE MINERS.

Appendix Q. CHINESE IN BALLARAT.

Appendix R. OFFICIAL AGENT'S WINDING-UP RETURNS.

Appendix S. THE DIGGERS' TEN COMMANDMENTS.

TABLE OF CONTENTS.

CHAPTER I.

BALLARAT BEFORE THE GOLD DISCOVERY.

First Exploring Parties.—Mount Buninyong.—Mount Aitkin.—Ercildoun.—Ballarat.—Lake Burrumbeet Dry.—Settling throughout the District.—First Wheat Grown.—First Flour Mill.—Founding of Buninyong.—A Wide Diocese.—Appearance of Ballarat.—The Natives. — Aboriginal Names. — The Squatters. — Premonitions of the Gold Discovery.   ...   .   1—13

CHAPTER II.

THE GOLD DISCOVERY.

California and the Ural.—Predictions of Australian Gold.—Discoveries of Old Bushmen.—Hargreaves and others in New South Wales.—Effects of Discovery at Bathurst.—Sir C. A. Fitz Roy's Despatches.—First Assay.—Esmond and Hargreaves.—Esmond's Discovery at Clunes.—Previous Victorian Discoveries.—Esmond's the First Made Effectively Public.—Hiscock.—Golden Point, Ballarat.—Claims of Discoverers as to Priority.—Effects of the Discovery.—Mr. Latrobe's Despatches.—His Visit to Ballarat.—The Licenses.—Change of Scene at Ballarat.—Mount Alexander Rush.—Fresh Excitements.—Rise in Prices.   ...   .   14—31

CHAPTER III.

FROM THE GOLD DISCOVERY TO THE YEAR OF THE EUREKA STOCKADE.

Great Aggregations of Population.—Opening up of Golden Grounds.—Character of the Population.—Dates of Local Discoveries.—Ballarat Township Proclaimed.—First Sales of Land.—Bath's Hotel.—First Public Clock.—Primitive Stores, Offices, and Conveyances. Woman a Phenomenon.—First Women at Ballarat.—Curious Monetary Devices.—First Religious Services. — Churches. — Newspapers. — Theatres. — Lawyers. — First Courts.—Nuggets.—Golden Gutters.—Thirty or Forty Thousand Persons Located.   ...   32—46

CHAPTER IV.

DIGGER HUNTING.

The Gold License.—Taxation Without Representation.—Unequal Incidence of the Tax.—Episodes of Digger Hunting.—Irritating Method of Enforcing the Tax.—Suspicions of Corruption among the Magistrates and Police.—Visit of Sir Charles and Lady Hotham.—Big Larry.—Reform League.—Murder of Scobie.—Acquittal of Bentley.—Dewes

Suspected.—Mass Meetings.—Burning of Bentley's Hotel.—Irwin's Narrative.—Arrest of
Fletcher, M'Intyre, and Westerby.—Re-arrest of Bentley.—Conviction of Bentley.—
Conviction of Fletcher, M'Intyre, and Westerby.—Demand for their Liberation.—
Increased Excitement.—Fete to the American Consul.—Foster.—Sir Charles Hotham.
—Arrival of Troops.—Troops Assaulted.—Bakery Hill Meeting.—Southern Cross Flag.—
Burning the Licenses. ...   .   47—64

CHAPTER V.

THE   EUREKA   STOCKADE.

The Last Digger Hunt.—Collision between the Diggers and Military and Police.—Southern
Cross Flag again.—Lalor and his Companions Armed, kneel, and swear mutual Defence.
—Irwin's Account.—Carboni Raffaello.—His Pictures of the Times and the Men.—More
Troops Arrive.—The Diggers Extend their Organisation Under Arms.--Lalor "Com-
mander-in-Chief."—Forage and Impressment Parties.—Original Documents.- Shots Fired
from the Camp.—The Stockade Formed.—Narrative of a Government Officer in the
Camp.—Attack by the Military and Taking of the Stockade.—Various Accounts of the
Time.—Raffaello's Description.—Another Tragic Picture.—List of the Killed.—Burials.
—Rewards Offered for the Insurgent Leaders.—Their Hiding and Escape.—Charge
Against A. P. Akehurst. — Proclamation of Martial Law. — Feeling in Melbourne.—
Foster's Resignation.—Deputation of Diggers.—Humffray Arrested.—Vote of Thanks to
the Troops.—Legislative Council's Address to the Governor.—His Reply.—Prisoners at
the Ballarat Police-court.—Royal Commission of Enquiry.—Trial and Acquittal of the
State Prisoners.—Humffray.—Lalor and his Captain.—Cost of the Struggle.—Subsequent
Celebrations.—Monument.—The Burial Places.—Death of Sir Charles Hotham.   65—107

CHAPTER VI.

POLITICAL   DEVELOPMENT.

Ballarat Politically Active and Influential.—New Constitution.—Humffray and Lalor
Elected.—Their Addresses.—Humffray in Trouble.—Lalor on Democracy.—Petition for a
Private Property Mining Law.—Neglect by the Parliaments of Mining Interests.—Pro-
bable Causes.—New Political Demands.—Votes of Lalor and Humffray.—Burial Expenses
of Governor Hotham.—O'Shanassy Chief Secretary.— Haines Succeeds with M'Culloch as
Commissioner of Customs.—O'Shanassy in Power Again.—Nicholson Cabinet.—Succeeded
by Heales with Humffray as First Minister of Mines.—O'Shanassy in Power Again.—
Succeeded by M'Culloch.—The Tariff.—Re-call of Governor Darling,—Darling Grant
Crisis.—Death of Governor Darling.—Grant to his Widow and Family.—Sladen Ministry.
—M'Culloch in Power Again.—Representative Charges.—Jones Declared Corrupt.—
Defeats Vale.—The Macpherson Ministry.—Its Resignation.—Macgregor's Failure.—
M'Culloch and Macpherson in Office together.—Michie Elected for Ballarat West.—
Local Court.—Mining Board.—Court of Mines.—Local Courts Wrongly Constituted.
—Mining Boards Not Now Necessary.—One Code of Mining Law Required.--Valuable
Services of the Earlier Courts and Boards.   ...   .   108—125

CHAPTER VII.

DEVELOPMENT   OF   MINING.

Block and Frontage Claims.—Election Excitements.—White Flat Company.—Opposition
to Extended Areas.—Such Opposition a Mistake.—Present Areas.—Progress of Mining

TABLE OF CONTENTS.   XV

Discoveries.—Increased Operative Difficulties.—Introduction of Machinery.—The Corner,
—Wide Operations of Ballarat Capital and Enterprise.—Occasional Excesses.—Koh-i-Noor,
Band and Albion Consols, Prince of Wales, and St. George Companies.—Transitions.—
Great Depression.—Fall of Two Millions sterling in Mining Stocks.—Equal to Fifty
Years' Purchase of the Annual Revenue of the City.—Or Two-thirds of the Annual
Revenue of Victoria.—Projects for Co-operation of Labor and Capital.—Old Mining
Institute.—School of Mines.—Mining Reform Association.—Miners' Association.—Mr.
Serjeant's Sabbath Observance Bill.—Tables of Gold Returns and Mining Statistics.—
Pre-eminence of the Ballarat District.—Westgarth on the Purity of Ballarat Gold.—Assays
of Ballarat Nuggets.—Table of Nugget Dates, Weights, and Localities.—Increasing pro-
portion of Quartz Gold.—The Future to be Chiefly Quartz Mining.—The Black Hill
Quartz Company.   ...   .   126—150

CHAPTER VIII.

THE   TOWN   OF   BALLARAT.

Area and Population of the Town.—Borough Statistics of Ballarat West, Ballarat East,
and Sebastopol.—Water Supply.—Hospital.—Benevolent Asylum.—Orphan Asylum.—
Churches. — Eistedfodd. — Schools. — Recreation Grounds. — Ballarat Cricket Club.—
Mechanics' Institute. — Public Library. — Chamber of Commerce. — Theatre Royal.—
Musical Societies.—Fire Brigades.—Ballarat Rangers and Cavalry.—Gas Company.—
Horticultural Society.—Agricultural and Pastoral Society.—Statistics of Produce and
Stock.—Meat Preserving Company.—Banks.—Mining Exchange.—The Gaol.—The
Camp.—Last of the Military.—Post Offices and Treasury.—Electric Telegraph.—
Explorers' Memorial.—Caledonian Society.—Hibernian Society.—Prince Alfred's Visit.
Magdalen Refuge.—Ladies' Benevolent Society.—Temperance Hall.—Alfred Hall.—
Railway.—Shire Councils and Road Boards.—Ballarat, Sandhurst, and Geelong.—Past
and Present Contrasts.   ...   .   151—185

ERRATA.

Page 110.—*For* Romano-British Caerlon *read* Romano-British Caerleon.

Page 118.—*For* Edwin Charles Jones *read* Charles Edwin Jones.

Page 136.—*In line* 11, *for* It raised, &c., *read* The Band of Hope Company raised, &c.

In line 20, *after* The No. 3 *read* Consols. *Also after* No. 4 *in next line.*

In line 27, *for* 1869 *read* 1868, *and for* United Hand-in-Hand and Band of Hope *read* Band of Hope. [It should have been stated also that the Consols Company has a No. 5 Shaft, which was sunk in 1868 at a cost of £2,000 4s 8d.]

Page 137.—*In line* 19, *after* expended the sum of £564,514 17s 9d *read* inclusive of dividends.

Page 144.—The table of returns by the Mining Department as to the value of machinery will afford the statistical student matter for comparison with our remarks at page 143 as to the incompleteness of such returns. Thus, for Ballarat, 358 engines with an aggregate of 9,829 horse-power are valued at £595,513 ; and, for Sandhurst, 186 engines with an aggregate of 1.949 horse-power, or less than one-fifth that of Ballarat, are valued at £427,867 !

HISTORY OF BALLARAT.

CHAPTER I.

BALLARAT BEFORE THE GOLD DISCOVERY.

First Exploring Parties.—Mount Buninyong.—Mount Aitkin.—Ercildoun.—Ballarat.—Lake Burrumbeet Dry.—Settling throughout the District.—First Wheat Grown.—First Flour Mill.—Founding of Buninyong.—A Wide Diocese.—Appearance of Ballarat.—The Natives.—Aboriginal Names.—The Squatters.—Premonitions of the Gold Discovery.

ALLARAT is one of the wonders of this century. Young in years its mutations have been many and rapid, and its marvellous progress has given to it a seeming antiquity beyond its urban years. Our task is to trace an outline of the rise and progress of this golden city. This task takes us back to days that seem, in the swift march of colonial events, to belong already to a remote antiquity. While the sailor-King William IV. was but newly buried, and Queen Victoria was still an uncrowned maiden; while only a few rude huts, sprinkled about the still uncleared slopes and gullies, failed to scare away the native animals that haunted the bush where the City of Melbourne now stands; while the pleasant borders of the Bay of Corio, where Geelong is to-day, were not graced by a single house, but only bore on their silent slopes a few scattered tents, a small band of settlers started from the Corio shore to explore the unknown country to the north-west. This was in the month of August, 1837. The party comprised Mr Thomas Livingstone Learmonth; Mr D'Arcy, a surveyor; Dr. Thompson, late of Geelong; Mr David Fisher, then manager of the Derwent Company, Tasmania; Captain Hutton, of the East

B

India Company's Service; and Mr Henry Anderson. With them
they took suitable equipment and provisions. From Bellpost Hill
they saw in the distance, north-westward, a mount, to which they
directed their course, steering their way by compass, and thus they
arrived at and ascended Mount Buninyong. From the Mount the
explorers saw fine country to the north-westward, Lake Burrumbeet,
and the distant ranges of the Pyrenees and the Grampians. An ocean
of forest, with island hills, was all around them, but not a speck visible
that spoke to them of civilisation. But the promising landscape
drew the explorers on westward and north-westward. They descended
the Mount, the party divided, their compass-bearings were not well
kept, the provision-cart failed to be at the appointed rendezvous,
and thus, broken into sections, the explorers found their way back
to the coast, some of them unable to find their provisions, and
therefore fasting by the way.

In January of the next year explorers set out again. The party
this time consisted of Messrs J. Aitken, Henry Anderson, Thomas
L. Learmonth, Somerville L. Learmonth, and William Yuille. The
starting point was Mr Aitken's house, at Mount Aitken, and thence
the explorers went towards Mount Alexander, which at that time had
just been occupied by a party of overlanders from Sydney, consisting
of Messrs C. H. Ebden, Yaldwin, and Mollison. From Mount
Alexander they followed the course of the Loddon, passed over what
has since been proved to be a rich auriferous country, and bore down
on a prominent peak, which the explorers subsequently called
Ercildoun, from the old keep on the Scottish border, with which the
name of the Learmonths' ancestor, Thomas the Rhymer, was
associated. Their course brought them to the lake district of
Burrumbeet and its rich natural pastures. The days were hot
but the nights cold, and the party, camping at night on an eminence
near Ercildoun, suffered so much from cold that they gave the
camping place the name Mount Misery. There was water then in
Burrumbeet, but it was intensely salt and very shallow. Next
year, 1839, Lake Burrumbeet was quite dry, and it remained dry for
several succeeding summers. It was covered with rank vegetation,
and the ground afforded excellent pasture after the ranker growth
had been burnt off. The country thus discovered was occupied
during the year 1838, and other settlers, pushing on in the same

direction, in a couple of years completed the occupation of all the fine pastoral country as far westward as the Hopkins River. The brothers Learmonth, Mr Henry Anderson, Messrs Archibald and W. C. Yuille, and Mr Waldie settled on the subsequently revealed gold-fields of Ballarat, Buninyong, Sebastopol, and their immediate vicinities. Some members of the Clyde Company, of Tasmania, visited the Western district in 1838, that company giving the name to the Clyde Inn, of the old Geelong coach road. They settled upon the Moorabool and the Leigh, Mr George Russell being the manager. Major Mercer, who gave the name to Mount Mercer, and Mr D. Fisher, were of that company. The Narmbool run, near Meredith, was taken by Mr Neville in 1839. Ross' Creek was named from Capt. Ross, who in those early days used to perform the feat of walking in Highland costume all the way to Melbourne. But in those times travelling was a more serious matter than in these days of railroads, coaches, cabs, and other vehicles, with good roads and a generally settled country. Then there were no roads, few people, and a thick forest, encumbered about Ballarat, too, with the native hop. Mr Archibald Fisken, of Lal Lal, was the first person to drive a vehicle through the then roadless forest of Warrenheip and Bullarook. In 1846 he drove a dog-cart tandem with Mr W. Taylor through the bush to Longerenong, on the Wimmera.

Messrs T. L. and S. L. Learmonth, whose father was then in Hobarton, settled their homestead on what is now known as the Buninyong Gold Mining Company's ground at Buninyong. Mr Henry Anderson, who was the earliest pioneer in what is now known as Winter's Flat, planted his homestead near the delta formed by the confluence of the Woolshed Creek and the Yarrowee, Messrs Yuille subsequently taking that homestead and all the country now known as Ballarat West and East and Sebastopol. These settlers gave the name to Yuille's Swamp, more recently called Lake Wendouree. The Bonshaw run was taken up by Mr Anderson, who named it Waverley Park, and Mr John Winter coming into possession shortly afterwards gave to it the present name, after his wife's home in Scotland. Messrs Pettett and Francis, in 1838 (as managers for Mr W. H. T. Clarke), took up the country at Dowling Forest, so called after Mrs Clarke's maiden name. Shortly after they had settled there Mr Francis was killed by one of his own

B 2

men with a shear-blade, at one of the stations on the run. Before
Mr Pettett took up the Dowling Forest run he was living at the
Little River, and a native chief named Balliang offered to show
him the country about Lal Lal. The chief in speaking of it
distinguished between it and the Little River by describing the
water as La-al La-al—the *a* long—and by gesture indicating the
water-fall now so well known, the name signifying falling water.
Mr Waldie subsequently took up country north-west of Ballarat,
and called his place Wyndholm, where he has resided ever since.
Messrs Yuille had settled originally on the Barwon, near Inverleigh,
but finding the natives troublesome they retired to Ballarat. Mr
Smythe, who with Mr Prentice held the run, gave the name to
Smythe's Creek, as Messrs Baillie had to the creek at Carngham,
their run there being afterwards transferred to Messrs Russell and
Simson. Mr Darlot also occupied a run there. Creswick Creek has
its name from Henry Creswick, who settled upon a small run there.
Two brothers Creswick had previously held country close to
Warrenheip. The Messrs Baillie were sons of Sir William
Baillie, Bart., of Polkemmet, Scotland. Mr Andrew Scott settled
with his family at the foot of Mount Buninyong, where he had
a snug run in which the mount and its rich surrounding soil were
included. Mrs Andrew Scott was the first lady who travelled
through this district. She drove across the dry bed of Lake
Burrumbeet in the year 1840. The country about Smeaton and
Coghill's Creek was taken up in the year 1838 by Captain Hepburn
and Mr David Coghill who came overland from New South Wales
with sheep and cattle, following the route of Sir Thomas Mitchell in
his expedition of exploration in Port Phillip in 1836. With them
came Mr Bowman, who also brought stock. He took up a run on
the Campaspe, while his companions came on further south. The
Murray was very low when they crossed, and the stock was easily
passed over. At the Ovens they found a dry river-bed ; Lake
Burrumbeet was also dry that year. When Messrs Hepburn and
Coghill had left sheep at the Campaspe and Brown's Creek on their
way, they pushed on, and from Mount Alexander they descried the
Smeaton Hills, and, continuing their journey, found and took up
the unoccupied country there. Smeaton Hill was called Quaratwong
by the natives, and the hill between the Glenlyon road and Smeaton

Hill was called Moorakoil. Captain Hepburn, a seafaring man originally, was one of the Hepburns of East Lothian, Scotland, and Smeaton was named by him after the East Lothian estate held by his relative, Sir Thomas Hepburn. Mr Coghill was the first to plough land at the creek which bears his name, and in which locality there now is found one of the broadest and richest tracts of farming land in Victoria. He brought with him overland a plough, a harrow, and the parts of a hand steel flour-mill. In 1839 he ploughed and sowed wheat, and thus grew and ground the first corn grown there. In 1841 Captain Hepburn erected a water-mill for corn on Birch's Creek ; that was the first mill of that kind. Birch's Creek was named after the brothers Arthur and Cecil Birch, who, with the Rev. Mr Irvine, came overland soon after Messrs Hepburn and Coghill, and settled at the Seven Hills. Besides the run at Coghill's Creek, taken up by Mr Coghill for some others of his family, Cattle Station Hill was also taken by him. This run lay between Glendaruel and the Seven Hills, and is now part of the purchased estate belonging to the Hepburns. The late Captain Hepburn long acted as a justice of the peace, and he was one of the squatters whom M'Combie mentions as having taken part in a meeting held on the 4th June, 1844, in front of the Mechanics' Institute, Melbourne, to protest against Sir G. Gipps' squatting policy, and to urge forward the movement for the separation of Port Phillip from New South Wales. The squatters mustered on horseback that day on Batman's Hill, and thence rode to the meeting in Collins street, the " equestrian order " thus giving an early example of the right freemen have, even in a Crown colony, to air public grievances publicly and fearlessly.

Lal Lal was taken up in the year 1840 by Messrs Blakeney and George Airey, the latter a brother of the Crimean officer so often and so flatteringly mentioned in Kinglake's " History of the Crimean War." In the same year, Messrs Le Vet (or Levitt) and another took up Warrenheip as a pig-growing station, but the venture failed, and some of the pigs ran wild in the forest there for years, and preyed on each other. After Messrs Le Vet and Co. had been there awhile, the run was taken up on behalf of Messrs Verner, Welsh, and Holloway, of the Gingellac run, on the Hume, by Mr Haverfield (at present the editor of the *Pastoral Times*), Le Vet and partner

selling their improvements for about £30.   Shortly after Mr Haver-
field came to Warrenheip, Bullarook Forest was occupied by Mr
John Peerman, for Mr Lyon Campbell.   The Mr Verner mentioned
above was the first Commissioner of the Melbourne Insolvency Court.
He was related to Sir William Verner, a member in the House of
Commons for Armagh.   Mr Verner took part, as chairman, at a
Separation meeting held in Melbourne on the 30th December, 1840,
and soon after that he left the colony.   Mr Welsh was the late Mr
Patricius Welsh, of Ballarat ; and Mr Holloway became a gold-broker,
and died at the Camp at Bendigo.   In the year 1843, Mr Peter
Inglis, who had a station at Ballan, took up the Warrenheip run, and
shortly after that purchased the Lal Lal station, and throwing them
both together, grazed on the united runs one of the largest herds
in the colony.   The western boundary of Mr Inglis' Warrenheip run
marched with the eastern boundary of Mr Yuille's run, the line being
struck by marked trees running from Mount Buninyong across Brown
Hill to Slaty Creek.   Mr Donald Stewart, now of Buninyong, was
stock-rider for Mr Inglis, on the Warrenheip and Lal Lal stations,
and superintendent during the minority of the present owner of Lal
Lal.   In 1839 Mr W. H. Bacchus brought cattle from Melbourne and
grazed them on his run of Burrumbeetup, the centre of which run
is now occupied by the Ballan pound.   There is a waterfall on the
Moorabool there, which, for its picturesque beauty, is well worth
visiting.   The run extended on the Ballarat side of the Moorabool
to about midway to the Lal Lal Creek.   Mr Bacchus still resides
in the same locality, his present station being known as Perewur,
or Peerewurr, a native name, meaning waterfall and opossums.   It
was originally held by Messrs Fairbairn and Gardner.   Buninyong
was a village, or township, long before Ballarat had any existence as a settlement.   The first huts were built at Buninyong in
the year 1841, by sawyers, splitters, and others, Mr George Innes
being then called the " King of the Splitters."   George Gab, George
Coleman, and others, were the pioneers in the Buninyong settlement.
Gab had a wife who used to ride Amazonian fashion on a fine horse
called Petrel, and both husband and wife were energetic people.
Gab opened a house of accommodation for travellers on the spot
where Jamieson's hotel was afterwards built.   The first store in
the neighborhood was opened at the Round Water Holes, near

Bonshaw, by Messrs D. S. Campbell and Woolley, of Melbourne, who almost immediately afterwards removed to a site next Gab's, at Buninyong, whose place they took for a kitchen. Gab then removed and built another hut opposite to the present police-court, and he opened his new hut also as a hotel. A blacksmith named M'Lachlan, with a partner opened a smithy opposite to Campbell and Woolley's store. This was the nucleus of the principal inland town then in the colony. In the year 1844 Dr. Power settled there, and built a hut behind what was afterwards the Buninyong hotel. He was the first medical man in the locality, and for years the settlers had no other doctor nearer than Geelong. The young township became a favorite place with bullock teamsters, who were glad to build huts there where they could leave their wives and children in some degree safe from aboriginal or other marauders. In the year 1847, the Rev. Thomas Hastie, the first clergyman in the district, came to Buninyong. His house, and the church in which he performed service, were built entirely by the residents in Buninyong, both pecuniary gifts and manual labor being contributed. Then, as now, the Messrs Learmonth were among the foremost movers in the promotion of the mental and moral, as well as material welfare of the people about them. Mr Hastie, in a letter to us, says :—

Before I came in 1847, the Messrs Learmonth had made several efforts to procure the settlement of a clergyman at Buninyong, but had failed, partly from want of support, but chiefly from their inability to procure one likely to be suitable. Overtures had been made to Mr Beazely, a Congregational minister then in Tasmania, and afterwards in New South Wales, but he declined them. The Messrs Learmonth were willing to take a minister from any denomination, and the circumstance that a Presbyterian clergyman was settled here arose from the fact that no other was available. Until after the gold discovery there was no minister in the interior, that is out of Melbourne, Geelong, Belfast, and Portland, but Mr Hamilton of Mortlake, Mr Gow of Campbellfield, and myself. For many years my diocese, as it may be called, extended from Batesford, on the Barwon, to Glenlogie, in the Pyrenees, and included all the country for miles on either side, my duties taking me from home more than half my time. Before I came the Messrs Learmonth had contemplated the establishment of a cheap boarding-school for the children of shepherds and others in the bush, but for prudential reasons they deferred the matter till the settlement of a minister offered the means of supervision. Immediately after I came the project was carried out, and subscriptions were received from most of the settlers in the Western district. The school was opened in 1848 by Mr Bedwell, £10 a-year being charged for board and education.

The gold discovery carried away the teachers, raised the prices of everything, and Mr Hastie had to see to the school and its 60 boarders himself; but through all the difficulties the school was maintained with varying fortunes, until at length it became the present Common-school near the Presbyterian Manse, with an average attendance of some 180 children.

What is now the boroughs of Ballarat, Ballarat East, and Sebastopol, was then a pleasantly picturesque pastoral country. Mount and range, and table land, gullies and creeks and grassy slopes, here black and dense forest, there only sprinkled with trees, and yonder showing clear reaches of grass, made up the general landscape. A pastoral quiet reigned everywhere. Over the whole expanse there was nothing of civilisation but a few pastoral settlers and their retinue—the occasional flock of nibbling sheep, or groups of cattle browsing in the broad herbage. There were three permanent water holes in those days where the squatters used to find water for their flocks in the driest times of summer. One was at the junction of the Gong Gong and the Yarrowee, or Blakeney's Creek, as it was then called, after the settler of that name there. Another was where the Yarrowee bends under the ranges by the Brown Hill hotel, and the other was near Golden Point. Aborigines built their mia-mias about Wendouree, the kangaroo leaped unharmed down the ranges, and fed upon the green slopes and flats where the Yarrowee rolled its clear water along its winding course down the valley. Bullock teams now and then plodded their dull, slow way across flat and range, and made unwittingly the sites and curves of future streets. Settlers would lighten their quasi solitude with occasional chases of the kangaroo, where now the homes of a busy population have made a city; it was a favorite resort of the kangaroo, and the present proprietor of Lal Lal and other settlers often hunted kangaroo where Main, Bridge, and other streets are now. The emu, the wombat, the dingo, were also plentiful. The edge of the eastern escarpment of the plateau where Ballarat West now is, was then green and golden in the spring time with the indigenous grass and trees. Where Sturt street descends to the flat was a little gully, and its upper edges, where are now the London Chartered Bank, the Post-office, and generally the eastern side of Lydiard street, from Sturt street to the gaol site, were prettily ornamented with wattles.

I often passed (says Mr Hastie) the spot on which Ballarat is built, when visiting Mr Waldie, and there could not be a prettier spot imagined. It was the very picture of repose. There was, in general, plenty of grass and water, and often I have seen the cattle in considerable numbers lying in quiet enjoyment after being satisfied with the pasture. There was a beautiful clump of wattles where Lydiard street now stands, and on one occasion, when Mrs Hastie was with me, she remarked, " What a nice place for a house, with the flat in front and the wattles behind!" Mr Waldie had at that time a shepherd's hut about where the Dead Horse Gully is on the Creswick road, and one day when I was calling on the hut-keeper, he said the solitude was so painful that he could not endure it, for he saw no one from the time the shepherds went out in the morning till they returned at night. I was the only person he had ever seen there who was not connected with the station.

The ground now occupied by Craig's hotel on one side of the gully that ran down by the " Corner," and by the Camp buildings on the other side, were favorite camping places in the pastoral days. Safe from floods, and near to water and grass, the spot invited herdsman and shepherd, bullock-driver and traveller, to halt and repose.

The aborigines were not numerous about Ballarat even in those early days ; a little earlier, however, as when Dowling Forest was taken up, they were more numerous and were often troublesome, being great thieves. Several of the adults were strongly marked with small-pox at the time the locality was taken up for pastoral occupation. The natives were considered inferior to the Murray tribes, and were generally indolent and often treacherous. From time to time they were troublesome to the settlers—as well to the good as to the bad. King Billy was the name given to the chief of the tribes about here, and that regal personage for many years wore a big brass plate bearing his title. He was chief of the tribes about Mounts Buninyong and Emu, and King Jonathan, of a Borhoneyghurk tribe, was his subordinate.

My brother and I (says Mr Somerville L. Learmonth) began by feeding and being kind to the natives, but not long after the establishment of our first out-station, on the way to Smythesdale, we were roused in the dead of night by the intelligence that Teddy, the hut-keeper, had been murdered. Some of the natives had seen the ration-cart on the previous day ; they watched until the hut-keeper went unarmed to the well for water, his return was intercepted, and one blow with a stone hatchet laid him dead at the murderers' feet. The hut was robbed and a shepherd brought to the homestead the sad intelligence.

A party started next day in pursuit of the natives, but I have often felt thankful that we failed in finding them.   On two occasions our men were attacked, but they resisted successfully and their assailants retired. Frequently small numbers of sheep were missing, but beyond this, and the stealing of small things when allowed to come near a station, the natives never injured us.   I attribute our immunity to having issued orders, which were enforced, that the natives should on no pretext be harbored about any station. They are most expert thieves.   I remember seeing a woman who was employed in gathering potatoes quietly raise a large proportion with her toes, and place the potatoes in her wallet, the others being openly put into the receptacle provided by the employer.   Another gentleman, surprised at the rapidity with which his crop withered away, examined and found that the tubers had been removed and the stems placed in the ground again.

The place where the Messrs Learmonth's hut-keeper was murdered was called Murdering Valley.   It is near the south-western boundary of the borough of Sebastopol, and was, a few years ago, the scene of a more horrible tragedy than that of the murder by the aborigines. Once in 1842 the natives were troublesome on Mr Inglis' run at Ballan.   They had offered some insult to a hut-keeper's wife and all the European force of the station turned out with tin kettles, pistols, sticks, and other instruments of noise and defence or offence—a great noise and demonstration were made to terrify the natives and thus that trouble was got over.   Mr Hastie says that when he first came to Buninyong the natives were " comparatively numerous."   They used to come to the manse for food, in return for which they would fetch or break up firewood.

Ballarat or, more properly, Ballaarat, is a native name, signifying a camping or resting place, *balla* meaning elbow, or reclining on the elbow ; all native names beginning with *balla* have a similar significance.   Buninyong, or, as the natives have it, Bunning-yowang, means a big hill like a knee—*bunning* meaning knee, and *yowang* hill.   This name was given by the natives to Mount Buninyong because the mount, when seen from a given point, resembled a man lying on his back with his knee drawn up.   The *Yow-Yangs*, by the Werribee, is a form of *Yowang*.   Station Peak, one of the Yow-Yangs, was called *Villamata* by the natives.   Warrengeep, corrupted to Warrenheip, means emu feathers; the name was given to Mount Warrenheip from the appearance presented by the ferns and other forest growths there.   Gong Gong, or Gang Gang, is an aboriginal name for a species of parrot ; Burrumbeet means muddy water, and Woady Yaloak standing water. Mount Pisgah, in the lake country, was first known as Pettett's Look-Out, and Mount Rowan as Shuter's Hill. Mount Blowhard had no name among the settlers until one of Pettett's shepherd-boys gave it that name, from having often proved the appropriateness of such a designation, since his experiences of windy days there had been frequent.

As a race the Australian squatters were brave and adventurous. Many of them were men of liberal education and broad and generous culture, and some were men bearing old historic names, as well as possessing the instincts and the discipline of gentlemen. Others were vulgar boors, whose only genius lay in adding flock to flock, run to run, and swelling annually the balance at their bankers. The first squatters took their lives in their hands, for they had to fight with various enemies—a treacherous native population, drought, hunger, and on all sides difficulties. Says Mr Coghill in a *viva voce* communication to us :—

Every day, I may say for ten years, I have been many hours in the saddle. I never had much trouble with the natives, only that they would sometimes thieve a little ; but I used always to make a point of going to them and talking to them as well as I could, and explaining to them that if they behaved themselves they would not be molested. I remember the bother we had with our first wool. We did not know how to get it down to ship, and we thought we would send it by way of Morrison's station, on the Campaspe. We had to cross the Jim Crow ranges, and we were a week among the gullies and creeks there before we could get a passage with our wool across the ranges.

The squatters were essentially explorers, and encountered all the risks of exploration. Over mountain and valley, through forest and across plain, they went where everything was new to civilisation. Passing by arid, treeless, grassless wastes, mere howling wildernesses of desolation, they pursued their way to tracts of boundless fertility, lands flowing, prospectively, with milk and honey, potentially rich in corn, and wine, and oil. Ever among the virgin newness of an unsubdued country, they steered their course by day guided by the sun or the compass ; at night, led by the skies, as, to quote the great New England poet's melodious, child-like conceit,—

Silently, one by one, in the infinite meadows of heaven,
Blossomed the lovely stars, the forget-me-nots of the angels.

This may seem to be a romantic view of the squatter, but it is a real one. It is as real as the cutty pipes, the spirit flasks, the night rugs, the camp fires, the rivalries, ambitions, generous hospitalities, and occasional meannesses of the race. Doubtless they sought their own good, but, however unwittingly, they actually became the beneficial occupiers of the land for others. The teeming hosts drawn hither afterwards by the more dazzling hopes of fortune, and becoming eventually, and not without reason, hostile to the squatter, were in great part fed by the countless flocks and herds which the pastoral pioneers had spread over the wide pastures of this fair and fertile home of all the nations. With what to the squatter must have seemed like rash and boisterous violence, the sudden tide of population dashed its confluent waves upon our shores, and the serried ranks of the new army of industry marched boldly in upon the domains of the squatter, rudely disturbed his quiet dreams of perpetual occupation, and added at once a hundredfold to the market value of all his possessions.

From the first pastoral settlement to the discovery of gold there was a wool-growing, cattle-breeding period of something more than one decade. In that period the courage and the enterprise of the squatters, the real pioneers of all our settlement, had achieved no little in the direction of the development of the value of the main source of all national wealth—the land. Mr M'Combie, in his " History of Victoria," remarks of the early years of settlement :—

During the ten years that the province of Port Phillip had been settled it had been daily progressing in population and wealth. Vast interests had been silently growing up, and new classes were beginning to emerge into importance. All depended upon the land. The first wealth of Port Phillip was acquired from pastoral pursuits, and nearly every person was either directly or indirectly engaged in squatting.

But while those " vast interests had been silently growing up," there had been occasional premonitions of a rapid and turbulent change. While the shepherds fed their flocks by night and by day, other voices than those of angels in the air were heard in some places. In some of the more picturesque nooks of the district traversed by the Pyrenees and their off-shoots, the solitary shepherd, or squatter, on one or two occasions, or oftener still, saw sudden visions of easily won and boundless immediate wealth. Where the broad belts of purple forest spread out, and fair green glades and glens and ravines stretched over the swelling ranges of the district, the bushman wandered from silence to silence that only the elements or the birds of the native woods ever disturbed. Then it was that the first whisperings were heard of the rich secrets of the unmeasured geologic ages, and the first gleams were caught of the visions that had in them, however dim and formless then, the promise of a more brilliant epoch. But it may be well supposed that those hardy pioneers recked not then, even as they knew not, of the troubles that would fall to the squatter with the sturdy democracy of the then coming time. They were lords of all they surveyed. Of all earth-hungerers they were, assuredly, among the hungriest, for, as Westgarth says, they had " a cormorant capacity for land." Over tens of thousands of acres of broad lands they roamed in the jocund spirit of undisputed occupation, and the still broader future lay unexplored, though even then the democratic invasion was imminent. The visions we wot of had been seen, but if seen were not all revealed. They were not at once blazoned forth to the public ear, but stealthily treasured or stealthily told, for instinct of change, of hope, of fear, more or less held back all who had seen the bright spectacle. The governing authorities heard of the things seen, and were offered proofs of the reality of the fateful discovery ; but the same instinct and horror of change restrained them also from giving the revelations to the world. But the secret had escaped for ever when the first glittering speck glared as a lured omen of evil, or lit up bright hopes that fell like a burst of sudden sunshine upon the silent, solitary settler. The new thing might be feared, or worshipped, fought against or cherished by the timid or selfish possessors of office and settlements, but it was to master all their purposes. Thus was foreshadowed the quicker entry of Australia among the peoples and the nations, the coming of population from all the corners of the earth to overrun the quiet haunts of the squatter and the shepherd, the beginning of new life, new interests, and a grander destiny for the whole continent.

CHAPTER II.

THE GOLD DISCOVERY.

California and the Ural.—Predictions of Australian Gold.—Discoveries of Old Bushmen.—
Hargreaves and others in New South Wales.—Effects of Discovery at Bathurst.—Sir C.
A. Fitz Roy's Despatches.—First Assay.—Esmond and Hargreaves.—Esmond's Discovery
at Clunes.—Previous Victorian Discoveries.—Esmond's the First Made Effectively
Public.—Hiscock.—Golden Point, Ballarat.—Claims of Discoverers as to Priority.—
Effects of the Discovery.—Mr. Latrobe's Despatches.—His Visit to Ballarat.—The
Licenses.—Change of Scene at Ballarat.—Mount Alexander Rush.—Fresh Excitements.—
Rise in Prices.

P O T E N T as was the wonderful lamp of
Aladdin, and magnificent as were its successes,
the power of gold has equalled in its marvellous
effects all that the warm orient fancy has pictured
for us in the Arabian Nights. Gold has done
even more than ever mere magician achieved. It
certainly has operated magically in Australia, and
in no part of the country has it created greater
marvels than in Ballarat. Everywhere the resist-
less charm operates similarly, but it is not everywhere that its material
results are alike notable. California and Australia have caught the
more gorgeous lights and colors, and though some dark shadows
mingle with the magnificence of the general results, the gold discovery in both countries has worked prodigies, and many of its
creations remain. They not only remain, but are in themselves
seminal powers forecasting greater wonders in the future. All that
lies in the unknown future of this continent must be connected with
the past and the present, and these, in their grander features, take
their form from the matrix in which they were born—the gold
discovery of the year 1851.

California electrified Europe and the United States by its gold
discoveries in the years 1848-9, and that event was soon followed by
the discovery of gold in Australia. Geologists who had studied

maps and noted the auriferous mountain lines of the Ural and California no sooner heard of Australian strata, and the bearings of the mountains and ranges, than the existence of gold in this island continent was predicted. In the older settlements, too, of New South Wales, the aborigines and the whites had occasionally stumbled upon glittering metals, as afterwards they did also in Victoria ; but it was the Californian prospector, Hargreaves, who first publicly demonstrated the existence of gold in Australia. Actually, the discovery by others seems to have occurred both in New South Wales and Victoria about the time of the Californian rush in the year 1849. From a despatch dated 11th June, 1851, to Earl Grey from Sir C. A. Fitz Roy, then Governor of New South Wales, we learn that some two years before then a Mr Smith announced to Sir Charles' Government the discovery of gold. A despatch from Mr Latrobe, the Governor of Victoria at the time of Esmond's discoveries, mentions the discovery of gold some two or three years previously in the Victorian Pyrenees. Smith was attached to some ironworks at Berrima. He showed a lump of golden quartz to the Chief Secretary in Sydney, and offered, upon terms, to reveal the locality of his discovery. The Sydney Government, if we may take the Governor's despatch as a guide, had some doubts both as to the veracity of the applicant and the propriety of making known his discovery even if a reality.

Apart (says Sir C. A. Fitz Roy) from my suspicions that the piece of gold might have come from California, there was the opinion that any open investigation by the Government would only tend to agitate the public mind, and divert persons from their proper and more certain avocations. ·

Then, on the 3rd April, 1851, Mr Hargreaves appeared upon the scene, Smith having vanished in refusing to " trust to the liberality " of the Sydney Government. Mr Hargreaves was a man of greater faith than Smith, and he disclosed the localities in which he had discovered the precious metal. The localities were near Bathurst. The news spread all over the colonies, and the Bathurst and adjacent districts were rushed, to the great terror of quiet pastoral settlers, and the annoyance of the respectable Government of Sydney. From the Governor's despatches to Downing Street, it appears that the official mind was much agitated what to do. Settlers advised absolute prohibition of gold digging, and the authorities were in doubt as to whether it might be safe to impose regulations and a tax.   Counsel's opinion was obtained as to the property of the Crown in the precious mineral, and ultimately a license tax of thirty shillings per month was levied upon the Bathurst diggers.   The Rev. W. B. Clarke, the geologist, gave excellent geological and political advice at the time, in the columns of the *Sydney Morning Herald*.   He sagaciously remarked that "the momentary effect of the gold mania may be to upset existing relations ; but the effect will be a rapid increase of population, and the colony must prepare herself for an important growth in her influence upon the destinies of the world."

The police despatches to the Sydney authorities described the miners as " quiet and peaceable, but almost to a man armed," wherefore the officer advised, " that no police power could enforce the collection of dues against the feeling of the majority."   Hargreaves came to the aid of the authorities as a man strong in counsel and Californian experiences.   A minute of Hargreaves' is worth noting— " There existed (he says) no difficulty in obtaining the fees in California."   But this was no marvel, as will be seen by the following revelation.   " All the people (he continues) at the mines are honest and orderly.   I was alcadi there.   If a complaint be made the alcadi summonses a jury, and the decision is submitted to.   A man found guilty of stealing is hung immediately."   This was not less direct as a system of jurisprudence than that practised, as Dixon and Dilke tell us, by the sheriff of Denver on the buffalo plains of America, where criminals had a very brief shrift and a quick nocturnal " escape" up the gallows tree.   Yet we do not learn that in Denver, or anywhere else in that part of America, " all the people " were either honest or orderly, as Alcadi Hargreaves says they were in California.   But then the Sydney prospector left his alcadiship in the early days, when the Arcadian simplicity of mining society had not yet lost the fresh bloom of what we will take to have been its early and honest youth.   The Bathurst diggers appear to have behaved pretty well on the whole.

In July, 1851, occurred what the *Sydney Morning Herald* called " a most marvellous event," namely, the discovery of a mass of gold 106 lbs. weight imbedded in quartz.   This made everybody wild with excitement.   The *Bathurst Free Press*, of 16th July, said— " Men meet together, stare stupidly at each other, talk incoherent nonsense, and wonder what will happen next." Some blacks in the employment of a Dr. Kerr found this prize, their master appropriated it, and gave the finders two flocks of sheep, besides some bullocks and horses. Possibly this was the basis of Charles Reade's great nugget incident in his "Never Too Late to Mend." It may be noted here that last November the discovery of a similar mass took place at Braidwood, in New South Wales. The weight of the specimen was given at 350 lbs., of which two-thirds were estimated to be pure gold. We may conclude this notice of the discovery of gold in New South Wales by quoting the first assay of gold as given in the Government despatches from Sydney, under date 24th May, 1851. This assay was as follows :—

HUMID PROCESS.		DRY PROCESS.	
Gold	91·150	Gold	91·100
Silver	8·286	Silver........................	8·333
Iron.........................	0·564	Base metal.................	0·567
	100·000		100·000

Or 22 carats, £3 17s 10½d per oz., plus 1 dwt. 16 gr. silver, value 5½d.

Victoria was not long behind New South Wales in finding a gold-field, and it soon caused the elder colony to pale its ineffectual fires in the greater brilliance of the Victorian discoveries. James William Esmond was to Victoria what Hargreaves was to New South Wales. Esmond, like Hargreaves, had been at the Californian gold-fields, and had an impression that the Australian soil was also auriferous. He left Port Phillip for California in June, 1849, observed that there were similarities in soil and general features between Clunes and California, and decided to return and explore his Australian home for gold. It chanced that Esmond and Hargreaves were fellow passengers on their return from California to Sydney. Esmond found gold on the northern side of the hill opposite to Cameron's, subsequently M'Donald's pre-emptive right, at Clunes, on Tuesday, the 1st of July, 1851, and gold was found about the same time at Anderson's Creek, near Melbourne. Esmond published his discovery in Geelong on the 6th of July, Hargreaves having preceded him in the sister colony by some two months. But we have seen that before Hargreaves there was a Smith, who would not accept the terms of the Sydney Government, and so disappeared. There was yet another discoverer earlier than the man of the Berrima

c

ironworks.   Mr John Phillips, late Government mineralogical
surveyor, and now mining and contract surveyor for the Government
at St. Arnaud, discovered gold in South Australia before any of the
explorers previously mentioned.   He announced his discoveries to the
authorities in South Australia and Port Phillip, and to Sir Roderick
Murchison, but neither of the local Governments acted upon his
discovery.   The discovery by Mr Phillips was about synchronous with
discoveries made by the Rev. W. B. Clarke, and had been foreshadowed in the geological predictions of Sir Roderick Murchison
and Count Strzelecki.   Mr Phillips got nothing for his pains, and
Esmond was less fortunate than Hargreaves in the matter of public·
recognition and reward.   To Hargreaves were voted £10,000 by the
Government of New South Wales, and subsequently £2381 by the
Victorian Parliament,* Esmond, after a hard fight, receiving a vote
of £1000 from the Parliament of Victoria, and some small public,
quasi-public, and private rewards besides.   But he did not receive
the amount all at once, though early proposed.   On the 5th
October, 1854, Dr. Greeves proposed, in the Legislative Council, a
vote of £5000 to Hargreaves, and in his speech he admitted that
Esmond was "the first actual producer of alluvial gold for the
market." The motion was carried. Mr Strachan moved, supported
by the late Mr Haines, and only seven others, an amendment for
giving £1000 each to Hargreaves, Esmond, Hiscock, Mitchell, and
Clarke, and £500 to a Dr. Bruhn, who was said by Dr. Greeves
to have advised Esmond as to the existence of gold in Victoria.
There was an earlier discovery than Esmond's in Victoria, asserted
by Mr J. Wood Beilby, as the repository of a secret from the person
who was said to have been the actual discoverer.   But Beilby does
not claim for public revelation, but only as the revealer to the
Government of the day.   In a pamphlet published by Dwight, of
Melbourne, in Beilby's interests as a claimant for State reward, the
following statement is found :—

Mr J. Wood Beilby establishes, by the production (from the Chief Secretary's office) of his correspondence with Mr La Trobe, and concurring
documentary evidence, the fact that, so early as 7th June, 1851, or some weeks
earlier than Mr Wm. Campbell, he informed the Government of the existence

of gold in workable deposits at the locality now known as Navarre, and in the ranges of the Amherst district. Mr B. does not claim to have been the original discoverer, but to have placed the information before Government, for the benefit of the public, at the critical period when its value in arresting the threatened exodus of our population to Bathurst was immense. Mr La Trobe was at first very incredulous, evidently not having been made aware previously, of the existence of gold as one of the mineral products of Victoria, as his reply, by letter of 11th June, 1851, demonstrates. Mr B., however, supplied further details of information, and, waiting upon him personally, so urged investigation, offering to share expenses, that Mr La Trobe organised a prospecting party, including Mr David Armstrong, then a returned Californian digger, afterwards gold commissioner, and the late Capt. H. E. P. Dana, attended by a party of native police ; Mr Commissioner Wright, resident at the Pyrenees, being nominated to act with the gentlemen of the party as a board of enquiry. From various causes the expedition was delayed starting from the Aboriginal Police Depôt, Narree Worran, until a few days before the publication of Mr Campbell's letter. But the news was made public. Although Mr La Trobe had requested Mr Beilby to abstain from further publication of the fact until the result of his investigations, the officials named to accompany the expedition, and their subordinates and outfitters, were not tongue-tied or bound to secrecy. It is, therefore, no matter of surprise that their intended prospecting trip to the Pyrenees was bruited far and wide ; and, as a sequence, their investigations forestalled by the discoveries at Clunes.

In or about 1847-8, William Richfould, the author of the discovery published by Mr Beilby, was a shepherd in the employment of Mr W. J. T. Clarke, at his upper outstation on the Heifer Station Creek, Navarre. He was an intelligent and observant man, and always looking for and preserving natural curiosities. He discovered water-worn gold in the crevices of a brownish slate rock, in the bed and sides of the creek close to the ranges, and also found a few specimens of gold in quartz upon the surrounding ranges. These specimens he from time to time disposed of. In 1848, finding himself followed and watched by his fellow servants too closely, and being at the time desirous of selling some valuable specimens, he journeyed westward, and meeting Mr Armstrong, an employee of S. G. Henty, Esq., at the Grange, he was induced to visit Portland, and disposed of his gold to merchants there, by whom it was sent to Tasmania as Californian gold ; being probably represented to them as such, the then current popular belief being that all gold deposits belonged to the Queen, and that its appropriation by an unauthorised person was punishable. Richfould then engaged as shepherd with Mr Beilby at Mount Gambier, and shortly after showed Mr B. some small specimens of gold he had retained, refusing, however, at that period, to give any information as to the locality of his discovery. Subsequently, in July, 1849, he divulged his secret to Mr B. on his pledge to keep it, unless its publication was required by public emergency, or the discoverer died. Richfould after this left Mr B.'s service, professedly to return to the scene of his discoveries. Nothing certain is now

c 2

known of his subsequent history, but his death was shortly afterwards reported in the Mount Gambier district.

Some two years before either Esmond's or Beilby's dates there was a discovery of gold at the Pyrenees asserted by one Chapman, who sold gold to a jeweller in Melbourne, named Brentani. Chapman was at that time shepherd at Mr Hall's station near the Pyrenees, the locality of the subsequently opened Daisy Hill diggings. Brentani and his trade hands made up a secret party with Chapman to go to the Pyrenees and get " a dray-load of gold." They went, but did not get the dray-load of gold, and Chapman mysteriously disappeared and was not heard much of again. Brentani and his men do not seem to have pushed their search or disclosed what they had heard, or seen, or done. M'Combie also mentions the finding of gold in quartz by W. Campbell, of Strathlodden (M.L.C.), in March, 1849, at Burnbank, and also at Clunes, near where Esmond subsequently made his more fertile discovery. Clunes was named by Mr Donald Cameron after a farm at Inverness in Scotland.

Mr Bacchus, of Perewur, in whose service Chapman had once been, chanced to meet Chapman in Sydney. Mr Bacchus wrote a letter on the 1st July, 1851, which was published in the *Argus*, and copied into the *Sydney Morning Herald* of the 23rd July, 1851, and in that letter he says :—

Chapman is an old servant of mine, and I have every reason to believe his story. He says he left Melbourne for Sydney because he felt himself watched and was regularly hunted for information as to where he had found the gold. He says he never took Brentani and Duchesne within miles of the place, and gives an excellent reason for not doing so. His story is plain and straightforward, and from his description of the place I think he might be able to put any one in the way of claiming the reward. He offers to show the exact place at which he picked up the piece of gold for the sum of fifty pounds and his passage from Sydney.

Mr Bacchus, writing to us with the above enclosure, states :—

About the same time I wrote to another person in Victoria :—"From what I have heard and seen of the description of country where gold is found in this Colony (N.S.W.) I have no doubt that it can be obtained in Lerderderg and other creeks running from Mount Blackwood and Bullencrook towards Bacchus Marsh." And so it was, a few weeks after. I give another extract of a letter to me from a friend in Victoria, dated in July, 1851 :—" Coming from one so well-known as yourself your letter in the *Argus* attracted great attention, and has been the means of preventing numbers from leaving here for Sydney. No end of people have set out in the direction indicated by you."

The reward referred to by Mr Bacchus was advertised by the Port Phillip Government, the disclosure of Hargreaves' discovery having compelled the Government here to abandon its previous policy of fear as to the possible consequences of such a discovery, as it was expected there would be a wholesale exodus to New South Wales. The Lerderderg locality has been proved, as Mr Bacchus states, to be auriferous, but the country there has not been very rich in the precious metal.

As soon as Esmond's discovery was known prospecting parties set out from the seaboard, and early in August the late Mr Hiscock found gold in the gully near Buninyong which now bears his name. The ground was poor and was abandoned as richer fields were soon discovered. The Ballarat gold-field was discovered by other prospectors, two only of whom are at present in Ballarat, namely—Wm. Woodward, a French polisher, living in Chancery lane (late Eureka street), Ballarat West; and Rd. Turner, a house decorator, living in Raglan street south, Ballarat West. Woodward was in Connor's party of six persons, namely— Connor, Woodward, Brown, Jeanes, Smith, and Thornton. Turner was with four others, namely—Dunn, Merrick, Wilson, and a man named Charlie, the party having, from Alfred Clarke, the name of the Geelong Mutual Mining Association. Merrick is now mining at Dolly's Creek, Connor and Brown are dead, Thornton was lately at Miners' Rest, and Dunn, Jeanes, and Smith are in Geelong. Both parties left Geelong for Clunes, but on the way met Alfred Clarke, who informed them of Hiscock's discovery, and they therefore began digging at Hiscock's Gully, but the ground did not pay. Woodward and Turner differ a little in some of their dates and facts, and appear in some sort to be rival claimants for the honor of the discovery of Golden Point. Woodward asserts for his party the exclusive right to whatever honor belongs to the discovery, while Turner claims for his party equal credit as being discoverers simultaneously with Connor's party. Woodward says the discovery was made by Brown on Monday, the 25th of August; Turner says it was made by himself and Merrick on Sunday, the 24th, and that Brown made his discovery on the same day. Woodward says that on the 25th Brown was sent out to prospect and returned the same day, saying he had found gold in every dishful

of dirt, and wanted men and the cradle to go with him.   On the
26th three others of the party went with Brown and the cradle,
and got 4½ oz. of gold for the first two hours' work.   That day they
first used the cradle, and for the first day's full work obtained
30 oz. of gold.   Woodward also says that Turner and Merrick's
party reached the Point on the Tuesday, but not earlier.   Turner
avers, on the contrary, that on the Sunday he and Merrick went
out to look—as advised by some diggers in Geelong returned from
California—for hills with quartz gravel and boulders.   They went
by way of Winter's Flat, ascended the ranges, found a ¼ oz. of
gold in a tin dishful of dirt, carefully concealed the traces of their
prospecting, returned to Buninyong, and told the news to their
partners.   He states that on the Monday both his party and
Connor's party left Buninyong for the Point, his own party being
bogged in Winter's Flat by the way, and part only reaching the
Point that night, the remainder arriving next day.   Merrick, as
Turner avers, commenced cradling on the Tuesday morning, for the
purpose of being able to say they were the first to do so.   They
obtained 9 oz. or 10 oz. of gold during the first week, being less
fortunate in that respect than Connor's party.   Turner admits
that Connor's party were the first to arrive on the Point, but he
says it was on Monday, and that a few hours later on the same day
some of Turner and Merrick's party were also there.   Both parties
agree that they were there together on the Tuesday, and that all
the men on the field then were only about half a score.   Dunn,
writing from memory at Chilwell, Geelong, on the 9th of February,
1870, sent the following letter to Turner :—

Dear Sir,—In answer to yours of the 8th inst., I shall give you a full and true
account of our gold prospecting, and the first discovery of Golden Point, as
follows:—1st. Richard Turner, James Merrick, Thomas Dunn, George Wilson,
Charles Gerrard, James Batty.   2nd. Started from town on Tuesday, 5th
August, 1851 ; met with an accident on Batesford Hill, the loaded dray
passing over the driver's stomach, left him at Mrs Primrose's with the Chinese
Doctor, proceeding on journey (for the Clunes) but stopped at Buninyong
near a fortnight.   The party getting dissatisfied, Wilson and I agreed to
go in search of better diggings, so we started from Buninyong on the Sunday
morning, 24th August, 1851, between 10 and 11 o'clock, with tin dish and
shovel to find the Black Hill ; reached there about 2 o'clock, saw Greenwood's
party with a few specks of the color, left the Black Hill about half-past three.
In coming over Winter's Flat, I says to George—" There is a likely little quartz

hill, let us try it before we go home." It was pouring of rain at the time. So with that I cut a square turf, then partly filled the dish and went to the creek to wash it. Oh, what joy ! there was about 10 or 12 grains of fine gold. So we left off, covered up with turf, and made for home as fast as possible through the rain ; reached home like two drowned rats ; started next morning early for our new discovery ; reached there in the afternoon ; had the cradle at work next morning. I firmly believe that I, Thomas Dunn, and George Wilson were the first men, and got the first gold on the little quartz hill now known as Golden Point. If there is any one that can dispute this letter let them come forward publicly like men. I remain, yours, &c.,

THOMAS DUNN.

From memory, in Ballarat, since giving us an oral statement, Woodward writes as follows as to the discovery :—

Connor, Woodward, Jeanes, Thornton, and Brown left Geelong Wednesday, 20th August, 1851. Smith arrived on Sunday, 24th August. Brown started (for new ground) Monday morning, 25th. Meeting on Monday evening to petition against paying license-fee for the month of September on account of gold not being sufficient to pay expenses. On the 26th Brown came back for three more men, horse and cart and cradle, and the two first hours' work gave 4½ oz. Commissioners arrived on Friday, 19th September, asking for Connor's party ; taking the pannikin up with the gold remarking—"This is a proof it will pay the license-fee." On the 20th Commissioner sends for Connor to pay the license-fee for the remainder of the month. After Connor had paid the license he was pelted with clay and bonnetted. A public meeting was held outside the bark hut in the hearing of the Commissioners, Herbert Swindells on the stump. Resolutions passed that no one pay the license for September, as we had petitioned against it. The meeting no sooner over than the (Commissioners') hut was rushed to pay the license, as them that did not pay would lose their ground—Conner's party receiving 16 feet square each, double the ground to what others had. Herbert Swindells was refused a license to dig on account of taking the stump at the meeting. A collection was made for him of 12 oz. of gold which he lost the same night. This is a correct list of facts. W. WOODWARD.

Merrick, writing from Morrisons Diggings, on the 24th February, 1870, to Mr James Oddie, says :—

As to the time or date of our arrival on Golden Point I do not remember, but as to the day and circumstances they are simply as follows :—I formed the party at first with the intention of proceeding to Esmond's Diggings, and on the road we tried Hiscock's Hill, found it would not pay, so we agreed at the end of the week to send George Wilson, one of our party, to the Brown Hill to see if Lindsay and party had found gold. If they had not we were to start for the Clunes on the Monday morning. George went up on Saturday or Sunday returning over Golden Point, the flat being flooded. He tried a dishful of gravel and got a nice prospect—some of the bits like small shots flattened.

When we had seen the prospect we determined to start for the place next morning early, so that we should not be noticed leaving. On our arrival at Yuille's Flat our cart got bogged, so three of our party, the carter, and horse, started for the Point, taking with them as many things as they could, leaving two of the party to mind the cart. When they got to the Point, to their surprise they found Connor's party just arrived. The cart was soon got up and the tents commenced putting up. Most of our party were for finishing tent and other odd jobs, and commence washing the next week, but I said, "No, for I intend to be the first that ever worked a cradle in this place." It was agreed I should, and I cradled the remainder of the week, but no other party began till next Monday or Tuesday following, except they tin-dished it. My party consisted of six men, but Mr Batty did not come up with us. Their names are as follow:—T. Batty, R. Turner, Dunn, G. Wilson, C. Fitzgerald, J. F. C. Merrick.

Thus was opened the gold-field of Ballarat, and the honor of discovery seems to be tolerably evenly balanced between the two claiming parties.   Turner does not, though Dunn does, assert priority of discovery for his party, and he admits that Connor's party were first on the Point on the first working day, Woodward making Tuesday and Turner making Monday to be that day. Merrick does not assert priority either, save as to the use of the cradle.   It may, perhaps, be held that the balance of priority inclines to the side of Connor's party, and it is said in support of Connor's claim that he was always regarded as leader of the diggers at the meetings held in those first days when the authorities made their first demand of license fees.   Then it is seen from Woodward's statement that the Commissioner recognised Connor's claim to priority, and gave the party a double area.   Swindells fared worse than our modern men of the stump, and appears to have been less mindful of No. 1 than his less scrupulous descendants.   It is worthy remark that none of these actual discoverers and openers of the Ballarat gold-field ever received any reward from the Government, though Hiscock had, and Esmond also, Hargreaves, however, as already stated, having the lion's share.   So far, it must be said, Victoria has acted with less liberality to her own children than to the stranger's.   As to Hiscock's gold cup, lately exhibited here as the product of gold got in Hiscock's Gully, Woodward affirms that the cup was not made of gold discovered there.

Other parties from the seaboard were quickly on the trail of the Golden Point prospectors, and Hiscock's Gully-workers soon repaired to the richer locality. On the 28th of August, among others who arrived at Buninyong, were Messrs James Oddie, Thomas Bath. Francis Herring, and George Howe, and they reached Golden Point on Monday, the 1st September. The news quickly got to Geelong, and on the 9th a good many people, including ministers of religion, doctors, merchants, and others, arrived. On the day following, the Clunes prospectors having heard of the richer discoveries, Esmond, Cavenagh, and others arrived from Clunes, and Esmond and Cavenagh found fifty pounds weight of gold in two days, that being the first sent down by escort, and Cavenagh being the first to send gold to England, where it realised £4 per oz. On the 19th of September Mr Commissioner Doveton, and Assistant-Commissioner Armstrong arrived with troopers, and on the 20th the first license was issued, Connor's party being the first licensees, and paying 15s each for the remainder of the month. The diggers did not relish the demand of license fees, and at a meeting held—Connor on the stump—the division was against paying the fees. But the decision was not adhered to in practice, for the licenses were taken out immediately. Turner, for his party, followed Connor's example quickly, for by that time jealousies of each other had arisen, the Clunes contingent being regarded with especial disfavor. Swindells, one of the Geelong diggers, mounted the stump in those early days and on one occasion he got the diggers to divide—Clunes v Geelong—and the balance of power being seen to be on the side of the latter and the presence of the authorities aiding also, peace was kept. The diggings were shallow and very productive, the rains were heavy, and two rude bridges erected, the first probably, over the Yarrowee by Connor's party, were washed away. By the time the first week was over there had gathered near 100 diggers at the Point, the riches unearthed there quickly attracting not only all the other prospectors, but setting the colony on fire with excitement from end to end. The quiet Ballarat sheep run, with its grassy slopes and shadowy glades, and its green valley where the Yarrowee poured its limpid waters, became suddenly transformed as by the wand of an enchanter. The Black Hill then looked upon the valley with a densely timbered head and face, whence its name was taken. The valley was thinly sprinkled with trees, and the ranges, with the spurs subsequently known as Golden Point, Bakery, Specimen, and Sinclair's Hills, were well timbered, while the western basaltic table land, where the Western borough is now, was moderately sprinkled with the usual variety of forest growth.   In a brief time all this was changed. Soon the solitary blue columns of smoke that rose from the first prospecting parties' camping places were but undistinguishable items amidst a host.   The one or two white tents of the prospectors were soon lost in crowded irregular lines and groups of tents that dotted the slopes and flats, or spread out along the tortuous tracks made by the bullock teams of the squatter.   The axe of the digger quickly made inroads upon the forest all round ; the green banks of the Yarrowee were lined with tubs and cradles, its clear waters were changed to liquid, yellow as the yellowest Tiber flood, and its banks grew to be long shoals of tailings.   Everywhere little hillocks of red, yellow, and white earth were visible as the diggers got to work, and in a few weeks the green slopes, where the prospectors found the gold of Golden Point, changed from their aboriginal condition to the appearance of a fresh and rudely made burial ground.   At first the upturned colored earth-heaps were but as isolated pustules upon the fair face of the primeval hills and valley, but they rapidly multiplied until they ran together, so to speak, and made the forest swards but so many blotched reaches of industrious disorder, the very feculence of golden fever everywhere in colored splotches with shadowed pits between.

Mr Latrobe, in a despatch at this date to Earl Grey, says :—

It is quite impossible for me to describe to your lordship the effect which these discoveries have had upon the whole community. Within the last three weeks the towns of Melbourne and Geelong and their large suburbs have been in appearance almost emptied of many classes of their male inhabitants. Not only have the idlers to be found in every community, and day laborers in town and the adjacent country, shopmen, artisans, and mechanics of every description thrown up their employments—in most cases leaving their employers and their wives and families to take care of themselves—and run off to the workings, but responsible tradesmen, farmers, clerks of every grade, and not a few of the superior classes have followed ; some, unable to withstand the mania and force of the stream, but others because they were, as employers of labor, left in the lurch, and had no other alternative. Cottages are deserted, houses to let, business is at a standstill, and even schools are closed. In some of the suburbs not a man is left, and the women are known, for self-protection, to forget neighbors' jars, and to group together to keep house. The ships in the harbor are in a great measure deserted, and masters of vessels, like farmers, have made up parties with their men to go shares at the diggings.   Both here and at Geelong all buildings and contract works, public and private, are at a stand-still.

Mr Westgarth, in his " Victoria in 1857," thus refers to what he saw of change in Melbourne when he returned from a visit to Europe :—

All had been changed into a wild and tumultuous development.   The waters of Hobson's Bay were scarcely visible beneath a forest of five or six hundred vessels.   The grassy glades of North Melbourne were now a hard and dusty surface, cut up everywhere with roads, and disturbed with the incessant noise of the traffic to the interior.

To extricate the deserted ships it was proposed to get Lascars from India.   Communication with the mother country was only possible haphazard in those days.   The Victorian Governor's despatches took six, and, in one instance, seven months to reach London.   His Excellency and all his following were perplexed by the whirlwind of auriferous excitement.   As his despatches stated, all classes felt the burning thirst for gold.   Sir J. Palmer, the present President of the Legislative Council, was one of the first diggers at Golden Point, and used to quarter at Lal Lal.   Among the first visitors were Lady A'Beckett, wife of the Chief Justice, with other ladies and gentlemen, who made a pilgrimage from Melbourne in a waggonette to see the new wonders.   The Governor, too, came upon the scene.   Clunes and Anderson's Creek had mildly aroused the authorities in Melbourne, and regulations to be enforced by the 1st of September were discussed for those places ; " but (writes the Governor to Earl Grey) before this could be done, they also were deserted, not from any real unproductiveness, but from the discovery of the new gold-field within a mile of the township of Boninyong."   This was the Hiscock's Gully ground, but that electric flash was speedily followed by the more brilliant discharges from Golden Point, " another locality (to cite the Governor's despatches again) producing the precious metal in far greater abundance in the valley of the River Leigh, about seven miles to the northward, into which a very large conflux of adventurers is pouring."   Under these circumstances the Government bestirred itself, sent up police, promulgated the right of the Crown in the gold, issued licenses, and so took the first feeble steps in the portentous and sometimes wayward path of gold-fields government.   The Golden

Point diggers did not like the licenses at first, but they soon took kindly to them, and 400 were issued within a few days.   His Excellency, writing on 10th October, stated that 1300 had been issued, and by the 30th October, 2246.   He saw the lucky diggers digging up the gold on the Point, and told Earl Grey there were 500 cradles at work, not fewer than 2500 persons on the ground, and 500 arriving daily.   He saw 8 lbs. of gold washed from two tin dishes of dirt, heard of a party that raised 16 lbs. at an early hour, and 31 lbs. in all that day, many parties of four sharing day after day 10 oz. per man.   "There can be no doubt (continues his Excellency) but that gold must rank as one of the most important, if not the most important, products of the colony, and that from this time forward a very considerable and valuable section of the population will be employed in realising it."

The Victorian Governor's foresight was true, for he was sagacious and the times were quickening.   He and his Ministers had only just begun to draw breath again after the Ballarat rush, had begun to discuss the propriety of raising the salaries of civil servants to meet the new state of affairs, had noted " business beginning to revive as many, physically and morally unfit for the austerities of the gold-fields, returned to their homes," when a second shock came to fright them from their re-assuring propriety.   The Mount Alexander diggings " broke out," as the expressive phrase had it, and the Governor once more took to horse and went to see the newer Eldorado, writing on 30th October to Earl Grey, and telling him " On my return to Melbourne the whole population was again excited."

The Mount Alexander rush was caused by a shepherd picking up a bit of golden quartz.   That led to prospecting, and a party having got £300 worth of gold in a seam of quartz, more prospectors arrived, and then the rich alluvial grounds were opened, and Ballarat itself was half deserted by rushers to the later field, and everything was turned topsy-turvy once more.   Poor Mr Latrobe at last got excited in his syntax.   Writing on 3rd December to Earl Grey, his Excellency said—

I must now apprise you that the progress and results of the successful search for gold in this (Mount Alexander) quarter, in the short interval which has since elapsed, has been such as completely to disorganise the whole structure of society, and it really becomes a question how the more sober operations of society, and even the functions of government may be carried on.

The Ballarat excitement was exceeded by that of the Mount Alexander rush, and the Governor informed Earl Grey that while there were about 6000 persons at the Ballarat rush, there were double that number in an area of 15 square miles at Mount Alexander. His Excellency forthwith proposed to put a pecuniary drag upon the wheels of this auriferous machine that was running away with the bodies and wits of the population. He proposed to double the license fee, as the Legislative Council would not sanction a special vote to meet the new exigencies of the Executive. A further ground for the proposal was, "the notorious disproportion of the advantages derivable under the license system to the public revenue, compared with the amount of private gain." His Excellency also hoped by this means to deter unfit men from going to the diggings—fond but delusive hope. The superintendent of police and the sheriff furnished their contributions to the bitter cup of the unhappy Governor, informing him that most of the police and warders and turnkeys of gaols had sent in their resignations. Nor was this all, for "many clerks in the public service are bent on the same course." Then the Governor applied to the Governor-General at Sydney for "an increase to the small military force stationed here, sufficient, I trust, happen what may, to place the gaols, stockades, and banks for the present in safety." Mr Latrobe wisely reminded Earl Grey that the preservation of order was more important than raising a great revenue, as thousands would flock to the colony, but good colonists would stay away if law became impotent to preserve peace and order. So he felt that he must have soldiers, not fearing that they would desert like the sailors to follow the seductive pursuit of gold. "Melbourne ought (wrote his Excellency) to be made the head-quarters of one regiment at least." In time this came about, and now, in less than two decades, we have talked of getting rid of both soldiers and the Home Government, and setting up absolutely for ourselves. The soldiers are already gone, and all the British empire is discussing the relations to be maintained between the parent State and her world-encircling colonies.

This modern outcome, however, had not appeared to the Government of 1851 as a probability. The Governor and his subordinates were busy regulating and licensing and escorting the diggers and their gold. "Boninyong," as the name was spelt in the despatches, was the head-quarters of the local authorities then. They issued a notice in October, having found that gold was accumulating, that "the escort will leave Boninyong every Tuesday morning at six o'clock; persons desirous of sending gold under the security afforded by this conveyance are to take care that it is forwarded to Boninyong not later than four o'clock p.m. of the Monday. Escort charge of 1 per cent. on washed gold, to be estimated at the rate of £3 per oz., and on gold mixed with a larger portion of stone at the rate of £2 10s the ounce." The Government authorities undertook no responsibility. Like the squatters, or small settlers, they advertised a sort of accommodation paddock on wheels, but took no responsibility. They had to take gold-dust in payment for licenses, for coin was scarce, and in the same month we find the Treasurer in Melbourne advertising for tenders for the purchase of 1500 oz. of gold.

In December the Government doubled the license fee, making it £3 per month, or £1 10s if the license was taken out after the 15th of the month. And this for a claim eight feet square for one man, or eight feet by sixteen for a party, and with a prohibition against digging within half-a-mile of every side of a homestead. Even these regulations were luxuries to be denied to civil servants unless they could show that their resignation of office had "not only been authorised, but was unattended with embarrassment to the Government." To work this machinery on the Ballarat, or "Boninyong," diggings there were gazetted in October :—William Mair, commissioner, salary £300 a-year; D. Armstrong, assistant-commissioner, salary £250; John Bell, clerk, salary £100 ; Henry Smith, inspector of police, salary £150 ; mounted and foot constables at 3s and 2s 9d per diem respectively ; and native police at the magnificent pay of 1½d per diem. For the Mount Alexander diggings there were Messrs Doveton, Lydiard, Dana, and Eyre, as commissioners, or police officers, and, as clerk, Mr W. Hogarth—now clerk of petty sessions in Ballarat.

The following table, showing the prices current at Ballarat, has been compiled from official returns, and will show the influence of the gold discovery on the value of the necessaries of life :—

ARTICLES.	QUANTITY.	DATES.							
		Jan. 1852.		May 1852.		June 1852.		Oct. 1852.	
		s.	d.	s.	d.	s.	d.	s.	d.
Flour	pound	0	6	0	6	0	10	1	3
Tea	,,	2	0	2	6	2	6	3	6
Sugar	,,	0	6	0	6	0	8	1	0
Meat	,,	0	3½	0	3	0	4½	0	5
Milk	quart	2	0	4	0				
Bread	pound	0	4½	0	6	0	9	0	10¼
Bacon	,,	3	0	2	6	3	0	3	0
Butter	,,	3	0	2	6	3	6	3	6
Potatoes	,,			0	3	0	5	0	8
Washing	dozen	7	0	6	0	6	0	8	0

The returns for the Mount Alexander diggings were more elaborate, as at the dates given that locality was the more important. It is, however, presumable that similar rates ruled in Ballarat for goods not included in the Ballarat table. The prices at Mount Alexander in October, 1852, were similar where both tables recite the same articles. We find that at Mount Alexander some handicraftsmen got as much as 25s per diem, oats were £3 per bushel, tobacco 10s per lb. ; while in Melbourne Wellington boots were quoted at from 50s to 60s per pair for imported, and from 75s to 90s for those made to order. The price of cartage from Melbourne to the diggings was from £100 to £120 per ton ; hotel charges were from 50s to 140s per week, and a horse at livery cost 15s a day, or 105s a week. And it must be remembered that these prices were paid for the roughest and rudest accommodation and service, while the qualities of goods could never in those days. be very closely or, at least, profitably scrutinised.

CHAPTER III.

FROM THE GOLD DISCOVERY TO THE YEAR OF THE EUREKA STOCKADE.

Great Aggregations of Population.—Opening up of Golden Grounds.—Character of the
Population.—Dates of Local Discoveries.—Ballarat Township Proclaimed.—First Sales
of Land.—Bath's Hotel.—First Public Clock.—Primitive Stores, Offices, and Conveyances.
Woman a Phenomenon.—First Women at Ballarat.—Curious Monetary Devices.—First
Religious Services.—Churches.—Newspapers.—Theatres.—Lawyers.—First Courts.—
Nuggets.—Golden Gutters.—Thirty or Forty Thousand Persons Located.

U R I N G the three years which passed between the December, 1851,—when the license
fee was raised from thirty shillings to sixty
shillings a month,—and the December, 1854,
when a rebel flag was hoisted at the Stockade, the
changes here had been vast and various. There
had been ebbings and flowings of population
between Ballarat and Mount Alexander and
other more newly opened gold-fields, and the
golden note which Hargreaves had struck in New South Wales
and Esmond in Victoria had been heard all over the world. From
every country under heaven there flocked to these shores men—
young and wifeless men for the most part—eager to engage in
the hunt for gold and fortune. Thousands upon thousands
came from Europe, Asia, Africa, and America, a mingled
motley host that swarmed upon the greater centres of gold-digging
enterprise, prospected for new grounds, or lingered upon the sea-
side to swell the urban populations. These gathering hosts rapidly
pushed forward the work of exploration. Slope and flat and gully
and hill-top were successively invested by the army of old-comers
and new-comers, before whose resistless march the forest gradually
fell, streets of canvas and shingles sprang into being, and thus,
where but a little time before the forest was thick, and bird and beast
were undisturbed, gold seeking became a wide-spread and permanent
industry. In February, 1853, the White Flat was rushed, and

before that time the upper part of Canadian Gully was opened. The Black Hill was already busily occupied, and the ground between that and Rotten Gully—the head of the Eureka Lead—was being taken up, the Eureka, so named by a medical man, being opened in August, 1852. During the next year or two the shallow grounds declined in importance, occasional discoveries of new reaches of such ground not sufficing to keep back the gradually growing importance of the deeper sinking on the Canadian, Gravel Pits, Eureka, and other golden gutters. Creswick was rushed in December, 1852, and ground down the Leigh and at Smythesdale was gradually opened thereafter. In Ballarat the population was located principally, indeed almost entirely, on the ground now traversed by the present streets of the eastern borough and along the lines of leads now built over, covered with gardens and yards, crossed by streets, or still lying outside the clustering houses and on the edges of the mingling boundaries of borough and bush.

Mr Latrobe, writing to Earl Grey on the 2nd March, 1852, said the population at Golden Point and " the outworks at Brown Hill" had " dwindled rapidly down to 200 steady licensed workers," averaging not more " than eight or ten ounces per man monthly." In the same despatch, however, his Excellency is pleased to express a belief—strengthened by the fact that the population had just then begun to increase and reached " 500 and upwards"—that when rain should come more people also would come, " and that it will be found that the 'Ballarat Gold-field' is far from being exhausted." His Excellency was, as we know, a good prophet. He was not always as accurate in his geography, for in a despatch dated 8th July, 1852, he informs Earl Grey that " a new working, called the ' Eureka,' nine miles from Ballarat proper, as well as two or three others were discovered in the month of May." In the Governor's view of the gold-field population there seems to have been not only a spirit of faith in the people, but, as became the son of the old Moravian missioner, of devotion towards God. In the despatch last cited, his Excellency says :—

On all hands it must be considered that the population at the workings, taken as a whole, are as orderly and well disposed as can be met with in any part of the colony. The comparative rarity of instances of grave outrage or of capital crime is a subject of great gratitude to God.

D

On the same day, in another despatch, the Governor adverts to the state of the Government and the exigencies of the new order of things, and again says his feeling is " that of thankfulness to God that so much has been achieved" in the way of preserving order. His Excellency over and over again bears testimony to the general good order maintained by the mining population, and that, too, " notwithstanding the extraordinary circumstances under which the multitude finds itself brought together, the passions and temptations of the hour, and the acknowledged insufficiency of the police to oppose physical force to any really serious outbreak or general disturbance." And when that which the Governor hinted at as possible had really become a fact, the *Argus* correspondent, writing from Ballarat on the 13th November, 1854, bears the following testimony to the good manners of the diggers on Sundays even in those exciting times :—

These Ballarat diggers are most extraordinary rebels. It struck me to remark particularly, and to enquire as to their conduct and observance of the Sabbath. Truly they have few advantages, precious little of the gospel offered to them, little either of education given ; no wonder, indeed, if they were vagabonds. But, as far as I could hear or see, the greatest possible order and sobriety, the utmost observance possible, I may say, of the Sabbath, has characterised their proceedings. Clean and neat in their diggers' best costume, they promenade over these vast gold-fields, their wives and children in their best frocks too ; but anything more calm or becoming or regardful of the day could hardly be witnessed in the best towns of even Christian Britain. How delightful would it not be to rule such men well ?

True, most truly, indeed ! But the writer need not have wondered if he had known that the great bulk of the population were of the best men of "the best towns of Christian Britain," men of invincible spirit, as well as of moral and law-abiding principles.

His Excellency's next despatch, dated the 31st July, 1852, enclosed a petition from the Legislative Council to the Queen, praying the establishment of a mint in Victoria, as " one of the richest gold-fields in the world." We have not yet got a mint any more than a law to legalise mining on private property, also petitioned for a year or two after the date last given. The Corporation of Melbourne backed up the Legislative Council's petition for a mint, but the Ballarat petition of 1855, for a private property law, fell then, as through all the succeeding years, upon an unsympathising Parliament and a careless metropolis. It is a coincidence worth noting, that the Melbourne corporation's petition for a mint was signed by the late Minister of Mines, Mr J. T. Smith, who had about that time begun his long series of mayorships of Melbourne.

The following table, compiled from various sources, including the compiler's own knowledge of several items, will give, as it were, a bird's-eye view of the opening of the several portions of the Ballarat field during the period ending December, 1854 :—

LOCALITY.	DATE.	LOCALITY.	DATE.
Clunes	1st July,.... 1851	Dead Horse Gullies ...	Early in.... 1853
Hiscock's Gully	August,..... 1851	Prince Regent	February,.. 1853
Golden Point	August,..... 1851	Sailors' Gully	Early in.... 1853
Canadian Gully	September, 1851	White Flat	Early in.... 1853
Brown Hill	September, 1851	Scotchman's Gully	Early in.... 1853
Black Hill	October,.... 1851	New Chum Gully	End of...... 1853
Little Bendigo Gullies	End of....... 1851	Black Hill Lead	Early in.... 1854
Eureka Lead	August,..... 1852	Gravel Pits Lead	Early in.... 1854
Red Hill Lead	November, 1852	Bakery Hill Lead	Early in.... 1854
Black Hill Flat	November, 1852	Gum Tree Flat	End of...... 1854
Creswick	Early in.... 1852		

The Ballarat township, now the Borough of Ballarat, was proclaimed towards the middle of the year 1852, the first sales of land being held in Geelong, Thomas Bath, now of Ceres Farm, Learmonth, being the first purchaser for business occupation. This was in November, 1852. The land obtained by Mr Bath was bought at the second sale, and consisted of portions of sections 1 and 2. Cobb's corner and the present town-hall site were sold at the same time, and were bought by Robt. Reeves, on which, subsequently, he forfeited his deposit. In the following year the land was put up again, and the corner was bought by Mr Bath for £250. The next lot, that now occupied by the Town-hall and District Court, was bought on the same day by P. W. Welsh, for £202, and the deposit on that lot was again forfeited. In the Appendix B will be found reports of the first land sales in Ballarat West and East.

Mr Bath built the first hotel in Ballarat, when all the Government dwellings were of canvas, or of slabs with bark roofs. It was erected in May, 1853, and licensed in the following month. At that time there was no other hotel between Buninyong and Lexton. But near the corner of Dana and Lydiard streets, now occupied by Holmes and Salter's law offices, a tent or hut was kept by one Meek, who

D 2

wrote pen and ink sketches of Victoria.   Meek, as became his name, did not make his business very prominent from a licensing point of view, and his establishment, by way of irony upon it or the police, used to be called " The Trooper's Arms."   The hotel built by Mr Bath in May, 1853, was of wood, in one story, and is now a private dwelling on Soldiers' Hill, the site of the original hotel being now occupied by the permament portion of the hotel now known as Craig's Royal hotel.   The wood for the first hotel was all brought from Geelong.   The two-story portion yet remaining was begun at the end of 1853, and finished in 1854.   The clock now in the wooden tower was then placed there, and was the first public clock in Ballarat.   Mr Biddle, now of Biddle's Saw-mills, supplied the hardwood for the building, the longer timbers having been cut in the hollow called the Crater on the western slope of Mount Buninyong.   He says he also suggested the placing of the public clock in the tower.   Mr Bath tells us that the cost of both buildings was enormous, for prices alike of material and transit were then excessive.   He paid £80 per ton carriage from Geelong, 40s to 45s per hundred feet at the pit for hardwood, as the indigenous forest timber is called, and £1 per hundred feet cartage from the saw-pits to Ballarat.   Mr Bath, in a letter to us, gives the following additional recollections :—

The roads in those days were frightful.   I have had goods on the road from Geelong above five weeks.   Mrs Bath came from Geelong by, I suppose, the first coach, and was three days and two nights on the road.   Watt ran a conveyance from Ballarat to Melbourne *via* Bacchus Marsh, stopping there one night, fare £7.   When I built in Ballarat there were not many hotels between Geelong and this—two at Batesford, then the Separation Inn, then Watson's at Meredith, and Jamieson's and Sellick's at Buninyong.   I have often ridden from Ballarat to Geelong without seeing a fence or meeting any person, but at those times I kept off the track.   I purchased a stack of hay in 1853 from Mr Darlot at the station at Sebastopol at £60 per ton, and I had to truss and cart it in the bargain, and this was hay of a self-sown crop and about half of it silver grass.   [While we copy this fine oaten hay in truss is sold in the Ballarat market at £2 10s per ton.]   I purchased oats in Geelong in 1850 at 2s per bushel, and at Bendigo in 1852 at £3 per bushel.   Some of the farming land in this district was sold in June, 1854, and I then commenced farming, cropping about fifty acres the first season.

On the 8th December, 1856, the first sale of frontages in Ballarat East commenced.   The sale had been preceded by much excitement relative to an absurd proclamation prohibiting the issue of licenses, or the carrying on of business within one mile of sold lands. After some agitation that ukase was withdrawn by the Government. The sales of the Main road frontages were continued for four consecutive days, and land now of little value then realised enormous prices. To return to 1852, we note that Mr Adams, late of Buninyong, had a store at the head of Golden Point, and he used to act as postmaster and convey letters from the diggings to the township of Buninyong, his store giving the name to the hill now known as Old Post-office Hill, where also the first Government Camp was situated, whence it was removed to the present locality. Mr Alfred Clarke, late of the *Geelong Advertiser*, acted as letter-carrier between Geelong and Buninyong in 1851. The first supply of stores to the early diggers was afforded by one Stirling's hawking dray, in October, 1851, and the first regular store was shortly after that opened by Mr Robinson, subsequently a member of the first town council of Geelong. Stirling and Sons' drays were the only conveyances at that time for either passengers or goods between Ballarat and Geelong. Stores, like dwellings, were rude, and often the storekeeper, like the digger, was surly. From his tent of calico or canvas, with its furniture of blankets, frying-pan, cradle, puddling-tub, pick and shovel, the digger went to the store where mutton, flour, boots, serge-shirts, moleskin trousers, tobacco, sardines, sugar, picks, shovels, billies, and other things were all found in one grand miscellany. Coin was rare, and the digger generally bartered his gold-dust for goods. Change there was none, and reckonings partook of the largeness of view which ignored minute calculations. Paper was scarce, and often the digger had to carry his groceries to his tent in box, billy, handkerchief, or shirt. The life was rough but eventful, not to say jolly, and as long as gold was got the digger was generally happy. If his pocket grew light and the authorities demanded license fees, he had to wash dirt enough to supply the required gold ; but if he failed in his search, or, worst of all, if health failed, he was of all men most miserable. There were no hospitals or asylums in that early day, and a woman was an absolute phenomenon ; so the sick man often died with nothing civilised about him but the awkward, if gentle, tending of his digging partners in the gold-hunting wilderness. And some fell

in utter loneliness, their bones when found being buried beneath
some drooping spray of peppermint about the slopes or gullies of
the gold-field.

   In those first days of digging-life, when womanless crowds
wrestled with the earth and the forest amid much weariness and
solitude of heart, the arrival of a woman was the signal for a cry
and a gathering. The shout, " There's a woman !" emptied many a
tent of besoiled and hardy diggers, for the strange sight evoked
instant memories of far-away homes : of mothers, wives and sweet-
hearts, and all the sweet affections and courtesies they represented,
and never with such eloquent emphasis as then. There was no man,
having the heart of a man, who did not bless the vision, while
many an eye was moistened with the sudden tear as love, hope,
disappointment, fear, struggled all at once in the homeless digger's
bosom. But recklessness often marked the life of the time, and the
brandy bottle of the grog-shanty killed some victims then as it does
in this later day. Unlicensed at first, the grog-sellers got licensed
afterwards, and did heavy trade with the heavy drinker, the more
moderate drinkers helping to swell the business to a large and highly
profitable aggregate. Prices of all kinds of goods and all kinds of
labor were enormously high. One publican in 1853, when cartage
from Geelong was £80 per ton, paid £1500 a week for cartage for
seven months running. This one man had at one time no fewer
than 122 public-houses or shanties either mortgaged to him or in his
own actual possession.

   From Mr Irwin's contributions to the *Ballarat Star*, more
expressly referred to in a subsequent chapter, we take the following
as confirmatory of some foregoing remarks :—

   During the earlier days of the rush to Golden Point a monetary arrangement
existed which would scarcely be long tolerated now-a-days. It was this, when
the purchaser went to a store for supplies he got as change either a Burnbank,
Colac, or other " note." These notes were simply rudely lithographed pro_
mises "to pay one day after sight," in Melbourne or Geelong, where the
principal store of issuer was, the amounts specified in the " notes," which
were of various amounts, from 5s upwards. Suppose a purchaser of goods had
got some of the notes from the Burnbank store and on the next occasion for
purchasing went to the Colac or Robinson's store, the persons in charge of the
latter would not accept of the notes of the rival establishment, to which the
holder of them must go unless he was willing to lose their value. The system
was an intolerable nuisance while it lasted, but it had soon to be abolished.

change for purchases being reduced to a minimum by the sale of so many
ounces or pennyweights of gold to the storekeeper, the balance, if any, being
made good by boxes of matches and the like, to the satisfaction generally of
both parties to the transaction. It is on record that very small potatoes,
reckoned at the rate of threepence each, served as small change to a storekeeper who is now one of the wealthiest of Victorian colonists.

The first woman who arrived among the diggers was a bullock-
driver's wife, whose husband had left his bullocks and turned to
gold seeking. Next came Mrs Thomas Bath, who was, in fact, either
the first woman, or among the first half dozen or so of women,
who settled on the gold-field. After her others came at wide
and dreary intervals in angelic similitude; but when the first
two years had passed, and the gold-field had acquired some elements
of permanency, women joined their husbands, sons, and brothers
already here, or came with new-comers, and thus gradually the
diggers' social life assumed a greater similarity to that of older
settlements.

The first meetings for the celebration of divine worship in public
were held by a few Wesleyans, who assembled in a mia-mia, or tent
of boughs, as for a Christian Feast of Tabernacles, in the White
Flat, where the smithie belonging to Mr John James, late M.L.A.,
now stands, near the intersection of Grant street and the Yarrowee.
For greater privacy these Wesleyans used to go from the tent of
boughs to the denser bush then adjacent, and, seated on fallen logs,
hold there the "class-meeting,"—that private service which is
peculiar to the Wesleyan family of Christians. They were after
that held in a hut on Winter's Flat, and in a tent at the White Flat,
when the Golden Point rush was at its height. One of those early
Wesleyan worshippers writes as follows :—

The first service was held on Sunday morning, the 28th September, on the
flat, preacher (local) Mr J. Sanderson, about one hundred present, text
Corinthians II, "Ye are bought with a price." Class meeting at two o'clock in
Sanderson's tent on Golden Point. Mr Hastie came, attracted by the singing,
and requested the aid of the singers, and waited half-an-hour, and took them
to his service at the Commissioners' Camp. Sunday following, 5th October,
Rev. Mr. Lewis, Wesleyan minister, from Geelong, preached on the flat at
eleven o'clock and at the Black Hill in the evening. Subscriptions for a chapel
rolled in and on the 12th November, in the afternoon, Mr Sanderson opened
the new chapel ; text 12th Chap. Isaiah, "Behold, God is my salvation." The
chapel was of saplings and boughs with tarpaulin over it, no pulpit. James

Oddie was at the opening service. The day was a very stormy one. Mr William Howell was the treasurer. A Mr Jones, of Tasmania, gave the first pound, and nuggets rolled in fast and furious. No other service was held in the building. The rush to Forest Creek took away the population the next week.

The social, if not aggressive, missionary spirit of Wesleyanism had earlier proof in Victoria than even in those services at Golden Point. M'Combie, in his "History of Victoria," has the following passage :—

In April, 1836, before the city of Melbourne existed, the Rev. Mr Orton, a Wesleyan minister of Van Diemen's Land, who had accompanied Mr Batman when that gentleman brought his family across Bass' Straits, celebrated divine service beneath the beautiful casuarina trees which adorned the crest of Batman's Hill. Those who assembled to worship upon this interesting occasion belonged to many races and countries ; they were a pretty fair average from the adjoining colonies and the islands of Great Britain. Mr Batman's Sydney blacks also attended, while not a few of the aborigines, who had been attracted by the preparations, had crowded in. The Church of England service was read, and an excellent discourse preached from the text, "Except a man be born again he cannot see the kingdom of God ;" and we have heard from one who was present that the first sermon delivered by a regularly ordained clergyman on the site of the great metropolis was striking and orthodox.

The Wesleyans discovered similar activity when, in 1852, the crowding hosts of gold-seeking immigrants could not find houses to enter in Melbourne, not even at the enormous rents then demanded. The Government was at its wits' end and did its slow and cumbrous best to procure shelter for the crowd, but Mr Latrobe thus refers to the Wesleyans in a despatch on 28th October, 1852, to Earl Grey :—

The Wesleyan body have the credit of taking the lead, by a very large collection, amounting, as I am informed, to near £2000, and the immediate commencement of a "Refuge for the Houseless," primarily for those in connection with their particular community, but in effect as far as their means will allow, for any who might be found to require it.

Some who joined in those tent or hut services, in the midst of the hot fever of the first rush to the marvellous riches of Golden Point, became active honorable men in our public life, and some are at this day filling positions more or less prominent in both ecclesiastical and secular life. The Rev. Thomas Hastie, of Buninyong, and the Roman Catholic Father Dunne, of Geelong, used to visit the diggings also and minister to their several flocks at irregular intervals.　The Wesleyans built the first place of worship, the site being on a knoll near Sinclair's Hill, and named by them Wesley Hill.　They then built a weatherboard church where the Eastern Town-hall now stands.　The Roman Catholics, Anglicans, and Presbyterians, were close upon the heels of the Wesleyans, and other denominations followed, the first church building in permanent materials being erected by the Wesleyans where their present school-house now stands at the corner of Lydiard and Dana streets.　The first church there was built towards the end of the year 1854, some stray bullets from the insurgent diggers on the flat falling among the workmen while the building was being built.　The late Rev. Theophilus Taylor was then superintendent minister of the Wesleyan Church here.　After holding services in what was then the police-court, in Ballarat West, the Church of England people built a small wooden church in Armstrong street, where worship was held till Christchurch was built in Lydiard street. The wooden church was afterwards a billiard saloon, and is now Pinkerton and Co.'s printing office.

Schools and newspapers sprang up, too, during these first three years, and the population increased from Governor Latrobe's hypo-thetical census of 6000 to over four times that number.　The bills of newspaper mortality showed a strong tendency in the early papers to early death.　Mr Alfred Clarke, as the representative of Mr Harrison (then proprietor of the *Geelong Advertiser*), attempted to bring a printing press here in October, 1851, for the purpose of bringing out a paper to be called the *Boninyong Gazette and Mining Journal*—for it must be remembered that Buninyong was then the only recognised settlement.　It was a township of some antiquity, and Ballarat was but an aboriginal name in the aboriginal bush, or in the hardly less barbarous diggings.　Clarke's dray with the press got bogged on the way up from Geelong, and in the meantime Clarke had a little feud with the commissioner of the day about the site selected on Old Post-office Hill, the press was packed off to Geelong again, and thus ended the first essay in the direction of newspaper literature here.　The *Ballarat Times and Southern Cross* was the first paper actually published in Ballarat, the first number being published on the 4th March, 1854, at an office in Mair street, opposite the Market Square.　Subsequently the *Times*

office was removed to Bakery Hill, near the intersection of the
present Victoria and Humffray streets, by the proprietor and editor,
the late Henry Seekamp. The paper lived for several years, and
died on the 5th of October, 1861. The *Leader* was the next
adventure. It was a joint-stock affair, and only made six appearances. The *Creswick Chronicle* was next brought out by Mr J. J.
Ham, an old colonist and experienced journalist. It died in the
bloom of early youth, after two or three issues only. In July,
1855, appeared the *Ballarat Trumpeter*, a gratuitous sheet, which
in 1856 was published as a tri-weekly, under the joint ownership
of Messrs Wheeler, Fletcher, and Evans. It lived about twelve
months, and was the nucleus of the *Ballarat Standard*. Then
came the *Star*. It appeared as a tri-weekly journal on the 22nd
September, 1855, under a joint-stock proprietary, with Messrs Samuel
Irwin and J. J. Ham as editors. After some four months it was
discontinued for a week, and then it re-appeared, having passed into
private hands in the interval, and in December, 1856, appeared daily
as at present. On the 10th November, 1856, the *Ballarat Standard*
appeared, and some time previously the *Nation*. The *Standard*,
owned by Messrs D. D. Wheeler and W. Cooper, was a tri-weekly,
edited by Mr W. Cooper (now of the *Portland Guardian*). It
made its last appearance on the 26th of the month in which it was
born. Mr Denovan, afterwards M.L.A. for Sandhurst, edited the
Nation, which peacefully expired after less than a dozen issues.*
In 1857 an attempt at the facetious was made, and a *Ballarat
Punch* appeared, and laughed at some of our follies, and chided
some of our sins. Mr Hasleham, then correspondent of the
Melbourne Herald, conducted the new comer through a portion of
its short and merry career, and Mr E. C. Moore designed a capital
title page for it that never appeared for want of the necessary wood
or stone gravers. The comic little paper had several owners and
editors, but none of them could make it live. Newspaper enterprise
then flagged for a while, until, on the 24th March, 1859, a little
company of adventurers brought out the *North Grenville Mercury*,
Mr M. G. Byrne, now a barrister, being editor. It was pluckily
maintained, first as a tri-weekly and then as a daily, in all for some
twenty weeks, when, after a hundred appearances, it was also
welcomed by the journalistic Capulets to their tomb. The *Tribune*

came next, appearing on the 21st of November, 1861, and ending on the 11th July, 1863, Mr Harrison, previously of the *Ballarat Times*, being the manager and editor, and at last sole proprietor. The *Ballarat Sun* arose on the 26th September, 1864, and appeared daily under the auspices of a joint-stock proprietory. After a troublous life and change of ownership, it sank below the horizon during the following year. Advertising sheets, distributed gratuitously, appeared and disappeared at intervals all the years after 1854, and on 25th of May, 1863, appeared the *Evening Post*, at once our first evening and first penny paper. It has had several changes of ownership. The *Ballarat Courier*, Messrs Bateman and Clark, proprietors, first appeared on the 10th of June, 1867, and the *Evening Mail*, the last-born of the newspapers, on the 6th of April, 1869. It was started by a band of printers, then, in the hands of the same company, was registered with an increased capital under the Trading Companies Statute, and is now in private hands. *Ballarat Punch* revived also, and struggled against fate till February, 1870, when it disappeared. It was started by Mr C. A. Abbot, who was both artist and editor, as well as proprietor. Buninyong, Creswick, Clunes, and Smythesdale now have papers of their own ; and even Sebastopol, the most juvenile of boroughs, has had its local newspaper. In recording this list of publications, we have travelled beyond the period set down at the head of the chapter, but have done so as being more convenient than otherwise.

The caterers for the amusement of the early diggers had ample patronage in those days. The first theatrical venture was in December, 1853, when a canvas house was set up in the Gravel Pits, the leading actress afterwards becoming the wife of the editor and proprietor of the *Ballarat Times*. A person named Clarke opened a similar theatre on the Eureka in February, 1854, and soon after that Mrs Hanmer opened a weatherboard theatre called the Adelphi, where the Tontine, and more recently called the Windsor hotel, afterwards stood in Esmond, now Durham, street east. The Charlie Napier, Montezuma, and Victoria theatres in Main street, all long since burnt down, speedily followed with larger accommodations and better performances. There came afterwards, drawn by the fame of the golden colony, some of the most accomplished histrionic artistes of the time. Catherine Hayes, Anna Bishop, Lola Montez, Brooke, Kean, Ellen Tree, Sir William and Lady Don, Jefferson, Celeste, Montgomery were among the brighter stars that have risen upon our auriferous horizon.   Lucy Chambers, an Australian by birth and a singer of European fame, has recently appeared in Victoria in opera, and Charles Mathews, the comedian, has also lately come to these golden shores.

The first magistrate sat of course at Buninyong. Mr Eyre was the officer, and he used to visit the diggings at intervals.   The finding of the first monster nugget at Canadian Gully in February, 1853, caused a new rush hither, and in that rush came Mr Adam Loftus Lynn, who was the first attorney that practised here.   After spending the months of February, March, and April in digging, he began to practise his profession on the 1st of May, his office being then opposite to the *Ballarat Times* office, and on the site now occupied by Mr Logan, watchmaker, Humffray street.   About six months after Mr Lynn had commenced practice, he was joined by Mr Ocock. After them came, in time, a forensic deluge. The first local County Court and Court of General Sessions were opened by the late Judge Wrixon, with Mr Francis Greene as clerk of the peace, in January, 1853, at Buninyong, the original style of the County Court being "The County Court of Buninyong and Ballarat." It retained this style till a year or two ago. The courts presided over by Judge Wrixon first sat at Ballarat near the end of the year 1853.   Mr Justice Williams opened the first Circuit Court in Ballarat on the 12th of December, 1856, in what was then the police court-house, the county court-house, and the place where the English Church service was performed.   The building stood in what is now Camp street, on the western side, where the street bends round by the present office of the Superintendent of Police.   In respect of the courts of law we have gone beyond the period set down at the head of this chapter, but we have done so by way of convenience to the reader.

By the end of the year 1852 the diggers on the gutters had begun to reach what was then called deep ground, and their vocation soon after that began, though rudely and tentatively, to assume more of the character of regular mining.   The year 1853 was rich in new discoveries, and a large number of gullies were then opened.   The

Canadian, opened early in 1851, was named from a man called Canadian Swift. The gully and issuing gutter were very rich, the first large nugget ever found being unearthed there about February, 1853. It weighed 1620 oz., and has never been surpassed in weight by any discoveries since, except by the Welcome nugget, found on the reef in some old ground on Bakery Hill on the 9th of June, 1858 (weight, 2217 oz.), and the Welcome Stranger, found at Mount Moliagul on the 5th of February, 1869 (weight, 2280 oz). A rich bend in the gutter known as the Jeweller's Shops, was about two hundred yards from where the nugget was found. The ground there was prodigiously rich in gold, heavy, lumpy, bright gold in profusion, and hence the name given to the spot. The gutter ran down the valley, and mingled with the other golden streams that met in the area formerly known as the Gum Tree Flat, into which also the Red Hill, Red Streak, Eureka, Bakery Hill, Gravel Pits, and their tributaries poured their golden wealth. Dr. Gibson, Muir, and others on the Gravel Pits gutter near the Prince Albert hotel (afterwards St. John's Presbyterian Church), and Rowland and party in Sailor's Gully, appear to have been among the first miners who slabbed their shafts throughout. Gibson's first essay was with frame and piles; but before that, in 1852, Mr Beilby and others used saplings to secure unsafe shafts, and others lined the shafts with slabs of bark placed vertically and fastened with sapling frames. The claims known as the Italians', where the Gravel Pits entered the Gum Tree Flat, were famous for their heavy deposits of gold. The Eureka, the Canadian, and the Gravel Pits leads, all opened just after the first rush to Golden Point, were the famous golden trinity that made Ballarat world-renowned. The Eureka ran from Little Bendigo southwards beneath the Yarrowee and the present railway, Humffray, Victoria, and Eureka streets, into Pennyweight Flat, where it was joined, near the present Charlie Napier, by the Canadian, both flowing with other leads into the Gum Tree Flat, where they were joined by the Gravel Pits and Bakery Hill, which ran from the foot of Black Hill across the present Humffray street and Victoria street to the general place of confluence in the Gum Tree Flat—that area of ground the eastern edge of which Main street now traverses. The combined lead, which was in fact the main ancient stream flowing over the primeval bed rocks, ran westward, and entered beneath the basaltic plateau of Ballarat West, just below the intersection of Sturt and Lydiard streets, where it took a southern bend, and received a tributary from Golden Point. This tributary, being the first registered gutter, gave the name to the main stream which flowed on westward and southward, receiving many tributaries in its course. This is, however, anticipatory in point of time. The year 1853 was marked by a vigorous prospecting. In that year, the whole range north and south of the Ballarat Flat was opened up. Prince Regent's, Sailor's, Scotchman's, and New Chum Gullies on the eastern slope of the Golden Point range, and Terrible, White Horse, Frenchman's, Chinamen's, and Cobbler's Gullies on the western slope, were in that year entered upon in their shallower portions. On the Black Hill side, besides that hill and the adjacent gullies and Little Bendigo, Dead Horse, Sulky, and other gullies on the way to Creswick were opened. Apropos of Frenchman's Gully, it may here be noted that Esmond, the Clunes gold discoverer, found a 70-oz. nugget in the shallow ground in 1853. In the following year, while Sir Charles and Lady Hotham were on a visit here, a nugget weighing 98½ lbs. was found in Dalton's Flat, and called the Lady Hotham after the wife of the Governor. By that time the quartz lodes at the Black Hill had been tested. Dr. Otway was the first adventurer there, and he erected a windmill as a motive power for reducing the stone. After that he procured Chilian mills, but neither process was successful. Mr George Milner Stephen followed Dr. Otway, and with similar results. The Port Phillip Company then came upon the scene, operating both at the Black Hill and on the ranges at Dead Horse, but with small success. That company soon found better fortune at the Clunes reefs, from which it still draws a large annual revenue.

Thus the three first years after the gold discovery saw some of the richest of the Ballarat gutters opened up, most of the rich shallow grounds once or twice dug over, a population of from 30,000 to 40,000 assembled, lines of streets thickly inhabited by dwellers in canvas or wood, churches, theatres, hotels, bowling alleys, dancing saloons, stores in plenty, and all the elements present of a rough, prosperous, young gold-fields settlement; while enterprising prospectors were still pushing out on every side, and adding fresh discoveries to those that had already made Ballarat famous in every part of the civilised world.

S.D.S.Huyghue del. 1854.

THE GRAVEL PITS, BALLAARAT.

SEP^t 1854

F.W.Niven, lith.

Plan of organisatione
for the Diggers of Ballarat.

Let every 7 men select a trust or sub officer,
who will be responsible for the immediate appearance,
if wanted, of the 6 men under his comand,
7 of those little détaichement's to form a company,
and to select a captaine. the captain to be
responsible for his company, and to keep the muster
rolls. 8/ companies to form a brigade. Every
company to select 3 member's, for the electione
of a military comissione, and a commander in
chief of the Ballarat forces. the captaine
of every company to appoint a meeting place
for the company, every trust officer to appoint
a place of meeting for his six men. The commander
in chief to appoint a meeting place for the
united forces, and to erect a flag staff for
giving the signal to assemble. &c. Vern
late aid de camp to Gen Miller

[left margin, written vertically] every company to pay the cost of a road to their military comission.

CHAPTER IV.

DIGGER HUNTING.

The Gold License.—Taxation Without Representation.—Unequal Incidence of the Tax.—Episodes of Digger Hunting.—Irritating Method of Enforcing the Tax.—Suspicions of Corruption among the Magistrates and Police.—Visit of Sir Charles and Lady Hotham.—Big Larry.—Reform League.—Murder of Scobie.—Acquittal of Bentley.—Dewes Suspected.—Mass Meetings.—Burning of Bentley's Hotel.—Irwin's Narrative.—Arrest of Fletcher, M'Intyre, and Westerby.—Re-arrest of Bentley.—Conviction of Bentley.—Conviction of Fletcher, M'Intyre, and Westerby.—Demand for their Liberation.—Increased Excitement.—Fete to the American Consul.—Foster.—Sir Charles Hotham.—Arrival of Troops.—Troops Assaulted.—Bakery Hill Meeting.—Southern Cross Flag.—Burning the Licenses.

O W N the swift stream of the brief years we now come to troublous times. At the root of all the troubles that led to the Eureka Stockade, lay the old tyranny of taxation without representation. When the gold discovery occurred, Victoria had not long been created an independent colony. It had become independent then only in the sense of separation from New South Wales, and in having a Lieutenant-Governor and a Parliament of its own. But that Parliament was not representative in more than a small degree. It was a single House, and largely composed of nominees of the Crown, the balance of members representing constituencies in which the masses, gathered and increasing on the gold-fields, had, not simply not a voice potential, but absolutely no voice at all. This was an injustice that was attended with more than the usual dangers that accompany wrong. The gold-fields inhabitants being outside the mystic circle of governing power were placed, *ab initio*, in an attitude of hostility to the constituted authorities. An unnatural separation was, so to speak, created by the law between the majority of the people and the Crown; and to give intensity to the danger, the people here were for the most part superior in mental and bodily capacities to the

average capacities of their fellow countrymen whom they had left
in their fatherlands. The courage and adventure which had made
them emigrants, and the physical strength which had enabled them
to weather the rude elements of early gold-fields life, were qualities
which made them valuable as freemen, but dangerous as slaves.
They were not the men tamely to brook the voiceless poverty of
political power which marked the ante-Eureka Stockade era; and
when to the absence of representation were added the insolence
of gold-fields officials, the indignities of quasi-martial regulations,
and dark suspicions of corruption, the elements of disorder rapidly
grew more and more menacing to the public peace, until, at last, it
needed only the proverbial want of tact in official routine to permit
the recurrence of irritations that fell like sparks upon prepared
combustibles. Then a flame burst out that was partially quenched in
blood, the black disorder of the conflagration being cleared away
only by that reform of grievances which has given to us what we
now possess.

When the European gold hunter arrived in Victoria, just after the
gold discovery, he no sooner found himself upon the gold-fields than
he was unpleasantly brought into contact with a Government in
the construction of which, and in the direction of whose policy, he
had no more voice than the naked aborigine he saw prowling about
the bush. Before he could legally put pick or shovel into the
ground, the digger had to pay a heavy monthly tax, levied upon him
by a Government and Parliament in which he was not represented.
At first for thirty shillings, then for sixty shillings, and then again
for thirty shillings per month, the digger obtained a license in this
or some nearly identical form :—

GOLD   LICENSE.

No.   185
   The bearer   , having paid to me the sum of
on account of the territorial revenue, I hereby license him to dig, search for, and
remove gold on and from any such Crown lands within the
as I shall assign to him for that purpose during the month of   185 ,
not within half-a-mile of any head station.
   This license is not transferable and must be produced whenever demanded by
me or any other person acting under the authority of the Government.
                          (Signed)   A. B., Commissioner.

In this we have the symbol of the grievances that roused the gold-
fields population. There was a heavy tax levied monthly by a

non-representative executive ; that tax was often oppressive in itself and unequal in its incidence, and it was often collected in so insolent a manner, that its unpopularity became a thousandfold greater.

Here, illustrative of the sport of license or digger-hunting, is an episode from a lecture by Mr. William Benson, once an escort-trooper in South Australia, then a reporter on the *Ballarat Times*, and now a mining surveyor. The lecture was delivered at a Working Men's Temperance Meeting, in the Alfred Hall, on Saturday, the 19th February, 1870 :—

I had been for some short time in 1853 occupied at the store of Messrs Hilfling and Greig, on the township, where the drapery establishment of David Jones and Co. now is. Not very well liking my employment, I was on my way to the labor office on Bakery Hill to offer for a stock-rider's billet. Being dressed in somewhat digger costume, and walking near where the Yarrowee bridge now is, I heard behind me a stentorian voice—" Hallo ! you fellow." I turned round. Speechless horror ! There, at full gallop, at the head of fifteen or twenty mounted troopers, with scabbards clattering and stirrups jingling, rode a stalwart black-looking chief of the digger hunters. " Hallo ! I say, you, Sir," thundered forth he, with a mighty flourish of his sword glittering in the beautiful sunlight, "have you got a license." Worse luck to me I never was a digger, even when gold could be got by pounds weight. Well, there flourished the sword of the mighty hunter, and there stammered I forth " No." At that moment up came the mounted and foot police. "Take this man into custody," shouts out the leader of the troop and off he gallops. I, in my simplicity, said the mighty hunter did not recognise me, he was a sergeant in the foot police at Adelaide when I was a government escort trooper there. " Well," says my custodian, " all I know is that I am going to take you to quod." This was the " logs," but all this time I was being taken away from the " logs " (or Camp lock-up), and near where the corner of Barkly street now is we there found another guardian of the spoil of the hunters, holding in terror of his formidable weapon a real digger whose clothes bespoke him to be a sojourner amongst the holes on the Red Hill. We were marched up the slope of Golden Point, the troopers and foot police far in advance ; but I refused to go further and sat down. One of the diggers near, espying my bespattered comrade in distress, calls out " Hallo ! mate, what's the row ?" " Got no license," grumbles out the Red Hill digger. " Can't you give bail?" sings out the charitable-minded questioner. " Not I," returns the other, " or I shouldn't be without a license." No more ado, but into his tent walks he of the charitable mind, and out he shortly comes and walking straight up to my fellow captive, thrusts into his brawny hand five £1 notes, saying "There's thy bail money," and off he walked. " Know you that man ?" said I to my astonished mate in misfortune. " Never saw him before in my life," he replied, " but he is a good fellow and one of the right sort."

E

Benson and his companion were both bailed, and, after the examination before the bench, the digger was fined in the amount of his bail. Benson escaped fine, and after some delay recovered his bail. Such episodes abounded, with variations in detail. From an unpublished manuscript by Mr R. M. Serjeant, descriptive of the times under discussion, the following comic picture is taken :—

We marked out a couple of claims on the Eureka, and one or two more at Prince Regent's Gully. On returning home one afternoon we found our gully (Specimen Gully) surrounded by the force on the hunt for licenses. I noticed our sod chimney smoking, and the hut door—an old flour sack stretched on a frame of wattle sapling—wide open, so I concluded Joe, our cooking mate, was about, and could not very well escape two of the police who were marching straight into the doorway. I had approached to within a few yards of the scene, license-paper in hand, when the traps stepped back, as I thought, rather hastily, and, to my surprise, were confronted on the threshhold by a smart, genteel-looking female, who politely enquired their business, and the next moment, espying me close in the rear, said—" Perhaps my brother can answer your enquiries, gentlemen !" The gentlemen, however, who were not among the rudest of their class, begged pardon, and turned on their heels in search of more easy prey, while I proceeded to introduce myself to my newly-found sister, whom I then saw throwing up her heels and cutting most unladylike capers round the dining table. In the course of the evening Joe intimated that as he had resolved never to take out a license, he should, if we had no objection, continue to wear his new style of attire, and that in future his name was to be Josephine.

Mr Serjeant gives us another lively view of the digger-hunting process :—

"Traps ! traps !! Joe ! Joe !!" were the well-known signals which announced that the police were out on a license raid, now becoming almost of daily occurrence. The hasty abandonment of tubs and cradles by fossickers and outsiders, and the great rush of shepherds to the deep holes on the flat as the police hove in view, readily told that there were not a few among them who believed in the doctrine that " base is the slave who pays." Hunting the digger was evidently regarded by Mr Commissioner Sleuth and his hounds as a source of delightful recreation, and one of such paramount importance to the State that the sport was reduced to an exact science. Thus, given a couple of dirty constables, in diggers' guise, jumping a claim, gentle shepherd approaches with dilapidated shovel on shoulder, and proceeds to dispossess intruders in summary manner. A great barney ensues : Constable Derwent and his mate talk big, a crowd gathers round, and "a ring ! a ring !!" is the cry. The combatants have just commenced to shape, when the signal referred to at the head of this paragraph rings through the flat. On come the traps in skirmishing order, driving in the stragglers as they advance, and supported by mounted troopers in the rear, who occupy commanding positions on the ranges. A great haul is made, and some sixty prisoners are marched off in triumph to the Camp, hand-cuffed together like a gang of felons, there to be dealt with according to the caprice or cupidity of their oppressors.

Irwin, in his letters to the *Geelong Advertiser*, corroborates Benson's account of the hunting mode, and gives, under date 23rd October, 1854, the following statement in explanation of resolutions adopted at a meeting in the Roman Catholic Chapel on Bakery Hill, expressive of sympathy with Father Smyth, and of indignation against Commissioner Johnstone :—

Some time since Mr Johnstone was in command of a license-hunting party, one of whom, named Lord, come up to a tent in which was John Gregory, a foreigner, on a visit of charity to some other foreigners whose language he knew. The trooper Lord ordered the "—— wretches" to come out of the tent that he might see their licenses. Gregory, the servant of the Rev. Mr Smyth, had no such document ; on seeing which the trooper, damning him and the priest, ordered him to come along. As Gregory is not very strong-limbed, he requested to be allowed to go to the Camp himself, as he was not able to follow the force while visiting the various diggings looking for unlicensed miners. So far right ; but on Gregory's appearing unwilling or unable to follow, the trooper ill-used him, and only let him off on Mr Smyth depositing £5 bail for his appearance. At the Police-office, after being fined £5 for not having a license, Gregory was going away, but was re-called. On re-appearing, the charge of wanting a license was withdrawn by Mr Johnstone, and one of assaulting a trooper put instead. For this he, a cripple, was fined the original £5 bail. In the whole affair the Rev. Mr Smyth was certainly treated with but little courtesy ; and the trumpery story of a cripple assaulting an able-bodied mounted trooper is too ridiculous to warrant serious attention.

Englishmen, free from crime, were at the mercy in those days of many demoralised and ruffianly policemen, who treated the diggers like felons, and were too often abetted by their superiors in this treatment of men thus practically deprived of two centuries of political progress. To these causes of irritation were added suspicions of corruption in the administration of the common law on the Ballarat gold-field, and this it was, as will presently appear, that precipitated the events which ended in the collision between the Queen's troops and the armed insurgents. Begun at Bendigo in 1853, the agitation against the gold-fields license tax, and for representation in Parliament, was quickly taken up in Ballarat, and was there pushed forward with more eventful incident to a more tragic conclusion. The outbreak was not that of a stupid, stolid,

E 2

ignorant peasantry in arms against hay stacks and threshing machines, but of a free-spirited, intelligent people, goaded to resistance by intolerable wrong, and guided—at all events during a portion of the period—by men of education and character among themselves, aided by a provincial Press created and sustained for the most part by men also from among their own ranks. When commissioners, magistrates, and troopers had got used to treat the diggers as people to be taxed and harried at pleasure, the offensive method of carrying out the obnoxious license law had grown so irksome that a reform of the whole system was irresistibly pressed upon the population. A Reform League was formed for the redress of grievances, and all the gold-fields supported the organisation. Towards the middle of 1854, Mr Latrobe's successor, Sir Charles Hotham, and Lady Hotham, visited Ballarat, and, in spite of the existing grievances, they were loyally received. In connection with the visit there was some prominence acquired by a gigantic Irish digger, called Big Larry, who, with a rougher Raleigh-like politeness, not only assiduously planked over muddy spots for the dainty feet of the Governor's wife, but sometimes carried that representative lady bodily over portions of the ground, and generally cleared a way for the visitors through the crowd of spectators. It may be that his Excellency and his Melbourne advisers were led, by the welcome given by the diggers, to misconstrue the mind of the gold-fields population, and to think that all the Camp officials, instead of a very small minority only, were proper men properly enforcing the law. Be that as it may, the Government not only maintained the law, but sought to enforce it with greater rigor. In October, 1854, the Government sent up an order that the police should go out two days a week hunting for unlicensed diggers. At that time there were four commissioners at Ballarat, between whom the field was parcelled out in four divisions; but the boundaries being ill-defined, the police often hunted over the same ground twice, and thus the rudeness which too often marked the process of license-fee collection was often repeated over and over again upon the same man in the same day.

While reform leagues and committees were organising during the years 1853 and 1854, the population educated itself to a certain degree in the discussion of grievances, and men came to the front as popular leaders, some of whom remain to this day in public life, as Messrs Humffray and Lalor, at present members of the Legislative Assembly. Others there were who, more gifted in committee than upon the public platform, quietly and effectively aided the reform movement, but never rose or sought to rise to the more prominent elevation of public celebrity. Many of these, also, remain with us to this day. " Digger hunting," as the collection of the license fee was called by the men on the gold-fields, continued incessantly, accompanied with frequent instances of official tyranny. Informers were employed by the authorities, and some of those men were mere creatures of the higher officials, and had histories that helped from the first to forbid confidence. The tide of irritation and discontent rose higher and higher, and the more excited of the population began to collect arms, to form leagues of their different nationalities, and to discuss the probabilities of open insurrection and a declaration of revolt from British rule. At length, in the latter half of the year 1854, a digger named James Scobie was killed in a scuffle at the Eureka hotel, on Specimen Hill (now Eureka street), kept by one Bentley, who was considered by the diggers to be a participator in Scobie's murder. The house was one of very bad fame, and Bentley was arrested and brought before a bench presided over by Mr Dewes, the police magistrate, who acquitted him. There were a few thoughtful men sitting in the court at the time, who saw the gravity of what they felt to be a glaring miscarriage of justice. One of them—Mr J. Russell Thomson— narrowly escaped committal for daring to urge that Bentley's was a case which should be sent to a jury. This acquittal aroused the population more than any single official act since the gold discovery, for the general belief was that Bentley was guilty, and that the police magistrate corruptly urged the acquittal because he was under pecuniary obligations to the prisoner. This opinion as to Dewes' embarrassments with Bentley is still held. Dewes fell before the popular storm, went to British Columbia, where he justified Victorian condemnation by committing embezzlement, and he ended his life by suicide in Paris. The exasperation caused by Bentley's acquittal gave a vigorous impetus to the agitations for reform. At an indignation meeting held on, or close to, the spot where Scobie was killed, Messrs J. R. Thomson, T. D. Wanliss, Peter Lalor, J. W.

Gray, W. Corkhill, Alex. M'P. Grant, and Archibald Carmichael
were appointed a committee to take steps for the collection
of money to defray the cost of a further prosecution of Bentley,
and so warmly did the public respond that £200 were
gathered in a very short time in Ballarat alone, when the
collections were stopped, as the Government, in the meantime,
moved in the business and offered rewards for the apprehension of
Scobie's murderers.   The collector of the moneys, Mr John W.
Gray, returned the subscriptions, after payment of some charges, and
thus that expression of indignation at wrong done was ended.
The other gold-fields ardently joined in the feeling prevalent here.
In Ballarat meetings were held on Sundays as well as on other days,
and on Saturday, 11th November, 1854, thousands of men gathered,
and flags and bands of music lent ominous life to the assemblage.
The leaders were in favor of moral force and a purely constitutional agitation ; but there were more fiery spirits than they.   One
of these—a compatriot of Scobie—on another occasion harangued
the crowd, and said the spirit of the murdered Scobie was hovering
over them and yearning for revenge.   The occasion referred to was
a meeting held near Bentley's hotel on the 17th October, when the
arrival of the police and military, and some injudicious acts by a
few bystanders, led to a collision with the police, the reading of
the Riot Act, and the burning of the hotel.   Some of the diggers
were arrested, and one was rescued on the way to the Camp.   Milne,
Sergeant-Major of police, a man held in general execration as an
unprincipled informer, was regarded as the right hand of the officials
in that business.

The subjoined extracts are from contributions to the *Ballarat
Star* by Mr Samuel Irwin, a gentleman who was an eye-witness of
the time and a daily recorder for the Press of what transpired.   His
letters to the *Geelong Advertiser* of those days gave very full and,
in the main, very accurate descriptions of the occurrences of the
time.   So far may their reliableness be assumed that not only have
no material contradictions been made, but, as the English Blue
Books demonstrate, Sir Charles Hotham adopted some of Irwin's
letters as portions of his despatches to the English Secretary for
the Colonies :—

As a matter of course, those who take an interest in the past of Ballarat have in a great measure to fall back on personal reminiscences, as but few of them have easy access to documentary evidence, so that most of what can be said or written under the circumstances partakes of the egotistical.

A good deal has been said of the means and persons by and through whom Bentley got into the good graces of some of the leading officials at the Camp. Little is positively known of the matter beyond those immediately concerned, but any one who had heard the tone in which Bentley asked a person standing one cold early winter's day in the verandah of the Police-court, after the court had closed, "Where is Mr Dewes?" could hardly have failed to note a more than usually free and easy manner on the part of the equestrian questioner. The reply was civil—" in the magistrate's room "—to which Bentley, dismounting, betook himself with all the confidence of one who knew the locality well. In a few minutes Mr Dewes and his visitor, then an applicant for a publican's license, appeared, and went into the large tent, just opposite the Police-court, where the former resided.

The license was in due time granted, the hotel was usually crowded, the bowling-alley and the free use of cards contributing among other inducements to attract a large number of customers, almost in a continuous stream by night as well as by day. Knowing the fact that the hotel was nearly always open, Scobie made for it, found it closed, created a disturbance to gain admission, was assaulted in consequence and died. The coroner's inquest which followed was far from partaking of that strict scrutiny and judicial aspect which on the whole are so characteristic of such proceedings, and so the suspicion already existent as to the purity of some of the camp officials became stronger. At length the supposed participators in the death of Scobie were brought before the Police-court, composed of Messrs Dewes, P.M., Rede, resident commissioner, and Johnston, commissioner. The prisoners, in the opinion of the majority of the bench, were free from blame, and were discharged, though Mr Johnston, the junior, dissented from the opinion of his seniors. He even was so decided in opinion as to the guilt of the prisoners that he took a copy of the depositions, forwarding them to Melbourne for the consideration of the Attorney-General.

It was decided to hold a public indignation meeting on the spot where Scobie had met his death, to protest against the miscarriage of justice, and to devise the ways and means for bringing the delinquents to a fair trial. The meeting was held and passed off quietly, though pretty strong language had been used. The camp authorities, dreading an attack they said on Bentley's hotel, but to provoke one asserted the discontented, sent the police to act as a guard over the building. The usual "chaff" was indulged in, and nothing serious was supposed to be imminent on the part of the leaders among the discontented. But it fell out otherwise. A youngster, one of the lads who used to wash "headings" from rich claims, in the reckless unthinking spirit of untamed boyhood, threw a stone at the lamp in front of the hotel. The stone struck the lamp and broke the glass. This was the spark which lighted the train. The long suppressed indignation broke forth in one long terrific yell of irrepressible indignation "down with the house, burn it." The demolition of the windows was effected in a moment, and the sound of the crashing glass added still more to the excitement of all present, even of those who either from disinclination for such work, or by reason of the intervening crowd, could not join in it. The house was soon occupied, the people swarming into it by door or window as came most conveniently to hand. Some of the camp officials who had still managed to keep some faith in their honesty in the popular breast— notably Mr Commissioner Amos, who was drowned in the London, aided by Mr M'Intyre, who subsequently was rewarded for having done this, by being arrested for having been an aider and abettor in the riot—tried all their persuasive powers to calm the excited and now well-nigh frantic assemblage. It was labor in vain. The long gathering hurricane had burst, and must career until its fury had been spent. In a few minutes the cry was that the rear or side of the premises towards the bowling alley was in flames. And so it was, but who caused the fire is among the secrets of that day.

How it should have been a secret seems remarkable if the description given by the *Argus* correspondent be considered. His narrative may, in the absence of a statement to the contrary, be taken as given by an eye-witness. He says :—

About half-past two or three o'clock in the afternoon, and when the crowd had increased to about 8,000 or 10,000, a man carried an armful of paper and rags to the windward end of the bowling-alley, and, placing them under the calico covering, deliberately struck a match and fired the building in the presence of the military. The cool, resolute manner in which everything was carried on resembled more the proceedings of the "Porteous mob" than of anything of the kind that has occurred since.

Contrasting with present rapidity of communication the tardy publication of the Bentley hotel burning in the towns on the seaboard is notable. The disturbance and burning happened on the 12th October, but it was not mentioned in the *Argus* till the 19th, and then only in a letter from Geelong dated the 18th, and saying the news had been "just received." The Ballarat correspondent of the *Argus* seems to have acted with considerable deliberation, for he did not write till the 18th, his letter appearing on the 23rd. To make the deliberation more judicial by contrast with facts, the letter began with the words, "the exciting events, &c."

Irwin's narrative continues :—

During the earlier stage of the proceedings it was evident that the owner of the hotel might not expect much mercy at the hands of those present, and he was therefore easily persuaded to mount a fleet horse provided for him, and make his way to the Camp, where he ensured his personal safety, and gave word that more assistance was needed by the authorities at the hotel. The hurried progress of the refugee messenger, as he sped along the main road coatless, if not hatless, spread the excitement among those at work on the Gravel Pits Lead, and they also soon added their numbers to the already large and fast increasing multitude. The quick march of soldiers from the Camp soon after Bentley's arrival showed the urgency of the case, and ere they had gained the foot of Bakery Hill, scarcely a man was on the Gravel Pits, save some miner whose excited fellows had forgotten that he was "below," or some storekeeper who could not procure a temporary caretaker for his goods.

It may be superstitious or otherwise to mention it, but it is nevertheless the fact that, just as the military entered Specimen Gully, while the force of the breeze had fashioned the flames from the ridge-board of the yet standing but wholly ignited roof into a fiery coombe or crest, a small black cloud rested over the Black Hill, and a few scattered heavy drops of rain fell. Possibly the excitement was so intense that but few noticed the occurrence. The rain-drops ceased, the cloud disappeared—the breeze lulled, and with a crash down fell the only yet standing portion of Bentley's hotel.

With the now well ascertained opinions of Sir Charles Hotham on subordination, it may be readily imagined that he was furious at this open revolt against the law and fully bent on avenging the outrage. He had plenty of willing tools ready to his hands, men who, to use the words of one of his class, "would swear a hole through an iron pot" to oblige a friend. They at last picked out three scape-goats. One was M'Intyre, now in comfortable circumstances in Glasgow, who had used his best endeavors to restrain the crowd at Bentley's from overt acts. Another was Fletcher, a printer, whose office was on the Main road, not far on the Eastern Market side of Twentyman and Stamper's. Fletcher, from all that can be learned, was not off the Main road the day of the fire, and certainly was not farther than the Prince Albert hotel in that direction. Westerby, the third man, has been asserted to be equally innocent with Fletcher in the transaction.

A meeting was held, and a committee was suggested to bail the prisoners. J. F. Coleman, now mining registrar at Staffordshire Reef, volunteered to act, and his example being speedily followed the number that had been named— nine—was soon got together. Some had advised that the meeting proceed to the Camp and release the prisoners by force. A milder course, however, was adopted, and the committee went to the Camp and offered bail. After enquiry bail was accepted. All this took time, and the crowd, which had promised not to come nearer the Camp than already stated, had crept up, first to the Yarrowee Creek, and finally to the brow of the hill in front of the present Mining Board-room. The police had been drawn up on the higher ground to meet this body of men, as they came towards the Camp. Experience had taught the Camp to be on the alert, and the whole force there was well in hand to prevent a second riot. While the bailbonds were being prepared, the angry hum of the crowd outside was distinctly heard inside the Police-court, and at one time the magistrates seemed to think the giving bail was but a ruse to temporarily distract the Camp, and, during a riot, release the prisoners by force. Fortunately the bail was concluded, and the committee with M'Intyre appeared. But a new difficulty was in store. In the anxiety to reach M'Intyre the crowd pressed forward, and, being kept back by the police, a collision would have been inevitable but that M'Intyre was hurried forward while the members of the committee spread their arms and good naturedly pressed their friends backwards. Returning down the Main road, revolvers were drawn and fired in defiance of the authorities. One of the revolvers went off in the excitement before its owner had raised the barrel over the heads of the crowd: in going off it somewhat seriously injured a man walking on the left hand of the person carrying it. Among the things advised was, now that M'Intyre was liberated, he should take to hiding. The adviser of this step was Kennedy, and the objector was one of the bondsmen, who happened to be present. To M'Intyre's credit be it said he refused, apart from the responsibilities of his bail, to hide for an hour. The trial and conviction of the three prisoners followed, which brings us to the celebrated DEMAND for the release of the prisoners, made by a deputation to Sir Charles Hotham.

A meeting on Bakery Hill had adopted resolutions demanding the release of the prisoners, the dismissal of Milne, and affirming the right of the people to full representation, manhood suffrage, no property qualification of members, payment of members, short Parliaments, abolition of the gold-fields commission and the diggers' and storekeepers' license fees. Messrs Hayes, Humffray, Holyoake, Black, Vern, Burke, Kennedy, and others were the speakers, and Hayes was in the chair. There had been a commission of enquiry into the Bentley hotel affair. The commissioners were Captain Sturt, Dr. M'Crea, and the magistrate Dewes, and they had closed their sittings on the day before the Bakery Hill meeting. That commission was looked on with mistrust by the diggers because of Dewes, whom, moreover, the Colonial Secretary, Mr Foster, had dismissed, or suspended, as a sop to the enraged population.

The commissioners went to Melbourne with their report. In December the trial of Westerby, M'Intyre, and Fletcher, the prisoners arrested for the burning of Bentley's hotel, was to take place in Melbourne, to which place the *venue* had been changed. Mr Humffray prepared the briefs for their advocate. Bentley had also, in the interim, been re-arrested for the murder of Scobie, and had, with some associates in the affray that ended in Scobie's death, been convicted. They were sentenced to three years on the roads. The original acquittal was attributed mainly to the medical evidence of

Dr. A. Carr, who was regarded as a colluding associate of both Dewes and Bentley. Solemn official condemnation of the Police Magistrate confirmed the popular denunciations of Dewes and some of his associates. Messrs E. P. Sturt, W. M'Crae, and F. A. Powlett, who had been appointed to enquire into the matters connected with the hotel, and to report on claims for compensation therewith connected, made the following statement :—

Influenced by the fact that to the Police Magistrate, and the misconduct of that public officer, may be attributed, in a great measure, the riotous assembly which led to such unfortunate results, your board are willing to recommend certain of the sufferers by the burning of Bentley's hotel to a consideration of their claims.

The trial of the alleged incendiaries ended in a conviction, and M'Intyre was sentenced to three, Fletcher to four, and Westerby to six months' imprisonment. The jury had recommended them to mercy, and, amid the applause of the bystanders in the crowded court, declared their belief that the outrage had been provoked by the improper conduct of the Ballarat officials. As to those officials, however, it must be remembered that, besides Dewes, there were Messrs Johnston and Rede on the bench when Bentley was examined, but Johnston not only voted for the committal of the prisoner, but forwarded copies of the depositions to the Attorney-General.

As soon as the conviction of Fletcher, M'Intyre, and Westerby was known in Ballarat, the Reform League sent Messrs Kennedy and George Black to Melbourne to "demand" the release of the prisoners. Black was then editor of the *Digger's Advocate*, and wrote vigorously for the popular cause. Kennedy was a man of rough, but moving eloquence. It was he who, at the meeting that ended in the burning of Bentley's hotel, declared that the murdered man's ghost was there yearning for revenge. As Saint Buonaparte, with pious fervor, proclaimed an alliance between Divine Providence and heavy battalions, so Kennedy, at one of the meetings of diggers, declared his preference of physical over moral force by reciting the rugged but vigorous couplet—

"Moral persuasion is all a humbug,
Nothing convinces like a lick in the lug!"

They reached Melbourne on the 25th November, Humffray, the secretary of the League, having, on the 23rd, been introduced by Mr

Fawkner, M.L.C., to the Governor, who had intimated that if a proper memorial were sent to the Government, the prisoners might be released.   The League secretary disapproved of the intemperate "demand" brought down by the delegates.   The Sunday was at hand and the secretary and the delegates, and Mr Ebenezer Syme, then of the *Argus*, and afterwards of the *Age*, spent part of the day discussing the position.   Meanwhile, rumors of an arrest of the delegates got current, the diggers at Ballarat resolved on a monster meeting, and the camp officials sent despatches for more troops.   On Monday, the 27th November, the delegates and Humffray waited on Sir Charles Hotham, to present the remonstrant petition.   His Excellency was attended by the Attorney-General, Mr (now Sir William) Stawell, and the Colonial Secretary, Mr Foster.   The "demand" was refused, but réforms were promised, and were said to be already begun.   It is worthy of record that in the course of the interview the delegates spoke of the mode of alienating the Crown lands as being inimical to the interests of the poor man.   Thus early had begun our not yet ended troubles in land administration.   The excitement in Ballarat now grew intenser, and the towns on the seaboard were alarmed with rumors of insurrection.   On the eve of the 28th, Mr Tarleton, the American consul, was feted at a banquet in Ballarat, and while the dinner was going on soldiers were arriving from Melbourne, and a collision had taken place between the soldiers, troopers, and diggers.   All that night the diggers were busy preparing arms and ammunition, the committee of the League sat night and day, the Camp bristled with sentries, and an eventful morrow was looked for. Irwin thus refers to the banquet given to the American consul :—

The dinner was supposed to be given by the Americans, then numerously resident in Ballarat, but most of the leading residents, of all nationalities, were also present.   Dr. Otway occupied the chair, and Messrs Resident-Commissioner Rede, and Acting Police Magistrate Hackett were invited.   Just as the toasts were about to be proposed, a message was conveyed to Mr Rede that an attack had been made on some troops coming from Melbourne when they had reached the workings on the Eureka Lead.   Mr Rede and Mr Hackett withdrew at once, and some time after Mr Tarleton also left, as the report was that several lives had been lost.   When the toast of "The Queen" was proposed a very significant fact was disclosed, namely, that for several minutes no one would respond to it.   The Resident Commissioner had originally been allotted the duty of responding to this toast, but he had left for the scene of the Eureka outrage. There were many business men and miners present who were British subjects, and yet they sat without the slightest attempt to manifest their loyalty, until Dr. Otway said if no British subject would volunteer for the duty, he himself would have to do so. At length a gentleman undertook the business, more pithily than originally saying, " While I and my fellow-colonists claim to be and are thoroughly loyal to our sovereign lady the Queen, we do not and will not respect her men servants, her maid servants, her oxen, or her asses." The last word, delivered with a hearty emphasis, was received with tumultuous applause. This incident tells more effectively than the most labored description could do what the state of public feeling was at the time it occurred.

Irwin himself was the " more pithy than original" respondent to the toast of the Queen.

In the Legislative Council, the Colonial Secretary, Mr Foster, in reply to a question from Mr Fawkner, did not appear to have realised the gravity of the crisis, and the *Argus* of that day compared the Secretary to Nero fiddling while Rome was burning. Yet, while the *Argus* was hounding Foster down as the one " black sheep," the diggers were hooting and groaning at the *Argus* as a " turn-coat," because that journal had condemned some of the wild doings of the outraged population. Foster was about the best abused man of the day, and he had eventually to leave office before the storm of popular indignation.

Reinforcements of horse and foot police were concentrated about this time at the Camp from the neighboring diggings, together with detachments of the 12th and 40th Regiments of the Line. On the 28th November the police were pelted, and the military, entering from Melbourne by the Eureka, were attacked by the diggers. The party in charge of the baggage was for a time cut off, and some of the waggons were overturned and rifled by the diggers in hope of finding fire-arms. In this, however, they were disappointed. Several soldiers were wounded and a drummer boy was shot in the thigh. The diggers followed the troops to the vicinity of the Camp, when the mounted police made a sortie, wounded several men, and drove back the crowd, the troops entering quarters in a panic-stricken and exhausted state at eleven o'clock at night. All night long the diggers kept fires burning, and made the night hideous with dis-charges of fire-arms and other noises. The military encampment was on the slope afterwards known as Soldiers' Hill, now forming part of the north ward of the Borough of Ballarat.   The attack upon the troops took place in the Warrenheip gully, within a few hundred yards of the spot where, a day or two later, the insurgent diggers erected their Stockade.   The onslaught upon the troops appears to have been unprovoked and savage, and it excited general disgust in the minds of the colonists everywhere out of Ballarat.   At Ballarat, also, the larger portion of the inhabitants regarded the affair as alike inopportune and disgraceful.   Indeed, the recognised leaders of the reform movement up to that time appear to have known nothing of the collision until it was actually over.   Raffaello, a writer whom we shall refer to again, calls it a " cowardly attack." In illustration of the fact that the general body of the diggers sought only the rights of freemen, and were not marauders or revolutionists, it may be stated that when the Government Camp at Creswick was almost emptied of both officers and men for the support of the authorities at Ballarat, hundreds of the diggers offered their services to Mr Commissioner, now Warden, Taylor for the protection of the gold deposited at the Camp.

A monster meeting was called by the League for the 29th of November, on Bakery Hill, at which some thousands were expected from Creswick, besides delegates from all the other gold-fields. For the movement had now become general, and emissaries had been sent all over the colony to enlist sympathy, procure help, and, in fact, make the rising national if not revolutionary.   Henry Holyoake, brother of the notable English Secularist, had been sent to Bendigo to raise the diggers there, but he learned at Creswick of the discomfiture of Lalor's force at the Stockade, and his martial occupation being thereby gone, he retired till more tranquil times arrived.   At the meeting of the 29th, Humffray and the delegates Black and Kennedy gave in their report of the conference with the Governor.   Raffaello says Lalor never addressed a meeting before that held on Bakery Hill on the 29th November, when he made his first speech in moving the calling of a meeting of the League for the next Sunday to choose a central committee,—the Sunday when the attack on the Stockade caused the collapse of all the physical force schemes then afloat.   Some 12,000 men, it is said, were present at the meeting on Bakery Hill.   A platform was erected, and on a flagstaff was hung the insurgent flag—the

Southern Cross. The flag had a blue ground, on which, in silver, the four principal stars of the constellation of the Southern Cross were shown. Hayes was again the chairman, and the site of the meeting was on and adjoining the area now occupied by Victoria street, between East and Humffray streets. Besides the committee of the League and the delegates, there were reporters on the platform, and two Roman Catholic priests—the Rev. Fathers Downing and Smyth. The Catholic bishop had also come to Ballarat to help to maintain peace. The delegates spoke, and Humffray, who still counselled moral force only, was denounced as a trimmer. He was also denounced for having waited upon the Government without authority from the League. A person named Fraser, among the crowd, also advised constitutional action, " and," says the *Ballarat Times*, " were it not for the influence of the chairman and his numerous supporters, the man would have been torn limb from limb by the infuriated people." How the people felt, and what they did and resolved to do, will best be gathered from the following resolutions, which were adopted unanimously, although the Rev. Mr Downing proposed an amendment against the burning of the licenses :—

Proposed by Mr Reynolds, seconded by Mr. Weekes—1. " That this meeting views with the hottest indignation the daring calumny of his honor the Acting Chief Justice, while on the bench, of the brave and struggling sufferers of Clare, Tipperary, Bristol, and other districts, on their endeavors to assert their legitimate rights ; and do hereby give the most unmitigated and the most emphatic denial to the assertions of his honor in stigmatising as riots the persevering and indomitable struggles for freedom of the brave people of England and Ireland for the last eighty years."

Proposed by Mr Lalor, seconded by Mr Brady—2. " That a meeting of the members of the Reform League be called at the Adelphi Theatre next Sunday, at 2 p.m., to elect a central committee, and that each fifty members of the League have power to elect one member for the central committee."

Proposed by Mr Frederick Vern, seconded by Mr Quinn—3. " That this meeting, being convinced that the obnoxious license-fee is an imposition and an unjustifiable tax on free labor, pledges itself to take immediate steps to abolish the same, by at once burning all their licenses. That in the event of any party being arrested for having no licenses, that the united people will, under all circumstances, defend and protect them."

Proposed by Mr G. Black, seconded by Mr Whatley—4. " That as the diggers have determined to pay no more licenses, it is necessary for them to be prepared for the contingency; as it would be utterly inconsistent, after refusing to pay a license, to call in a Commissioner for the adjustment of such disputes, and this meeting resolves whenever any party or parties have a dispute, the parties so disputing shall each appoint one man. The two men thus appointed to call in a third, and these three to decide the case finally."

Proposed by Mr Murnane, seconded by Mr Ross—5. "That this meeting will not feel bound to protect any man after the 15th December who shall not be a member of the League by that day."

Proposed by Mr Humffray, seconded by Mr Kennedy—6. "That this meeting protests against the common practice of bodies of military marching into a peaceable district with fixed bayonets, and also any force, police or otherwise, firing on the people, under any circumstances, without the previous reading of the Riot Act, and that if Government officials continue to act thus unconstitutionally, we cannot be responsible for similar or worse deeds from the people."

Bonfires were made of licenses, guns and revolvers were discharged, and League-tickets of membership were issued to the crowd. Troops were under arms in the gully beneath the Camp all the time in readiness for an outbreak.

THE GOVERNMENT CAMP, BALLARAT, 1854.——TROOPS ARRIVING FROM MELBOURNE.

From a Sketch by S. D. S. Huyghue.

CHAPTER V.

THE EUREKA STOCKADE.

The Last Digger Hunt.—Collision between the Diggers and Military and Police.—Southern Cross Flag again.—Lalor and his Companions Armed, kneel, and swear mutual Defence. —Irwin's Account.—Carboni Raffaello.—His Pictures of the Times and the Men.—More Troops Arrive.—The Diggers Extend their Organisation Under Arms.--Lalor "Commander-in-Chief."—Forage and Impressment Parties.—Original Documents.—Shots Fired from the Camp.—The Stockade Formed.—Narrative of a Government Officer in the Camp.—Attack by the Military and Taking of the Stockade.—Various Accounts of the Time.—Raffaello's Description.—Another Tragic Picture.—List of the Killed.—Burials. —Rewards Offered for the Insurgent Leaders. — Their Hiding and Escape. — Charge Against A. P. Akehurst. — Proclamation of Martial Law. — Feeling in Melbourne.— Foster's Resignation.—Deputation of Diggers.—Humffray Arrested.—Vote of Thanks to the Troops.—Legislative Council's Address to the Governor.—His Reply.—Prisoners at the Ballarat Police-court.—Royal Commission of Enquiry.—Trial and Acquittal of the State Prisoners.—Humffray.—Lalor and his Captain.—Cost of the Struggle.—Subsequent Celebrations.—Monument.—The Burial Places.—Death of Sir Charles Hotham.

ALLARAT has not been famous alone for its golden wealth. It has historical fame also, as the site of the collision, in the year 1854, between the Queen's troops and armed diggers at the Eureka Stockade. All the gold-fields of Victoria were moved by discontent under grievances, both legislative and administrative, during the period anterior to the affair at the Eureka; but the resistance to the authorities culminated at Ballarat. The general grievances were heightened there by some particular incidents. These were, in effect, but the occasion under the impulse of which a section of the mining population sought violently to enforce complaints which derived their gravity from other causes. All the grievances afterwards redressed would have been redressed without the bloodshed at the Eureka Stockade; but that tragical event intensified the momentum of the crisis. It exemplified the rashness of a few diggers, and the greater blunders of the Government, but it also expedited the reforms

F

which were eagerly desired by the whole population. If the armed insurgents who were attacked by the soldiers on the memorable Sunday morning in December, 1854, were wanting in the calm sagacity which has always won reform under British rule, they were for the most part not wanting in personal courage, and the result of their policy, as we have intimated, did certainly hasten the coming of those reforms whose fruits the whole colony now enjoys. For all this, then, let the gold-fields men who fell at the Stockade be honored. They stood up, with their lives in their hands, for freedom ; and in that we may well forgive the mistakes they committed, and the follies they purposed. Of the soldiers who fell, their record is in the roll of the army whose traditions are a history of which the race is proud.

With incredible want of prudence the authorities chose the juncture, marked by the meeting of the 29th November, for a more irritating display than usual of the so-long condemned practice of " digger hunting." On the 30th November the last raid of this kind in Victoria occurred, under the direction of Commissioners Rede and Johnston, and the authorities by that act destroyed the remaining influence of the friends of moral force action among the diggers. The police, supported by the whole military force available, with skirmishers in advance and cavalry on the flanks, formed on the flat south of the Camp and advanced upon the Gravel Pits, as the Bakery Hill diggings were called. This cleared the swarming crowd of diggers collected there, the diggers retiring as the troops advanced. At certain parts of the Main road, however, the diggers made a stand, and received the troops with a running fire of stones and occasional gun-shots. The troops took some prisoners and returned to Camp, and soon after that the Southern Cross flag was again hoisted on Bakery Hill ; the diggers knelt around the flag, swore mutual defence, implored the help of God, and then began to drill. New leaders came to the front, as the advocates of moral force were discomfited by the authorities and the more turbulent insurgents. Peter Lalor, a native of Queen's County, Ireland, a son of the late member of the House of Commons for the same county, was chosen " commander-in-chief " of the insurgents, and issued warrants and manifestos. A fiery-spirited Italian, named Carboni Raffaello, was another who then acquired prominence. He afterwards wrote a quaint polyglottic book, entitled " The Eureka Stockade : The Consequence of some Pirates Wanting on Quarter-deck a Rebellion." We shall meet with him presently. Irwin, in his communications to the *Ballarat Star*, says with respect to this last digger-hunt, and he speaks nearly always as an eye-witness and often as an actor in the business :—

By the time that the camp authorities had retired, the men from the Eureka arrived, a good many of them, Lalor among the rest, being armed. A short consultation took place, all work was suspended, and the Southern Cross flag was hoisted on Bakery Hill. The popular indignation was intense. A mass meeting was held on Bakery Hill, where Lalor, gun in hand, mounted the stump and swore in his followers. The method of swearing-in was by uplifting the right hand, and was very impressive as taken by the hundreds who encircled their leader. Immediately after the swearing-in the names were taken down, and the men formed into squads for drill. The drilling was kept up with but little intermission to a late hour, and was now and then renewed up to the capture of the Stockade. As might naturally be anticipated, the Government had its emissaries among the insurgents, and but little was said or done which was not soon reported to the authorities. Immediately after the soldiers, &c., had retired to the Camp on 30th November, two or three members of the committee met in the committee-room at the Star hotel, and wrote a letter to the delegates who had gone that day to Creswick. The letter detailed the occurrences of the day, and solicited the aid of the miners of Creswick, and was directed to the delegates by name " or any MAN on Creswick." When the messenger arrived at Creswick he gave the letter to Black, and he read it to a large meeting he was addressing. It was immediately determined to render the required assistance; and a large body of men, headed by Kennedy, started for Ballarat, taking the direct way through the ranges. Kennedy was armed with a sword, and some of those who accompanied him from Creswick give an extraordinary account of how he flourished the sword about his head and speechified to his followers during a violent thunderstorm that happened that night. The Creswick contingent gradually dwindled away as they had but indifferent accommodation, and the majority of those who still remained left for home on the evening before the capture of the Stockade.

The *Melbourne Herald* correspondent states that the Creswick men marched out with a band, or singing the song " The Marseillaise." It was but a straw, but it showed how the current of men's thoughts and feelings was flowing.

Carboni Raffaello, in his book, shows that he had had a liberal education, and was gifted with a warm poetic temperament, with considerable shrewdness of observation and faculty for description. But he lacked discretion sometimes, and he seemed to be always

F 2

perplexed with suspicions and mysteries, besides being oddly
egotistical.   He is sometimes a mystery himself, and, in his style,
often amusingly incoherent, but his narrative has color and fire
and incisiveness, and will make itself read.   He hits off a man
with a few sharp touches that live in the mind's eye.   Here is one,
a portrait of Kennedy :—

Thomas Kennedy was, naturally enough, the lion of the day. A thick head,
bold, but bald, the consequence perhaps not of his dissipation, but of his
worry in bygone days. His merit consists in the possession of the chartist
slang ; hence his cleverness in spinning a yarn, never to the purpose, but
blathered with long phrases and bubbling with cant. He took up the cause of
the diggers, not so much for the evaporation of his gaseous heroism, as eternally
to hammer on the unfortunate death of his countryman Scobie, for the sake of
"auld lang syne."

Raffaello calls Irwin "a rattling correspondent, who helped to
hasten the movement fast enough."   He gives the following picture
of the Catholic priest :—

Father Patricius Smyth, a native of Mayo, looks some thirty-five years old,
and belongs to the unadulterated Irish caste, half-curled hair, not abundant,
anxious semicircular forehead, keen and fiery eyes, altogether a lively
interesting head.

The *Ballarat Times* of the day he calls "a plant of cayenne
pepper," and gives the following extract from that journal of 18th
November, 1854, interlarded in his peculiar style with remarks of
his own :—

We salute the League [but not the trio, Vern, Kennedy, Humffray] and
tender our hopes and prayers for its prosperity [in the shape of a goodly pile of
half-crowns]. The League has undertaken a mighty task [the trio 'll shirk it
though], fit only for a great people—that of changing the dynasty of the
country [Great works]. The League does not exactly propose, nor adopt, such
a scheme, but we know what it means, the principles it would inculcate, and
that eventually it will resolve itself into an Australian Congress [Great
works ! !].

Here is Raffaello's account of the Leaguers' preparation for the
digger-hunt of the 30th November :—

Quos Vult Perdere Deus Dementat.—What's up ? a license hunt ; old
game. What's to be done ? Peter Lalor was on the stump, his rifle in his
hand, calling on volunteers to "fall in" into ranks as fast as they rushed to
Bakery Hill, from all quarters, with arms in their hands, just fetched from
their tents. Alfred, George Black's brother, was taking down in a book the
names of divisions in course of formation, and of their captains. I went up to

Lalor, and the moment he saw me, he took me by the hand saying, "I want you, Signore ; tell these gentlemen *(pointing to old acquaintances of ours, who were foreigners)* that if they cannot provide themselves with fire-arms, let each of them procure a piece of steel, five or six inches long, attached to a pole, and that will pierce the tyrants' hearts." Peter of course spoke thus in his friendly way as usual towards me. He was in earnest though. The few words of French he knows, he can pronounce them tolerably well, but Peter is no scholar in modern languages ; therefore he then appointed me his aide-de-camp, or better to say his interpreter, and *now I am proud to be his historian.* Very soon after this, all the diggers "fell in" in file of two abreast, and marched to the Eureka. Captain Ross, of Toronto, was our standard-bearer. He hoisted down the Southern Cross from the flagstaff, and headed the march. Patrick Curtain, the chosen captain of the pikemen, gave me his iron pike, and took my sword to head his division ; I "fell in" with John Manning, who also had a pike, and all of us marched in order to the Eureka. I assert as an eye-witness, that we were within one thousand in the rank with all sort of arms, down to the pick and shovel. We turned by the Catholic church, and went across the gully. Of this I have perfect recollection : when the "Southern Cross" reached the road, leading to the Eureka on the opposite hill, the file of two abreast crossing the gully, extended backwards up to the hill where the Catholic church stands. I took notice of the circumstance at the time. We reached the hill where was my tent. How little did we know that some of the best among us had reached the place of their grave ! Lalor gave the proper orders to defend ourselves among the holes in case the hunt should be attempted in our quarters. The red-tape was by far too cunning this time ; red-coats, traps, and troopers had retired to the Ballarat Camp, and wanted a "spell." We determined, however, to put an end to their accursed license-hunting, mock riot-act chopping, Vandemonian shooting down our mates in Gravel-pits.

Vern is always ridiculed as a vain, boasting, "long-legged, sky-blathering Vern." Lalor he loves as "he is the earnest, well-meaning, no two-ways, non-John-Bullised Irishman," wherefore "more power to you, Peter, old chummy ! Smother the knaves ! they breed too fast in this colony." Of the meeting on the 30th November, he says Lalor administered the oath to some 500 armed diggers, as follows :—"We swear by the Southern Cross to stand truly by each other, and fight to defend our rights and liberties." Dr. Kenworthy, Raffaello seems to regard, as did many more, as a go-between with the Camp authorities and the diggers. He was, in fact, regarded as a spy.

As soon as the news of these doings reached Melbourne, the Government sent up all the remaining available troops, with men-of-

warsmen, horse and foot police, four field-pieces, and a number of
baggage and ammunition waggons.   Lieut.-Colonel Valiant, and
subsequently Sir Robert Nickle, Commander-in-Chief of the Forces,
and Colonel Macarthur, Deputy Adjutant-General, proceeded to
Ballarat in command of the troops.   The diggers who drilled
under *their* commander-in-chief, meant, many of them at least,
nothing less than revolution and a republic.   Lalor had a " minister
of war," named Alfred Black, who, or his brother, had drawn up a
Declaration of Independence.   This was drawn up in a store kept
by one Shannahan ; Black, Vern, M'Gill, Raffaello, Curtin, Lessmann
(a German), Kenworthy (an American medical man), and others
being present.   Black was subsequently killed while working as a
quartz miner.   Lalor having been, to Vern's disgust, elected Commander-in-Chief, " orders of war " were issued by him for arms,
ammunition, and impressment, and he sent out picquets to enforce
them, and prevent their being made a cover for robbery.   It
appears, however, that ammunition was not abundant in the
Stockade, the foraging parties of the insurgents to the contrary notwithstanding.   A pistol was picked up in the Stockade loaded with
powder and quartz pebbles, in lieu of ball or smaller shot, showing
as may be assumed, that the diggers were not rich in the usual
materials of destruction.   One of the foragers' receipts for a
military levy reads as follows :—

Received from the Ballarat Store 1 Pistol, for the Comtee X. Hugh
M'Carty—Hurra for the people. Another :—The Reform Lege Comete—4
Drenks, fouer chillings ; 4 Pies for fower of thee neight watch patriots.—X. P.

The night-watch patriots were some of the insurgents told off to
patrol the diggings, for now there was, *de facto*, civil war.   The
Government authorities were in a fortified camp on the western
plateau, and the insurgents were organising and fortifying on the
eastern grounds.   Before us lies the tattered remnant of a triple
receipt given by the subscribers to the firm of Bradshaw and
Salmon, then carrying on business in the Main road, Ballarat East.
It will be seen that Esmond the gold discover was one of the
foragers for ammunition, the time being imminent when a deadly
use was to be made of the materials collected.   Mr Leake, from
whom we receive the document, and who, later, had joined Bradshaw's firm, writes :—"I cannot call to mind much about the matter,

only I have a distinct recollection of Mr Moran threatening to shoot me if I did not 'hand over quick,' and I have very little doubt my life would have been taken that night only for Esmond." The "patriots" were getting stern and peremptory as the times got bracing. But Esmond was not one of the most fiery of the insurgent officers, and he appears to have had a memory for friends as well as a sense of what was judicious. He once rescued Irwin, the correspondent of the *Geelong Advertiser*, who writing of Esmond and himself in the following passage says :—

One night, that of Friday, 1st December, a gentleman who had occasion to go down the Main road, when he came in front of the old Charlie Napier hotel, found some hundred men drawn up two deep there. Passing down the one side of the men, he sought to discover if he had any acquaintance among them. Not having found one he passed up the other side, until he arrived where the person, a lieutenant, who was in charge stood. The gentleman being unknown to any of the party, was asked his business there, and his account of himself not being deemed satisfactory he was arrested, to be subsequently conveyed to head quarters to be dealt with. It soon transpired that the captain of the detachment, with a few men, was in the hotel searching for arms, and that he was momentarily expected to come out. When he did come out he spoke to the prisoner, who was an old and intimate friend, and, not knowing that he was under arrest, asked him to go into the hotel and have a drink. The lieutenant began to fidget. The explanation was soon made, the misunderstanding being got over by the lieutenant, under a threat from the captain of having him arrested, going into the hotel when he, the captain, the late prisoner, and one or two more came to a better understanding while drinking a few glasses of champagne.

Here is the triple receipt :—

30 Novr. 1854.

eved from Bradshaw,

n   12 lbs Powder, @ 6/ ℔.

£3 12 0 to pay.

J. W. Esmond.

1 Pistol flask, 7/6.

John C. Murnane.

1 Box Revolver Caps, 6/

Moran.

Comitte.

Murnane fell down dead one day while working at a shaft on Esmond's Lead, and Moran either fell or threw himself overboard when on his way hence to India.

On the 1st December—says a Government officer then in the Camp—the

Government took final measures to meet assault. Every Government employee was armed and told off to his post, and sentinels and videttes were placed at several points. The principal buildings of the Camp, including the present Mining Board-room, in Camp-street, were fortified with breastworks of firewood, trusses of hay, and bags of corn from the commissariat stores, and the women and children were sent for security into the store, which was walled with thick slabs, and accounted bullet-proof. A violent storm of rain, with thunder, commenced as these arrangements were completed, and the mounted police, soaked through with the rain, spent the night standing or lying by their horses, armed, and horses saddled ready for instant action. At 4 a.m. on Saturday, 2nd December, the whole garrison was under arms, and soon after daylight a demonstration in force was made towards Bakery Hill without opposition. We heard to-day that the insurgents were visiting the outlying stores and demanding arms. Bodies of men are seen drilling near the Red Hill. No work is now carried on throughout the entire diggings, and every place of business is closed. A mounted trooper from Melbourne with despatches was fired at near the Eureka line, where, through the information of spies, it is known that a stockade is being erected.

To this pass had the gold discovery, "digger hunting," and irresponsible government brought the place where less than four years before there was nothing but pastoral silence and solitude. The Eureka Stockade was at first intended more as a screen behind which the diggers might drill than as a fortification. It was an area of about an acre, rudely enclosed with slabs, and situated at the point where the Eureka Lead took its bend by the old Melbourne road, now called Eureka street. In the picture published at the *Ballarat Star* office the middle of a line drawn from Mount Warrenheip, in the centre back ground, to the chimney from which smoke is issuing on the right of Sturt street, would indicate very nearly the site of the Stockade. The site, as is shown on the map herewith, lay about midway between what are now Stawell and Queen streets on the east and west, and close to Eureka street on the south. To preserve the site from alienation to private hands, and to help to keep alive the memory of the spot, the borough council of Ballarat East has it in contemplation to enclose the ground as a public reserve. At the time of the fight the lead had not then been traced so far, but the "shepherds" were there with their shallow pits, and one or two claims were sinking. The Stockade included some of those holes, as well as some diggers' tents, where the staff and other officers and men of the insurgent force had their quarters. Pikes were forged in the Stockade, and

V. R.

Colonial Secretary's Office,
Melbourne, 2nd December, 1854.

THE

Lieut. Governor

Having heard that some evil disposed persons are endeavouring to excite the Mining Population of Ballaarat to a riotous and violent course of action His Excellency calls upon *all* **BRITISH SUBJECTS** *not only to*

ABSTAIN

From Identifying Themselves

With these persons, but to render support and assistance to the Authorities, Civil as well as Military, who are now at Ballaarat for the protection of life and property.

By His Excellency's Command,

JOHN MOORE,

ASSISTANT COLONIAL SECRETARY.

BY AUTHORITY: JOHN FERRES, GOVERNMENT PRINTER, MELBOURNE.

Le Consul de France

Aux Français Residant

DANS LA COLONIE DE VICTORIA.

Au milieu des troubles qui agitent les mines de Ballaarat, le Consul de France croit devoir recommander a ses compatriotes de s'abstenir de toute manifestation qui aurait pour but de meconnaitre *l'autorite des representants de la Reine dans la Colonie de Victoria.*

Ils ne doivent pas oublier qu'ils sont dans un pays ami de la France, et que le premier devoir d'un etranger est de respecter l'autorite du pays qui lui donne l'hospitalite.

Si les Français ont des plaintes ou des reclamations a adresser au Gouvernement Colonial ils peuvent les transmettre en toute confiance au Consul de France qui saura leur faire rendre justice.

Fait au Consulat de France, le 3 Decembre, 1854.

COMTE DE MORETON DE CHABRILLON.

BY AUTHORITY: JOHN FERRES, GOVERNMENT PRINTER, MELBOURNE.

arms and ammunition had been largely collected. Several companies of riflemen and pikemen were formed, and a military insurgency established. The mass of the diggers did not support this armed resistance, but friends, and, it is said, enemies also, dropped into the Stockade at all hours of the day and night of Saturday the 2nd of December. Friendly butchers brought cart-loads of beef to the rendezvous, and Lalor's men lay about the fires cooking, burnishing arms, or engaged in other warlike business. Lalor, it is said gave " Vinegar Hill" as the night's pass-word, but neither he nor his adherents expected that the fatal action of Sunday was coming, and some of his followers, incited by the sinister omen of the pass-word, abandoned that night what they saw was a badly organised and not very hopeful movement. Father Smyth and Messrs Humffray and George Black were in the Stockade during the Saturday, and heard a project made to assault the Camp, it being declared that 2000 diggers could be got for the purpose, and the Camp easily taken. The three persons just mentioned did what they could to dissuade from the proposed attack on the Camp, and so left the Stockade. Mr Budden, J.P., a Canadian, and a schoolfellow of Ross, heard of the approach of the troops and police on the Sunday morning, and hastened from his tent near the Stockade to advise Ross to withdraw from the hopeless struggle. Challenged by the insurgent sentries, Budden succeeded at length in getting within the Stockade and endeavored to prevail on Ross to leave the place, warning him that the Government force was approaching and that resistance would be useless and fatal. Ross, however, refused to desert his comrades. The firing soon began, Budden escaped by precipitate flight to his tent, and Ross was fatally injured. All the day, on Saturday, Lessmann was out, by Lalor's orders, in quest of a horde of vagabonds who were using the name of Lalor's " minister of war " as a cover to thievish raids upon storekeepers and others. Lessmann's and other outposts of night videttes were off duty just before daybreak on the 3rd, no attack being anticipated, but Lalor, Ross, Vern, M'Gill and other leaders were there.

We will now let the Government officer speak again from the Government Camp :—

Before daylight on the 3rd December a force, consisting of 276 men of all arms, including a strong body of cavalry, mustered quietly and left camp with the purpose of attacking the Stockade. At early dawn they reached the neighborhood of the position sought, and the advanced files were fired at by a sentinel posted within the Stockade. The order of attack was now given, and the detachment of the 40th Regiment, led by Captain Thomas, the chief officer in command, made a quick advance upon the double breast-work which formed the stronghold of the insurgents. After several vollies had been fired on both sides, the barrier of ropes, slabs, and overturned carts was crossed, and the defenders driven out, or into the shallow holes with which the place was spotted, and in which many were put to death in the first heat of the conflict, either by bullets or by bayonet thrusts. The foot police were first over the barricade, and one, climbing the flagstaff under a heavy fire, secured the rebel flag. After burning all the tents within the enclosure, and in the immediate vicinity, the troops returned to camp, and carts were sent out for the dead and wounded. The latter thus obtained immediate medical aid. They were covered with blood, and were mostly shot in the breast. The number of insurgents killed is estimated at from thirty-five to forty, and many of those brought in wounded afterwards died. Of the troops, three privates were killed, and several wounded, one of whom died. Two officers were wounded, and one, Captain Wise, died. Among the arms taken in the fight were pikes of a rude construction, made on the spot, and furnished with a sort of hooked knife to cut the bridles of the cavalry. The dead were buried the same day in the cemetery. The bodies of the insurgents, placed in rough coffins made hurriedly, were laid in a separate grave, the burial service being performed by the clergymen to whose congregation they belonged. At night we were again under arms, as constant rumors of an intended attack kept us on the alert. This is exhausting work, and a severe trial, especially for the military, as the men have had no rest for several nights. Indeed, no one within the lines has undressed for the last four nights at the very least.

4th December.—The funerals of several of those who fell at the Stockade and were removed by their friends, took place to-day. They were attended by several hundred men who marched three abreast up the Main road and past the Camp, during which the garrison was under arms. 7 p.m.—A number of insurgents, favored by a clouded moon, crept up under cover of the nearest tents beyond the palisade, and fired from several points upon the sentinels. This caused a sudden alarm, everyone flew to his post, and a general discharge took place, resulting, as was believed, though erroneously as to the deaths, in the death of a woman and child in one of the tents, and in the wounding of three men on the road adjoining, who unfortunately happened to be passing at the time. One of these was brought in from the road in front of the mess-house (now Mining Board-room), and died a few days after.

5th December.—This afternoon, to our great joy, the advance guard of the relief from Melbourne, commanded by Major-General Sir Robert Nickle was seen defiling from the ranges, and soon after, the whole body, escorted by squadrons of cavalry, and accompanied by a seemingly endless string of baggage-waggons traversed the diggings, and piled arms within the lines. This force consists of 800 men, together with a large party of sailors from H.M.S. Electra, and four field pieces.

6th December.—The district is placed under martial law, and in obedience to a General Order, the inhabitants have brought in a large quantity of fire-arms.

9th December.—The General attended to-day at a tent specially erected on the flat below the Camp, to swear in special constables ; but with, as I believe, one solitary exception, no one came forward to support the Government, and the object failed. Nevertheless, the handful of persons assembled heartily cheered for the British army. This was the period of the siege of Sebastopol, the false rumor of the capture of which had just arrived.

22nd December.—Captain Wise was buried this day with military honors. Since the time when his death became known, many flags throughout the diggings were lowered half-mast out of respect to this officer, who had been stationed here previously, in command of the enrolled pensioners, and was a general favorite with the people.

2nd January.—A soldier, who was shot in the face, died this morning. All further apprehension of an outbreak having ceased, the Major-General and staff, with a portion of the field train and the navy, have returned to Melbourne, leaving about 800 men in garrison to await eventualities. Confidence is being now generally restored. The gold-field again presents its usual thronged and lively aspect, and the streets of the township are no longer deserted, or traversed by grim patrols of mounted troopers.

1st April.—The prisoners taken at the Stockade, and tried in Melbourne, were acquitted on the charge of high treason, which is considered a triumph to the popular cause. And thus terminated the agitation which caused such loss of life and property to those prosecuting mining and commercial operations on the Ballarat gold-workings.

Thus far goes the narrative of an intelligent eye-witness within the Government Camp. He is evidently in error as to the hour when shots were fired into the Camp on the night after the affair at the Stockade. At 7 p.m. it would be daylight. The statement as to the firing upon the Government Camp on the evening of the 4th is traversed altogether by one who was here then and is still here. He says :—

The soldiers were not fired upon, though they might report so to save themselves. The soldiers on guard on Soldiers' Hill, being either in drink or strongly excited, wantonly and savagely, without orders and without provocation, fired into the Flat. They came rushing out of the large tent like madmen, firing and re-loading, and firing again irregularly at the tents, not even a corporal commanding them. They turned round and fired at me two·

or three shots though they saw me in a different direction from that whence the insurgents are said to have fired.

Some allowance must be made for the opinions formed by men in sudden emergencies like this when general alarm prevailed. That shots were exchanged between the Flat and the Government Camp appears unquestionable.

As has been seen, the attack by the authorities was unexpected, and thus both men of war and men of peace were found within the Stockade, while insurgents were absent who would otherwise have been present. There were over a hundred armed men in the Stockade, including Lalor, the chief, and a company of pikemen, and a company of musketeers, under Ross, Vern, Lynch, and Esmond. James H. M'Gill, another leader, had been previously absent on the ranges with some riflemen, ostensibly for the purpose of opposing the troops expected from Melbourne. There were diggers working at their claims also within the Stockade. One of the captains under Lalor thus describes the affair:—

I was on guard and saw the military at the same time that the alarm was given by a digger working on a brace hard by. They were then at the point where the gully, running down from the Stockade, joins the head of Specimen Gully. I called out to Vern, and Vern called Lalor. We got under arms immediately, some 200 about. The first shot was fired from our party, and the military answered by a volley at 100 paces distance. Then there was a volley from the Stockade. The military sent out scouts on foot, and the troopers surrounded the Stockade, the party on foot being covered by the fire from the force posted on the high ground in the rear of the Free Trade hotel. Captain Wise led the scouts on foot, who broke into the Stockade where Lalor was, on the side fronting to Specimen Gully. They got in, and the firing, and piking, and bayonetting went on, and the "rebels" got into disorder and rushed into some tents and a blacksmith's shop on one side of the Stockade. The troopers fired the tents, and the rest of the military now came up. The sun had now risen, and about twenty minutes had passed since the first shot was fired. Then two soldiers appeared on the other side with bayonets fixed. Warden Amos' horse, which we had taken with the warden before, was between me and them, and I fired my revolver. One fell, and the other drew back. I then fired a second shot at the soldiers, my men in the tent cheering at the time. I then said, "I'm off," and wheeled round to go out of the Stockade, but met some troopers and retreated, and ran into a butcher's shop close by. The military had now taken the Stockade, and they took away the prisoners they had. I was in the chimney, and so escaped, as they did not search. Most of our men were Irishmen. The soldiers now went off with their prisoners, and the Stockade, slabs, tents, and all were on fire.

The correspondent of the *Melbourne Herald* saw the retreat of the military with their dead, wounded, and prisoners. He says further :—

I was attracted by the smoke of the tents burnt by the soldiers, and there a most appalling sight presented itself. Many more are said to have been killed and wounded, but I myself saw eleven dead bodies of diggers lying within a very small space of ground, and the earth was besprinkled with blood, and covered with the smoking mass of tents recently occupied. Could the Government but have seen the awful sight presented at Ballarat on this Sabbath morning—the women in tears, mourning over their dead relations, and the blood-bespattered countenances of many men in the diggers' camp—it might have occurred to His Excellency that *"prevention is better than cure."*

M'Combie, in his "History of Victoria," gives the following account of the attack on the Stockade :—

On the night of the 1st December lights were observed in the tents of the diggers ; and signals were repeatedly exchanged, and shots fired at the sentries, who were driven in. The officer in command found a large number of insurgents organising, drilling, and equipping themselves. The spies had seen their leaders telling them off in companies, and heard one of the commanders say to the people that those who had no other arms should get an iron spike placed on a pole, as "that would find the tyrants' hearts !" The officer in charge issued a public notice that no light would be allowed after eight o'clock ; that no discharge of fire-arms would be tolerated upon any pretence ; and that persons disobeying these orders would be fired at. On the same day Mr Commissioner Amos arrived at the Camp at Ballarat, with information that the diggers were occupying an entrenched camp at the Eureka, in considerable force, with the avowed intention of intercepting the troops under the Major-General, then hourly expected to arrive from Melbourne. During the whole of that day the insurgents had possession of the diggings, and were busy levying contributions on all classes, giving the orders of their "minister of war" in payment. The officer in command prudently refrained from molesting any of their detached parties. He was unable to attack the insurgents during the day, as he could not leave a force behind to protect the Camp, and resolved upon a night surprise. Circumstances favored this bold attempt. The insurgents had not contemplated any active measures on the side of the authorities until the main body of troops and the commanding-officer had arrived. It was Sunday morning, and a very great portion of them were away, and those who remained had dined late, and some, no doubt, had drank deep. They were surprised by the gallant commander of the Queen's troops, Captain Thomas, who resolved to seize the favorable opportunity of delivering a most effective blow against them. The insurgents were posted in a very advantageous position, in a fortified camp, or rather stockade, at the Eureka. It rested on a gentle eminence, and was of considerable strength. The leaders were, however, not very deeply skilled in military engineering, for it was much too large, and was not protected by proper bastions or outworks to aid the defenders in a general assault. Under all disadvantages, the diggers would have repulsed the military had the attack not been made at a time when it was totally unexpected, and when the great body were absent. The officer upon whom the responsibility of this enterprise rested was Captain Thomas, and he planned and carried out the whole affair with creditable ability and vigor. He was assisted by Captain Pasley, R.E., who bravely advanced with the skirmishers and directed the assault. The military were fortunate in having Mr Commissioner Amos to act as their guide ; being well acquainted with the locality, he led the troops to the exact spot where the operations were to commence. The force under Captain Thomas reached the ground just as the morning begun to dawn. There were present 30 men of her Majesty's force [40th], under Lieutenants Hall and Gardyne ; 70 mounted police, under Sub-Inspectors Furnell, Langley, Chomley, and Lieutenant Cossack ; 65 men of the 12th Regiment, under Captain Quendo [Queade] and Lieutenant Paul ; 87 men of the 40th Regiment, under Captain Wise and Lieutenants Bowder [Bowdler] and Richards ; 24 foot police, under Sub-Inspector Carter ; making a total of 100 mounted and 176 foot.

When the body arrived at about 300 yards from the entrenchments the detachments of the 12th and 40th Regiments extended in skirmishing order ; the mounted force moved to the left of the position and threatened the flank and rear of the insurgents. The main body now advanced boldy to the attack. We have no means of ascertaining the exact number of men in the Stockade, but they could not have out-numbered the Queen's force. They stood to their arms manfully as soon as the alarm was sounded, and when the military were at a distance of 150 yards they poured in a tolerably effective fire upon them. The commanding-officer now directed the order to fire to be sounded, and throwing in a steady fire on the camp in front, the military advanced in unbroken order, undaunted by the continuous discharge with which the insurgents received them. As the troops were likely to be severely handled, the reserves and foot police were now brought up for the struggle ; a sharp fight was kept up for some time, but, in consequence of the ammunition becoming scarce amongst the insurgents, their fire slackened, and in a few minutes the military carried the entrenchment at the point of the bayonet. The engagement lasted about twenty-five minutes ; the rebel leaders fought well, Mr Peter Lalor having been wounded in the breach and left for dead in the Stockade, and several others cut down at their posts. The loss to the Queen's force was considerable, including Captain Wise, who, in leading his men to the attack, was severely wounded and died in a few days afterwards ; Lieutenant Paul was also severely wounded. The loss among the insurgents was variously estimated, but there could not have been fewer than thirty killed on the spot, and a great many wounded. There were 125 prisoners taken in the Stockade. The commander-in-chief of the " forces of the Republic of Victoria," as they were styled, named Vern, a Hanoverian by birth, escaped, and a reward of £500 was offered for his apprehension. Mr Lalor, the other

leader, who fell within the Stockade, lost his right arm in the engagement.
On the Tuesday the troops under the command of the Major-General arrived
on Ballarat ; and they were not there a minute too soon, for a large body of
insurgents were in arms at Creswick.   There can be no doubt, however, that
the victory at the Eureka had very much raised the spirits of those who
supported the Government, and in a corresponding degree dispirited all connected with the insurgents, and the officer in command unquestionably deserved
credit.   He exercised a wise discretion in attacking them, instead of waiting
until they became the aggressors.   Indeed, most of the colonists who were
unfavorable to the authorities, and their system of administering the law on
the diggings, were compelled to condemn this open attempt to overthrow the
Government.   The Legislative Council, then in session, presented an address of
sympathy to his Excellency, which was of the following tenor : that, having
been placed in a painfully embarrassing position since his arrival in the colony,
he was entitled to the sympathy and support of the Legislature.   Sir Charles
Hotham was very far from inexperienced in affairs of State importance.   He
was particularly happy in his reply.   The firm resolve to suppress the in-
cipient revolution was softened by the readiness with which he offered to
redress those grievances which the diggers had complained of.   He said
it would be his constant endeavor to conduct the government with the
utmost possible temper ; he said the time for military rule had passed ;
but when there was an outbreak, and that caused by foreigners—men who
had not been suffered to remain in their own country in consequence of the
violence of their character—then Englishmen must sink all minor differences, and unite to support the authorities.   The Government, however, fared
rather differently when a direct appeal was made to the people.   A public
meeting had been called by requisition, to consider the best means for pro-
tecting the city during the crisis at the diggings.   The principal agitators in
this matter seemed to be the members of the Legislature, who took a large
share in the proceedings of this public meeting.   The resolutions proposed
were received with such ill-concealed dissatisfaction, that, after the Mayor had
declared two of them to be carried, the opponents of the Government interfered,
and such confusion prevailed that the gentleman who presided vacated the
chair, which was occupied by Dr. Embling, and a series of resolutions diame-
trically opposed to the proceedings of the Executive, and demanding an
immediate settlement of the differences between the Government and the
diggers, were carried with the utmost enthusiasm.   Mr Frencham, who has
been already alluded to as one of the discoverers of gold in Victoria, spoke on
behalf of the diggers, and told the people they "must go forth with their
brother diggers to conquer or die."   The Government demonstration having
terminated in so very unsatisfactory a manner, another meeting was convened
on the following day "for the assertion of order and the protection of constitutional liberty."   It took place on a large open space of ground near St.
Paul's Church, at the corner of Flinders lane.   From 4000 to 7000 people were
present, the chair being filled by Henry Langlands, Esq., one of the largest

employers of labor in Melbourne.   The speakers were Messrs Blair, Owens,
Fawkner, Fulton, Frencham, Grant, Cathie, and Embling.   The resolutions
condemned the whole policy of the Government, and declared that, while dis-
approving of the physical resistance offered by the diggers, the meeting could
not, without betraying the interests of liberty, lend its aid to the Executive
until the coercive measures they were attempting to introduce should be
abandoned.   The result of this meeting had very considerable weight with the
Executive, and the same afternoon a *Government Gazette* extraordinary appeared,
in which was a proclamation revoking martial law on Ballarat.

The repulse at the Stockade did not depress the diggers, and a body of about
1000 armed men was, at this time, collected together on the Creswick road.
It was very fortunate that Sir Robert Nickle, who had now assumed the command, was an old and experienced officer.   He immediately restrained the
violence of the police and military, and held several parleys with the disaffected
diggers, in which he strongly urged them to return to their duty.

Some literal errors in M'Combie's narrative we have corrected
in brackets.   He is wrong also as to the diggers not being depressed
by the affair at the Stockade.   The action of Sunday entirely
demolished the schemes of the insurgents.   There was no such
gathering either on the Creswick road as that mentioned by
M'Combie.   Archdeacon Stretch, of the English Church, bore
witness to the peaceable aspect of affairs at Creswick.   The
Geelong Advertiser, of the 11th December, states that the Archdeacon had been on "a conciliatory tour in the district, and
reports the 25,000 diggers of Creswick Creek to be under the
physical charge of three policemen."   The three constables were
enough, and no clearer evidence seems necessary to show how little
disposed the general population there was to armed resistance to
the authorities.

Here is Raffaello's description of the attack on the Stockade :—

Remember this Sabbath Day (3rd December) tō Keep it Holy.—I awoke.
Sunday morning.   It was full dawn, not daylight.   A discharge of musketry—
then a round from the bugle—the command "forward"—and another
discharge of musketry was sharply kept on by the red-coats (some 300 strong)
advancing on the gully west of the Stockade, for a couple of minutes.   The
shots whizzed by my tent.   I jumped out of the stretcher and rushed to
my chimney facing the Stockade.   The forces within could not muster above
150 diggers.   The shepherds' holes inside the lower part of the Stockade had
been turned into rifle-pits, and were now occupied by Californians of the I. C.
Rangers' Brigade, some twenty or thirty in all, who had kept watch at the
"outposts" during the night.   Ross and his division northward, Thonen and
his division southward, and both in front of the gully, under cover of the slabs,

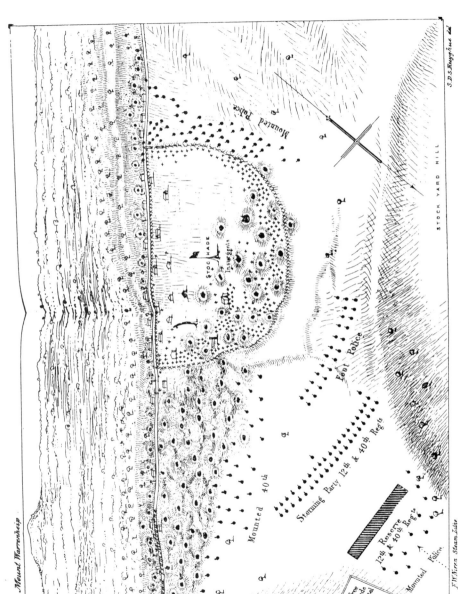

PLAN OF ATTACK ON THE "EUREKA STOCKADE" — 3RD DECEMBER, 1854.

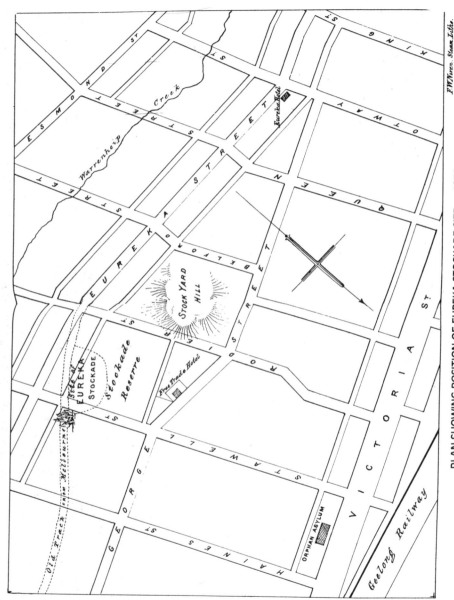

PLAN SHOWING POSITION OF EUREKA STOCKADE SITE – 1870

answered with such a smart fire, that the military who were now fully within range, did unmistakably appear to me to swerve from their ground ; anyhow the command " forward " from Sergeant Harris was put a stop to. Here a lad was really courageous with his bugle. He took up boldly his stand to the left of the gully and in front : the red-coats "fell in " in their ranks to the right of this lad. The wounded on the ground behind must have numbered a dozen. Another scene was going on east of the Stockade. Vern floundered across the Stockade eastward, and I lost sight of him. Curtain whilst making coolly for the holes, appeared to me to give directions to shoot at Vern ; but a rush was instantly made in the same direction (Vern's) and a whole pack cut for Warrenheip. There was, however, a brave American officer, who had the command of the rifle-pit men ; he fought like a tiger ; was shot in his thigh at the very onset, and yet, though hopping all the while, stuck to Captain Ross like a man. Should this notice be the means to ascertain his name, it should be written down in the margin at once. The dragoons from south, the troopers from north, were trotting in full speed towards the Stockade. Peter Lalor was now on the top of the first logged-up hole within the Stockade, and by his decided gestures pointed to the men to retire among the holes. He was shot down in his left shoulder at this identical moment ; it was a chance shot, I recollect it well. A full discharge of musketry from the military now mowed down all who had their heads above the barricades. Ross was shot in the groin. Another shot struck Thonen exactly in the mouth, and felled him on the spot. Those who suffered the most were the score of pikemen, who stood their ground from the time the whole division had been posted at the top, facing the Melbourne road from Ballarat, in double file under the slabs, to stick the cavalry with their pikes. The old command, " Charge ! " was distinctly heard, and the red-coats rushed with fixed bayonets to storm the Stockade. A few cuts, kicks, and pulling down, and the job was done too quickly for their wonted ardor, for they actually thrust their bayonets on the body of the dead and wounded strewed about on the ground. A wild " hurrah ! " burst out, and the " Southern Cross " was torn down, I should say, among their laughter, such as if it had been a prize from a May-pole. Of the armed diggers, some made off the best way they could, others surrendered themselves prisoners, and were collected in groups and marched down the gully. The Indian dragoons, sword in hand, rifle-pistols cocked, took charge of them all, and brought them in chains to the lock-up. The red-coats were now ordered to " fall in ; " their bloody work was over, and were marched off, dragging with them the " Southern Cross." Their dead, as far as I did see, were four, and a dozen wounded, including Captain Wise, the identical one, I think whom I speak of in relating the events of Tuesday evening, November 28. Dead and wounded had been fetched up in carts, waiting on the road, and all red-things hastened to Ballarat. I hastened, and what a horrible sight ! Old acquaintances crippled with shots, the gore protruding from the bayonet wounds, their clothes and

G

flesh burning all the while. Poor Thonen had his mouth literally choked with bullets ; my neighbor and mate Teddy More, stretched on the ground, both his thighs shot, asked me for a drop of water. Peter Lalor, who had been concealed under a heap of slabs, was in the agony of death, a stream of blood from under the slabs heavily forcing its way down hill.

A correspondent of the *Geelong Advertiser*, not Irwin, gives the following tragic picture of what he saw :—

The first thing that I saw was a number of diggers enclosed in a sort of hollow square, many of them were wounded, the blood dripping from them as they walked ; some were walking lame, pricked on by the bayonets of the soldiers bringing up the rear. The soldiers were much excited, and the troopers madly so, flourishing their swords, and shouting out—" We have waked up Joe ! " and others replied, " And sent Joe to sleep again ! " The diggers' Standard was carried by in triumph to the Camp, waved about in the air, then pitched from one to another, thrown down and trampled on. The scene was awful—twos and threes gathered together, and all felt stupefied. I went with R—— to the barricade, the tents all around were in a blaze ; I was about to go inside, when a cry was raised that the troopers were coming again. They did come with carts to take away the bodies. I counted fifteen dead, one G——, a fine well-educated man, and a great favorite. I recognised two others, but the spectacle was so ghastly that I feel a loathing at the remembrance. They all lay in a small space with their faces upwards, looking like lead ; several of them were still heaving, and at every rise of their breasts, the blood spouted out of their wounds, or just bubbled out and trickled away. One man, a stout-chested fine fellow, apparently about forty years old, lay with a pike beside him ; he had three contusions in the head, three strokes across the brow, a bayonet wound in the throat under the ear, and other wounds in the body—I counted fifteen wounds in that single carcase. Some were bringing handkerchiefs, others bed furniture, and matting to cover up the faces of the dead. O God ! sir, it was a sight for a Sabbath morn that, I humbly implore Heaven, may never be seen again. Poor women crying for absent husbands, and children frightened into quietness. I, sir, write disinterestedly, and I hope my feelings arose from a true principle ; but when I looked at that scene, my soul revolted at such means being so cruelly used by a government to sustain the law. A little terrier sat on the breast of the man I spoke of, and kept up a continuous howl ; it was removed, but always returned to the same spot ; and when his master's body was huddled, with the other corpses, into the cart, the little dog jumped in after him, and lying again on his dead master's breast, began howling again. ——— was dead there also, and ———, who escaped, had said, that when he offered his sword, he was shot in the side by a trooper, as he was lying on the ground wounded. He expired almost immediately. Another was lying dead just inside the barricade, where he seemed to have crawled. Some of the bodies might have been removed—I counted fifteen. A poor woman and her children were standing outside a tent ; she said that the troopers had surrounded the tent, and pierced it with their swords. She, her husband, and her children, were ordered out by the troopers, and were inspected in their night-clothes outside, whilst the troopers searched the tent. Mr Hasleham was roused from sleep by a volley of bullets fired through his tent ; he rushed out, and was shot down by a trooper, and handcuffed. He lay there bleeding from a wound in his breast, until his friends sent for a blacksmith, who forced off the handcuffs with a hammer and cold chisel. When I last heard of Mr Hasleham, a surgeon was attending him, and probing for the ball.

Raffaello speaks in fierce language of his treatment in the "lousy logs." He was taken with the other State prisoners to Melbourne :—

On passing through the Eureka I got a glance of my snug little tent, where I had passed so many happy hours, and was sacred to me on a Sunday. There it lay deserted, uncared for. My eyes were choked with tears, and at forty years of age a man does not cry for little.

In his 77th chapter he gives the following account of the killed and wounded at the Stockade :—

Requiescat in Pace.—Lalor's Report of the Killed and Wounded at the Eureka Massacre, on the morning of the memorable Third of December, 1854 :—The following lists are as complete as I can make them. The numbers are well known, but there is a want of names. I trust that the friends or acquaintances of these parties may forward particulars to *The Times* office, Ballaarat, to be made available in a more lengthened narrative. KILLED :— 1, John Hynes, County Clare, Ireland ; 2, Patrick Gittins, Kilkenny, Ireland ; 3, — Mullins, Kilkenny, Limerick, Ireland ; 4, Samuel Green, England ; 5, John Robertson, Scotland ; 6, Edward Thonen (lemonade man), Elbertfeldt, Prussia ; 7, John Hafele, Wurtemberg ; 8, John Diamond, County Clare, Ireland ; 9, Thomas O'Neil, Kilkenny, Ireland ; 10, George Donaghey, Muff, County Donegal, Ireland ; 11, Edward Quin, County Cavan, Ireland ; 12, William Quinlan, Goulbourn, N.S.W. ; 13 and 14, names unknown, one was usually known on Eureka as "Happy Jack." WOUNDED AND SINCE DEAD :—1, Lieutenant Ross, Canada ; 2, Thaddeus Moore, County Clare, Ireland ; 3, James Brown, Newry, Ireland ; 4, Robert Julien, Nova Scotia ; 5, — Crowe, unknown ; 6, — Fenton, unknown ; 7, Edward M'Glyn, Ireland ; 8, no particulars. WOUNDED AND SINCE RECOVERED :—1, Peter Lalor, Queen's County, Ireland ; 2, name unknown, England ; 3, Patrick Hanafin, County Kerry, Ireland ; 4, Michael Hanly, County Tipperary, Ireland ; 5, Michael O'Neil, County Clare, Ireland ; 6, Thomas Callanan, County Clare, Ireland ; 7, Patrick Callanan, County Clare, Ireland ; 8, Frank Symmons, England ; 9, James Warner, County Cork, Ireland ; 10, Luke Sheehan, County Galway, Ireland ; 11, Michael Morrison, County Galway, Ireland ; 12, Dennis Dynan, County Clare, Ireland. (Signed) PETER LALOR, Commander-in-Chief.

How many others owed their death to the Stockade attack can

hardly be stated.   Some lingered long, and died of wounds received
there.   The Melbourne *Herald* of the 12th May, 1856, reported:—

Amongst the deaths of recent occurrence at the Benevolent Asylum is that
of Frederick Coxhead, native of London, lawyer's clerk, and 24 years of age.
He sided with the insurgents at the memorable battle of the Eureka Stockade
at Ballarat, and received a gun-shot wound.   Compression of the brain ensued,
and an abscess then set in which terminated fatally on Sunday.

The authorities were under the impression that Vern was the
insurgent leader, and as Vern, and Lalor, and Black, the " minister
of war," escaped the grip of the assaulting force, rewards were
offered for their apprehension.   For Vern, as the presumed chief,
£500 were offered, and for Lalor and Black £200 each.*   None of
them were ever arrested.   Black was not present at the affair of the
3rd.   Lalor had been severely wounded, and was supposed at first
to be dead.   He was covered up by a pikeman with slabs, till the
soldiers retreated with their prisoners, when he left his hiding
place, weary and faint with pain and loss of blood.   Having made
good his escape, he was, after divers troubles, secreted at a friendly
hut on the ranges, where friends ministered to his necessities.   On
the night of the 4th he was conveyed to Father Smyth's house,
where his arm was amputated by Dr. Doyle.   Women may live
nearer to the invisible than men, and be more rich in gifts of
spiritual vision.   Dreams and presentiments are sometimes theirs
when the stronger sex see and hear nothing.   It was said that
Lalor's betrothed in Geelong—whom he afterwards married—saw
him "in a vision of the night" or early morning of the 3rd
December, wounded and bleeding before her.   It was further said
that her vision was a tolerably accurate picture of his actual
condition.   In an age of vote by ballot and much hard iron
machinery Puck's declaration has been realized in the electric
telegraph, and, still, "there are more things in heaven and earth than
are dreamt of in our philosophy."   To leave the speculative for
the known, it will suffice here to record that search for the fugitive
chiefs was made, and Lalor, who had many narrow escapes, was
hidden in various places by his friends till the storm had blown over,
when he was removed to Geelong, and underwent further surgical
operations, the authorities appearing to have given over the pursuit.

* The copies of the placards interleaved here and elsewhere are photo-lithographic re-
productions of the originals issued by the Government.

V. R.

NOTICE!

GOVERNMENT CAMP, BALLARAT, DEC. 3RD, 1854.

Her Majesty's Forces were this Morning fired upon by a large body of evil-disposed persons of various nations, who had entrenched themselves in a Stockade on the Eureka, and some Officers and Men killed or wounded.

Several of the rioters have paid the penalty of their crime, and a large number are in Custody.

All well-disposed persons are earnestly requested to *return to their ordinary occupations*, and to *abstain from assembling in large groups*, and every protection will be afforded to them by the Authorities.

Robt. Rede,
RESIDENT COMMISSIONER.

GOD SAVE THE QUEEN!!!

PRINTED AT THE "TIMES" OFFICE, BAKERY HILL, BALLARAT.

V. R.

PROCLAMATION

By His Excellency SIR CHARLES HOTHAM, Knight Commander of the Most Honorable Military Order of the Bath, Lieutenant Governor of the Colony of Victoria, &c., &c., &c.

WHEREAS by a Proclamation bearing date the fourth day of December, in the year of Our Lord One thousand eight hundred and fifty-four, Martial Law was proclaimed to be in force from and after the hour of *Twelve o'clock at Noon on Wednesday, the sixth day of December, One thousand eight hundred and fifty-four,* within the following limits, that is to say: Commencing at the junction of the Yarrowee River and Williamson's Creek, thence by a straight line to the junction of the Lal Lal Rivulet with the Moorabool River; thence by that river to its source, in the great Dividing Range; thence by that range to the boundary of the county of Carngham, at Baillie's Creek; thence by a line south-westerly to the township of Ripon, and by that boundary south-westerly to the junction of the River Yarrowee with Williamson's Creek aforesaid: Now therefore I, SIR CHARLES HOTHAM, the Lieutenant Governor aforesaid, do hereby proclaim and declare that *no arms, ammunition, munitions of war, food, or supplies, shall from and after the said last mentioned day be brought, without my consent, within the limits aforesaid;* And I do hereby notify the same to all subjects of HER MAJESTY in the Colony of Victoria.

Given under my Hand and the Seal of the Colony, at Melbourne, this fourth day of December, in the year of Our Lord One thousand eight hundred and fifty-four, and in the eighteenth year of Her Majesty's Reign.

(L.S.)   CHAS. HOTHAM.

By His Excellency's Command,

JOHN FOSTER.

GOD SAVE THE QUEEN!

BY AUTHORITY: JOHN FERRES, GOVERNMENT PRINTER, MELBOURNE.

V. R.

PROCLAMATION

By His Excellency SIR CHARLES HOTHAM, Knight Commander of the Most Honorable Military Order of the Bath, Lieutenant Governor of the Colony of Victoria, &c., &c., &c.

WHEREAS bodies of Armed Men have arrayed themselves against Her Majesty's Forces and the constituted authorities, and have committed acts of open rebellion: And whereas for the effectual suppression thereof it is imperatively necessary that Martial Law should be administered and exercised within the limits hereinafter described: Now I, Sir Charles Hotham, Governor of the said Colony, with the advice of the Executive Council thereof, do hereby command and proclaim that Martial Law, from after Twelve of the Clock at Noon on Wednesday, the sixth day of December instant, and until the same be administered and exercised against every person and persons within the said limits who shall at any time after the said four consent are of rebellion, any reason, treasonable or seditious practices, or other outrage or misdemeanor whatever within the following limits, that is to say: Commencing at the junction of the Yarrowee River and Williamson's Creek, thence by a straight line to the junction of the Lal Lal Rivulet with the Moorabool River; thence by that river to its source in the great Dividing Range; thence by that range to the boundary of the county of Ripon, and by that boundary south-westerly to the township of Carngham, at Baillie's Creek; thence by a line south-westerly to the junction of the River Yarrowee with Williamson's Creek aforesaid: And I do hereby, with the advice aforesaid, order and authorize all Officers commanding Her Majesty's Forces to employ them with the utmost vigor and decision for the immediate suppression of the said rebellion and officers, and to proceed against and punish every person and persons acting, aiding, or in any manner assisting in the said rebellion and treason, according to Martial Law, as to them shall seem expedient for the punishment of all such persons. And I do hereby especially declare and proclaim that no sentence of death shall be carried into execution against any such person without my express consent thereto; And I do hereby, with the advice aforesaid, notify this my Proclamation to all subjects of Her Majesty in the Colony of Victoria.

Given under my Hand and the Seal of the Colony, at Melbourne, this fourth day of December, in the year of Our Lord One thousand eight hundred and fifty-four, and in the eighteenth year of Her Majesty's Reign.

(L.S.)   CHAS. HOTHAM.

By His Excellency's Command,

JOHN FOSTER.

GOD SAVE THE QUEEN!

BY AUTHORITY: JOHN FERRES, GOVERNMENT PRINTER, MELBOURNE.

Ross had died from wounds received on the Sunday morning, and Vern escaped, and hid in various places till danger passed away with the subsequent acquittal of the State prisoners. M'Gill's story is that he and some others, not thinking all was over when they fled, repaired to Creswick with a view to get out of harm's immediate way, and to secure two field-pieces that were said to be on Captain Hepburn's property at Smeaton. That project was soon abandoned, and M'Gill had to disguise himself and fly. He was met at the Springs by Mrs Hanmer and another, who furnished him with woman's attire, in which he travelled by coach to Melbourne on the 5th, passing Sir Robert Nickle and his troops on their way up near the Moorabool. By advice of the since notorious G. F. Train, then Melbourne agent for the White Star Company's line of ships, M'Gill, disguised afresh in man's attire, went on board the *Arabian* as an officer of the ship. In the meantime Train and other American citizens interposed on behalf of their compatriot, whose youth—he was then about twenty-one years old—they pleaded in bar of grave punishment. Train sent to M'Gill one day, got him ashore, took him to Sir Charles Hotham's at Toorak, and after a brief interview the Governor, who expressed surprise at M'Gill's youth, bowed them out hopefully. Train next informed his client that the Government would not interfere to prevent his escape if he left the colony forthwith. M'Gill, however, still by the ever-vigilant Train's agency, was passed on as an invalid to the health officer's quarters at Port Phillip Heads, where he remained until the acquittal of the State prisoners practically proclaimed liberty to all the compromised. It was rumored at one time that M'Gill shot Captain Wise, then that he was pardoned because he saved Captain Wise's life in the Stockade, then that he was let off because he was an American. What happened to him because of his nationality cannot be precisely known. He avers that he neither shot Captain Wise nor saved him from any threatened harm. As to his Americanism, it is certain that a strong feeling existed at the time against what was considered a fear of American influence on the part of the Government. It is equally certain that the Government attributed the outbreak in a great measure to the treasonable schemes of concerting foreigners then in Ballarat and active in the agitations of the time.

That intelligent witness of most of the incidents during the whole agitation, upon whose papers in the *Ballarat Star* we have so freely drawn, makes the following statement relative to the later scenes in the drama :—

After the capture of the Stockade, it may well be imagined that there was a good deal of flight and hiding indulged in, and some singular incidents could be narrated in reference thereto. Lalor, Esmond, and others, some of them immediately, and others from time to time, found their way to Geelong, where they were secreted by various friends. The local police knew where most of the Geelong fugitives were, but as most of them had influential friends they were not molested, the more so as the Government said they had quite enough of the insurgents in their clutches. Messrs Black and Kennedy started in company to make for Geelong. The latter, in his usual self-opinionated way, assured his companion that he knew all about the road to Geelong by way of the Mount Misery Ranges. How the fugitives took a pair of scissors and "barberised" each other, exchanging clothes, and generally disguising themselves, need not be minutely detailed. At last, towards evening, Kennedy acknowledged he was lost, though after a time a smoke was seen, and was soon found to be from an encampment, a sort of out-station depôt or rural retreat for some of the rowdy boys of Ballarat. Kennedy was for being very mysterious, but Black frankly told the men that he and his companion were in some trouble—what he did not say—with the Government. He also let them see that he had plenty of money, and gave them £5 to get some stores. The messengers who went for the stores returned on the Monday evening, bringing a bottle of wine. How a decent fellow of the party took Black's side when some of his mates would have ill-treated him—how Black and Kennedy separated, the latter going bullock-driving—and how Black, meeting with other fugitives, at last got up to Melbourne, where his friends secreted him—would fill columns, but these things are more of a private or personal than a public interest. Mr Seekamp was arrested on the Monday after the capture of the Stockade, he having £105 on him, and about to go to Bendigo. An extraordinary issue of the *Ballarat Times* was in course of publication when Mr Seekamp was arrested. Hearing of his arrest, a friend called at the *Times* office and found a quiet enough account of the capture of the Stockade, wound up by about a "stickful" commencing thus, "This foul and bloody murder calls to high Heaven for vengeance, terrible and immediate," &c., &c. The copies that had been already printed were taken away and burned, all save one, which probably by this time has shared the same fate. After the acquittal of some of the State prisoners and the release of the remainder of them, those who had not been apprehended, and for whom large rewards had been offered, were in a somewhat anomalous position. Virtually they were as free from blame and as little hindered as others from going about, but actually they had the reward hanging over them, and some of them, at least, might tempt a needy man to assassinate them, as the reward was for them "dead or alive." Well, a land sale was advertised to be held in the old Police-court on the Camp. Some of the allotments were at Glendaruel, and Lalor had decided to purchase some of them. Of course, he could do so by an agent, but he preferred a bolder course, for, to the astonishment of his friends, all of whom by this time knew where he was, he appeared publicly on the day of the land sale, went to the Police-court to bid for the allotments, and when asked who's the purchaser gave his name in the usual way. There was no more secrecy after this; the matter was reported to head-quarters, and the rewards were withdrawn in an early number of the *Government Gazette*.

Very barbarous excesses were charged against some of the troopers and other members of the civil arm, and one Powell was declared to have been murdered in cold blood, by Arthur Purcell Akehurst, a Government officer, but the officer was acquitted by the jury at the trial. Raffaello and the journals of the day give particulars of this very ugly episode. Wanton wounding of mere spectators or unresisting insurgents was alleged to have been perpetrated, and it was gravely suspected that some wounded men were burned alive when the troopers fired the tents. One of the wounded spectators was Frank Arthur Hasleham, then acting for the correspondent of the *Geelong Advertiser*. Hasleham, in a memorial for compensation, described himself as " a native of the good town of Bedford, and son of a military officer, to wit, William Gale Hasleham, who bore His Majesty's commission in the 48th Foot at Talavera." He was compensated by the Government subsequently, and after some years' sojourn here he went home to England. Some twenty-three who fell were buried by their friends, and the anniversary of the day was kept up with gradually decreasing demonstration.

On Monday, the 4th December, 1854, the Government issued a proclamation placing the "district of Buninyong"—for the old name with slightly changed spelling still prevailed over that of Ballarat— under martial law. On the same day, in the afternoon, an extraordinary *Gazette* was issued, calling on " all true subjects of the Queen, and all strangers who have received hospitality and protection under her flag to enrol themselves, and be prepared to assemble at such places as may be appointed by the civic authorities in Melbourne and Geelong, and by the magistrates in the several towns of the colony." Simultaneously a reward of £500 for Vern's apprehension, was offered, as the authorities not only thought he was the commander of the insurgents, but were haunted by another delusion,

born of a rumor, that Vern and some associates were erecting another
stockade in the Warrenheip forest.   The metropolis was frightened
from its propriety by the aspect of affairs at Ballarat.   The
Herald reported on the 4th that "One time it was said that
an invading army of diggers was marching upon Melbourne,
intending a general sack and pillage ; next, that portions of the
road were beset with guerilla parties anxious to have a shy at
any detached troops and police who might happen to pass.   *   *
Throughout the day there was almost a constant swearing-in
of special constables at the police-office."   Deputations waited
upon the Governor, declaring their loyalty.   Meetings were convened in the metropolis, some to sympathise with the diggers, others
to rally round the law and the authorities.   Thus were the distant
places shaken by the collision of that early Sunday morning at
Ballarat.   The poor diggers, in truth, wanted neither "sack nor
pillage," but only to be treated as freemen, and to be governed by
laws made by parliaments in which they had free representation,
and not by laws enacted by a nominee legislature, and insolently,
and sometimes corruptly administered by men irresponsible to the
people.   Yet, as has been said before, there were rash and foolish
and disloyal men among the insurgents.   To them, and them alone,
may be fairly applied the words of Sir C. Hotham in reply to one
of the deputations to whom he spoke of "designing men who had
ulterior views, and who hoped to profit by anarchy and confusion."
But such men are found in all uprisings, and their presence in this
one neither justified the wrongs of the times nor deprived the
resistance of freemen of its inherent virtue.   The Melbourne alarm,
however, was not without fruit.   The sympathy meetings were
attended by large masses, and men of all classes united in con-
demning the misrule which had caused the outbreak.   It chanced
that just about this time the members of the Melbourne bar were
roused by an attack by the *Geelong Advertiser* upon one of their
brotherhood, who was accused of conduct unbecoming a prudent
lawyer and a true gentleman.   Then the barristers rushed to arms
and fought on platforms in their brother's behalf, and while their
weapons were yet keen-edged and bright the lawyers gathered also
to the larger battle then waging between the gold-fields population
and the Government.   At a mass meeting held on the 13th January,

PORTRAIT OF MR. PETER LALOR, M.L.A.

To the Right Worshipful the Mayor
of Melbourne

Sir

We the undersigned inhabitants
of Melbourne considering the
unsettled state of a portion of
the diggings and the necessity of
taking measures for the better
protection of the city and
upholding the cause of law
and order hereby request your
Worship to convene a public
meeting of the citizens tomorrow
without delay for the above purpose

Henry _____ M.L.C.
William Nicholson M.L.C.
J. J. _____ Faulkner M.L.C.
Thomas _____ Engineer
John _____ M.L.C.
Augustus F. _____ M.L.C.
Frank Murphy M.L.C.
John Stevenson ~~_____~~
~~George Annand~~ M.L.C.
Decr 4th 1854.

                              of the Citizens
I hereby call a Public Meeting
for the purpose above stated
at the Mechanics Institution at
one o'clock precisely on to-morrow
Tuesday the 5th December

                    J. T. Smith Mayor

1855, in Swanston street,—where the St. Paul's schools now are,—
the State prisoners being yet untried, a petition for a general amnesty
was adopted. In that petition the true cause of the rising, in so far
as its moral force phases had gone, was set forth as follows :—

The recent unhappy outbreak at Ballarat was induced by no feeling of
disaffection to the person of her Majesty, and by no traitorous designs against
the institutions of the monarchy, but purely by a sense of political wrong, a
loss of confidence in the local administration of law, and an irritation
engendered by the injudicious and offensive enforcement of an obnoxious and
invidious tax, which, though legal, has since been condemned by the Gold-
fields Commission.

Thousands of people in Ballarat subscribed a similar petition, but
the Government refused the amnesty. The whole colony felt the
rising to be serious. The Executive was certainly alarmed, and on
the 7th December Mr Foster, the Chief Secretary, gave way before
the popular storm and resigned office. Foster was a member of the
Vesey family in the Irish peerage. To him, as the prime spirit
in the Legislative Council and Cabinet, great odium attached, for
he was regarded as the mainstay of the system of misrule and
nomineeism, and his resignation was, therefore, judicious if not
necessary. It is probable that Sir Charles Hotham, however, was
more directly responsible for the policy of the time than, to judge
from the general feeling against Foster, was supposed by the population generally. Mr Samuel Irwin furnishes some evidence, or
hints of evidence, in support of this probability. He says, in
his contributions to the *Ballarat Star* on the Eureka Stockade
affair :—

Those who take an interest in these matters and have the requisite leisure
might, among other documents, refer to the evidence given before a select
committee of Parliament in the case of Mr Foster when he sought to gain his
pension. From the evidence in this case they will find that a very unwilling
witness says Sir Charles Hotham had made up his mind before he left England
what course he would pursue, and that he had even in sight of the English
coast, said that the unruly gold-finders wanted "blood letting." The
expression may not be literally correct, but at all events it signified that he
would adopt repressive measures on his arrival. The same evidence—dragged
from an unwilling witness—also went to show that Sir Charles Hotham used
to correspond with the Resident Commissioner on the gold-fields in cypher and
without the advice or even the knowledge of Mr Foster. This much in justice
to the reputation of one of the best abused men of the time referred to, who,
whatever other sins he was guilty of, was not so of one-half of those then laid

to his charge. The burning of Bentley's hotel, as may be imagined, created
no small consternation in the official mind. With the now well ascertained
opinions of Sir Charles Hotham on subordination, it may be readily imagined
that he was furious at this open revolt against the law and fully bent on
avenging the outrage.

Mr Haines succeeded Foster, and the Legislative Council a
day or two afterwards passed an Act of Indemnity for the declaration
of martial law. The Act of Indemnity was passed on the 15th
December, and on the 11th and 18th the Government offered rewards for the apprehension of Vern, Lalor, and Black.

Judge Wrixon and some barristers were at Bath's hotel on the
4th December, in readiness to open the General Sessions, but though
the gaol was full of prisoners the sessions could not be held, because
the Court-house had been turned into a guard-room, and jurymen
could hardly be got together in that time of disturbance. The
Melbourne Herald had sent up a special correspondent, and on the
4th December he described his view of the position of affairs. He dis-
covers a solemn sense of the importance of his office, asserts anxiety
to preserve a just neutrality, but feels bound to declare " it would
appear that the Government officials here are determined to lose no
opportunity of prolonging that animosity which it should be their
duty to obliterate for ever." That it was their duty is certain, and
it would have been well had they quickened duty with honest
endeavor. The *Herald's* ordinary, or " own," correspondent also, on
the 8th December, while the martial law recently proclaimed was
still in force, takes occasion to denounce the civil officers of the
Government Camp by contrasting their rule with that of the military
régime. He says :—

The martial law administered by Sir R. Nickle is about as far superior to
the Commissioners' law, under which we have been so long laboring, as it is
possible for anything human to be. Had Sir R. Nickle arrived here a few days
before, the bloodshed of last Sunday would have been avoided.

There is ample reason for adopting this writer's view of the
situation. If the military rule was strong and odious because of its
nature, and the reflection of wrong which it threw upon the diggers,
it was also free from the still more odious and exasperating insults of
the rule of civilians enforcing an irksome law with cruel impertinence
and harrassing personal injuries. The proclamation of martial law
was objected to at the time as unconstitutional, and some protests

were made. Whether the proclamation was right or wrong, it is a notable fact that it did not cover the attack of the military upon the diggers in the Stockade. That tragedy was enacted without the reading of the Riot Act or the sanction of the existence of martial law, the proclamation being made on the day after the Stockade action. Another anomaly was the holding a coroner's inquest on one body only. The time was, it seems, out of joint in many particulars.

On the 6th December a large meeting of diggers was held on Bakery Hill, Mr Thomas Williams in the chair. Humffray was there and Dr. Wills, father of the brave explorer who perished with Burke. Coleman and Mosterd were there, who afterwards were elected members of the Local Court. Resolutions were adopted whose tone showed the influence of the fiery blast of Sunday morning, and the rigor of martial law. They were mildly drawn, but with a double meaning, apparently, being applicable to either the authorities or the insurgents according to the mind of the interpreter. Here are the resolutions :—

Moved by Mr Donald, seconded by Mr W. Levy—"That this meeting views with regret the proceedings of the last week, rendering it necessary to assert the sovereignty of law and order by the sacrifice of so many lives and the proclamation of martial law."

Moved by Mr Mosterd, seconded by Dr. Wills—"That this meeting considers the late appeal to arms to have been uncalled for, and pledges itself to use every constitutional means to restore tranquility and good feeling on the Ballarat gold-fields."

Moved by Mr J. F. Coleman, seconded by Mr Ingram—"That this meeting hopes that the officer in command of her Majesty's forces at Ballarat will act with as much forbearance and humanity as the circumstances may admit of : otherwise the lives of many innocent persons may be sacrificed."

Moved by Mr Harris, seconded by Mr Douglass—"That when the present excitement shall have ceased, we will pledge ourselves in a constitutional manner to have our acknowledged grievances brought before the Legislative Council of the colony."

Moved by Mr J. B. Humffray, seconded by Mr W. B. Robinson—"That a copy of the resolutions passed at this meeting, signed by the chairman, be forwarded to his Excellency Sir Charles Hotham immediately. That a deputation be appointed to wait on his representative at Ballarat, and present him with a copy of the same."

Moved by Mr Dyte, seconded by Mr Willern—"That the following gentlemen be the deputation to the Camp : Mr Thos. Williams, chairman ; Rev. P. Smyth ; Messrs Homffrays (Humffray), Donald, Mosterd.

The deputies were not very flatteringly received, for the *Herald* correspondent says Humffray was arrested, and the others were told by Mr Commissioner Rede and Captain Pasley "that they could not receive such resolutions as they were not sufficiently eulogistic of the Government." This is probably rather a comment by the correspondent than a statement in terms of a naked fact. It is not probable that the Camp officials were so far demented as to make so very silly a speech ; but the resolutions appear at any rate to have been rejected. As to Humffray, though he thus fell among the Camp Phillistines, peace-advocate though he was, he had been received at the meeting "with loud and protracted cheering." He conjured the diggers to refrain from further violence, and declared that he had put his life in jeopardy during his moral-force campaign against the insurgents and the authorities. He was liberated on the following day. It is worth noting that on the same day as this Bakery Hill meeting was held, a "monster meeting" was held on St. Paul's Church Reserve, Melbourne, Mr Langlands in the chair, when the following motion, moved by Mr David Blair, was seconded by Mr Fawkner and adopted :—

"That the constitutional agitation at Ballarat has assumed its present unconstitutional form in consequence of the coercion of military force, and that matters would not have been precipitated to their present issue but for the harsh and imprudent re-commencement of digger-hunting during the period of excitement."

It is impossible to avoid concurrence in the latter portion of the resolution. The later digger-hunts were ordered by Sir Charles Hotham, and were his cardinal blunder. His excellent intentions, and his lucid and unanswerable expositions of the duties of a Government in relation to the maintenance of law and order, are all as idle judgments of sagacity after the event. He was not a great politician nor politic, and his military instincts knew nothing of concession or compromise with a people clamoring against both law and administration. This must be remembered, as well as the equally obvious fact that his Excellency had difficulties of many kinds to overcome, when we come presently to one of the Governor's special deliverances upon the Eureka collision.

Reverting to the meeting in Melbourne, it may be stated that one resolution by Mr Grant, late Minister of Lands, proposed that Messrs Fawkner, Strachan, O'Shanassy, Cooke, Fulton, Dr. Owens, and Westgarth, be a body of delegates to act as a commission of arbitration and adjustment between the authorities and the diggers. The meeting objected for awhile to Mr Fawkner. Possibly this was because on the previous day, in the Legislative Council, that vigorous old "conscript father" had carried the following resolution, so entirely true in its eulogies and censures, if a little loose in construction :—

That the thanks of this House are due to the officers and men of her Majesty's 12th and 40th Regiments, sent last week on duty to Ballarat, for their truly soldierlike and highly commendable forbearance in receiving the hootings and violent assaults of a mob of worthless idlers, whom no man can class as true diggers : the merits of the forbearance and the steady patience of men bearing arms in their hands wherewith to repel assaults, stamps those troops and their commanders as truly British troops.

After some discussion the meeting consented to Mr Fawkner being one of the delegates, but added to the list the name of Mr Cathie, who afterwards became member for Ballarat East in the Legislative Assembly. The Government declined to entertain the proposition, but the Commission of Enquiry appointed by the Government to report on gold-fields' grievances comprised several of the gentlemen nominated at the meeting.

On the 6th December the following resolution was carried in the Legislative Council, on the motion of Mr Miller, seconded by the Colonial Secretary (Foster), who had resigned, but still held office:—

That the Lieut.-Governor, having been placed in a painfully embarrassing position since his arrival in Victoria, is entitled to the sympathy and support of this Council, and it pledges itself by every means in its power to aid him in restoring and maintaining law and order."

Mr Miller, in moving the resolution, regretted the injuries suffered by innocent men in the trouble, but said it was "patent that all this disaster had been brought about mainly by the off-scourings of the foreigners collected on the gold-fields from every nation." The Colonial Secretary agreed with this, but Mr Myles, a member for Grant, opposed the motion, and, says the reporter for the *Herald*, "attacked the policy of the Government in a speech in which he had not the sympathy of a single member of the House." Mr Haines said "the time selected for the outbreak was exceedingly bad—a

time when the Government proposed to look into all grievances."
Unhappily for the reputation of the Government, there will always
stand out in bold relief the steady pursuit of a policy of irritation
and non-compromise until the latest moment. The authorities were
too late in their "proposals to look into all grievances." They
over-estimated the force of the insurgent, and under-estimated the
weight of the moral-force movement, failing to see the expediency
of a frank and earnest entertainment of the complaints made so long
and so constitutionally. Small at the best, ill-organised, and ill-
provided, the armed diggers' party would have never had heart to
take the position it did take had not the authorities disarmed the
larger body of peaceful agitators, and provoked hostilities by the
peculiarly despotic action taken in the last license-collecting raid.

The Legislative Council, on the 6th of December, presented an address to his Excellency embodying the motion submitted by Mr
Miller, and adopted almost unanimously by the House. Sir Charles
received the Council at Government House, himself and chief officers
of State attired in the Windsor uniform. To the address of the
Council his Excellency read the following reply :—

Mr Speaker and Gentlemen,—It is with no small pride and satisfaction that
at a moment of unusual difficulty the Legislative Council of Victoria have
assembled themselves around the Governor, and enabled him to proclaim to
the world that with one voice, and one mind, and one heart, we are resolved to
maintain the law. I assure you, gentlemen, that my utmost endeavors have
been used to stave off and prevent the difficulty which has arisen, but is now,
I am thankful to say, rapidly disappearing.

I am desirous, if you will grant me time, to touch upon these points lightly,
in order to show to you that my words are not lightly uttered, not spoken without some consideration. Before the deputation came from the gold-fields, the
Eureka riots broke out, and the burning of Bentley's hotel ensued. Immediately the discharge of Bentley and the other men was sent to the Attorney-
General [now Chief Justice Stawell], he saw that the authorities had taken
the wrong course, and he came out post haste to Toorak, and recommended
most strongly that the men who had been prisoners should be again brought
to trial. We had then received no representative of any sort or kind from the
diggers of Ballarat. Immediately instructions were sent down to bring Bentley
and his associates to trial, and shortly after that we heard that the fire had
taken place at the Eureka hotel.

Mr Speaker and Gentlemen,—I wish to establish the fact, that the Government had given orders to enquire into the manner in which the former trial

had been conducted before any representative from the diggers of Ballarat had been received, and before any violence had ensued.

Of the trial of the men engaged in the burning of the hotel I shall say but little, excepting to observe that the sentence was most lenient.

There were reasons which induced us to imagine that the conduct of the authorities at Ballarat had not been entirely what it ought to have been, and a commission was sent down with very stringent instructions to enquire into the whole case, and bring the offenders, of whatever degree they might be, prominently to notice. The result of that enquiry was, the magistrate [Dewes] was dismissed, the sergeant-major [Milne] was also dismissed (or rather will be placed under punishment and then dismissed), and that the coroner was most severely reprimanded for some injudicious expressions which he made use of. Now, Mr Speaker and gentlemen, I do not think that that shows there was a Government in power which was unwilling to listen to the voice of the people.

The commission returned, the military were withdrawn, and there was every probable appearance of order and tranquility at those diggings, when suddenly we found it necessary to send down an overwhelming force in consequence of the reports we received from Ballarat. The Camp was threatened, and reports reached us that the Camp was not safe an hour, and then the time arrived when it became absolutely necessary that some vigorous steps should be taken and a decisive blow be struck. With regard to the opinion which I formed of the manner in which the authorities acted, I shall allow my own despatches to speak for themselves.

His Excellency then read copies of his despatches to the Resident-Commissioner at Ballarat, in which he approved the action taken on the morning of the 3rd December, ordered secure holding of the prisoners, announced the proclamation of martial law, directed the apprehension of all the speakers at the license-burning meeting, and enjoined "the propriety of forbearance, caution, and temper towards the mining population." He continued:—

I was anxious to have those despatches read, to show that whilst we have on the one hand endeavored to the utmost of our power to uphold law and order, yet, the very moment it was feasible, we revert to the original state of things ; and martial law, which is repugnant to every Englishman, and especially so to every colonist, will cease as soon as possible, and I most anxiously hope that there may not be again occasion to revert to it. * * * I am satisfied that the time for military law and rule by violence has gone, never more to be recovered, and it ought not to be recovered. But, gentlemen, the moment there is an outbreak, and that caused, not by Englishmen, but by foreigners — men who are not suffered to remain in their own countries in consequence of the violence of their characters and the deeds they have done—I, for one, say that whenever that happens, the Englishmen of Victoria must rally round the Government, and must to a man sink their private differences, and forget the causes of difference which to Englishmen are inherent, and which, to a certain extent, are the blessings of our Constitution, and must rally round the authorities, liking or disliking them, and put that outbreak down.　As long as I am at the head of the Government I will endeavor to prevent these foreigners agitating to disturb the good order which generally exists in Victoria, and preventing the honest and industrious portion of the population from continuing at their work.　*　*　*　We will redress all grievances, if possible, maintain order, and keep prominently before us the fact that our endeavors will meet with their reward in the way that the Legislative Council and the Speaker at their head have shown.

Mr Speaker and Gentlemen,—I most cordially thank you for your expressions of feeling, and I hope from the bottom of my heart that whatever circumstances may arise, I may not be found wanting.

Good Yorkshire pluck at the bottom of the Yorkshire sailor's heart, no doubt, but a terrible buzzing bee in his bonnet as to "these foreigners."　A seeming slip of the pen, too, about the time for rule by violence being gone "never to be recovered," and the slip is instantly corrected, for the time " ought not to be recovered." Excellent sentiment !　Had it been practised as well as preached there had been no need of slaughtering men in the early Sunday morning light, nor of the " overwhelming force," the martial law, and all the abortive show of arrests, examinations, and trials for high treason and sedition.

Sir Charles was energetic in the business of the time.　Some of the Government proclamations were written from end to end by his own hand.　He was also brave and honest, but it would seem there never entered the head of that naval officer the conception that he was dealing with a different body of men from those that formed the laboring or even yeoman class upon his native wolds. It is likely that he had been, like many English gentlemen of rank and estates, accustomed to regard the masses as so much rent-producing material.　But he had to learn that Victorian diggers were of quite different mettle.　They were well described in a letter of the Bendigo correspondent of the *Herald* on the 30th November, who wrote of the Government officials and diggers :—

They have to meet hardy men, whose open-air occupations, thorough independence, and well-trained sinews give them a noble daring and a generous impetuosity.　Free of all masters, with a knowledge that they can obtain gold whenever they choose to work, they possess all the self-reliance of the mountaineers.

Governor Hotham had learned nothing of the spirit of larger

freedom which was abroad here, and was soon to be begotten afresh in the fatherland as we see it now. He appeared not to have divined the presence here of the germs of a bold democracy, germs even then fast approaching the bursting point under the united influence of a fertile soil and a freedom-inspiring atmosphere, bursting into fruit, to be garnered here and shared, through the sympathy of race and the quickening of constant inter-communication, by the still struggling and ever enfranchising people of the mother country. One open declaration of a willingness to hear and enquire through the medium of men in the confidence of the gold-fields population, would have sufficed to prevent all the bloodshed and all the heart-burnings that outlived the Eureka tragedy itself. But the Government would not stoop to such a method of conquering its few enemies and of assisting its multitudinous friends. Old country hauteur, with new exasperations, was persevered in, blood was shed, and then the Government gave all the diggers wanted, and Sir Charles Hotham died, a victim to the anxieties caused by the troubles that might have been avoided but for official blindness, blindness that was fatal to life and peace for a time, but powerless to hold back those rights which greater wisdom would have earlier conceded.

In the fragments of hours which the writer has spent amongst old newspaper files he has felt as if making a pilgrimage, after a long absence, through an old burial ground. "The years that are fled knock at the door and enter." The local dead have been continually before him, but speaking or acting in some of the many affairs of life. The vehemence of speech and intense interest and vitality of action over what, seen in the present distance, seem to be matters narrow and trivial, contrast strangely and in-structively with the silence of the now departed actors and talkers. Names forgotten—names even of acquaintances and friends—are re-corded on these yellowing and fragile sheets, and as they re-appear, one by one, they almost startle sometimes by the rush of many memories which they produce. To a newspaper writer it is similar, but more solemn, less merely curious, than the sudden meeting, in some strange journal printed, it may be, thousands of miles away, a paragraph from his own pen and quoted from paper to paper till it has reached the far distance and comes back again upon

H

him by some chance of affairs as an old but forgotten face, with features sometimes distorted by violent handling or worn by attrition of time and change. This is like a sudden note of music or odor of a flower recalling a past hour: the other is like the loud re-echoing of thunder among the hills when the listener had thought the last far-off reverberation had for ever died away. The first sonorous burst which awed him by its grandeur seems then to be heard again, and the first emotions are re-awakened. Such is the power that lies in these dry records which the printer's art has preserved, and such the seeming remoteness of the yet near past in the swift evolutions of events in a young and growing and active colonial settlement.

The newspapers of the day present to us a sorry procession to the Ballarat Police-court on the 8th December and following days, before Messrs Sturt and Webster. The prisoners taken in and about the Stockade were brought up, while their wounded comrades still lay bleeding hard by in the rude Camp-hospital. There came Timothy Hayes, large, portly, jovial, humorous, wayward, egoïste, the Irish chairman of the Bakery Hill meetings, whom the military arrested on their march back from the Stockade. He was not much of a fighter, but he had a wife of spirit. Lieutenant Richards, who ordered his arrest, deposed:—" After the arrest, the prisoner's wife came up and said if she had been a man she would not have allowed herself to have been taken. Then, addressing witness, she said 'why did not you come yesterday when the men were ready for you.'" Less happy marital days than these came to Hayes and his spouse afterwards, but they do not belong to this History. There came the little red-haired, fire-eyed Italian, Raffaello, to confront the "spy" Goodenough, his accuser. Defeated, but not cowed, Raffaello shot lightnings of indignation at the Crown witness, and afterwards wept tears of manly agony as he was taken past his little tent on his way to trial at Melbourne. No saintly shape, " robed in white samite," or radiant with heavenly glory, ever appeared more pure than did the diggers' cause to Raffaello's vision. Whatever else may be said of him he was true to it, as he saw it, and to the last, even when a tragical and inglorious end seemed a not improbable fate. There came also Manning, the *Ballarat Times* reporter, who had thought the sword could better serve than the pen to right the wrongs of the time. There came, too, another, the little editor of big words, Seekamp. " *C'e un'uómo ardito sènza prudènza*" Raffaello would have said. He was accused of sedition. Editorial lunacy might have been as appropriate an accusation. At least so it seems to the calmer reason of later days. Some of Seekamp's wonderful deliverances were read in court from the *Ballarat Times* of the 18th and 25th November. Here is one. *Ex pede Herculem.*

It is not for us to say how much we have been instrumental in rousing up the people to a sense of their wrongs ; we leave that to the public and the world. * * The coming Christmas is pregnant of change, for on next Wednesday will be held such a meeting for a fixed determinate purpose as was never before held in Australia. The Australian flag shall triumphantly wave in the sunshine of its own blue and peerless sky over thousands of Australia's adopted sons. * * And when the loud pœan of

> Now's the day and now's the hour,
> See the front of battle lour,

shall have pierced the blue vaults of Australia's matchless sky, from the brave men of Ballarat on next Wednesday at Bakery Hill, there will not be one discordant voice in the sublime and heroic chorus. * * * Go forth indomitable people ! gain your rights, and may the God of creation smile down propitiously upon your glorious cause ! FORWARD PEOPLE, FORWARD !

Though such appeals as these serve now to provoke a smile, they did not seem so ludicrous to the men whose blood was up in those hot days of agitation. A wild feeling of poetry as well as of anger fired the breasts of many then, and that which now reads like fustian was at that time perused with fierce delight and accelerated emotion. To judge from the *Herald* report the dealing with Seekamp's exalted language lifted reporter and printers above the common prose of business. The reporter calls the presiding magistrate "his Lordship," and the printers mixed up with the report two or three dreary paragraphs from the painfully dry details of debate in the Legislative Council of the previous day. Humffray too, the cautious peace-advocate, may have been inspired by the ardent phrases of the " seditious " editor, for we shall see by-and-bye that even he infused some of the music of sounding phrases into his first political address to the Ballarat electors of the coming days. Lalor, the real chief, and Vern, the supposed chief, of the insurgents, were still lying under cover, with the Government rewards over their heads. Of these something more anon. The magistrates committed the prisoners for trial on the charges of treason and sedition.

Four days after the historic Sunday, a Royal Commission of Enquiry, consisting of William Westgarth, chairman ; John Pascoe Fawkner, John Hodgson, John O'Shanassy, and James Ford Strachan, members of the Legislative Council ; and William H. Wright, Chief Commissioner of Gold-fields, was appointed to investigate the whole grounds of the agitation which had been thus tragical in its results. On the 14th December the commissioners met at the Imprest Office in Melbourne, and four days afterwards they opened their commission at Bath's (now Craig's) hotel, Ballarat. The evidence taken by the commissioners comprised a vast mass of important information touching the wrongs and the requirements of the diggers ; and the report of the commissioners, while it demonstrated the brutality of some of the subordinates, and the folly of the authorities generally, and chid the excesses of the insurgents, led to a speedy amelioration of the social and political condition of the gold-fields population.

On All-Fool's Day, 1855—so grim, sometimes, is the irony of the fates—the men arrested by the authorities and indicted for high treason were acquitted, a fitting day on which to record such a verdict upon the bloody business which had all along been marked by much folly on both sides. There were thirteen men arraigned by the Attorney-General's indictment of treason. First named was Timothy Hayes, the bland chairman of the Bakery Hill meetings. To him succeeded Carboni Raffaello, John Manning, John Josephs, Jan Vennik, James Beattie, Henry Reed, Michael Tuohy, James Macfie Campbell, William Molloy, Jacob Soranson, Thomas Dignam, and John Phelan. Sixty-four witnesses were set down in the Crown brief, and three panels of jurymen numbering 178 men in all were summoned for the trial. Henry Seekamp, the editor and proprietor of the *Ballarat Times*, had been previously tried for sedition, and being found guilty, " with a very strong recommendation to mercy," he was released on his own recognisances. Seekamp was a little man, but a pugnacious writer, and was often in trouble. He used sometimes to " set up " his own " leaders," concocting them as he " set " them, and he was said to write occasionally under inspiration from the source whence tradition tells us Dutchmen have drawn courage. Lola Montez horsewhipped him once in Ballarat for an unpleasant notice he wrote of her theatrical doings. One morning, long after the Stockade tragedy, Seekamp's prophetic soul was seen to have burst forth in a ludicrously inconsequent declaration that something would happen, " when Ballarat shall be Ballarat, and give laws to all the world." People then smiled and wondered. Now, after his life's brief and very fitful fever, poor Seekamp has joined the majority. He had some more judicious editorial coadjutors later in his journalistic career, but at the time of Westgarth's visit as chairman of the Royal Commission, it was no wonder he could find cause to write afterwards—" We found here a local newspaper—of course at war with the authorities, local and general—and we amused ourselves with the violent style of the ' leaders.'"

The State prisoners were defended gratuitously by Mr B. C. Aspinall, who thus earned an honorable celebrity. With him in the defence were several of our foremost barristers. A general amnesty, in effect, followed the acquittal, and the Government even compensated both friends and foes who had suffered. Lalor, the chief man of war, and Humffray, the leading man of peace, on the popular side, were returned to the first Parliament held under the new Constitution which, with all their follies and excesses, the fighting men of the insurgents had done so much to obtain, and which the men of peace have done so much more to consolidate and improve. Humffray was the first Minister of Mines, a new department of the State for the control of the chief industrial industry of the colony. The department has not proved so useful as was expected, and public opinion, which has seen the actual power to lie mainly in the hands of Mr Brough Smyth, the permanent Secretary for Mines, has here and there, but on hardly good grounds, grown in favor of an abolition of the department. Lalor has held a seat in Parliament from the date of his first election until the present day, and for a long period held salaried office as Chairman of Committees in the Legislative Assembly. He filled that office with credit to himself and the House, and whatever may be said against him it will be admitted that he has shown practical and suggestive, if not constructive, faculty as a legislator. He is now, and has for a long time been, with occasional vacillations, one of the

most conservative, that is, constitutional, members of Parliament ; as
if, so to speak, justifying his resolute rebellion under arms by his
generally steady maintenance in peace of that constitutional freedom
which he and his colleagues of the Stockade fought to obtain.   The
next chapter, however, will refer more in detail to political affairs.

The insurgent commander at the time of the Stockade collision
was in the prime of early manhood, and his brown hair, blue-
grey eyes, broad face, and rather heavy brows were those of a
handsome presence.   Not more than about twenty-five years old,
full six feet in stature, broad-chested, and generally well proportioned, and possessing a rather impulsive temperament, he
was just the man to embody the physical-force-spirit of the movement.   Raffaello was a shrewd restless little man, nearly forty
years old, under the middle height, with reddish hair and red beard
cut short, and small hazel eyes that had ever a fiery twinkle
beneath a broad forehead and rather shaggy eyebrows.   An Italian,
a Catholic, possessing others besides his mother tongue, his sanguine
temperament pushed him into the thickest of the struggle, and his
political sympathies being democratic and unmixed with English
leanings, he was one of the readiest to carry the rising to the
extreme limit of revolution.   Humffray was then a young man, too,
possessing the patriotism and more than usual of the caution of
Welshmen.   Darker in complexion than either Lalor or Raffaello,
he also differed from them in stature.   He was about the middle
height, moderately stout in frame, and had a well poised head and
a comely face.   His voice was musical, and he possessed a readiness
of utterance which made him one of the foremost of the advocates
of peaceable reform.   To that phase of the struggle he adhered,
but his caution at times led him to cross the more ardent purposes
of others, who used to accuse him of trimming—an ancient
and easy method of denouncing, and often of no worth.   In this
case there seems no ground for supposing Humffray ever to have
been disposed either to abandon a legitimate, or to sanction an
illegitimate agitation for a redress of grievances.   Vern was a
Hanoverian, warm, rough, uncertain, without the discretion, weight,
and tact that Lalor possessed.   Vern had a large ambition for
cheap military glory, and, like the great Napoleon, had a stern
unconquerable scorn of facts.   Emerson says, somewhere, that

Napoleon's genius was boundless in that direction, and before us lie letters in Vern's hand which demonstrate his great ability and daring in that peculiar walk of life.   And this, too, while he declares in one of the letters that his motto had "always been *fiat justitia et si pereat mundus.*" But Vern may be credible sometimes, nevertheless.   In a letter to the *Star*, dated 2nd October, 1856, he defends Humffray from charges of "treason" against the diggers, and says he was one of the first to attend on Ross when wounded, besides having kept Vern's hiding place secret when he could have had £500 for revealing it.   To those who were intimate with the men and the time, the following letter—a literal copy—will be regarded as characteristic of the writer's general frame of mind :—

Mr Lalor.

My dearest friend !

Once more enjoing the blessings of freedom, and having returned to the colony free from danger, I hasten to address you.   I hear that you was seriously wounded and maimed for life.   We are taking steps to subscribe in Melbourne for a man who has so bravely risked his life in defence of the miner's rights.   My friend, would to Heaven you had taken my advice on Friday, or would to Heaven we would have had men more true and honorable in our ranks.   I have positive information, and hold a correspondence in my hands now, from an officer in the insurgent army, and Mr. Furnell, late of H.M.A.—as soon as I can fathem the infamous plot, I shall avenge the murder of Ross and Capt. Potts, late of our ranks, and the world will be to hot to hold me and Lieut. Col. M.

Did you read my letter dated Albury, signed E. W. and S. F., it was a reply to Capt. Thomas' despatch.   I am sorry that it should have cost 22 lifes, or 23 including Capt. Pott's, to convince the diggers of the ridiculuous absurds of such a foolish outbreak as the late Ballarat affair.   Do you remember the delegates from Slaty Creek and their letter, as also M.Gill's reply to that letter, I have it from the best authority, that that was a plot.   We was sold to the government for £800.   Would to God I had seceded from the movement, or that you had taken my advice, and been discreet in your trust to strangers.

I charge M'Gill with treason before God and men, and woe to him if we meet again.   I wish I had never accepted the command after your resignation on Saturday morning, and then Sir Toorak could never have offred £500 for my apprehension.   The affair has produced good, but what a cruel, useless, wantan sacrifice of humane life, did it involve.   You have seen now that my advice was good, and that it was to permature a period for such a movement as you unfortunatly provoked.   Vengeance is now the only thing that is left to me, and I shall do my duty cooly but not foolishly.

Your

sincere friend,

Melbourne, 7 | 4 | 55.

F. VERN, late of Ballarat.

This letter shows a little of what Raffaello calls "sky-blathering," for Vern was one of the wildest and least reliable of the physical force party. Lalor did not surrender, nor Vern accept the command. The letter is a raving symptom of Vern's delight in illusions. When peace returned Vern took to mining, and in 1856 he was tried in Ballarat for "rioting at Black Lead on the 7th April," and sentenced to three months' imprisonment. The so-called riot was a combination, actively exerted, to fill up the holes sunk by "jumpers" upon claims held under the frontage regulations, then just become law. One of the witnesses at the trial said— "I heard Vern say, 'If any man stops us from filling up the claims, I shall make a dead cock of him, by my God!' At the same time he pulled out a revolver." They were out-spoken men in those days here. Black had a light complexion, was tall, thin, sanguine, gentlemanly, irresolute; but, the occasional perturbations of some "sin of fear" apart, was true and faithful as became a gentleman, and one having, in the Raffaello dialect, "a belief in the resurrection of life." M'Gill was a young American, fuller of ardor than of trusty courage and sagacity. Ross was of another stamp; he was a Canadian, bold, brave, and trusty: about twenty-eight years old, of middle height, true as the steel of the axe that felled his native forests, he was one of the best loved men of those that fell. He was shot in the attack on the Sunday morning, and was removed by friends to the Star hotel that then stood in Main street, where he soon died. Esmond, was another who, with a few others, took the more prominent positions in the struggle. His prominence was only comparative, and was essentially local.

In March, 1856, a return of the cost of the strife between the insurgents and the Government was laid before Parliament. The Deputy-Commissary General's figures showed the military expenditure to be £26,733 18s 6d, which, by deducting the cost of the military in Melbourne on their ordinary footing, was reduced to £12,050. To this were added extra police charges, and the sum of £4689 4s 0d voted in compensation to sufferers. With regard to the compensations voted, it is to be remarked that Lalor and Humffray both interposed on behalf of the claimants. Lalor was specially active. The *Star* of the 22nd and 25th March, 1856, had the following reference to the part taken by the insurgent chief, then become a representative of the gold-field in Parliament :—

To Mr Lalor's exertions we must attribute this successful result. * * We can only consider as an additional grace to the triumph, that he who was the foremost to defend our rights, has also been the principal instrument in recovering compensation for wrongs inflicted.

On the 3rd December, 1856, there was a small procession to the site of the Stockade, about two hundred people assembling. Mr John Lynch, who was a mining surveyor, a native of Ireland, and one of Lalor's captains in the Stockade, mounted a tree-stump and read an oration, the opening sentence of which was as follows :—

Sensible of the debt of gratitude we owe to the memories of the brave men who fell victims on the fatal 3rd December, 1854, in their efforts to resist the oppression and tyranny of the then existing Government, we meet here to-day, the second anniversary of that disastrous day, in solemn procession, to pay to their manes the only tribute in our power, the celebrating with due solemnity the sad commemoration of their martyrdom.

When Lynch's oration was finished, a march was made to the cemetery. The *Star* of that day reads thus :—

The persons present formed in procession, two and two, headed by Mr Esmond, carrying a pole draped in sable, with black crape streamers. Next came Messrs Seekamp and Lessmann, bearing garlands of flowers, and followed by the committee and the general procession. Nearly all the persons present wore crape on the left arm, and many more also wore crape on their hats. As the procession proceeded along the Eureka and Main road its numbers swelled to nearly three hundred, the line reaching from the Colonial Bank to the bridge, while numerous outsiders accompanied the processionists. Arrived at the cemetery, the procession walked round the spot where the bodies of the men who fell on the fatal Sunday morning are interred, and, returning to the monument erected to their memory, the apex of the monument was crowned with the garlands borne in procession. An oration by Dr. Hambrook followed, every person standing with head uncovered.

At this time the enthusiasm of the days of agitation had not all disappeared. There were left swelling bosoms and big words that the least opportunity brought into play. An emotional writer in the *Star* of the 9th February, 1856, drawing attention to a meeting, to be held that day on Bakery Hill, to discuss measures for the erection of a monument to the men who fell at the Stockade, ended his appeal with the following burst of fervor :—

The man on Ballarat who fails to swell to-day's meeting should be, in its most perfect reality of chains, dungeons, and degradation, a victim of slavery !

It does not appear that the enthusiasm of the time was very practical, for the only monument ever erected was a gift by the man who constructed it and undertook its erection. Oratory, however, was cheap, and at that time most of it was, no doubt, as sincere at the moment as it was plentiful.

In a despatch by Deputy Adjutant-General Macarthur we read of Captain Wise that " his remains are to be buried with the honors due to his rank, in the graveyard at Ballarat gold-field, beside those of the three other meritorious soldiers which lie there interred." Alas! the honors have not been very gratefully echoed by later survivors. Mr Westgarth was in Ballarat on that day. He says :—

The day was hot and dusty as the cortege moved along to the place of burial, a slightly rising ground nearly a mile from the township. This rural cemetery was still wild and open, no fence having as yet been placed around it, for even this is an expensive process at a gold-field. But some excuse appeared for this apparent negligence, for the ground had evidently been but recently devoted to its present purpose, as the small number of graves amongst a large population indicated.

Since that time the city has spread out its arms all around the " rural cemetery." The place has been enclosed ; it has well-kept paths, flower borders, handsome monuments, and it is crowded to overflowing with those who have fallen in this part of

The world's broad field of battle.

There is, too, a new and larger cemetery now, enclosed, ornamented, and already in part peopled with the silent ones. The place in the old cemetery where the military were buried is like a neglected wilderness, a disgrace to the place, which the municipal authorities might well remove by introducing order and ornament where all now speaks of neglect and ruin. The spot where some gathered bodies of the insurgents lie is neatly enclosed, and has upon it a simple monument and sepulchral urn, sculptured, engraved, and given by James Leggat, of Geelong. A few years after Scobie's death a broken bluestone pillar was erected to his memory by his brother in the old cemetery.

On the last day of the year 1855, at half-past twelve o'clock of the day, Sir Charles Hotham died at Toorak. His disease was dysentery, and his death was attributed to the harassing anxieties which accompanied the crisis. He is the only Victorian Governor who has yet died while in office here. His remains were buried in Melbourne. Governor Hotham failed, no doubt, to understand the gold-digging population. His mistakes were due to a want of sympathy with the democratic instinct inherent in all aggregations of free British colonists. His intentions, we may well believe, were to do his duty dutifully. That duty he conceived to be to rule with a high hand a people whom, though complimented by him upon occasion as peaceable and law-abiding, he practically regarded as a froward race of vagabond gold - hunters, mixed with demagogues and escaped and liberated convicts from the adjacent penal settlements. What wonder, then, that he, an aristocrat, a naval officer used to peremptory command, with such views heightened, too, by occasional excesses of language and action amongst the miners, should fail to comprehend all at once the policy required for the redress of wrongs which some of his own subordinates on the gold-fields had first intensified and then misrepresented. Divining only a part of the truth, Sir Charles Hotham was betrayed into a misconception of the crisis. As his predecessor had discovered "designing" men in the journalists of his day, so Governor Hotham found the gold-fields troubles to be the product of the schemes of "disaffected" men, and that idea whelmed all other conceptions of the causes of the outbreak. The Governor was partially right. There were among the insurgents men who hated British rule with a hereditary hatred. There were Irishmen who felt that feeling, and there were foreigners who had no special sympathy, if any at all, with British government ; but even those men never desired or aimed at rebellion until they were maddened with the excitement of the agitation which sought, at least in its earlier stages, nothing but the clear and rational redress of plain and insulting wrongs. Here, even those who elsewhere may have been the least loyal were disposed to peace and submission, no matter whence they came, and it was nothing but the haughty folly of officials that precipitated what has been called rebellion ; for it was clear to demonstration that it was not so much the law, or the want of law, as the unwise administration of law that provoked the rising of the gold-fields population.

CHAPTER VI.

POLITICAL DEVELOPMENT.

Ballarat Politically Active and Influential.—New Constitution.—Humffray and Lalor Elected.—Their Addresses.—Humffray in Trouble.—Lalor on Democracy.—Petition for a Private Property Mining Law.—Neglect by the Parliaments of Mining Interests.—Probable Causes.—New Political Demands.—Votes of Lalor and Humffray.—Burial Expenses of Governor Hotham.—O'Shanassy Chief Secretary.—Haines Succeeds with M'Culloch as Commissioner of Customs.—O'Shanassy in Power Again.—Nicholson Cabinet.—Succeeded by Heales with Humffray as First Minister of Mines.—O'Shanassy in Power Again.— Succeeded by M'Culloch.—The Tariff.—Re-call of Governor Darling.—Darling Grant Crisis.—Death of Governor Darling.—Grant to his Widow and Family.—Sladen Ministry. —M'Culloch in Power Again.—Representative Charges.—Jones Declared Corrupt.— Defeats Vale.—The Macpherson Ministry.—Its Resignation.—Macgregor's Failure.— M'Culloch and Macpherson in Office together.—Michie Elected for Ballarat West.— Local Court.—Mining Board.—Court of Mines.—Local Courts Wrongly Constituted. —Mining Boards Not Now Necessary.—One Code of Mining Law Required.—Valuable Services of the Earlier Courts and Boards.

 H E acquittal of the State prisoners was an earnest of the fuller fruition of the reform struggle. It was not merely an acquittal of the insurgent diggers, but a justification of the basis of the whole reform movement, and a condemnation of the system of tyranny whose stupid and insulting administration had provoked such bloody reprisals. The report of the Commission of Enquiry averred that the diggers had been "governed three times over," and declared that if the insurgents had been guilty of excesses, they had been goaded thereto by bad laws badly enforced. The remedy suggested was the government of the people by the people through a fairly representative Parliament. Thence came our present Constitution and all its benefits in the form of a manhood franchise and local self-government.

Thus, to the wild delirium of the early gold hunting time there succeeded the troubles of the Eureka Stockade, and then, with the gift of constitutional freedom, there came the noble or ignoble rage of party politics. Ballarat has always held a prominent position in politics. The sturdy men who fought through all the agitations that led up to and followed the Eureka Stockade seemed to have given a character of influence to the electorates that were the outcome of those early struggles. But some of those earlier fighters were soon left behind. The current of politics ran a turbulent race in keeping with the swift march of colonial affairs generally. Some men who rose to early fame and bade fair to ride firmly upon the waters of public life have drifted upon lee shores and made wreck of health and reputation. Others have been out-faced by newer and bolder, if not better, men, and have fallen back among the shadows of private life. The simple aims and earnest honesty of most of the earlier agitators have given place to complications of policy and, too often, to the mere self-seeking of cunning men who trade upon the weaknesses and the vices common to society everywhere, and nowhere so potent as in a democracy where the passions and prejudices of all classes have full play.

We may as briefly as possible trace the course of those later events, besides glancing at some anterior passages of colonial history which were the prelude to those which relate more closely to our story. On the 25th July, 1828, the British Parliament passed an Act giving larger powers to the Governments of New South Wales and Van Dieman's Land, and in 1837 the Government of Australia was created. On the 5th August, 1850, the Government of Victoria was constituted. One-third of the members of the Legislative Council, the only House of Legislature then, to be nominated by the Crown, and the other two-thirds by the inhabitants of the territory, separation from New South Wales taking place on the 1st July of the following year. The Victorian " Act to Establish a Constitution in and for the Colony of Victoria," was reserved on the 25th March, 1854, for royal assent, was assented to on the 21st July, 1855, and was proclaimed in Victoria, and came into operation on the 23rd November, 1855. By that Act the old and partly nominee Council was abolished and two Houses were created—a Legislative Council and a Legislative Assembly, both wholly elective, the Council having thirty members, chosen from six provinces, and the Assembly sixty members, chosen from thirty-seven districts. Pending the royal assent to that Act, however, five representatives from the gold-fields had been added to the old Council.   This was done in pursuance of of a recommendation from the Gold-fields Commission after the quickening time of the Eureka Stockade, and Lalor and Humffray were chosen to represent Ballarat.   About the same time Messrs Samuel Irwin, John Victor, and William Bradshaw were appointed justices of the peace in Ballarat.   They were men of the times and of the mines, and their appointment was one of the immediate fruits of the agitation for reform of administrative as well as legislative abuses.   Irwin has already appeared in this narrative ; Victor is now principal of Grenville College, Ballarat.

The first printed election addresses of Lalor and Humffray were as different as the men.   Lalor's was brief and plain as a word of command from a military man.   In his short address it was natural he should say—

I am in favor of such a system of law reform as will enable the poor man to obtain equal justice with the rich one, which at present I believe to be impossible.

Humffray's was more verbose and rhetorical, full of wise saws, and bristling with sentiments and statistics.

I respond (he said) to the call readily, because I am anxious to enter St. Patrick's Hall, and have the high privilege of joining in the patriotic chorus which will form at once the requiem of the present irresponsible system, and be the herald of a glorious future for Victoria.

The printers of that day printed "golorious future," as if, facetious in their work, they wished to qualify the pacific agitator's eloquence by a suggestion of what, in the language of American politicians, is called "high falutin."   We, however, may rather suppose he had only caught some distant echos of the songs of the bards of his native land as, in the ancient times, they sang in "patriotic chorus" among the hills of long unconquered and ever romantic Cymry. Born in Montgomeryshire, near the source of the Severn, and not far from the head waters of old Usk that runs from the Brecon hills by valley, and glen, and crumbling castle walls, close past the site of hoary Romano-British Caerlon, thence to mingle its waters with those of the British Channel not very remote from the mouths of broader Severn and the more picturesque Wye, Humffray may have seen visions of the past and the future, in which poetry and politics became curiously blended.   Lalor was not so much given to visions and poetry, if his later life be the test.   He was directer, more practical, more commercial. However, youth and hope are immortal, and Humffray, at the time under discussion, was nearer than now to the days of "unbounded hope and heavenly ignorance." He may have penned his first political manifesto with the "March of the Men of Haerlech" ringing in his ears, or under other remains of the inspiration of his legendary forefathers who, if poets speak truly, were, some of them, in youth, as "damsels-errant," and used to

> Ride
> Arm'd as ye see, to tilt against the knights
> There at Caerleon.

Humffray had spirit and could assert himself in time of pressure. On the 26th March, 1862, a "monster meeting" was held in the Town-hall, Ballarat East, to express indignation against Humffray and John Cathie for their votes in favor of a ten years' extension of the Squatters' Leases. Popular indignation is often accompanied by imputations of corruption, and by insulting assumption of almost despotic authority over the very reason and will of the representative. A display of this temper in the electorate seems to have occurred, for Humffray retorts upon some scandals of the kind. He did not appear before the meeting, but a letter from him was read in which were the following passages in wholesome assertion of rational freedom in the representative :—

> I wish it to be distinctly understood that I claim now, as I ever have claimed, the most unfettered freedom in the exercise of my judgment while recording my votes ; as I would not, for one hour, occupy the humiliating position of a mere delegate, and vote according to order. * * As to the vile insinuations of corrupt motives which have been made against me, I know, and am known in Ballarat East too well to suppose for one moment that they will discredit any but their authors. Thus much, however, I will say, that if the price of a man's representing a constituency is that he must submit to an inquisition, by public meetings, into the state of his private affairs, whenever slanderous enemies choose to misrepresent and stigmatise his votes as venal, no human being of any spirit will consent to debase himself so far as to become a member.

Humffray fell, and Cathie too, before the storm ; Cathie, who was no mean stump orator, upon occasion, having had the courage to tell the tumultuous meeting that "the thing which shows me I have done right is the noise and not the reason that greets me." In all Humffray's public career he carried himself, as Hamlet puts it, "indifferent honest," not descending to the cunning arts of falsehood which have in later years carried away many constituencies captive. Later, he went the way, though less noisily, that the Netherlands Brederode went, and his influence consequently declined.

When the first Parliament was elected under the new Constitution Act, the Ballarat members were again elected, Lalor for Grenville district, including Ballarat West, and Humffray for North Grant, including Ballarat East.

There was one time, in December, 1856, when Lalor was held to have belied his previous democratic action. A new Electoral Act, brought in under the Constitution, the advent of which the Eureka affair had done much to hasten, was before Parliament, and the 4th clause proposed a renewal of the property qualification for the franchise. This was opposed by the country generally, as manhood suffrage was demanded as the people's right. It was certainly a fair demand and not illogical, as a sequence to the principles declared by the gold-fields reformers when Lalor was one of the most popular advocates of liberty. But Lalor voted for the obnoxious clause in the Act and brought a storm upon himself. In a letter to the *Ballarat Star* on the 1st January, 1857, he defended himself against the attacks of that journal and the complaints of his constituents. He said :—

I would ask those gentlemen what they mean by the term " democracy ? " Do they mean Chartism, or Communism, or Republicanism ? If so, I never was, I am not now, nor do I ever intend to be a democrat. But if a democrat means opposition to a tyrannical press, a tyrannical people, or a tyrannical government, then I have ever been, I am still, and I will ever remain a democrat.

Lalor held that " freehold suffrage is virtually manhood suffrage," and on that ground he justified his vote. No doubt he had grown more sober since the days in the latter half of 1854, when a programme of principles not much unlike Chartism, and a Declaration of Independence were adopted by the agitators of the day. His defence shows that he had the courage of his opinions, whether they were new or old, and suggests a feeling of the necessity of some such correction of the unequal action of a purely numerical majority, arrived at in the ordinary way, as proposed by Hare in his scheme for the representation of minorities. But he also went the length of advocating an Upper House of nominees instead of elected representatives. He even then cited that advocacy as a proof of his never having advocated "thorough democracy." That such an opinion as to the Upper House should have been held within twenty-four months of the Eureka agitation by the armed leader of that rising is one more instance of the mutability of human feeling if not of change of opinion. Lalor may not have had any very well-reasoned opinions on constructive politics when he took up arms against the rule of a Government and a partially elective single House of Parliament, but there is little ground for doubting that at that time his sympathies were in favor of as wide a liberalism as was espoused by those of his subsequent constituents who condemned his vote on the 4th clause of the Electoral Act in December, 1856.

In June or July, 1857, Messrs John Yates, Alfred Arthur O'Connor, and John Cathie were appointed delegates to represent Ballarat in the Land Convention in Melbourne. The Convention was called at the instance of the Victorian Land League, a body sitting in the metropolis, and the immediate cause of the Convention was the general opposition in the country to the Land Bill then before the Legislative Assembly, and for his vote on which Mr Lalor was called to account by the electors of North Grant. The first sitting of the Convention took place at Keeley's Australasian hotel, Melbourne, on the 15th July, Mr Thos. Loader, chairman of the League, presiding. Mr Wilson Gray, a barrister, declared the Bill before Parliament to be a fraud upon the people, as it gave the squatters a too great grasp upon the public territory, and he announced the three great principles of the Convention as to land legislation to be—First, perfectly free selection ; second, uniformity of price ; third, open pasturage on all unalienated lands. These principles became the basis of the Convention's action, and steps were taken at once to arrest the progress of the Bill before the Assembly. The reform of Parliament was another part of the Convention programme, the delegates declaring for manhood suffrage, no-property qualification of members, and a limitation of the duration of the Houses of Parliament to two years for the Assembly, and four years for the Council. The doings of the Convention went a good way towards indoctrinating the people generally with the principles of land legislation, which later received, in great part, embodiment in actual law. On the 16th July, Mr Wilson Gray

I

was elected president of the Convention, and two other barristers, Sir George Stephen and Mr Prendergast, were elected vice-presidents, the first act of the president being to call on the delegates to make their deliverances. He said he must first call for the delegates " of Ballarat, that monarch of gold-fields," and forthwith Messrs Yates, O'Connor, and Cathie were called upon. When that series of Convention sittings was over, a public meeting was held in the Victoria Theatre, Ballarat East, to receive the delegates on their return. Mr Humffray presided, and he and the delegates were received with great acclamations, Humffray's vote against the Bill being contrasted with the contrary vote of Lalor, " the recusant member for North Grant." About that time, too, a pecuniary testimonial was being subscribed for Humffray, and meetings were being held and requisitions signed to procure Lalor's resignation, as he had been acting, to quote the *Ballarat Star* of that day, " in the license of constant and unvarying opposition to the wishes of his constituents." The feeling against the Land Bill was strong, and a petition signed by 17,745 persons at Ballarat, and one from Sandhurst, signed by 11,875 persons, were sent to Parliament expressing the opposition of the subscribers. In leaving this reference to the Land Convention it may be remarked that many of the delegates, including Gray, the President, were afterwards elected to seats in the Legislative Assembly.

As we are still, after more than thirteen years have passed, without a law to legalise and regulate mining on private property, it may be noted that on the 4th March, 1857, Humffray moved, in the Legislative Assembly, " that the petition presented from the miners and storekeepers of Ballarat, praying for immediate legislation on the subject of mining on private property, be printed." The records of Parliament inform us that " the motion was agreed to." All the Parliaments since then have been alike unmindful of the subject thus prayed for, as the miners have too often been content to feed upon the dry husks of pleasant charlatanry and passionate party, instead of seeking the pure and wholesome grain of honest and effectual statesmanship. By so much, and only so much, can the Parliaments be acquitted of neglect of the chief producing interest of the colony. While this narrative is being prepared for the press, Humffray is again moving in Parliament for legislation on private property mining.

The old adage that a people is governed as well as it deserves to be governed has very few exceptions in illustration of the rule. One great all-sufficing cause of the neglect of mining interests in Parliament was the change that came in the political constitution and in mining itself. That double change placed power in the hands of the wages class, and converted mining from a field of independent fortune seeking for all alike into a field for the exercise of capital and the employment on wages of the class that held in their hands the balance of political power. There thus arose the curious position that on the gold-fields themselves mining questions came to be of secondary political importance, as those who were most able to suggest a mining policy were out-numbered by those who only, or mainly, looked for wages, and who were led to vote for men who supported any policy that seemed to promise abundant employment and a wage-rate well maintained. The political agitations that followed the introduction of manhood suffrage and its accompaniments were therefore marked by all kinds of cries but mining ones. Though the mines were still the backbone of the country's prosperity, the men who worked in the mines on wages were separated in sympathy from the capitalists who were nearly the whole exploiters of the mines; and theology, or protection, or free-trade, or cheap lands, or some other hustings cry, or some absorbing passion of party was generally the moving impulse to the exclusion of questions relating to mining law and administration. In the earlier days of the gold-fields men were of one heart and soul, and on all public questions then current there was an irresistible unanimity, for all were more nearly on a level in industrial value and in relation to the chances of fortune. The difference between the two times was natural, and the Parliamentary results equally natural, for not even democracy can prevent a war of classes, or make the greater to be always the wiser number.

While, however, this change in the aspect of gold-fields politics had taken place, there had also come with the diversion of power some prevision of a still remoter change. The demand of the majority for protection and cheap land disclosed an instinct prescient of coming necessities. It was felt that though the mines had been, and still were, the chief producing interest in the colony, their importance had, relatively, declined. It was further seen that this decline must inevitably continue, and that for the increasing population new sources of labor and wealth must be developed. Hence the cry for protection that local manufactures might be created, and for cheap land that fresh fields might be opened for the employment of labor and the founding of new homes for the people.

That which the Protectionists desired the Free-traders also desired —the creation of new industries. But, in the differences upon the economical question there arose so fierce a fight of party that hurtful issues, foreign to the original ones, were raised as ancillary to victory rather than to the elevation of public opinion or the consolidation of a pure and stable scheme of economical politics. This made openings for new men, banished old ones from the political arena, and, in conjunction with the change that had come in the relations of capital and labor at the mines, caused questions of purely mining significance to occupy a subordinate and even neglected position.

In the moribund nominee Council Mr Haines was the last Colonial Secretary as successor to the abused John Leslie Fitzgerald Vesey Foster, or "Alphabetical Foster" as he was sometimes designated from the multiplicity of names he bore. Mr Haines also formed the first Government under the New Constitution of November, 1855. He was beaten on the 4th March, 1857, on a question of finance; Lalor and Humffray voting, as they generally have, on opposite sides of the House. Lalor on that occasion was with the defeated Government, and Humffray against it.

There was one notable occasion on which Lalor and Humffray voted together. This was in the old Legislative Council on the 10th January, 1856; a part of the proceedings relative to the burial of Sir Charles Hotham being reported as follows :—

Mr Fawkner moved that the sum of £1500 be appropriated for funeral expenses, which were estimated to amount to £500, and the remaining £1000 would amply suffice for the erection of a monument.

Mr Lalor was quite willing to defray the funeral expenses, but objected to the erection of a monument. THE MEMORY OF THE THIRTY INDIVIDUALS WHO MET THEIR DEATHS AT BALLARAT WOULD BE A STANDING MONUMENT TO THE MEMORY OF SIR CHARLES HOTHAM.

Mr Grant moved an amendment that the vote be limited to £500, funeral expenses only. He said the House ought to be just, and remember those for whom NO MONUMENT HAD BEEN ERECTED, AND FOR WHOSE WIDOWS NO SYMPATHY WAS EXPRESSED. What could they inscribe on his monument? Not his political character.

Mr Humffray seconded the amendment.

The amendment was lost, only the gold-fields members and one or two more, eight in all, voting for it. The emphasised words are so printed in the *Ballarat Star* of the date.

On the 11th March, 1857, a new Cabinet was declared, with Mr O'Shanassy as Chief Secretary, and Foster (whom Williamstown had returned) was Treasurer in that Ministry, which hardly lived two months. Its defeat was on personal grounds rather than on any question of policy proposed. Lalor and Humffray still voted one against the other on that occasion. Haines then came into power again. This was in April, 1857, and he had with him Mr M'Culloch as Commissioner of Customs. That Ministry was defeated on the 23rd February, 1858, on a question of extension of the franchise ; Lalor and Humffray being still opposed to one another. On the 10th March O'Shanassy formed his second Government. This Ministry was defeated on the 22nd October, 1859, on the ground of a general want of confidence ; Lalor voting against, and Humffray for the Government. On the 26th October, the Nicholson Administration was announced, with Wm. Nicholson Chief Secretary. On the 21st November, 1860, that Ministry was displaced also on a vote of general want of confidence; Lalor and Humffray still preserving their relative positions. Lalor, however, had now changed his constituency and sat for South Grant, which seat he has held ever since ; Humffray and Cathie sitting for Ballarat East, and J. R. Bailey (who shortly afterwards was Postmaster-General in the Nicholson Administration) and R. M. Serjeant for Ballarat West. These changes were synchronous with an alteration in the electoral districts, Grant and Grenville being divided into several districts of which Ballarat East and Ballarat West were two. In 1860 R. Gillespie and R. H. Locke were elected for the district of Grenville, which included Buninyong and the localities adjoining the Ballarat proper districts on the south and west sides.

On the 29th November, 1860, the Heales Ministry was announced, with Richard Heales Chief Secretary ; and Humffray,

Minister for Mines. This ministry was defeated on the 12th
November, 1861, in a debate on the Budget ; and the next day a
coalition ministry was announced, with O'Shanassy Chief Secretary. This coalition cabinet was displaced on 23rd June, 1853, on
the Land policy, both Lalor and Humffray voting with the defeated Government. In the meantime Bailey and Serjeant had
been displaced in Ballarat West by Duncan Gillies and W. C.
Smith. For Grenville A. A. O'Connor was returned with Gillespie
in 1862, and in 1863-4 he sat with M. M. Pope, T. Randall succeeding O'Connor in 1865. W. Frazer, once of the Ballarat
Local Court, and J. T. Smith sat for the Talbot district, in which
Creswick and Clunes are included.

On the 30th June, 1863, the first M'Culloch Administration was
formed, with J. M'Culloch Chief Secretary. On the 11th March,
1868, this Ministry tendered its resignation on the question of a
grant to Sir Charles Darling, who had been removed from office
as Governor of Victoria on the ground of indiscretions during disputes between the Houses of Parliament over the Tariff. The
" Darling Grant Crisis," as it is still called, was a dispute between
the opposing parties as to a grant of £20,000 proposed to the
re-called Governor. The party opposing the grant came to be
known in Victorian politics as Constitutionalists, whilst the supporters of M'Culloch's policy called themselves Loyal Liberals.
While the dispute was pending Sir Charles declined the grant,
and so the battle ended. He has since died, and all parties here
united in voting an annuity of £1000 a-year to his widow, and a
sum of £5000 in trust for her children.

While these events were transpiring electoral changes had come
about. In 1865, Charles Dyte and Edwin Charles Jones were
returned for Ballarat East. The former retains his seat, but in
1869 Jones was defeated by Humffray, who holds his seat still,
though Jones lodged an unprosecuted petition against his election.
For Talbot Frazer still sits also. His fame may be found in some
of the least creditable records in *Hansard* and the public journals.
For Ballarat West Gillies and W. C. Smith sat till 1865, when
Smith was replaced by W. M. K. Vale, who held the seat till 1869,
when, while Commissioner of Customs in the M'Culloch Ministry,
he resigned in order to contest the seat against Jones, the defeated

of Ballarat East. Jones had ousted Gillies, but, while Minister of Railways and a colleague of Vale, he had been turned out of Parliament on a charge of corrupt practices, both sides of the House—his own colleagues in office as well as the Opposition—voting for his expulsion. With great intrepidity he declared his innocence, invoking God's name at a public meeting in support of one particular averment of innocence, and he boldly sought at the hands of the Ballarat West constituency a rehabilitation of his tarnished reputation. Vale resigned his seat to contest the election, as he declared, in the interests of parliamentary purity, and he was beaten by Jones, who had a large majority among the Welsh miners of Sebastopol. Vale had ceased to be as popular as he had been, and the assistance he derived in the contest from his old political opponents, no doubt raised party feeling, and caused the election to be determined at least as much from party spirit as from a regard to the greater issue propounded to the electorate. What helped Jones's cause was, the general belief that if he was guilty, others still unpunished were as bad as he, and a suspicion in many minds that Vale's contest was the result rather of envy or spite than of a sincere regard for political honesty and purity of Parliament. Jones and his accusers have since then let the matter lie undisturbed. The Assembly, as being unused to such great moral efforts, has quietly borne many taunts from without in relation to corruption, and Jones has been permitted to sit unmolested.

The M'Culloch Ministry having, as we have seen, resigned on the Darling Grant dispute, a Ministry was announced on the 6th May, with Mr Sladen as Chief Secretary, Mr Gillies being Minister of Lands in this Administration. It was on the occasion of Gillies seeking re-election on acceptance of office that Jones had ousted him prior to his own expulsion from Parliament. The Sladen Ministry was defeated on the 10th July, 1868, on a vote of supplies, and Mr M'Culloch then returned to power. This Ministry was displaced in September, 1869, by a coalition of Constitutionalists and Loyal Liberals on the ground of want of confidence. A Government was then formed with J. A. Macpherson Chief Secretary. This Ministry was defeated on the Budget, and on the 31st March, 1870, the Government resigned. Some of their own supporters deserted them, including several Constitutionalists, and

after some time spent in negotiations by several members of the
House, and notably by Mr John Macgregor, who had moved the
hostile motion on the Budget, Mr (now Sir James) M'Culloch again
returned to power, and with him Mr Macpherson, the deposed Chief
Secretary, who accepted office as Minister of Lands.   The new
Attorney-General, Mr Michie, was returned unopposed for Ballarat
West, taking the seat vacated by Mr John James, who had been
elected to the seat vacated by Mr Vale in his contest against Jones.
James, at a meeting in the Alfred Hall—when Michie met the
electors on his unopposed return—"took credit to himself for having
done a noble act.   He had done something to raise the Ballarat
electorate—in fact, more than had been done for years," in giving
up political life in favor of his more illustrious successor.*

To revert to more exclusively local self-government, the course of
Local Court and Mining Board history may now be swiftly traced.
On the 14th of July, 1855, James Ryce, Robert Donald, Carboni
Raffaello, John Yates, William Greene, Edward Milligan, John Wall,
Thomas Chidlow, and Henry R. Nicholls were chosen—at a meeting
of the diggers near Lalor's stump, the old trysting place during the
previous year's agitation—to serve in the first Local Court granted
under the reformed *régime*.   A day before this Mr C. W. Sherard,
the resident-officer for the Government, had attempted to hold the
election from the top of a dray near the site of the late Charlie
Napier, but the crowd was too great for the space available, and
hence the resort to Bakery Hill, where the election was had by
show of hand.   There was no other way practicable then, for the
times were primitive and the circumstances pressing.   These
courts were the first fruits of the reform movement.   They
were presided over by wardens of the gold-fields—the old
commissioners with a new name and smaller powers—and the
members and electors of the courts were men holding miner's-
rights, documents issued annually in lieu of the old license.   The
Local Courts had power, not only to make local regulations, but to sit
as absolute and unappealable courts of judicature upon cases brought
under the regulations they framed.   This was a fatal error in constitution, and in the course of time the defect became generally

---

* A list of Members of Parliament, with the votes recorded for each, is given in
Appendix B.

apparent, and led eventually to the abolition of the Local Courts and the creation of the Mining Boards as at present existing. The first sitting of the first Ballarat Local Court was on the 20th July, 1855, and the last sitting of the last court was on the 30th April, 1857, Mr Warden Sherard being the first chairman. To him soon succeeded Mr Warden Daly, who filled the office as long as the court existed. The first clerk to the court was Mr Bowker, who was followed by Mr Harrington, and after him came Mr John Miskelly, who held the office till the courts were abolished. Fresh parliamentary legislation in 1857 created the present Mining Boards and Courts of Mines, the Mining Boards having power to elect their own chairmen, and being invested with merely legislative and some trifling administrative functions. His Honor Judge Rogers was the first judge appointed in the Ballarat Court of Mines, and he has held office ever since, presiding as well (since the death of Judge Wrixon) over the County Courts and Courts of General Sessions for this district. With the abolition of the Local Courts and the establishment of Courts of Mines, there came also the Wardens' Courts, dealing with applications for forfeited ground, and with mining disputes of all kinds eventually, appeal in all cases lying to the Courts of Mines. The first Ballarat Mining Board was elected on the 27th February, 1858, and Messrs James Baker, John Yates, Alfred Arthur O'Connor (for Ballarat Proper), William Frazer, Robert Lamb (for Buninyong), Duncan Gillies, Robert Critchley (for Smythesdale), Joseph Reed (for Creswick), —- Martin (for Blackwood), and William Butcher (for Stieglitz) were the members, James Baker being chosen chairman. Mr Harrie Wood was appointed clerk, and he has held the office ever since. The first meeting of the board was on the 9th March, 1858. The Local Court members were remunerated by the fees paid in the cases brought before the courts in their judicial capacity. The Mining Boards receive each a Government subsidy of £500 a-year. The courts were more intensely local bodies than are the boards. The boards preside over and legislate for large districts, but the courts had very small areas of jurisdiction, nearly every mining centre, small or large, having its own court and its own regulations.

In looking at the mixed powers of the Local Courts and their great number, we see the cause of their abolition. The conjunction of the legislative and judicial functions did not work satisfactorily, and the multiplicity of courts being followed by a multitude of varying regulations, another element of dissatisfaction was found to quicken the desire for further reform. Hence arose the present Mining Boards and Courts of Mines, the former legislating for districts in which previously, perchance, half a score of Local Courts had exercised their anomalous union of jurisdictions, and the latter exercising judicial functions over areas coterminous with the mining board districts. In the present day the want of still further reform is felt. To the Mining Boards is now raised an objection similar in part to that raised against the Local Courts. As the larger views and wants of the miners required the abolition of the Local Courts in order to do away with vexatiously numerous and conflicting regulations, and get rid of the inconvenient union of powers in the courts, so now the abolition of the Mining Boards is held to be desirable as a means of getting one uniform code of mining law for the whole colony. Popular freedom is now perfect, and popular power so absolute, that the form of local self-government existing in the Mining Boards can no longer be regarded as essential to local interests. On the contrary, the general feeling of the mining communities all over the colony now is that the profitable pursuit of mining will be best helped by a code that shall be applicable to the whole colony, shall leave the pursuit as free as possible from trammels of all kinds, and thus at once facilitate the investment of capital, and give new fields to the operative industry of the working miner.

But it must not be inferred from this that either the Local Courts or the Mining Boards performed no services of value to the gold-fields. Both have done much good. They were creations of the times, and served the times faithfully. As experiments they proved defective, but their work has been a part of our mining progress, and will remain an honorable portion of colonial history. The miners showed almost invariably a singular sagacity in the selection of representatives in these local bodies, and some of their earliest favorites have continued to hold positions of credit and prominence up to the present day. Some 1600 cases were adjudicated upon by the Ballarat Local Court during its twenty months' existence. Many of these involved large sums of money, and were complicated in their issues, yet few substantial complaints were made against the decisions delivered by the raw magistrates thus newly called by the will of the miners from their ordinary and so different avocations. Besides its judicial work, the court made laws, granted certain claims and water-rights, and licensed " amalgamations," or unions of companies. The court also, in its primitive sense of duty, fought long with the lawyers, whom it tried ineffectually to exclude from practising before the court. In this romantic attempt to do without lawyers the whole court was unanimous, excepting Mr H. R. Nicholls, who dissented on the ground of illegality. Though justified by the ultimate issue of the struggle, he had to bend before the popular will of the hour, and so resigned his seat.

It is worth while to exhibit in the light of these modern days the literal merits of this quaint antique question. On the 25th September, 1855, Carboni Raffaello, on behalf of his colleagues, sent a letter to the *Ballarat Star* with the following enclosure :—

Local Court, Ballarat, September 25, 1855. Present—James Ryce, Edward Milligan, Robert Donald, John Wall, William Green, Thomas Chidlow, H. R. Nicholls, Carboni Raffaello. Proposed by Mr Donald, and seconded by Mr Chidlow :—" That in all cases where attorneys or members of the Legal professions are employed, either to advise or plead, during the hearing of any case in this court, the court shall have power to adjourn all such cases to any time, and from such time to time as the members may see fit. Also, that this be made public in the local papers in their first issue."—The above proposition was carried by a majority of eight. The following protest was then handed in by Mr H. R. Nicholls, the ninth member of the court :—" I beg to enter my protest against this resolution, inasmuch as the law officers of the Crown have decided that this Court has no power to prevent solicitors so advising their clients during the hearing of their case. The course adopted by this Court in adjourning such case is, I consider, unwise and unfair, inasmuch as it does not in any way tend to settle the question, and is likely to cause much injury both to the complainant and defendant in such cases."

As a pendant to this now amusing episode in Local Court life, the following will serve to show that the same men could be unanimous sometimes, could speak out with Spartan bravery, and could, with a touching and egotistical earnestness, magnify their office. The Court had passed a regulation extending the areas for eight men " on the deep wet leads of this district " to twelve feet square, and had sought the intervention of the Government

to sanction regulations to stop the "system of shepherding or
holding claims in reserve of 24 feet square by individual men, boys,
and often children! aye, and even women!!" The Goverment
did not respond and, on the same day that Raffaello wrote to the
Ballarat Star, the Court wrote an indignant letter to the Colonial
Secretary from which the above quotations, notes of admiration
and all, and the subjoined are copied :—

> It is with feelings of regret and dying confidence in the Government, that the
> members of the Local Court have observed the indifference with which the
> Executive Government has treated these and other matters of paramount in-
> terest to the miners. We are alone the sinews of the entire colony, aye, even
> very life. It is remarkable that attention could be given to the members of
> the bar who wish to force their eloquence and learning upon us for a fee! to
> capitalists owning engines among us, &c.; and not have sufficient time to say
> yes or no to the affair of the Ballarat miners, inasmuch as the further con-
> sideration of the Executive Government, or even of the Legislative body, on
> matters upon which their knowledge must be second-hand, can throw no
> further light upon the subject.

Then followed a request for an expression of the "intention of
the Government with regard to the regulations submitted for their
consideration," and all the nine members signed the manifesto.
The document seems to have about it the odor of the old Bakery
Hill meetings. No mere "blatherskiting," that, as Raffaello
would have said. But, then, those tribunes sat there, not more
than nine brief months away from the Eureka bloodshedding, and
Raffaello still less distant from the Melbourne goal and Court of
High Treason. His blood at any rate had not cooled, and there
was still revolt in the general air at the least hint of adverse
action or inaction, for the Government and the Parliament had not
yet been popularised. There was yet much to do before there was
full freedom and perfect self-government.

Then the members had a few other smart tussles with the
wardens and the Government, battling like real tribunes of the
people; now for a rain-proof house to sit in, and smooth forms to
sit upon; now telling a resident-warden to mind his own business;
and now calling on the Government to look after the court chairman, or the governor of the gaol. Indeed, it is not too much to
affirm, that if the Parliament of the colony had been—in relation
to the gold-fields—composed of men as honest in intention and as

earnest in endeavor as have been the Local Courts and Mining Boards, the main industry of the country would not be suffering now from the want of suitable laws. It is probable that the scandalous neglect by the Government and the Parliament is also owing, in some degree, to the sense of limited responsibility caused by the existence of local boards of legislature ; and in this view it may fairly be said that the existing Mining Boards can in no way so well serve the mining interest as by securing their own abolition in assisting the central authorities to prepare one code of mining law for all Victoria.

The Mining Statute of 1865 created a new court, called "The Court of the Chief Judge of Courts of Mines," to be presided over by a judge of the Supreme Court. In its appellate jurisdiction the orders of the court were final. Besides appellate and original jurisdiction, special cases were reserved for the judges by the inferior courts. Mr Justice Molesworth was appointed Chief Judge, and has ever since held the office.

CHAPTER VII.

DEVELOPMENT OF MINING.

Block and Frontage Claims.—Election Excitements.—White Flat Company.—Opposition to Extended Areas.—Such Opposition a Mistake.—Present Areas.—Progress of Mining Discoveries.—Increased Operative Difficulties.—Introduction of Machinery.—The Corner. —Wide Operations of Ballarat Capital and Enterprise.—Occasional Excesses.—Koh-i-Noor, Band and Albion Consols, Prince of Wales, and St. George Companies.—Transitions.— Great Depression.—Fall of Two Millions sterling in Mining Stocks.—Equal to Fifty Years' Purchase of the Annual Revenue of the City.—Or Two-thirds of the Annual Revenue of Victoria.—Projects for Co-operation of Labor and Capital.—Old Mining Institute.—School of Mines.—Mining Reform Association.—Miners' Association.—Mr. Serjeant's Sabbath Observance Bill.—Tables of Gold Returns and Mining Statistics.— Pre-eminence of the Ballarat District.—Westgarth on the Purity of Ballarat Gold.—Assays of Ballarat Nuggets.—Table of Nugget Dates, Weights, and Localities.—Increasing proportion of Quartz Gold.—The Future to be Chiefly Quartz Mining. —The Black Hill Quartz Company.

 H E course of local legislation has been the sign of progress in mining, and all other local development has been involved in the prosperity of our chief industry. Two kinds of claims have for some years been in existence, one called "block" and the other "frontage" claims. The block claim is a fixed area, with bounds ascertained from the first; the frontage is a claim with a given width on a lead, or gutter, with boundaries changeable as to direction according to the course of the lead. In California and at Golden Point in 1851, the system of parallel claims, with frontages to water for washing purposes, was in vogue, and hence the application of the term frontage to the deep workings in Ballarat at a later date. Up to the year 1856, however, the block claim system had been exclusively the rule here. The original area of eight by eight feet per man, established by the Latrobe Government, was enlarged as the sinking increased in depth and the miners obtained the power to make their own regulations. But so long as the areas were small and fixed there was a great waste of

labor, time, and money, as, out of a group of many claims, only a
few could be upon the gutter, or auriferous alluvium.   In the first
days of gutter-sinking, too, the miners sank only for the gutter, the
value of the reefs, as the banks of the gutters were called, not
having been at that time ascertained.   This led to the abandonment
of shafts and ground the moment the gutter itself was known to
be outside such ground, and to the practice of " shepherding," or
holding claims unworked pending the proving of the gutter course
by the workings in more advanced claims.   When, however, the
ancient river-beds had been traced by the miner from their shallow
sources into greater depths beneath the surface, the sinking of
shafts became a more serious and more expensive business, and the
waste accompanying chance-sinking became obvious so long as the
areas remained too small to ensure the presence of the gutter.   At
length arose an agitation by some of the miners for the abolition of
block claims on deep leads, and the adoption of the system of
frontage or parallel areas, ensuring a given length of gutter to
each claim.   The proposal was warmly contested, and led to
breaches of the peace and more general disturbance than had
occurred since the affair of the Eureka Stockade.   Mr John Finlay
first suggested the adoption of the frontage system in 1855 in
letters to the *Ballarat Star*, under the signature of " Peeping Tom."
Mr Bacon, who was then in partnership with Mr James Baker at
Sebastopol, soon gave the proposition a more substantial form, and
after that Mr Baker espoused the cause so heartily, and fought for
it so ably and so persistently in print and on platform, that he
made the project peculiarly his own.   So much so was this the case
that for a long time the frontage regulations were known as the
Bakerian regulations.   As already stated the new scheme was
opposed.   The Sebastopol miners who had to sink through rock to
get to the gutter felt the need of the protection from risk which
the frontages promised, but the miners on the shallower and richer
grounds of the older portion of Ballarat retained their liking for
the old block system.   The Local Court itself was divided upon
the question, and resolved to refer the decision to the miners as
an election issue.   Bands of music, flags, and processions were a
part of the outward and visible signs of commotion evoked by the
issue raised.   After preliminary election struggles the members of

the court resigned to test the question by a general ballot of the
miners.   A hustings was erected near the present site of the Ballarat
gas-works, and the result was a decisive victory for the frontage
advocates.   This was on the 14th July, 1856.   The triumphant
party raised a shout of victory as they moved off up the then open
slope on the east side of Lydiard street, and the miners in the
minority showed their sense of defeat by chasing their opponents
up the slope and hurling blows and missiles in all directions.   A
riot seemed imminent, but mounted troopers rode up, dispersed the
mob, and patrolled the streets to maintain the peace.

Since then the depth of mining has increased and with it the areas
of claims, while unforeseen complications of titles arose as different
gutters were discovered and frontage boundaries intersected each
other.   During the last few years this led to a great deal of litigation,
and as the original argument for frontage claims had lost its force
when the extended areas ensured to each claim a portion of the
gutter, there gradually arose a demand for the abolition of frontage
and a return to blocks.   This cycle was run in the course of one
decade, and now all our deep lead mining companies have, wherever
possible, converted their holdings into blocks, held, in many
instances, by leases from the Crown, or by consolidated miner's-
rights, the price of the ordinary right having been reduced from
twenty to five shillings a-year.

The first proposals to largely extend the areas for mining claims
were violently opposed.   In the year 1856 Messrs C. Kinnear, H.
R. Nicholls, Phelps, and M'Murdoch, applied to the Local Court for
a recommendation of a lease of five acres in the White Flat, and the
court for a long time refused concession.   After a long fight and
many attempts to impose restrictions on the applicants, the court
gave way, and the White Flat Company was started—the first large
venture established here, the basis being co-operation of labor and
capital.   Mr Kinnear soon after that negotiated terms for the formation of the Clunes Company, which eventually became the present
Port Phillip and Clunes Company.   He has been an active projector
of mining adventures, and is at present chairman of the United

Hand-in-Hand and Band of Hope Company. Then, soon after the White Flat Company was started, Mr A. A. O'Connor, in the Local Court, proposed extended frontage areas, and he was opposed on the ground that the available auriferous area was a fixed quantity, that new-comers were arriving, and that the miner had enough ground to ensure him a fair wage. Events have justified the foresight of the advocates of extended areas, as immensely increased difficulties have made large outlay of capital necessary, and larger areas equally indispensable.

The areas tenable as mining claims under the bylaws of the Mining Board are limited by the bylaws, but areas held under lease are limited only by the terms of each lease. The latest bylaw of the Ballarat Mining Board limits a quartz claim area to 750 feet in width, with a length of 100 feet to each man. Alluvial claim areas are determined by the depth from the surface to the bed rock on which lies the golden drift or gutter. The latest bylaw ordains that a claim for one person shall be an area not exceeding half an acre, where the depth does not exceed 50 feet ; over 50 and not over 100 feet, one acre ; over 100 and not over 150 feet, two acres ; over 150 and not over 200 feet, five acres ; over 200 and not over 300 feet, nine acres ; over 300 feet, not more than thirteen acres. But a clause of doubtful legal value in the bylaw provides that anybody shall be entitled to take possession of any number of claims not exceeding fifty, the technical meaning of the word " claim" being that area of ground which the bylaw defines as the maximum to be taken up by one man. The explanation of the contradiction is an endeavor to provide for mining enterprise in practice, wherein most persons are interested in several ventures, and may be registered as original holders of several areas. Apropos of registration, it may here be stated that in every district claims are registered, priority of application and taking up determining the right. Mr Harrie Wood is the chief registrar for Ballarat.

As was seen in the previous chapter, the Local Court had to take the Government to task for its inattention to some rules proposed in the matter of shepherding. There was cause for the Local Court

interposing in the matter.   On the 27th December, 1855, the
Ballarat Star declared " we are not above the mark when we
estimate the shepherds at 4000 or 5000 men, or about one-fourth of
the population."   But there was no frontage system then, nor areas
large enough to warrant sinking on the areas then in vogue on the
rock leads until the course of the gutter was known.   Hence the
dilemma.   The miners had just traced the Frenchman's Lead beneath
the Sebastopol plateau with its superincumbent deposits of clay and
basalt.   On the 26th December they held a meeting, and a proposal
by Mr Bacon, " that parties of twelve should have 34 feet allowed
them along the supposed lead," was rejected in favor, not of a
demand for larger areas, but of a petition to the Local Court " to
propound rules which shall permit shepherding on this difficult lead,
and obviate the deplorable consequences of jumping, riot, and
tumult."   This feeling against extended areas lasted for years, as
has been already noted.   The *Ballarat Star*, in the article quoted
from above, did not hint at larger areas as a cure, but proposed that
the miners shepherding claims a-head should agree to some sort of
co-operative plan of testing the course of the lead.

While all these legislative changes were going on the character
of mining operations underwent remarkable mutation.   Excepting
in old shallow grounds where the " hatter," as the single worker
was called, or the small party of co-operative miners worked, the
tub and cradle and windlass, those signs of early digging days, had
disappeared.   The alluvial gutters that had been found within the
Ballarat East basin and on its sides, as well as those afterwards
discovered on the western slopes, as White Horse, Frenchmans'
Terrible, and Cobblers, had, by the year 1857, been traced beneath
the basaltic deposits of the western plateau.   Instead of having
to sink through from 100 feet to 180 feet of diluvial clays and
drifts merely, the miners now had to go in some cases more than
double the greater depth, to blast through successive layers of dense
basaltic rock, and to encounter heavy flows of water in the rocks
and drifts.*   The Inkermann, Redan, and some tributaries still later

---

* The section of the Nelson and Wellington shaft was furnished to us by Mr Surveyor
Davidson, and has been chosen because it happened to be one showing the whole of the
deposits through which the miner had to sink, and the shaft bottoming in the golden
gutter, or washdirt.   The rocks above the gutter are basalt.

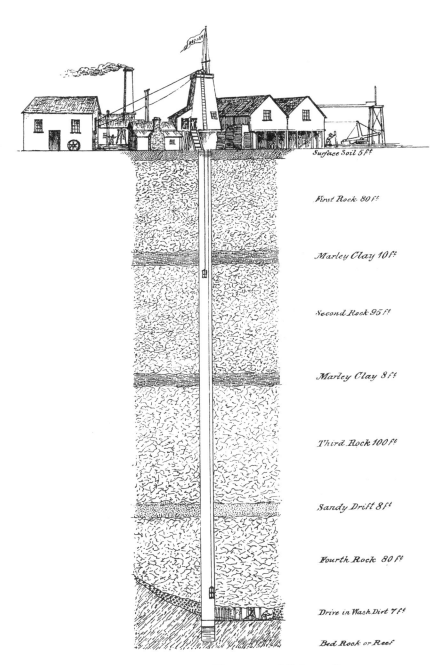

Surface Soil 5 ft

First Rock 80 ft

Marley Clay 10 ft

Second Rock 95 ft

Marley Clay 8 ft

Third Rock 100 ft

Sandy Drift 8 ft

Fourth Rock 80 ft

Drive in Wash Dirt 7 ft

Bed Rock or Reef

SECTION OF THE NELSON & WELLINGTON Cos SHAFT. SEBASTOPOL.
Scale - 80 feet to an inch.

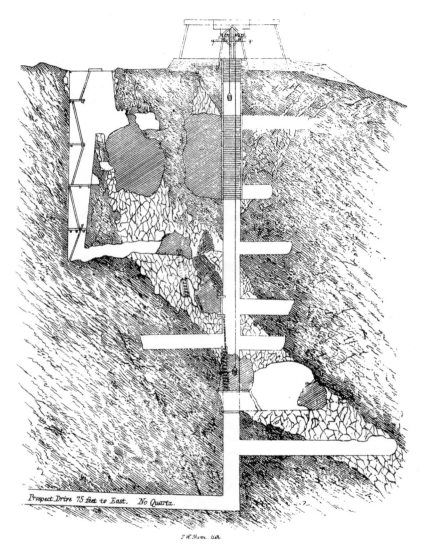

Prospect Drive 75 feet to East. No Quartz.

F. W. Niven. Lith.

QUARTZ REEF OLD POST OFFICE HILL, BALLAARAT.

Scale 24 feet to an inch.

discovered belonged to the same category of rock mining, and involved similar difficulties and hazards.

The following table shows, approximately, the order of discovery after the year 1854. Before the dates given as to the leads mentioned there had been workings in the shallower portions, but the dates refer to the discovery of well-defined gutters or leads in the deeper ground :—

LOCALITY.	DATE.	LOCALITY.	DATE.
Inkermann Lead	Early in.... 1855	Esmond's Lead	August....... 1856
Red Streak Lead	March....... 1855	Malakoff Lead..............	August....... 1856
Frenchman's Lead	June 1855	Mount Pleasant Lead ...	August....... 1856
White Horse Lead	June 1855	Miners Right Lead.........	September.. 1856
Asches Lead	June 1855	Cobblers Lead...............	October...... 1856
Gum Tree Flat	July 1855	Milkmaids Lead.............	November.. 1856
Terrible Lead..................	August...... 1855	Redan Lead	End of....... 1856
One-Eye Gully	September. 1855	A1 Lead.......................	July ...,..... 1857
Pennyweight Flat............	September. 1855	Rush to Carngham.........	October 1857
Dead Horse	Early in.... 1856	Haphazard Lead............	Some time in 1857
Nightingale Lead	February... 1856	Swamp Lead..................	Ditto ....: 1857
Golden Point Lead	May 1856	Paddy's & Crawfish Leads	Ditto 1857
Caledonian Lead	June 1856	Woolshed Lead	May........... 1858
Rush to Browns..............	June 1856	Essex Lead	June 1858
Lady Barkly Lead............	July 1856	Native Youth Lead........	July........... 1868

During the ten years after the Stockade year, a good deal of auriferous ground was opened down the valley of the Leigh as far as the Durham Lead. The Scotchman's, Black Lead, Stone Quarry, Sodawater, Devonshire, Goldseekers, Franklin, Victoria, and Welshman's Leads were during that time opened, as also the Union Jack and others at Buninyong. Well-defined leads in the Smythesdale, Scarsdale, Linton, Haddon, and some other fields in that part of the district were also discovered. Nearly all these, and Creswick likewise have, with varying fortunes, continued to yield gold from deep gutters up to the present time.

No longer able to carry on his vocation by mere manual labor and simple co-operative organisation, the miner had to invite the co-operation of capital and to employ expensive steam machinery. On the Eureka the first engine was worked on 3rd October, 1855, and before that date isolated attempts to use steam power had been made; but for a long time the miners opposed the introduction of machinery and capital. Mr Wood tells us, in his notes published in Mr Brough Smyth's " Gold-fields of Victoria," that when Messrs Talbot and others put up an engine near the spot now intersected by Bridge and Peel streets, to work a shaft on the Gravel Pits Flat there, " a body of men proceeded to the claim for the purpose

of smashing the engine, but were prevented from doing so by Mr
Talbot, who had provided himself with fire-arms, and threatened to
shoot the first man who approached." Some few years after this,
namely, in March, 1859, engines and horses were introduced below
the surface. The Burra Burra Company erected a four-horse power
engine below for hauling, and it was reported at that time that
thirty pounds weight of gold were taken from the excavation made
for the erection of the engine—an area of thirty feet by seven. At
the same date a Welsh Company in Paddy's Gully, Winter's Flat,
used horses below ground. Since then both engines and horses have
been used in several of the larger mines.

So long as the grounds worked were shallow and rich the opposition to machinery was in some sort tenable, but as soon as
gold-seeking assumed the features already described as belonging
to rock-lead mining, the use of capital and machinery became a
necessity. The eight feet square claim, bottomed at from two to
twelve feet, and exhausted in as many hours sometimes, when
Governor Latrobe first saw the gold hunters of Golden Point in
1851, has now grown to an area of hundreds of acres, held by
hundreds of shareholders in an incorporated company, often worked
by several large deep shafts, at each of which is an extensive plant
of steam machinery, with the best possible shaft apparatus, the
mine traversed by a network of tunnels and tramways, and taking
many years to exhaust even approximately of its auriferous deposits. The tub, cradle, tom, whip, and whim are out of date and
inapplicable to the claims now held by our large rock-lead companies, save only that the windlass or the whim is still sometimes
used in initial operations. Many thousands of pounds sterling are
spent in the mines of to-day before gold is ever reached by the
miner. The United Hand-in-Hand and Band of Hope Company
was said, by deputations before the Government lately, to have
expended over £300,000 without having paid a dividend. Whole
forests have been felled to supply firewood to our steam
engines, and timber for the mines below. Our companies call
for tons of candles at a time, and in some instances have gas
to light up the dark recesses of their mines. To draw the trucks
of ore along the extensive iron roads in their mines they have
studs of horses snugly housed in the warm bowels of the earth.

Engineers, engine-drivers, clerical managers, clerks, mine managers, captains of shifts, troops of miners, boards of directors, all belong to the working staff of our mines of to-day. The surface works at a single shaft involve an outlay of thousands of pounds in some instances, where there are engines, boilers, tramways on the ground, tramways in the air, lofty poppet-heads, with braces supported by ponderous beams and uprights, and housing to shelter all the costly portions of the plant. In the sinking of a single shaft many thousands of pounds are sometimes expended. The outlay is similar in many instances, whether the mine be a quartz or alluvial one, and in several of our mines, as notably in the Prince of Wales mine, Sebastopol, both quartz and alluvium are being worked, the steam-driven iron batteries working simultaneously with the steam-driven iron puddlers in extracting the gold from the original matrix and the alluvium respectively. And this character of the mining of to-day applies as well to all the suburban or intra-district fields, as Creswick, Buninyong, Haddon, Smythesdale, Linton, Clunes, Carngham, Blackwood, Egerton, Gordon, and Stieglitz.

But the mining adventure of Ballarat is not limited by the field of Ballarat proper, or even the wide territory indicated by the other fields within the district. The Corner, as the Ballarat Mining Exchange is called, is nearly as well known, in this part of the world as the London Exchange, or the Paris Bourse, or the New York Wall street. The capitalists of the Corner have exploited fields in every colony in Australasia, not excepting Tasmania and New Zealand, and, having engaged in enterprises beyond the compass of even the enormous wealth of the district, have traversed the world and laid under contribution the gigantic monetary accumulations in the English market. The commanding position of Ballarat as the head-quarters of Australian mining enterprise is plainly demonstrated in J. H. Were and Co.'s "Complete List of the Mining Companies of Victoria," issued in the latter half of the year 1868. In that work 529 companies were tabled, and of that number 196, or over one-third of the total, were situated within the Ballarat district. Of the other two-thirds it may be safely estimated that nearly or quite one had been created by the Ballarat Corner, so that two-thirds of the whole of the mining adventure of Victoria, to say nothing of extra-colonial companies, had their locality or were

projected in the district of which Ballarat is the centre. So ardent
has been the spirit of enterprise that it has more than once
paralysed the local market by the excessive exactions it has made
upon the monetary resources of the district, and the many dis-
honest schemes and mere bubble projects which have been placed
before the public in times of speculative excitement have done
much to weaken the confidence reposed by the investing public
in the remunerative nature of mining adventure.

Gradually we have seen pass away the early co-operative plans of
working, when sinking was comparatively easy, the areas small,
and shares were divided into halves, quarters, eighths, and so forth,
according to the supposed value of the ground, when capital was
found by furnishers of materials, and by "sleeping" partners holding parts of shares, and we have seen incorporated companies spring
into existence with large subscribed capitals, and subsidised by
banks on mortgages when the subscribed capital was insufficient.
The Corner was a logical sequence to these transitions, and the
race of brokers, jobbers, managers, and auditors followed also as of
due course, until mining has become more absolutely dual in its
character than ever before, the operative and the speculative phases
of the industry being now more than ever apart, yet having, it is
true, points of contact while maintaining a generally obvious dis-
tinctness.

Before giving some figures illustrative of the aggregate auriferous
value of the field of Ballarat, it may be well to give some particulars of a few leading companies as samples of the enterprise of
existing individual mining corporations in the present stage of our
gold-field's history. The past has seen many large successful
ventures, a list of the names only of which would occupy large
space ; the future may see more ; the present has many of such
enterprises, and of these last we shall give a few examples. But
before giving figures of current or very recent dates, we may cite an
instance or two of good fortune among the older co-operative parties.
Mr Wood's "Notes" furnish us with the figures we shall cite as
to those parties, and partially, also, as to later companies. One of
the richest alluvial tracts in Ballarat East was the Gum Tree Flat,
the basin into which, as has been seen, so many of the earlier discovered leads emptied themselves. At that spot, according to

Wood's "Notes," one party of six obtained 112 lb. of gold in ten weeks. Belcher and party of eight made £3000 each in four months. Eight Frenchmen obtained £2500 each in five months. The "Hell Fling Mob" obtained a similar amount each, and the "Sanctified Mob" £1500 each. These are only specimens. The working of the Eureka, Red Hill, and Canadian gutters, with their "Jewellers' Shops," their nuggets, their rich "pockets," their reefs or gutter-banks, often as rich as the gutters, supplied many instances of large individual successes.

The Koh-i-Noor Company, on the Golden Point Lead, commenced operations early in the year 1857, began driving in the latter half of 1858, and paid the first dividend on the 25th June, 1859, the company being a co-operative one until March, 1864, when it was incorporated under the Statute; the area of the claim is 170 acres. There are 4 shafts, 8000 feet of drives, 2 steam engines, 3 boilers, 4 puddling machines, and the usual other belongings to a first-class company's plant, the total estimated value of which plant is £22,000. The company had expended £286,845 19s 6d up to November, 1869; had won 147,570 oz. 15 dwt. 7 gr. of gold, value at £4 per oz., £590,283; and had paid £304,460 in dividends. It must be noted that Ballarat gold has realised generally more than £4 per oz., but we have adopted that as a sufficiently accurate basis of calculation. The company had at one time a larger steam plant than it has now, and has been one of the very best ventures ever launched upon the alluvium of this gold-field.

The Band of Hope and Albion Consols Company is a corporation formed by two companies, the Albion Company on the Frenchman's Lead, and the Band of Hope Company on the Golden Point Lead. The Albion Company was the first which tested ground in Victoria by boring operations before sinking. The first bore was commenced under the auspices of Messrs Elder, Campbell, and others, on the 21st June, 1856, when what is now the borough of Sebastopol, and the greater portion of the borough of Ballarat West, were still unreclaimed bush country. The company began its shaft on the 4th of June, 1858, sinking through clays, drifts, and basaltic and schistose rocks to a depth of 475 feet. By the year 1868 the company had obtained gold realising £254,144, had paid £117,995 in calls, and £90,921 in dividends. The Band of Hope Company began sinking in March, 1858, after previous boring. Unusual difficulties were encountered in heavy flows of drift and rock-water, for it took the company five years to sink the No. 1 shaft 340 feet, and put in a drive 180 feet, the shaft not being sunk to its present depth of 400 feet till April, 1866. In September of that year the company united with the Hand-in-Hand Company to work certain portions of the two companies' claims. The company procured the heaviest engines obtainable, lighted its mine with gas, and carried on operations upon the grandest scale then known here. It raised 700 tons of washdirt a day, and obtained as much as 1637 oz. of gold from one day's washing. Having bought and expensively altered the shaft of the extinct Golden Gate Company on the Redan Lead, it began, after boring, to sink a third shaft south of the Smythesdale road in November, 1865, and on the 26th September, 1866, a fourth shaft was begun in the centre of the Redan Racecourse. Up to the date of union with the Hand-in-Hand Company the Band of Hope Company had spent £29,565 on the No. 1 shaft, and £101,955 on alterations in and driving from the No. 2 shaft. The No. 3 shaft cost £11,859 in sinking, and the No. 4 shaft a nearly similar sum, and in all over £3000 were spent by the company in boring operations. Up to a date a few months previous to joining the Albion Company, the company had excavated and washed two and a half millions of cubic feet of auriferous alluvium and schist, from which 161,943 oz. of gold were obtained, value £656,869, yielding in dividends £388,000. On the 7th March, 1869, the United Hand-in-Hand and Band of Hope Company united with the Albion Company, forming the incorporated Band of Hope and Albion Consols Company ; capital £449,000, in 22,450 shares of £20 paid up ; area held, about 400 acres. The company's plant included 11 engines, 14 boilers, and 16 puddling machines, besides buddles. In September, 1869, nineteen horses were employed in the underground works of the mine, 900 men, exclusive of splitters and others in the bush, were employed by the company, and the monthly expenditure of the company in working the mine was £10,600, the value of the plant being estimated at over £20,000. Up to the 1st of November, 1869, gold of the value of £438,000 had been won, and £170,620 had been paid in dividends, the balance of £267,380 having been expended in working the mine, and carrying on the general business of this the largest mining company in Victoria.

The Prince of Wales Company, on the Cobbler's Lead, commenced operations in October, 1859, and occupied nearly 4 years in sinking its first shaft, which is 387 feet deep. A second shaft was subsequently sunk and abandoned, a third shaft having been sunk to a depth of 410½ feet, passing through four deposits of basaltic rock. This company has strong and costly machinery, both for alluvial and quartz mining—a rich quartz lode having been discovered in the mine. Of alluvial ore the company raises on an average 1500 trucks a day. There are 6 steam engines, 9 boilers, 9 puddling machines, a battery of 16 square-head stamps, a battery of 40 round-head revolving stamps, and all the necessary appendages to a complete crushing plant. The total value of the company's plant is estimated at £30,000. The number of men at work in November, 1869, was 376, and the monthly amount of wages and salaries was £2825. Up to October, 1869, the company had expended the sum of £564,514 17s 9d, and had won 128,486 oz. 1 dwt. 4 gr. of gold, value £521,915 6s 4d, the capital paid up being £33,734 8s 8d, and the aggregate of dividends paid being £233,999 9s 4d.

The St. George and Band of Hope United Company is a union of two companies, on the Woolshed and Band of Hope Leads originally, but occupying other leads as well subsequently; capital £120,000, in 6000 shares of £20 paid up. The company holds about 250 acres, and has four shafts: No. 1, sunk by the original St. George Company; No. 2, by the St. George United Company; No. 3, purchased from the Guiding Star Company; and No. 4, purchased from the Red Jacket Company. The claim extends from the Redan Lead on the north, in the borough of Ballarat, to the Defiance Lead on the south, in the borough of Sebastopol. There are two levels in the mine, the length of the drives in the upper being 2789 feet, and in the lower 9280 feet, about ten acres of ground being actually worked. The company has 5 engines, value £2000; pumps, value £1500; 9 puddlers, value £4900; 9 boilers, value £3150; other plant and stock swelling the total value to the sum of £18,000. The number of men employed ranges from 75 to 380 per week. Up to November, 1869, the mine had yielded gold to the value of £296,362, and had paid £71,100 in dividends. The company is engaged in driving on the bed rock between Ballarat and Sebastopol, and adding to its plant, the cost of which works will amount, when completed, to near £20,000.

The instances we have cited show what a vast transition has taken place in the miner's vocation since the days of the early shallow digging, and even the deeper and richer digging of the days when the Eureka, Canadian, and Gravel Pits were in their glory. The immense outlay in labor and plant before gold is reached now contrasts strangely with the easily won fortunes of the earlier days. If the classical digger ot the Eureka were here now he might exclaim, " Oh ! mihi præteritos referat si Jupiter annos;" interpreting it auriferously to mean, " Oh ! that the gods would give us back the Jewellers' Shops and the Italians' holes of the bygone days." And some yearn for even an earlier time than that. For to an old goldfields man, weary with the hope deferred, and the many losses of deep sinking, the memory of the first diggings, or the sight of a little shallow-ground "rush" now, is like a sweet vision of childhood coming back to bless the world-worn old man in his desolateness and sadness of heart. The shallow-ground days were blythe with rapid golden successes, the joyous energy of independence and hope, and a continuous and hilarious change ; but now the mines are filled with men who have to plod on at their dull and ever dangerous routine year after year upon a small wage, while capitalists win or lose upon the labors of the men who in the primitive days would have scorned to call any man master.

A shareholder in the Great North-West Company, on the Dead Horse and confluent leads in that promising and important portion of the Ballarat field, would be able very emphatically to illustrate the transition referred to. That company took up its claim in August, 1862, began boring on the 9th September, 1862, and commenced sinking on the 8th September, 1863. The rocks, clays, and drifts abound in water, and though over six years have gone by the shaft is not yet bottomed. The pumping machinery is the heaviest, perhaps, in the district, and was at one time throwing up 2,880,000 gals. of water a day, the engines being ponderous and built up in strong masonry. Mr Wheeldon the manager, has introduced peculiar and valuable improvements in the pumping apparatus. The company has lost largely by fire, has had immense difficulties in sinking, and has been compelled, after spending over £40,000 upon the shaft, to resort to re-organisations, to London capital, and to a partition of its large territory for the purposes of obtaining means to carry on its mere sinking operations without greater embarrassment.

Since the foregoing particulars relative to the companies named have been in type, material changes have taken place in some of the mines. In some cases expenses have been reduced, and portions of the mine let to tributors. By the courtesy of Mr Serjeant, the manager of the Band of Hope and Albion Consols Company, the following additional particulars respecting that mine are available. Since the dates previously given, the company's No. 3 and No. 5 shafts have been let on tribute, No. 3 at 48 per cent., and No. 5 at 25 per cent. for six months, and at 30 per cent. for twelve months thereafter. The company, therefore, has only two shafts now at work in its own hands. At these about 500 men are employed, and the rate of wages has been altered as compared with the rate in November, 1869:—Captains, from £3 5s per week to £2 10s ; facemen, from £2 5s to £2 2s ; truckers, bracemen, platmen, puddling-men, laborers, from £2 2s to £2 ; sluicemen, from £3 to £2 10s ; engine-drivers, 8s 4d and 7s 6d per day—"Sunday gratis" when required. There are eight boilers now in use, eight puddling-machines, nine horses, and the monthly expenditure now is £5000.

At the present moment, as for some months past, the town and district are suffering from a depression caused by the reckless spirit of gambling at the Corner, by the responsive tastes of a hopeful public, and by the natural operation of the progress of mining, by which last the alluvial grounds have been in great part exhausted. The large sums lavished upon mere paper claims, and the heavy demands upon capital caused by a too great extension of adventure have so far prostrated the ability of the district that a general collapse has ensued, to the partial or total pecuniary ruin of scores of families, and a very general depreciation of property of all kinds, and notably of mining stock. In 28 mining companies whose offices are in Ballarat, and whose mines are in or near the town, the depreciation in the market value of stock—comparing prices in July, 1869, with those in May, 1870, has reached the sum of £1,042,000. At least another million sterling must be added for depreciation in other stocks besides the companies specified. These calculations are furnished by a gentleman familiar with the market, and they do not include the losses in call-paying. In April last the Melbourne *Leader* estimated the depreciation in 45 given companies' stocks to be £1,016,000 in March, 1870—as compared with March, 1869. The same journal mentioned also, as a coincidence, that during the same term the stock of the Commercial, National, Colonial, Victoria, and New South Wales Banks had depreciated £689,370. The depreciation in mining stock, as cited above, amounts to £2,042,000 sterling—a sum equal to two-thirds of the annual public revenue of Victoria. The gravity of this fact, and the relation of mining to what is called real property, will be seen from a comparison with some estimates of municipal revenue and town property. The mining depreciation is very nearly equal to fifty years purchase of the total revenue of the boroughs of Ballarat West, Ballarat East, and Sebastopol, and is more than equal to eight years purchase of the whole real property in the city. The total annual revenue of the three boroughs at the last returns given amounted to £49,833, which multiplied by 50 gives the sum of £2,491,650. The total rateable value of the three boroughs, per similar returns, was £251,428, which multiplied by 8 gives the sum of £2,011,424.

This state of things in mining has hastened the consideration of the question—which must have pressed itself upon public attention, in any event, before long—of a re-adjustment of the prices of both labor and capital. The cry has arisen for a reduction of wages and of interest on capital, as it is felt that business men cannot pay the old rent-scale, and mining must decrease unless wages are also lowered. It has been computed by practical men that with lower prices ruling, there is hardly a lode of quartz in all our hills, nor an acre of alluvial ground, that will not pay for working, and thus be established for an incalculable term a steadily prosperous mining industry.* In times gone by there have been fluctuations, but it is

* The illustration of the works in the Old Post Office claim has been supplied by the lithographer, and is similar to the one furnished for Smyth's book. It does not show the most extensive of our quartz works, but gives a fair picture of the occurrence of lodes and the manner of working.

now felt that alluvial mining in the district cannot sustain the population at the present prices. Hence, a month or two ago, a project was started for forming a company to test our quartz lodes at a thousand feet below the surface, with a view to ascertain if at that level they were gold-bearing, and would promise, therefore, a permanent field for the operations of labor and capital. This project, after a burst of enthusiasm in public meeting and the formation of a committee to draw up a scheme, died, the committee making no sign. While this is being written other projects for tribute or co-operative mining are being discussed by a committee, which is also to report on the revival of a chamber of commerce here. In the earlier days many projects ancillary to mining had been projected, had lived a short day, and then died. In 1856 a Ballarat Industrial Institute was projected, "for the purpose of exhibiting productions of art and science tending to promote the mining, manufacturing, agricultural, and general interests of the district." It had its public acclamations; Mr Daly, the chairman, and Mr Miskelly, the clerk of the Local Court, were the head and tail of the project, and the Government, in January, 1858, granted five acres of land conditionally to the Institute. The Institute died an early death, and the block of land granted—which was in Sturt street, opposite to the Hospital—has long since been bought from the Crown and covered with private buildings. In December, 1859, a Mining Institute was formed for reading and discussing papers on mining; Mr James Baker was the president. He read his inaugural address in the Mining Board-room on the 6th December, and a few other papers were read thereafter, including one by Mr H. R. Nicholls, on "Mining Accident Prevention," in which he laid down the principle, since then generally adopted, that the only way to reduce accidents to a minimum is to make mining companies responsible. After a few meetings this Institute fell asleep, was awakened for a brief period in November, 1860, when two or three more papers were read, and then death ensued. To-day there are no fewer than three several mining organisations of recent birth—a School of Mines, a Mining Reform Association, and a Miners' Association.

The School of Mines was projected a few months ago by Messrs Harrie Wood, the clerk, and Bickett, a member of the Mining Board, and supported by the Mining Board as a body. The Government

has given the use of the old Court-house, between Wesley Church
and the gaol, on the east side of Lydiard street, for the purposes of
the school, and repairs and alterations in the building are now
being made to adapt it to the requirements of the new school.
Judge Rogers from the first gave valuable help, drew up a constitution, and drafted a bill for the incorporation of the school.
The borough councils and other local bodies voted money towards
the preliminary expenditure, the members of the Mining Board
and their secretary, Mr Wood, still giving, as the first movers
in the matter, a watchful support to the movement. The draft of a
constitution by Judge Rogers has been provisionally adopted, pro-
viding for classes, professors, and lectures, and giving to students on
examination certificates of efficiency in mining engineering, mining
surveying, metallurgy, chemistry as applied to mining, theoretical
and practical mining. His Excellency the Governor of Victoria is
visitor, Sir Redmond Barry is president, Judge Rogers is vice-president, and Sir Redmond Barry, Henry Rivet Bland, and Somerville
Livingstone Learmonth are trustees and treasurers. The visitor,
president, and six members of the council are elected for life, the
full council comprising twenty-nine members is made up as follows :—
The president and vice-president, six life members named by the
Crown, the chairmen of the seven mining boards of Victoria, and
fourteen members elected by the governors of the school. The
nominees for Crown appointment as life members of the council are
the president, vice-president, Sir James M'Culloch, Duncan Gillies,
M.L.A., Professor M'Coy, and Harrie Wood. A letter from Sir
Roderick Murchison to Sir Redmond Barry has lately been published,
in which the eminent geologist advises for the Ballarat school a
similar curriculum to that of the London school. The Mining
Reform Association is an organisation to procure the reduction of
mining rents, and the reform of many proved evils in mining law.
The Miners' Association is an organisation of working miners, for
the purpose, among other things, of obtaining a lien law to secure
wages, relief from Sunday work, the enjoyment of public holidays,
and a better management of mines. It may be mentioned here that
as long ago as 1858 Mr R. M. Serjeant, then recently a member of
the Local Court, drafted a bill to prohibit any one from " disturbing,
or removing any soil, earth, rock, or stone on the Sabbath Day,"

under penalty of fine or imprisonment, and without appeal from the petty sessions. His object was declared to be the prevention of "atheists and quibblers" from coercing their more Sabbath-observing mates into labor against their will on the Sunday. He, however, proposed to allow the miner to bale water and look after machinery on the Sunday. This also was an abortive project. The bill never came to maturity. The latest proposals, as we have seen, are for an organisation of capital and labor to work, at lower rates of wages and with shares in the mine, ground that will not pay with the existing wage rate. To this complexion have affairs come, and there is little room for doubt that some phase of this proposition will mark the mining of the future. The principle suggested is, in a word, a system of tribute with proposals for a general co-operation between labor and capital upon conditions suited to the times.

In attempting to show the aggregate produce of gold of this or any other district in the colony, great difficulty is at once encountered, and it is found that all figures must be merely approximate. For several years nothing like statistics of gold yields were attempted by the Government, and up to the present day it is impossible to arrive at more than probable aggregates and comparisons. One thing, however, amid all the dubiety of gold-field statistics, has long since been irrefragably established, namely, the superior auriferous wealth of the Ballarat district over all the other mining districts of Victoria. A few figures will illustrate this. The return for 1868 of the value of mining plant in the several districts gave the following comparisons:—Ballarat, £706,393 ; Sandhurst, £418,738 ; Beechworth, £283,445; Castlemaine, £277,248 ; Maryborough, £227,348. The subjoined table of companies registered in the Courts of Mines up to the end of 1868 illustrated the metropolitan character of Ballarat in another fashion :—

DISTRICTS.	No. of Companies.	No. of Shares.	Nom. Capital.
Ballarat	908	1,347,924	£10,579,711
Beechworth	641	1,240,731	5,935,419
Sandhurst	188	3,057,433	3,100,350
Castlemaine	431	771,524	2,270,176
Maryborough	195	873,048½	1,805,410
Ararat	94	105,667	662,429
Gipps Land	14	25,165	77,710

Subjoined is the tabular summary for 1869, issued by the Mining

Department, from which it will be seen that the mining collapse has told heavily upon the returns, but, that up to the latest statistical date, Ballarat maintained its position as the leading field :—

DISTRICTS.	No. of Companies.	No. of Shares.	Nom. Capital.
Ballarat....................	135	402,492	£1,555,300
Maryborough	87	332,554	1,157,656
Beechworth	53	240,086	772,875
Ararat	45	153,060	606,160
Sandhurst..................	44	643,636	583,686
Castlemaine	39	131,686	298,414
Gipps Land	20	80,746	261,136

The returns for the quarter ending 31st March, 1870, give the subjoined comparative table relative to the steam machinery at work on the Victorian gold-fields, this return also demonstrating the pre-eminence of the Ballarat field, while showing also the decline caused by the depression in mining affairs :—

DISTRICTS.	ALLUVIAL MINING.		QUARTZ MINING.			Approximate Value of all plant.
	No. of Engines.	Horse Power.	No. of Engines.	Horse Power.	No. of Stamp-heads	
Ballarat	214	6,374	144	3,455	1,256	£595,513
Sandhurst	35	518	151	2,724	1,431	427,867
Beechworth	47	752	69	939	1,099	302,257
Maryborough......	63	1,235	109	1,991	720	279,211
Castlemaine	31	552	134	2,291	995	262,070
Gipps Land	2	12	39	659	489	134,199
Ararat	15	224	35	879	397	124,110

The tables of gold exported from the Colony of Victoria give the following aggregates in ounces for the years from 1851 to 1869 inclusive :—

YEAR.	OUNCES.	YEAR.	OUNCES.
1851	145,146	1860	2,156,660
1852	2,218,783	1861	1,967,420
1853	2,676,345	1862	1,668,207
1854	2,150,730	1863	1,626,872
1855	2,751,535	1864	1,544,604
1856	2,985,991	1865	1,543,801
1857	2,762,460	1866	1,479,194
1858	2,528,478	1867	1,433,687
1859	2,280,950	1868	1,657,498

Total, 35,578,451 ounces ; value, £142,313,804 sterling.

From these returns it will be seen that the year 1856 was the culminating one. From that year to the year 1867 inclusive there was an annual decrease in the gold yield, with a recovery in 1868 of over 200,000 oz., or an increased produce worth nearly a million sterling. But the tables for 1869 show a return to the decreasing scale. For the three quarters ending 30th September, 1869, the aggregate exports were 1,011,856 oz.; the Customs returns for the year 1869 making the actual total exports of Victorian gold to be 1,340,838 oz. The Ballarat banks bought for the year 285,647 oz. of gold, or over one-fifth of the total exported, and to which total not only the six old mining board districts of Victoria but the newer one of Gipps Land contributed. The local banks were not the only purchasers in that year. The Melbourne merchants sometimes competed with the banks and bought the entire produce of some of our richest mines. The departmental returns for the quarter ending 31st March, 1870, show that the exports for the quarter were 357,184 oz. 5 dwt., which is above the average for the previous year. It may be safely stated that Victoria has produced one hundred and fifty millions of pounds sterling worth of gold since the Ballarat gold-field was discovered, and it is pertinent to the general issue to find out, as nearly as possible, how much of that magnificent aggregate Ballarat has contributed. And in speaking of Ballarat in this relation it must be understood that we speak of the district. While the district includes Clunes, with a company like the Port Phillip Quartz Company, which has yielded over a million sterling from the ground where Esmond found his first gold, it would be unfair to ignore the relation of the figures cited. By the end of 1859 the Port Phillip Company had realised over eleven hundred and fifty thousand pounds worth of gold, thus eclipsing all other quartz mines in the world except the St. John del Rey in Brazil, now unworked. The New North Clunes Company is another instance of success, and its returns may be compared with some statistics published a few months ago by the London *Times*, showing the aggregate dividends declared by British and foreign mines in the year 1869. The New North Clunes mine began to yield gold on the 5th of October, 1867, and up to the 8th of June, 1870, the total yield was 51,467 oz. 0 dwt. 20 gr.; value, £208,620 13s 2d. In 1868 the company declared five dividends, amounting to

K

£22,616 ; in 1869, twelve amounting to £61,680; and this year six have already been paid, amounting to £37,008, or in all £121,304. The only company in the *Times* list that approaches the New North Clunes is the foreign mine Don Pedro, which paid, in 1869, £61,500, or £180 less than the New North Clunes. The British list given by the *Times* numbers 52 companies, averaging a fraction over £6000 each, or less than a tenth of the New North Clunes payment; while the eleven foreign mines averaged a fraction over £12,022, or less than a fifth of the New North Clunes dividends. Clunes may certainly, after this, be entitled to hold up its head among the gold fields of the whole world. And Ballarat, it cannot be doubted, either as an isolated compact centre, or as a name for a district of which it is the centre, represents the richest field in Victoria. What the whole colony did in ten years was shown by a pyramid of gilded wood sent to the London Exhibition of 1862 by Mr J. G. Knight. This pyramid showed the size in mass of the Victorian gold exported from the 1st October, 1851, to the 1st October, 1861. It measured 1492½ cubic feet, and represented 26,162,432 oz., or 800 tons 17 cwt. 3 qr. 7 lb. of gold ; value, £104,649,728 sterling. But it has always been difficult to get at the district yields very accurately.

So long as the escorts were maintained district returns of more or less accuracy were possible, and we now cite them as follows, comparing with those of Ballarat the Sandhurst or Bendigo returns, that district being the only one that ever claimed rivalry with Ballarat :—

BALLARAT.		BENDIGO.	
	ozs.		ozs.
1853	319,099	1853	609,728
1854	584,957	1854	661,749
1855	769,429	1855	429,933
1856	920,351	1856	451,588
1857	686,263	1857	
1858	502,948	to	
1859	467,223		
1860	556,207	1860	2,152,993
Total......... 4,806,477		Total......... 4,305,996	

In this table we have, in the absence of returns at hand, assumed that Bendigo produced as much during the last four years tabled as during the first four years, though it is known that

that field did not produce in an equal ratio. Yet, after assuming in her favor what is not true, we find that Ballarat stood half a million ounces, or two millions of pounds sterling a-head of the northern field. Since the dates tabled the gulf has at intervals widened much, and Ballarat has so far outstripped all other districts as to enable us to say we may defy detraction and assert for this district the proud distinction of being the richest gold-field in the world. The last year's return of gold for Ballarat and Sandhurst show that the two places may be regarded as having, probably, kept a tolerably even distance apart in the race of productiveness. The Sandhurst banks bought 225,258 oz. of gold during the year 1869, or 60,389 oz. less than was received by the banks in Ballarat, and if the difference be multiplied by eight, the number of years in the comparative table above, it will be seen that the aggregate for that term is close upon the half million ounces we have reached in the tabled estimate. During the first three months of 1870, the Ballarat banks bought 82,941 oz. of gold, whereas the quarterly average of 1869 was only a fraction over 71,414 oz., and the Sandhurst average for 1869 only a fraction over 55,051 oz., but Sandhurst is now producing heavier yields.

Mr Westgarth, in his "Victoria in 1857," bears testimony to the superior quality and yield of this field, and to the enterprise of its miners. He says at page 182 :—

Ballarat gold for its purity excels the gold from any other Australian field. Ballarat, indeed, takes the position alike of the oldest gold-field of any note, and that which has yielded the largest quantity of the precious metal. From the month of September, 1851—when the Government first established the armed escorts—to the end of 1856, there was sent down from Ballarat by these conveyances, no less than 2,801,729 ounces of gold, of the value, in consideration of its purity, of upwards of £4 per ounce. It was at Ballarat where the spirit of enterprise was most prevalent.

The subsequent years have not, certainly, lessened, unless relatively, the importance of this metropolitan gold-field in respect of either its auriferous productions or the busy enterprise of its inhabitants.

The great purity of the Ballarat alluvial gold was early discovered. It has always commanded the highest rates in the bullion market. The assay of gold won from the Band of Hope and Albion

K 2

Consols mine for the half-year ending June, 1869, was 23 carats 2½ carat grains fine, and for the half-year ending December, 1869, 23 carats 2⅜ carat grains fine. Some assays of nuggets show similar purity. The Welcome Nugget assay was 99·20 pure gold = 23 carats 3¼ carat grains fine. The Nil Desperandum gave an assay 98·80 pure gold = 23 carats 2⅞ carat grains fine. Thus, whether in large lumps or small particles, the gold found in the alluvium or drift of the ancient water-courses, or on the banks of those water-courses, is ascertained to be nearly free from all impurity, while gold in the matrix, quartz, is always charged more heavily with the baser elements.

As the origin of gold is still a mystery, unsolved by science or experiment, each student has his own theory. Some hold that gold is the product of electric action, some of vaporific sublimation, others of precipitation. The modes of its occurrence, the principle which governs its purity in and out of the matrix, and other items in the arcana, remain nearly as they were to the unlettered digger of the first days. Our most erudite savans, indeed, can say but little more about gold than was expressed by the old diggers, who pretended to no very clear vision of the subject, and said—"All we can say is, that where it is, there it is !"

In Smyth's "Gold-fields of Victoria," from which we have taken some of the above assays, we find nearly all the particulars tabulated below in relation to large Ballarat nuggets. We have had to supply omissions and correct some errors in dates in Smyth's tables :—

LOCALITY.	When Found.	Gross weight Troy.			
		lb.	oz.	dwt.	gr.
Black Hill	14th October 1851	7	6	0	0
Canadian Gully	20th January..... 1853	93	1	11	0
Canadian Gully	22nd January..... 1853	84	3	15	0
Canadian Gully	31st January..... 1853	134	11	0	0
Canadian Gully	February.... 1853	30	8	0	
Canadian Gully	———— 1853	30	11	2	
Canadian Gully	February.... 1853	11	11	15	
Eureka	7th February.... 1854	52	1	0	0
Dalton's Flat, Canadian, "Lady Hotham"	8th September.. 1854	98	1	17	0
Bakery Hill	6th March........ 1855	47	7	0	0
Bakery Hill	March........ 1855	40	0	0	0
Union Jack Gully, Buninyong	28th February.... 1857	23	5	10	0
"Nil Desperandum," near Black Hill Lead	29th November.. 1857	45	0	0	0
"Welcome," Bakery Hill	9th June.......... 1858	184	9	16	0
Koh-i-Noor Claim	27th July.......... 1860	69	6	0	0
Koh-i-Noor, "Sir Dominick Daly"	February........ 1862	26	0	0	0
Koh-i-Noor, other nuggets	Feb. 1862 to May 1869	62	8	0	0
Webbville, Buninyong	1st August....... 1869	12	0	0	0

Though the gold yield from the whole of the Victorian fields has declined, the falling off is mainly from the alluvial grounds. For the six months ending May, 1870, forty alluvial companies returned in this district 106,651 oz., and twenty-seven quartz companies returned 46,709 oz.; total for the six months, 253,360 oz. This shows that the quartz yield was about three-sevenths, or nearly half, as much as the alluvial yield. Twelvemonths before that the proportion was one-third, and every year traversed in a backward series increases the relative magnitude of the alluvial yield, until the first few years of mining are reached when the gold yield was almost entirely from alluvial grounds. The increasing proportion of quartz to alluvial yields is more clearly seen in the general yields of the whole colony. The Government statistics for 1869 make the approximate totals to be—alluvial, 810,777 oz.; quartz, 530,061 oz.; thus showing the quartz produce to be over three-fifths that of the produce of alluvia. The same returns make the yield from Ballarat district quartz mines to be 104,148 oz. 19 dwt. 9 gr., or an average of 8 dwt. 3·91 gr. from 255,173 tons; and, from Sandhurst district quartz mines, to be 108,677 oz. 17 dwt. 2 gr., or an average of 10 dwt. 4·31 gr. from 213,516½ tons, thus showing that while in alluvial produce Ballarat is admittedly the first field, it is also not very far behind the best of the quartz fields of the colony. As to the several divisions into which the Ballarat mining district is divided the following table, taken from the Mining Surveyor's returns for the quarter ending 31st March, 1870, will show their present relative values as producers of quartz gold. As bearing, however, on the averages, it must be stated that the highest individual averages in the surveyor's tables were on small parcels of quartz. Thus the highest was 1 oz. 17 dwt. 14·22 gr. on a lot of 27 tons in the Blackwood division. The next was an average of 1 oz. 5 dwt. 20·40 gr. on a lot of 50 tons in the Creswick division. This last division includes Clunes where the quarterly average of the Port Phillip Company on 11,734 tons was 3 dwt. 19·01 gr., and of the New North Clunes Company on 7447 tons 15 dwt. 20.95 gr. The table will show the general averages and totals of the divisions for the quarter ending 31st March, 1870, exclusive of gold from pyrites

and quartz tailings, and exclusive of certain yields not obtained by
the registrars :—

DIVISION.	Tons Crushed.	Average.		Total Yield.		
		dwt.	gr.	oz.	dwt.	gr.
Ballarat Proper	14,602	3	14·02	2,617	1	21
Creswick and Clunes	25,801	7	21·63	10,193	9	12
Smythesdale	976	5	9·93	264	4	0
Buninyong	5,300	4	3·49	1,098	11	0
Gordon	4,473	12	0·68	2,690	3	0
Stieglitz	2,250	10	9·10	1,167	14	0
Blackwood	4,295¾	11	14·98	2,496	13	3
Totals and General Average	57,697¾	7	2·77	20,527	16	12

The future of the gold-fields is, no doubt, to be one chiefly
of quartz mining.   And, in this relation, every advance in the
mechanical and chemical sciences as applied to mining is of course
an addition to the realisable value of our lodes.   Already the quartz
lodes, when worked with economy and skill, pay fairly even when
poor.   Ballarat supplies a notable instance in the Black Hill Company's operations.   In the mineral statistics for 1869, issued by the
mining department of the Victorian Government, occurs the following
passage :—

As illustrating the present condition of the Victorian gold-fields in regard to
the management of mines and the character of the machinery and appliances
for reducing and treating auriferous quartz, the following statement, furnished
by the district mining registrar of Ballarat, is highly interesting and valuable.
He says:—"The Black Hill Quartz Mining Company at Ballarat began work
in January, 1862, and from that time to the end of December, 1869, embracing
a period of eight years, they have obtained the quantities of quartz and gold set
down hereunder :—Quartz crushed, 250,575 tons ; gold got therefrom, 36,185
oz. 15 dwt. 19 gr. : average per ton, 2 dwt. 21·31 gr.; total value of gold,
£145,541 6s 3d ; total amount of dividends paid, £21,730.   (Being 10 per cent.
per annum on the capital.)   The last dividend was paid in December, 1868."
This simple statement affords abundant encouragement to those who possess
the knowledge and skill which are required in mining for quartz and in treating
vein-stuff, and is worthy the consideration of those who say that our appliances
for saving fine gold are defective, and that a new invention is the urgent
requirement of the day.   It would appear, judging from the results obtained at
Black Hill, Clunes, and other well managed mines and reducing works, that
judgment and care and fidelity alone are needed to give excellent returns from
even poor quartz.

CHAPTER VIII.

THE TOWN OF BALLARAT.

Area and Population of the Town.—Borough Statistics of Ballarat West, Ballarat East, and Sebastopol.—Water Supply.—Hospital.—Benevolent Asylum.—Orphan Asylum.— Churches. — Eisteddfod. — Schools. — Recreation Grounds. — Ballarat Cricket Club.— Mechanics' Institute. —Public Library. — Chamber of Commerce.— Theatre Royal.— Musical Societies.—Fire Brigades.—Ballarat Rangers and Cavalry.—Gas Company.— Horticultural Society.—Agricultural and Pastoral Society.—Statistics of Produce and Stock.—Meat Preserving Company.—Banks.—Mining Exchange.--The Gaol.—The Camp.—Last of the Military.—Post Offices and Treasury.--Electric Telegraph.— Explorers' Memorial.—Prince Alfred's Visit.—Magdalen Refuge.—Ladies' Benevolent Society.—Temperance Hall.—Alfred Hall.—Railway.—Shire Council's and Road Boards. —Ballarat, Sandhurst, and Geelong.—Past and Present Contrasts.

THE town or city of Ballarat must be said to comprise the borough of Sebastopol, as there is no break in the continuity of streets actually built upon and inhabited. From the northern boundary of Ballarat West borough to the southern boundary of Sebastopol borough the distance is five miles and a quarter, and from the western boundary of Ballarat West borough to the eastern boundary of Ballarat East borough the distance is four miles. These distances are measured along the central thoroughfares, where the whole alignment, with immaterial exceptions, is built upon. Thus, starting from the eastern boundary at the Canadian and going to the western boundary at Alfredton, the traveller passes along Main, Bridge, and Sturt streets, and performs a journey of a few hundred yards over four miles. This is a distance as great if not greater than that in London from Hyde Park Corner to the Bank, that from Westminster Bridge by water to the Tower, or that from the Elephant and Castle, south of the Thames, to Highbury Park in the north. It is as great as the distance in Melbourne from the University to the Junction at St. Kilda, or from the Spencer street railway terminus by way of the streets to the junction of the

Merri Creek with the Yarra Yarra on the eastern boundary of Richmond. In starting from the northern boundary of Lydiard street and passing to the southern boundary at Bonshaw, the traveller. performs a journey of five miles and a quarter and traverses Lydiard, part of Armstrong, Skipton, and Albert streets. This long stretch of street is represented in London by the distance from Hyde Park Corner past the Bank and Whitechapel to the Mile End road, from the Elephant and Castle to the New River reservoirs, or from Westminster Bridge by water, to Limehouse Reach. In Melbourne it is equal to a walk from Flemington to St. Kilda, or by water from the mouth of the Yarra Yarra to Richmond. The traveller while traversing the Ballarat thoroughfares mentioned passes along the two central lines of streets of a city with over 40,000 inhabitants, 56 churches, 3 town-halls, 477 hotels, many other large public edifices, over 10,000 dwellings, 84 miles of made streets, 164 miles of footpaths, 15 miles of pitched channelling, property of the rateable value of a quarter million sterling, and yielding a yearly municipal revenue of £50,000, exclusive of a water-supply revenue of £15,000. He will pass over the two centres of a city comprising an area of 9400 acres in extent, where lie 60 miles of water mains, 50 miles of gas mains, and over 3000 lineal yards of stone flagging. He will see about him long reaching lines of stately buildings, and elegant shops, and large manufactories, including 11 banks, 8 iron foundries, 13 breweries and distilleries, 3 flour-mills, and other manufactories, all within the town boundaries ; while everywhere around him where less than twenty years ago there was only the wild solitude of the primeval forest, the works of mining companies, the fertile farms, and the hum of commerce will reveal at once the secret of the power which has created this great prosperity.

This large and populous city, whose area and population and annual revenue would absorb those of several English cathedral cities, is situated 50 miles west from the shores of the Port Phillip Bay, and at an elevation of 1437 feet above the sea. Its western half is spread over a basaltic table land, the foot of whose eastern slopes is traversed by the Yarrowee Creek, which for a part of its course is the boundary between the boroughs of Ballarat West and East. Its eastern half is spread over schistose ranges and made-hills of auriferous detritus, and includes the oldest inhabited portions of the city. From it issued the leads or gutters of golden drift which are now being worked beneath the elevated plateau of the western portion of the three boroughs.

The borough of Ballarat West is the oldest of the three boroughs. It was constituted a municipality on the 17th of December, 1855, and on the 14th of January, 1856, the first council was elected, consisting of Messrs Jas. Oddie, Robt. Muir, Jas. Stewart, M.D., Wm. Tulloch, Alex. Binney Rankin, John Smith Carver, and Patrick Bolger. James Oddie was the first chairman for 1856-7, and Joseph Comb and Samuel Baird were the first town-clerk and town-surveyor, both clerk and surveyor having held office up to the present date. The subsequent chairmen were James Stewart, M.D., 1858-9 ; William Collard Smith, 1860-1 ; Robert Lewis, 1862-3. In October, 1863, the municipality became a borough, the last chairman of the municipality being chosen first mayor of the borough. The mayors since then have been Matthew Campbell, 1864 ; Joseph Attwood Doane, 1865 ; Gilbert Duncan, 1866 ; Thos. Davey, 1867-8 ; James M'Dowall, 1869 ; Thos. Cowan, 1870. The first council chambers were of wood, erected by Messrs Doane and Ringrove on the site of the District Police-court in Sturt street, and were destroyed by fire. The erection of a new town-hall with granite front, from a design by Mr C. D. Cuthbert, having been decided on, the foundation of the first portion was laid by Mr John Robinson Bailey, M.L.A. for Ballarat West, on the 16th of August, 1860. The builders were Messrs Evans and Barker, the contract being for £4900, and the new building was opened on the 1st February, 1861. The borough council afterwards decided on a change of plan, and competitive designs were obtained, and finally the council ordered that a design by Mr Lorenz be adopted, subject to variations to be designed by Mr Oakden, the borough architect, under whose superintendence the present hall is being erected. The initial letter at the beginning of this chapter shows the upper portion of the centre and tower. The contractor for the works was Mr Cowland, for the sum of £16,767, the contract to be

completed by the end of 1870. On the 14th January, 1870, Thomas
Cowan, the mayor, laid the new memorial stone of the town-hall
His worship in his address on that occasion made the following
statement :—

The Sturt street frontage will occupy a space of 153 feet. The principal
entrance to the municipal offices, will be in the centre under the tower,
which will stand right out to the front so that the stone which has just been
laid will also be the foundation stone of the tower. This tower is to carry the
Alfred Memorial Bells which have already arrived in Ballarat. They have
been cast by Messrs Mears and Stainbank, of Whitechapel, and competent
judges have pronounced them to be the finest peal that has come to these
colonies. There are eight bells in all, pitched in the key of E flat, and the
largest—the tenor bell—is 4 feet 3 inches in diameter, and weighs 23 cwt.
The total weight of the eight bells is nearly 4½ tons ; the weight of the eight
bells in St. Patrick's Cathedral, Melbourne, being only 3½ tons. The Alfred
Memorial Bells are valued at £1,180. In addition to the bells, the tower will
contain a splendid illuminated clock, with four dials, each 9 feet in diameter,
and which, besides striking the hours and quarters, will ring a chime every
hour on fifteen small musical bells, that will be placed in the roof of the tower.
The centre of the clock face will be 95 feet above the street, and the total
height of the tower about 135 feet. It is to be observed that the building now
in progress will leave nearly half the town-hall reserve unoccupied, the depth
of the ground being 132 feet, and the depth of the building only 70 feet, so
that if at any future time it should be decided to erect a spacious public hall,
there will be a site available for the purpose of 120 feet by 70 feet.

The first assessment was in 1856, and showed that there were
then 267 tenements within the municipality, and 297 vacant lots,
the whole valued at £40,061. On this assessment the council
struck a rate of sixpence in the pound, which the Government
disallowed, and a shilling rate was then struck. Among the
applications to the Government by the first council were requests
for a site for a mechanics' institute, for a market place, for public
gardens, for the removal of buildings where Sturt and Lydiard
streets now intersect, and for the formation of Sturt street. Sturt
street, which is now made throughout its whole length, is three
chains wide, and is ornamented with elegant shops, churches, and
gardens. All the other streets are one chain and a-half wide.
The borough comprises an area of 2880 acres, and has now property of the rateable value of £148,522, every year showing an

increase until now it nearly quadruples the return for the first year. The progression has been as follows :—

Year.	Tenements.	Rateable Value.	Year.	Tenements.	Rateable Value.
1856 ...	564	£40,061	1864 ...	3474	£95,686
1857 ...	810	32,088	1865 ...	3571	98,172
1858 ...	1430	41,015	1866 ...	3948	112,580
1860 ...	2608	54,500	1867 ...	4191	114,757
1861 ...	—	72,058	1868 ...	4839	132,538
1862 ...	2788	82,721	1869 ...	5365	148,522
1863 ...	3451	102,434	1870 ...	6196	207,763

There are within the borough 86 streets, of which a length of 45 miles is made. There are also 90 miles of footpaths, 10 miles of pitched channelling, 3000 lineal yards of flagging, over 4000 dwellings, 287 hotels, 28 churches, 3 steam flour-mills, 6 iron foundries, 1 tannery, 1 gas-works ; besides a town-hall, a theatre, a mechanics' institute, a post-office, a police-court, a gaol, and other government offices. Estimating the population at the rate of $4\frac{1}{2}$ to each dwelling the total population of the borough is about 20,000 persons, the borough council having a revenue from all sources of £26,722 for the year 1869.

Ballarat East was proclaimed a municipality on the 5th May, 1857, and on the 1st June 1857, the first council was elected, consisting of Messrs Daniel Sweeney, John Gibbs, William M'Crea, Richard Belford, William Bramwell Robinson, William Bickham Rodier, and Geo. Clendinning, M.D. Mr Rodier was chosen chairman, and Mr Jno. Campbell was appointed town-clerk. The municipality became a borough in October, 1863. Following Mr Rodier as chairman of the municipality there were Messrs Richard Belford, 1858 ; William Scott, 1859 ; George Clendinning, M.D., 1860 ; William Scott, 1861 ; Charles Dyte, 1862 ; and Frederick Young, 1863. As in Ballarat West, so here, the last chairman became the first mayor of the borough. His successors have been respectively Messrs John Fussell, 1864 ; George Clendinning, M.D., 1865 ; Emanuel Steinfeld, 1866 to 1869 ; and Edward Eastwood, 1870. The municipal council held its meetings in several rented houses during the earlier years of its existence, but in 1861 the present town-hall was built by Messrs Irving, Glover, and Co. for the sum of 2877 11s 6d, Mr C. D. Cuthbert being the architect. The borough includes an area of 4320 acres, and has rateable property valued at £80,554. The first assessment on the books was in 1860, when the number of dwellings was 2470, amount of assessment not obtainable. The returns for the subsequent years are as follow :—

Year.	Tenements.	Rateable Value.	Year.	Tenements.	Rateable Value.
1861 ...	2982	£75,656	1866 ...	2928	£62,066
1862 ...	2714	80,244	1867 ...	3045	64,378
1863 ...	3070	80,001	1868 ...	3290	68,032
1864 ...	3226	74,423	1869 ...	3767	76,587
1865 ...	3126	74,561	1870 ...	3992	80,554

There are within the borough 25 miles of streets made and formed, and about 50 miles of footpaths, 16 churches, 140 hotels, about 3000 dwellings, a town-hall, a theatre, a fire brigade establishment, a brewery, candle, and other manufactories, a police-court, and a public library. Bridge, Main, and Humffray streets are what in the first days were bullock tracks; the former street is one of the busiest and handsomest in the city, and Victoria street is as wide as Sturt street, and, like it, planted with trees. Estimating the population of the borough at 4½ to each tenement the total population is about 14,000, the borough council having an annual revenue from all sources of £15,813 18s 3d, as per returns for 1869.*

The borough of Sebastopol was proclaimed in October, 1864, and the first election of councillors took place on the 12th December, 1864, when Messrs F. F. Beverin, Thomas Dickinson, John Edwards, Ricd. Miles, Ellis Richards, John C. Rowlands, Geo. C. Robinson, Geo. Tait, and Isaac Vickers were elected. Mr John Wall, formerly of the Local Court and a mining surveyor, was appointed town-clerk and surveyor, and still holds those offices. The mayors of the borough have been Messrs Beverin, 1865-6 ; Vickers, 1867 ; Dickinson, 1868 ; Whittaker, 1869 ; Edwards, 1870. The following are the assessments for the several years since the formation of the borough :—

Year.	Tenements.	Rateable Value.	Year.	Tenements.	Rateable Value.
1865 ...	440	£6,028	1868 ...	1245	£16,680
1866 ...	751	9,040	1869 ...	1661	22,352
1867 ...	1030	14,231			

* In Appendix D will be be found reports of the first sales of town lots in Ballarat West in 1852, and of the sales of the Main road frontages in 1856-7-8-9.

The borough comprises 2200 acres, 14 miles of made streets, 24 miles of footpaths, and contains a town-hall and police-court, a mechanics' institute, 12 churches, 50 hotels, and about 1600 dwellings. The town-hall was built, the first part by Messrs Thomas and Cope, cost £630 ; and the second part by Messrs Taylor and Ellis at a cost of £1056, after a design by Mr J. A. Doane, the building being opened on the 19th of March, 1869, when a banquet was given and several members of the Cabinet of the day were present. Estimating the population of the borough at $4\frac{1}{2}$ persons to each dwelling, the total population will be somewhat over 7000, the borough council having a revenue from all sources of £7298 5s 9d for the year 1869.

In December, 1852, the first attempt was made at water-supply. The Government Camp authorities then here employed men to build a small dam across the Gnarr Creek at the spot where the creek runs on the northern side of Mair street, close under what is now the railway terminus hill. The little dam intercepted the overflow from Yuille's Swamp and the Gnarr Creek drainage, and served mainly for the Camp use. Yuille's Swamp, or as it is now called Wendouree Lake, was for some years the only source of supply, but as the town grew that reservoir was found to be insufficient, and steps were taken to secure water reserves in the Bullarook Forest on which to construct reservoirs for the permanent supply of the town. The boroughs of Ballarat West and East united in a scheme of water-supply, whose magnitude and excellent organisation are unequalled in the colony save by the metropolitan supply. Mr Richard Belford, when chairman of the Municipal Council of Ballarat East, was one of the first proposers of a supply of water from the forest, and owing to the steps taken then the question was at intervals agitated until the supply was carried out to its present limit. When Mr J. B. Humffray was Minister of Mines in 1861, Mr Kirk, who owned the first reservoir made in the forest for mining purposes, offered the reservoir to the Government for the use of Ballarat, and Mr Humffray eventually promoted the purchase, and sent Mr Engineer Bagge to report on the repairs necessary. Subsequently Mr Engineer Palmer, who became the first engineer for water-supply, was employed to survey the forest with a view to the construction of additional

reservoirs for a more liberal supply. Before this a commission for
the whole town had been proposed in a circular by the Eastern
Council, but the proposition was not then entertained, and when Mr
Palmer made his survey there were grave doubts entertained as to
the wisdom of adventuring upon the larger scheme. Mr Palmer
held that the scheme was practicable and would pay, and he con-
ferred with Mr H. R. Nicholls, of the *Ballarat Star*, who urged the
adoption of the larger supply upon the attention of Mr C. Dyte,
then chairman of the Eastern Council. Mr Dyte did not fall in with
the representations made, and Mr W. C. Smith, of the Western
Council, was then appealed to. He was convinced by the arguments
used, and he became one of the earliest and ablest municipal advocates of the scheme of water-supply. Every year helps now to
confirm the wisdom of those who sought betimes to provide a
good supply of this essential element in urban health, wealth, and
comfort. The borough councils having had joint possession
of Kirk's dam given to them in June, 1862, pushed the business
of supply with energy, procured loans of money and grants
of water-shed reserves from the Government, until at the present
date the Ballarat and Ballarat East Water-Supply Committee has
under its control reserves of land comprising an area of 3000 acres,
three dams—Beale's, Pincott's, and Kirk's, with an aggregate storage
capacity of 294,000,000 gallons, 60 miles of mains, conveying water
by special services to 5000 houses, 40 manufactories, and 16 mines,
and producing an annual revenue of £15,000. Chairmen of the
Water Committee are chosen from the borough councils, whose
members form the committee. The present engineer is Mr C. H. O.
Bagge, and Mr W. Thompson is the secretary and treasurer. A
fourth dam has been projected, the site to be on the Gong Gong
Creek below Kirk's dam. The cost of this new reservoir is estimated
at £103,676, and its storage capacity at 1,076,703,805 gallons,
submerging the whole of the present hamlet of Fellmongers, whose
houses and other improvements have been purchased by the Water-
Supply Committee. Up to the end of May, 1870, there had been
expended in water-supply a sum of £167,576 7s 7d, part of which
has been obtained on debentures issued by the borough councils, and
it is proposed to raise part of the cost of the new reservoir in a
similar manner.

VIEW OF BA
Weste
Ta

ARAT 1858.

Ballarat is rich in charitable and other public institutions. The District Hospital, in Drummond street, corner of Sturt street, an edifice in the classic style, is the earliest of the public charities, sick and injured people having at first been housed in huts at the Government Camp. The wounded men at the Eureka Stockade* could not be provided with proper accommodation, and that led to the taking of steps for building a hospital. Messrs Lynn, Henry Foster (Superintendent of Police), W. B. Rodier, J. Daly (Warden), R. Lewis, and others, mentioned as among the first officers of the hospital, started the movement. When the building was begun the site was in the bush, and some people lost their way in returning to their homes in what is now Ballarat East and the parts adjacent to Lydiard street. The foundation stone of the first portion of the hospital was laid on Christmas Day, 1855, by Mr James Daly, police magistrate and warden, the architect being Mr J. Robertson. The foundation stone of the remainder of the south wing was laid on New Year's Day, 1866, by Mr Henry Cuthbert, with masonic honors, Mr Charles D. Cuthbert being the architect. The foundation of the centre, or Alfred Memorial, was laid on Queen Victoria's birthday, 1869, by Mr Robert Lewis, and was opened on the next anniversary of the day; Mr J. H. Jones being the architect of the centre, and of the completing north wing, not yet erected. The edifice stands on a reserve of five acres on the highest part of the western table-land. The names of the first committee of management and of the first staff of officers are as follow:—Messrs J. A. Douglas, president; W. B. Robinson and J. Oddie, vice-presidents; M. Elliot, J. Oddie, H. Foster, J. Dixie, and A. B. Rankin, trustees; J. Dixie, treasurer; R. Muir, R. B. Gibbs, W. C. Smith, C. H. Edwards, S. Irwin, J. Cummins, G. Butchart, W. Moore, J. Daly, D. Oliver, A. B. Rankin, and M. Elliot, committeemen; T. Doyle, J. Stewart, R. J. Hobson, and C. J. Kenworthy, honorary medical officers; H. Foster, hon. secretary; T. Hillas, resident-surgeon; J. Garrard, dispenser and house-steward; Mrs Garrard, matron. The presidents since have been Messrs W. B. Robinson, A. L. Lynn, A. Drury (four times), W. H. Foster, J. M. Strongman, R. Lewis (three times), and J. O'Meara. The present resident surgeon is Mr Owen, the secretary Mr Burrows,

* See Appendix E as to the insurgent flag and some other Stockade matters.

the collector Mr Geo. Moore, and the matron Mrs Bishop.   The house contains 185 bed-spaces, the last report returning 1033 as the number of patients admitted in the year 1869, and 5372 as the number of out-patients.

The Benevolent Asylum, on a five-acre reserve fronting Ascot street, was the next of the public charities.   It is a palace in the Elizabethan style, with well-kept grounds, a magnificent home such as the English poor have never dreamt of in their wildest flights of fancy.   The foundation stone of the first portion was laid on St. Patrick's Day, 1859, by F. Gell, D.P.G.M., with masonic honors, the architect being Mr Christopher Porter; builders, Messrs Evans and Barker ; cost £3765 4s 2d.   The first building was opened on the 20th February, 1860.   The foundation stones of the subsequent portions appear to have been laid without ceremony.   Mr J. A. Doane has been the architect of all those portions of the Asylum which have been built since the first.   The second portion was built by Mr J. Francis at a cost of £2907 15s, and was opened on the 10th June, 1862.   The third, or north centre portion, was built by Mr J. Hope, at a cost of £2016 8s, and was opened on the 26th August, 1863.   The fourth or north wing portion was built by Mr F. Nicholls at a cost of £2127 1s 5d, and was opened on the 19th March, 1867.   The fifth or southern wing—a lying-in hospital— was built by Messrs Irving, Glover, and Co. at a cost of £2712 10s 2d, and was opened on the 27th of July, 1869.   The first committee sat in 1857 as the almoners of the " Ballarat Visiting and Benevolent Association," and consisted of Mr R. Smith, president ; the Revs. P. Madden, J. Bickford, J. Potter, J. Strongman, G. Mackie, and Niquet ; Messrs W. C. Smith, R. Belford, W. Frazer, R. Ocock, J. H. Dunne, J. Oddie, M. J. Cummins, M'Ivor, A. Dimant, D. Morris, Martin, S. Donnelly, Tristram, A. Dewar, W. Dimsey, J. Dodds, Crane, H. Wood, I. Wheeldon, R. Davidson, R. Lewis, Brameon, A. Davies, Lockhart, Gripe, and Talbot, committee-men ; A. S. Park, hon. treasurer ; A. A. Tarte, hon. secretary.   The presidents of the asylum since then have been Messrs R. Lewis (six times), J. Twentyman, W. Scott, J. A. Doane (three times), and J. Oddie.   Mr and Mrs Boughen have been master and matron from the first.   The present secretary is Mr Peter Cazaly, and Dr. M'Farlane is the medical officer.   The charity provides a home for old age and chronic invalids, and rations to out-door patients, the members of committee undertaking to visit the out-door claimants for relief, and generally to supervise the administration of the funds. On the 6th of December, 1869, there were 195 patients in the home, and 816 patients were receiving out-door relief, the number of in-door patients, exclusive of children, since the opening of the asylum having been 1655, and the outlay for the ten years from 1859 to 1868, having been £68,202 10s 2d. Beds are made for 274 in-door patients in the present building.

The District Orphan Asylum is in Victoria street, and is a plain edifice, designed by Mr H. R. Caselli. It was established in 1865, the licensed victuallers of Ballarat having been, with Mr W. Redfern Watson at their head, foremost in its promotion, assisted very nobly from the first by the friendly societies of the town and district. The foundation stone was laid on the 8th of December, 1865, by Mr James M'Culloch, then Chief Secretary of the colony, and the building was opened on the 8th of July, 1866 ; cost to date, £7500. Mr R. W. Watson was the first president, and Mr and Mrs John Finlay the first master and matron. Mr R. B. Gibbs was the second president, Mr W. Scott is the present president, Mr and Mrs H. B. Sadlier the present master and matron, and Mr H. Davies the secretary. In December, 1869, there were 80 children in the asylum, the building having accommodation for 200.

On Crown lands near the western boundary of the city, and near the Botanical Reserve, is a building where vagrant or deserted children are supported by the State.

Of the many churches in Ballarat, those in permanent materials, as brick and stone are called, may be particularised. Every communion had earlier churches of wood, and at the present time most communions have churches both of wood and of brick or stone ; but the more perishable buildings are gradually disappearing as churches, and this record only refers in detail to the more durable edifices.

Of these the Anglican communion has six, of which Christ Church, in Lydiard street, is the oldest of all existing ecclesiastical edifices here in permanent materials. It is a Gothic structure, built of basaltic stone, the nave designed by Backhouse and Reynolds, and the transepts by Mr E. James, and was begun in 1854 during the incumbency of the Rev. J. R. Thackeray, the foundation stone being

L

laid by Archdeacon Stretch. At that time the building was not carried on. In the year 1857 the nave was built, the Rev. John Potter, the present incumbent, being then also the minister. It was opened on the 13th of September, 1857, by the Revs. P. Homan and J. G. Russell. The transepts and chancel were added in 1868, and were opened on the 6th of May of that year. The transepts and chancel cost £1792, and the earlier portion over £2000. The school-house of brick, which stands north of the church, was built about the same time, and opened on the 1st of October of 1868. St. Paul's, in Humffray street, a Gothic design, built of brick, has been re-built, in part, and was opened in its present state in April, 1864; architect, Mr L. Terry. The original body of the church was built for a school, the foundation stone being laid on the 17th of May, 1858, by Mr J. B. Humffray, who then said it was "the first stone foundation laid for educational purposes in Ballarat East." The tower was built and the church enlarged in 1862, but in 1864 the site of the church subsided in consequence of mining operations beneath, and the building was taken down. The present church was then erected, the Rev. R. T. Cummins incumbent, the old tower remaining, and the church built west of the tower instead of east as before. St. John's, a Gothic design, in Armstrong street north, built of brick, and designed by Mr L. Terry, was begun on the 15th of March, 1864, the Dean of Melbourne laying the foundation stone. It was opened on the 29th of February, 1865, by the Rev. C. T. Perks. On the 16th of November, 1869, Archdeacon Stretch laid the foundation stone of additions to the church, which were opened on the 11th of March, 1870, the Rev. G. W. Watson being the incumbent. St. Peter's, in Sturt street west, Gothic design, built of basaltic stone, was begun on the 16th of November, 1864, Mr B. H. Hassell laying the foundation stone. Mr C. D. Cuthbert was the architect, and the nave, the only part yet built, was opened on the 11th of June, 1865, the Rev. W. H. Adeney being the incumbent. St. James', Little Bendigo, Gothic, built of brick, and designed by Mr H. R. Caselli, was opened by the Dean of Melbourne on the 17th of July, 1864, the Rev. G. C. Allanby being the incumbent. Holy Trinity, Albert street, Sebastopol, built of brick, and designed by Mr H. R. Caselli, was begun in September, 1867, Archdeacon Stretch laying the foundation stone. Since then two bays and a chancel have been added, a memorial stone being laid by Miss Kate Bray in January, 1870, the Rev. Gualter Soares, minister. The Assembly of the Anglican Church has appointed a committee to report on a proposal made to divide the diocese of Victoria and found a Ballarat bishopric.

The Roman Catholics have one church, that in Sturt street. It is a design in Flamboyant Gothic, and is the largest and most beautiful Gothic edifice in the town. The materials are basaltic stone, with freestone enrichments. Bishop Gould laid the foundation stone of the nave and side-aisles on the 7th of February, 1858, the Revs. P. Madden and R. F. X. Fennelly being the resident ministers; architects, Messrs Shaw and Dowden. The pillars of the nave were erected in 1861, and the building, as far as the point now intersected by the transepts, was opened by the bishop on the 8th of November, 1863, Dr. Shiel, Archdeacon of Ballarat (now Bishop of Adelaide), being then resident here. The transepts, side chapels, chancel, and sacristy are now being built after drawings by Mr Denney, Dean Moore being the clergyman in charge. The present contract does not include the building of the tower and spire, the erection of which is reserved for the future. The nave and aisles cost £12,000, the present contract, with a contract for roofing-in, will amount to a similar sum, and £1500 were spent on the iron fence round the reserve, the total outlay to date, including the completion of the portion now building, being £25,500.

The Scottish Presbyterians have three churches. St. Andrews, in Sturt street, is a Norman design by C. D. Cuthbert, built in basaltic stone, with an ornate freestone doorway. The foundation stone was laid on 1st of December, 1862, by the Rev. W. Henderson, the minister. While being built a portion of the walls was blown down in a gale on the 3rd of August, 1863. The church, unfinished as at present, cost £3150, and was opened on the 15th of August, 1864. Two small congregations had existed before the original St. Andrew's one, which latter worshipped in the wood building adjoining, now occupied by the Ballarat College, under R. O. M'Coy, principal. The two earlier ones belonged respectively to the Synod of Victoria and the Free Presbyterian Church of Victoria. The remnants of these two joined in one, making the St. Andrew's congregation under the charge of the Rev. W. Henderson, the wooden church being opened

L 2

on the first Sunday in May, 1858. Soon after that nearly all Presbyterian bodies in Victoria united as the Presbyterian Church of Victoria, and the congregation of St. Andrew's joined that union. Ebenezer, United Presbyterian, in Armstrong street south, built of basaltic stone, and designed by H. R. Caselli, was begun on the 10th of December, 1862, the minister of the congregation at that time, the Rev. R. T. Walker, laying the foundation stone. The church was opened on the 21st of June, 1863. Doveton street Church, United Presbyterian, built of brick in 1866, and opened in June of that year, was then a Welsh Congregational Church, designed by carpenters T. Lewis and J. Thomas. It is now the property of United Presbyterians, under the pastoral charge of the Rev. R. T. Walker, who opened his pastorate there on the 15th of August, 1869. The congregation of St. John's, Presbyterian Church of Victoria, at present worshipping in the Alfred Hall, has accepted a design by Mr Oakden for a permanent church, to be built.

The Free Church of England has one building, dedicated to St. Thomas, built of brick, in Macarthur street west, designed by J. R. Burns. It was opened on the 19th of July, 1869; minister, the Rev. C. W. Collins.

The Welsh Presbyterians have one church. It is in Albert street, Sebastopol, is built of basaltic stone, and was designed by H. R. Caselli, the foundation stone being laid on the 3rd of March, 1865, by Mary, wife of Ellis Richards, a deacon of the church. The church was opened on the second Sunday in April, 1866, by the Revs. R. T. Walker and W. Henderson in the English language, and on the next Sunday by the Revs. Messrs W. M. Evans, Farr, Roberts, and J. Evans in the Welsh language.

The Welsh Baptists have a church of brick in the reserve at the corner of Lydiard and Armstrong streets. It was built in 1858 for the use of Welsh Baptists, with whom also worshipped other dissidents from the episcopal communion. The Revs. J. Farr and L. Llewellyn were the first ordained ministers.

The Primitive Methodists have four churches. One of brick in Humffray street, the foundation stone of which was laid by Mr J. Richardson on the 9th of April, 1860. The church was designed by J. Buckle, and was opened on the 8th of July, 1860. One of brick in Burnbank street, designed by W. Benson. Mr J.

Richardson laid the foundation stone on the 6th of June, 1864, and the building was opened on the 5th of August of the same year. One at the south east corner of Eyre and Lyons streets, designed by J. A. Doane, and built of basaltic stone. Mrs M. D. Morgan laid the foundation stone on the 10th of May, 1868, and the church was opened on the 23rd of October of that year. One of brick in Beverin street, Sebastopol, designed by J. A. Doane. The foundation stone was laid on the 23rd of June, 1868, by the Rev. S. Bracewell, and the church was opened on the 27th of the following September.

The Wesleyans have ten churches. Wesley Church, in Lydiard street, built of basaltic stone, was designed by Backhouse and Reynolds ; cost, £5000. The foundation stone was laid by his Excellency Sir Henry Barkly on the 17th January, 1858, and the church was opened on the 18th of July of the same year, the first sermon being preached by the Rev. D. J. Draper, who was drowned in the *London* steamer, that foundered in the Bay of Biscay on the 11th January, 1866. The change of prices between 1854 and 1870 is shown in the fact that £2500 was the cost of the original schoolhouse at the corner of Lydiard and Dana streets, a small, plain, low-walled building of rotten sandstone from the Black Hill, and basaltic boulders. A similar building could now be erected for a fifth or a sixth of the cost. Barkly street Church, of brick, cost £1933, was completed on the 5th of May, 1860 ; J. A. Doane, architect. There was no ceremonial laying of the foundation stone. Neil street Church, of brick, cost £1400, was completed on the 16th of March, 1867 ; J. A. Doane, architect. The foundation stone was laid by the Rev. W. L. Binks. Wendouree Church, of brick, cost £475, was finished on the 16th of June, 1860; J. A. Doane, architect ; the Rev. J. Bickford the officiating minister. Sebastopol Church, of stone, in Cheshunt street ; first part opened in March, 1864, completed on the 22nd of May, 1869 ; foundation stone laid in August, 1863, by the Rev. W. Taylor, of California ; J. A. Doane, architect ; the Rev. J. S. Waugh officiating minister. Little Bendigo Church, of brick, cost £611 ; J. A. Doane, architect ; foundation stone laid by Mrs D. Morgan, completed on the 25th of June, 1865. Mount Pleasant Church, of stone, cost £980 ; foundation stone laid by the Rev. J. S. Waugh, completed 16th September, 1865 ; J. A.

Doane, architect.   Pleasant street Church, of brick, cost £1700;
officiating minister, Rev. W. L. Binks; architect, J. A. Doane;
completed on the 24th of June, 1867.   Golden Point Church, of
brick, cost £850 ; foundation stone laid by the Rev. W. L. Binks;
architect, J. A. Doane; completed on the 29th of June, 1867.   Brown
Hill Church, of brick, cost £714 ; foundation stone laid by George
Smith; architect, J. A. Doane ; completed on the 22nd of March,
1869.

The Bible Christians have four churches.   Armstrong street
Church, of brick ; foundation stone laid in December, 1860, by Mrs
Frederick Baker, opened on the 3rd of March, 1861 ; F. O. Korn,
architect.   Skipton street Church, of stone ; foundation stone laid
on the 8th of August, 1865, by the Rev. John Orchard, opened on
the 25th of March, 1866 ; H. R. Caselli, architect.   Grant street
Church, of brick ; foundation stone laid on the 19th of December,
1865, by the Rev. W. H. Hooker, opened on the 18th of March, 1866 ;
designed by carpenter S. H. Lugg.   Humffray street Church, of
brick ; foundation stone laid on the 30th of October, 1866, by the
Rev. James Lowe, opened on the 20th of January, 1867 ; designed
by carpenter S. H. Lugg.

The Hebrew Synagogue in Barkly street, of brick ; cost £900,
was designed by T. B. Cameron.   The foundation stone was laid
on the 25th of January, 1861, by Mr C. Dyte, M.L.A., and the opening
service was celebrated on the 18th of the following March, the Rev.
Mr Isaacs, minister.

The Baptist Church, of brick, in Dawson street, opposite to St.
Patrick's, was designed by J. A. Doane, and cost £3591.   The
foundation stone was laid on the 23rd of October, 1866, by the Rev.
Isaac New ; pastor, the Rev. W. Sutton, and the building was
opened on the 6th of November, 1867.

The Congregational Church, of brick, at the corner of Dawson
and Mair streets, was designed by J. A. Doane, and cost £800.
The church that now is was designed for a school, the site adjoining
being reserved for a church.   The present building was opened on the
21st of March, 1862 ; the Rev. Mr Gosman, minister ; present pastor,
the Rev. J. J. Halley.   The first church was of wood, in Sturt street,
and opened on the 6th of June, 1857.   It was sold in September, 1861,
to Mr Boyd, the printer, who still occupies part of the premises.   In

October, 1856, the Rev. Mr Poole held the first services here, and in December, 1858, the Rev. Thomas Binney visited Ballarat. The church in Sturt street, west of the hospital, built in brick from a design by Mr Flude, cost £1309. The foundation stone was laid by Mr Vale, M.L.A., on the 18th of December, 1866, the Rev. J. M. Strongman being the minister. It was opened on the 9th of May, 1867, and the present minister is Mr F. L. Wilson.

Disciples of Christ Chapel, of brick, in Dawson street, designed by J. A. Doane; cost of building, £540; fittings, vestry, and extras, £185; land, £75; total, £800; opened in June, 1865.

The Society of Friends has a meeting-house in Grant street, the attendance ranging from ten to twenty members. The Wroeites have a tabernacle in Dyte's Parade. The Unitarians have no organisation here now. A few years ago they had a chapel in East street, and afterwards they met at the Mechanics' Institute, but the services have for some time been discontinued.

The Welsh inhabitants of Victoria have for some years held their annual festivals called Eistedfodda. The first was held in Ballarat on Christmas Day, 1855, in what was then a Welsh Chapel, but is now the engine-house of the Ballarat Fire Brigade in Barkly street.

Schools, secular and Sunday, are attached to nearly every denominational edifice, but only the Anglican, Wesleyan and Hebrew communions have school buildings in permanent materials. The National School at the south-west corner of Dana and Doveton streets, and the Common school in Humffray street, are in brick, and are under the direction of local trustees and the Central Board. There are many private schools. The two larger ones are called Grenville College and Ballarat College. The former is an elegant and spacious edifice in brick and cement in Holmes street, the latter is the old wooden church originally used by the St. Andrew's Presbyterian congregation. The principal of the Ballarat College is Robert O. M'Coy. Of Grenville College John Victor is the principal, and Henry B. de la Poer Wall is the vice-principal. There are two other private schools of some prominence—the Ballarat Commercial College, in Errard street, principal James Dimelow; and the Catholic College, in Raglan street, principal John W. Rogers.

Recreation Grounds have been provided in both boroughs. In the West are the Botanical Gardens, the Park, and the Cricket Reserves of the boroughs of Ballarat and Sebastopol. In the East are a reserve at Mount Pleasant, a Gymnastic Reserve near Brown Hill, and the Oval between Peel street and Soldiers' Hill. This last reserve is the oldest and most popular place of resort for cricket. The Ballarat Cricket Club was founded in 1856, when Daniel Sweeney (captain), Henry Davies, and some other of its present members were active promoters of the club. On the 29th of October, 1856, the club had its first practice on the then open flat near the present Oval. To secure the present reserve the club and the borough council have worked together generally, the club spending large sums in making the Oval what it now is—one of the finest cricket grounds in Australia. At the pavilion is treasured a rude lightwood bat, one of the first played with by the club. In the Cricket Reserve the Ballarat Bowling Club has a green. The first president of this club was Donald Macrae.

The Mechanics' Institute, in Sturt street, was born in April, 1859, in a little wooden house between Humffray and Barkly streets, in Main street, and its first reading-room was opened, as was afterwards the Ballarat East Public Library, in the engine-house of the Ballarat Fire Brigade. On the 20th of April, 1859, the first committee was chosen as follows :—Messrs J. B. Humffray, president ; A. Anderson and R. Belford, vice-presidents ; J. Stewart, M.D., T. S. Learmonth, H. R. Caselli, F. Young, and W. C. Smith, trustees ; G. G. Mackay, treasurer ; C. Dyte, W. H. Batten, R. Lewis, J. Cathie, D. O'Connor, J. M'Dowall, R. Mitchell, W. Frazer, J. Dodds, W. B. Withers, W. Cooper, and D. Oliver, committeemen ; Mr W. H. Batten was subsequently elected secretary, and has held office ever since. The presidents have been J. B. Humffray (two years), A. Anderson, T. Lang (two years), C. Lister, F. C. Downes (two years), and Joseph Jones (three years). Mr Anderson is now president for the second time. The first stone of the first part of the Sturt street building was laid with masonic honors by Mr H. Cuthbert on the 28th of September, 1860, and on the 19th of December the present reading-room was opened. The completed building, designed by J. H. Jones, is one of the largest and handsomest in the town. It was opened for a fine arts exhibition by his Excellency the Governor on the 21st of July, 1869. There are 1100 members on the roll, and near 9000 vols. in the library.   In May, 1870, while Haydon's "Aristides" yet hung in the hall of the Institute, General Tom Thumb and his companion dwarfs were exhibiting themselves there to large crowds. A writer to the *Ballarat Star*, himself an artist, remembered Haydon's wail of despair in his diary, and pointed out the coincidence that 24 years afterwards, and 16,000 miles away from the Egyptian Hall, the picture and the dwarf were again in contact, and again the dwarf the more popular.

The Public Library, in Barkly street, was established in 1862, and is open free to the public.   The building is handsome outside, and the interior library hall very elegant.   The foundation stone was laid by Sir Redmond Barry on the 21st of January, 1867, and the cost of the building and fittings was about £3500.   There are nearly 7000 vols. in the library.   The first president was Mr Emanuel Steinfeld, and the first librarian Mr Miller, Mr Frederick Young having been the first chairman of committee.   The present president is Mr Rosenblum, and the librarian Mr J. Fitzherbert.

The Ballarat Chamber of Commerce was first proposed publicly in 1856.   On the 5th of August, in that year, a meeting was held at the Montezuma hotel, Ballarat East, Mr R. Muir in the chair, when it was agreed that a Chamber should be established to watch over the commercial interests of the town, and Messrs J. B. Humffray, R. Muir, W. B. Robinson, H. Harris, W. B. Rodier, R. B. Gibbs and C. H. Edwards were appointed a committee to prepare rules and report.   Thereafter followed meetings of committee, and letters and deputations to the Governments of the day about a site for the building and other matters.   The first site proposed was on the south side of Sturt street near the Mechanics' Institute, but eventually the Chamber obtained a site on the opposite side of the street where the building now stands.   The building is in the Italian style, from a design by Backhouse and Reynolds, accepted in 1859.   The Chamber obtained the fee-simple and the property was held in shares, the shareholders guaranteeing to the Chamber the use of a room for its business.   After a few years the Chamber died out of usefulness and then out of existence, the shares in the property got into fewer hands and the ownership is now almost entirely in the hands of T. Lang and Co. and R. B. and S. Gibbs, merchants. All this did not come about without many bickerings among the projectors and shareholders, and allegations of sharp practice against some of the more active members of the proprietary. On the 13th of May, 1870, a meeting was held at the Alfred Hall, Mr E. Steinfeld in the chair, when it was resolved to revive the Chamber. That meeting was followed by others, and a Chamber has again been constituted; president, E. Steinfeld; vice-president, Joseph Jones; treasurer, Cornelius Lister; committeemen, F. C. Downes, A. Anderson, H. B. Chalmers, H. Smith, D. Turpie, L. S. Christie, J. T. Irving, J. Walker, T. Davey; secretary, George Perry.

The Theatre Royal, in Sturt street, was built after a design by Backhouse and Reynolds, and has a tolerably effective classical elevation with a bold Corinthian portico. It is at present the handsomest theatrical elevation in Victoria. The foundation stone was laid on the 20th of January, 1858, by Gustavus V. Brooke, tragedian, who was drowned in the *London* on her voyage hither in January, 1866. The building cost over £8000, and was the project of a joint-stock company. The drama has paid its exploiters but fitfully here, and the theatre has had many proprietors. It was at length bought by the Ballarat Temperance League in October, 1864, for £3000, from Rowlands and Lewis, then owners. The purchasers failed to pay the money, and Mr Walter Craig afterwards bought the building for less than £3000. He sold it to the present owner, Mr R. S. Mitchell, and at this moment (June, 1870,) Mr and Mrs Charles Mathews are performing there.

The Ballarat Philharmonic Society was formed on the 5th of March, 1858, at a meeting held in the Miners' Exchange, Mr D. Oliver in the chair, when Austin T. Turner was elected conductor, A. Fleury leader, D. Oliver secretary, A. Oliver treasurer, and Dr. Kupperberg, E. Towle, Bruun, Franz, Lake, Doane, Stoddart, Gates, Sayers, and Stower committee-men. The first performance was of the "Messiah" at the Montezuma Theatre on the 23rd of June, 1858, another concert being held the next evening in W. C. Smith's sale-room now Jones and Papenhagen's stores in Sturt street. The society died in 1863, but was afterwards revived as the present Harmonic Society with Mr J. Robson as conductor, to whom the original conductor has succeeded. It gives two performances annually, on Christmas Day and Good Friday respectively, and sometimes an intermediate concert. To its original repertoire the society has recently added opera in English. The Liederkranz and Liedertafel were German societies, and occasionally gave public vocal performances. In 1866 a Choral Society was formed with a person named Schmidt as conductor, but the society has disappeared.

There are three volunteer fire brigades. The Ballarat brigade was established in 1856 in Ballarat East, which part of the town has in past years suffered much from large fires, some sixty houses and a theatre having been swept away by one conflagration, and the same sites having over and over again been covered with the ashes of igneous ruin. The station of this brigade is in Barkly street ; there are 40 members and a complete apparatus. The Ballarat West brigade was established in 1859, after a previous brigade had been formed, only to disband again when the municipal council of the day refused to vote the supplies desired. There are 52 members and a complete apparatus ; the head station being in Sturt street. Now and for a long time both the elder brigades have been liberally subsidised out of the rates, though the insurance companies have never supported these valuable bodies as they ought to do. The Sebastopol brigade was formed in June, 1868. It is subsidised by the local borough council, but has not yet got into quarters of its own, though it has acquired a complete apparatus.

The volunteer corps of Ballarat Rangers is the outcome of a movement in the year 1857. On the 23rd of October, 1857, a meeting, convened by Mr Ocock, was held at Bath's, now Craig's hotel, Ballarat West, "to consider the propriety of establishing a rifle corps in this district." Mr A. Davies presided, Mr Cooper acted as secretary, and Messrs Davies, Wilkes, Coleman, Cooper, Daly, Ocock and Major Wallace (then sheriff), were appointed a committee to prepare a memorial to the government. On 21st of July, 1858, the consent of the Government to the enrolment of a corps was received, and on the 26th of July a meeting was held in the Shakspeare hotel, Main street, Ballarat East, Mr W. B. Rodier in the chair, when the name "Rangers" was rejected, and it was agreed that the name should be the "Ballarat Volunteer Rifle Regiment." The regiment was to consist of four divisions of infantry and two of cavalry. On the 9th August the first meeting of enrolled members was held at the Shakspeare hotel. At this meeting Mr Richard Belford, who had been then, or was soon afterwards, elected Lieut.-

Colonel, presided, and it was reported that there were sixty-five members on the roll. The rules were referred to the committee for revision, and on the 24th of August Mr Belford presided at another meeting, held at Bath's hotel, when Major Wallace, a half-pay officer of the line, was elected adjutant, Foster captain, Daly first lieutenant, and D. Sweeney second lieutenant of infantry ; and Alley captain, and A. Kelly and A. Davies first and second lieutenants of cavalry ; Mr Rodier acting as treasurer, and Mr Just as secretary. Mr Belford subsequently resigned office, and Major Wallace became the chief. The name of the corps also was changed to its present name, " Ballarat Rangers." The corps now consists of three companies of infantry ; Nos. 1 and 3 being manned in Ballarat West and East respectively, and No. 2 in Clunes and Creswick. The cavalry force of the colony, called the Prince of Wales Light Horse, is a distinct arm of the service now, and a troop exists in Ballarat. Of the Ballarat Rangers the present commissioned officers are :—1st Company : W. C. Smith, major ; J. Johnston, W. Henderson, and R. W. Musgrove, captains ; W. P. Whitcombe, assistant-surgeon. 2nd Company :—P. Keatch, captain, Creswick detachment ; B. Jessup, captain, and L. Le Gould, lieutenant, Clunes detachment. 3rd Company :—J. T. Sleep, captain commandant ; A. M. Greenfield, captain and adjutant ; J. Ivey, captain ; T. Hillas, assistant-surgeon ; A. J. Boulton, lieutenant. Of the Ballarat troop of cavalry E. C. Moore is captain, J. H. Mount lieutenant, and G. Nicholson assistant-surgeon.

The Gas Company is a private corporation, and was established in 1858, with a capital of £35,000. It has a freehold of about $3\frac{1}{2}$ acres in the heart of the town, a very large plant, with a gas-making power of 1,500,000 cubic feet per week, and storage for 210,000 cubic feet. The company has spent £65,000 on its works, and has over 50 miles of mains laid about the city. There were 1200 consumers at the end of 1868, that year's income being £24,689. The first board of directors were Messrs John Hepburn, M. J. Cummins, R. Belford, J. Gibb, R. B. Gibbs, E. A. Wynne, J. Stewart, M.D. The engineers have been Messrs Jones, father and son, and the secretaries Messrs Binsted and Figgis. Exactly 100 days after the turning of the first sod for the erection of the company's works, gas was first turned on at the main for the

supply of the town.   This opening of the works was performed by
Mr J. B. Humffray on Saturday evening, 17th July, 1858, and the
newspapers speak of the " brilliant devices " illuminating the gas-
works and other parts of the town as soon as the gas was turned
on.   Wesley Church was the first public building lit by this company.   A year or so before the company was formed there was gas
made by a Mr Courtis out of gum leaves, or gum leaves and oil or
fat mixed.   Courtis lit Christ Church, Bath's hotel, and other
places—his works being at the rear of Lydiard street buildings on
the slope between Albert street and Lydiard street.   The Gas Company reported at its first half-yearly meeting that it had purchased
" Courtis' pipes and customers " for £300.   About the same time
that Courtis was illuminating the western borough, gas of a similar
kind was made by Mr John Gibbs for the Charlie Napier Theatre
in Ballarat East.   An equivalent to the conversion of swords into
ploughshares and spears into reaping hooks was attained in laying
the first gas mains in Ballarat.   Some of the cartridges sent up by
the Government for use during the Eureka troubles were left in
store at the Camp, and were sold by the government auctioneer.
They were bought by Mr James Oddie who buried the powder and
sold the bullets to A. K. Smith, the contractor for the Gas Company, who used the lead in soldering the joints of the gas mains.

     The Ballarat Horticultural Society was formed in 1859.
On the 11th October of that year there was a meeting at Bath's
hotel, present : Messrs Ocock (in the chair), T. Lang, W. Elliott,
R. U. Nicholls, C. Tunbridge, B. Hepburn, and F. Binsted, when
preliminaries were discussed.   On the 18th of the same month
another meeting was held, at which Dr. Kenworthy (of Eureka
Stockade fame) presided.   The society was then formally constituted with Dr. Kenworthy president, Dr. Richardson, vice-president, T. Lang treasurer, F. Binsted secretary, and W. Elliott, G.
Smith, W. Appleby, R. U. Nicholls, R. Ocock, J. Tugwell, and W.
H. Foster committeemen.   The society held its first exhibition on the
25th of November, 1859, in W. C. Smith's sales-room in Sturt street,
near the south-east corner of Doveton street.   Now, the society has
for its president Mr R. U. Nicholls, for its vice-president Mr N.
D'Angri, and for its secretary Mr W. Harvie in place of Mr Elliott
(resigned).   There are 350 members on the roll, and the wide

expanse of the Alfred Hall is hardly large enough for the display of the society's exhibits at its spring and autumn shows.

Though we are only able to look as with a hurried glance at urban Ballarat, the local reader, looking with us as he reads, will perceive much more than is actually set down here. What he is told here will suggest to him much that is untold. We might have narrated somewhat touching the unsurpassed fertility of the agricultural tracts of Learmonth, Warrenheip, Bullarook, Smeaton, and Buninyong, whose farms are the glory of the district, and whose products fill our markets with the necessaries of life. The soil about Bullarook, Smeaton, and Learmonth has been compared to the inexhaustible deposits in the famous valleys of the Mississippi, so rich, deep, and mellow. The merino wool of Ercildoun is known in every market in the world for its unsurpassed, if equalled, fineness, strength, and beauty. Our Agricultural and Pastoral Society, and those of adjacent localities show, at their annual exhibitions, the marvellous rapidity of development which marks modern settlement. All the newest inventions in machinery and implements are in use by our pastoral and agricultural settlers, and finer grain is raised nowhere. In dairy produce improvement is wanted, but in horses, cattle, and sheep our breeders are famous. The Ballarat Agricultural and Pastoral Society assumed that style on the 3rd of May, 1865. Previously it was called the Ballarat Agricultural Society merely. The first record we find of it is a report of a meeting held at the George hotel on the 14th of June, 1856, Mr Robert Muir in the chair, when arrangements were made for the first ploughing match, which was held on Mr Baird's farm on the 10th of July, 1856. The records of the society show that on the 15th of August, 1856, a meeting was held in the old Council Chambers, in Sturt street, when Messrs R. Muir, J. M'Dowall, T. Bath, R. Dickson, Butchart, J. Stewart, M. D. Haydon, J. Baird, W. Sim, and Bilton were appointed a committee with R. Dickson secretary. Mr Archibald Fisken, of Lal Lal, is now president; Messrs Gilchrist, Cowan, and Bacchus are vice-presidents ; and Messrs Fisken, Morton, Dalgleish, and M'Intosh represent the society at the Victorian Board of Agriculture. The society held its first exhibition of produce on the 12th of March, 1859, in the old brick building called the Corn Exchange in the Market square. Learmonth and

Burrumbeet had a certain localisation of the society there until the 2nd of April, 1860, when a unification took place and the society was known as the Ballarat Society. In December, 1854, a proposition of union with the Western District Agricultural and Pastoral Society was made, but it was not carried out. The first National Grain Show was held in the Ballarat Society's yards on the 22nd and 23rd of October, 1868. The present secretary of the Agricultural Society, Mr Simon Morrison, states that he learns that the first ground broken in the Burrumbeet district was by Messrs Robertson and Ross, after whom came Messrs Strachan and Beaton. On the Learmonth side Messrs J. Medwell, G. G. Morton, J. Baird, J. M'Intosh, and Moore were the first. Medwell is said to have put the first post in the ground at Learmonth and turned over the first acre of ground for a crop of potatoes. The magnitude of the pastoral and agricultural interest of the district is reflected from that of the demands of the town markets. As an index to both it may be recorded here that the inspectors of the Ballarat cattle-yards and produce markets make the following returns of stock and produce passed through the yards and markets for the terms stated :—During the year 1869 there passed the cattle-yards 28,613 cattle, 2717 calves, 537,333 sheep, 50,731 lambs. During the first three months of 1870 of cattle there were 8334, calves 524, sheep 264,976, and lambs 15,896. During the first four months of 1870 there were passed through the produce market, of oats 167,152 bushels, of wheat 90,888 bushels, of barley 32,531 bushels, of hay 4466 tons, of potatoes 940 tons, of straw 564 tons.* During the first four months of 1870 the cattle-yards produced a revenue to the borough treasury of £1520 16s 11d, and the produce market a revenue of £792 1s. The trade in horses is almost entirely confined to the private yards of Hepburn and Leonard, O'Farrell and Son, and Macleod and Co. During the first four months of 1870 O'Farrell and Son sold 1107 horses, estimated average value £12 ; Messrs Hepburn and Leonard, during the same time, sold 780 horses, and Macleod and Co. 159, in all 2046.

---

* See Appendix F for Tables of Agricultural Statistics, showing that the country taken up by the first pastoral settlers around Ballarat now produces over a fifth of the entire grain crops of the colony.

The surplus live stock of the squatter which used to be boiled down for tallow is now converted, by several processes, into a valuable addition to the world's dietary and to the list of articles of exchange between the nations. Mr Barnes, deceased, of Ballarat, started a process by which meat was cooked by steam and then hermetically sealed in tins. Messrs Eddington and Co, established a meat preserving business at Windermere, near Ballarat, which was successful. On the 6th of June, 1870, a meeting was held at Craig's hotel, Ballarat, the Mayor in the chair, when it was decided to establish a Ballarat company. On the 9th of June another meeting was held at the same place, Andrew Anderson, J.P., in the chair, when the offer by Eddington and Co. of their plant was accepted by the Ballarat company, and it was decided to issue a prospectus forthwith. The company computes its preserving capacity at 100,000 lbs weekly, and expects to give employment to 250 people.

The Banks are all clustered in Lydiard street at or near the intersection of that street with Sturt street. The Bank of Australasia, Union, London Chartered, National, Colonial, New South Wales, Victoria, Commercial, and Ballarat Banking Company all have buildings more or less elegant and costly whose architectural prominence attracts the notice of every visitor to the town. The designs for these edifices are generally some phase of Italian.

The Mining Exchange at the " Corner," adjoining the Mechanics' Institute, was first opened as an exchange in October, 1857. It afterwards was used as a gold office by the Union Bank, and the Welcome Nugget was exhibited there. The premises were then leased by a firm of drapers, and subsequently they were altered and were opened in October, 1865, as at present.

The Gaol, at the southern end of Lydiard street, was commenced in 1856 by Gray, a builder, whose contract was for £9000. In 1857 a wooden stockade, surrounding the site, was blown down during a gale ; another was erected and then removed as useless. New extended plans for the gaol were prepared in 1858, and a second contract was begun in December of that year by Evans and Barker, builders, the contract being for £4000. Then, such is the genius of government architects for blundering, the plan was condemned, and Evans and Barker contracted for £9000 more to alter what had been done, so as to make the gaol plan radiating. Then there was a contract let to Williams and Young at £9000 for the erection of boundary walls and certain offices, the establishment as it now stands being completed early in 1862, at a total cost of between £40,000 and £50,000. The present Court-house, south of the goal, was opened in 1868; the older Court-house, injured by subsidence of the site, being now the School of Mines.

The Police and Warden's Offices are, as they have been ever since the removal from Old Post Office Hill, on the Camp Hill, now no longer a green mound, but cut up by streets and nearly covered with buildings. The present warden, Mr James Grant Taylor, and Mr Huyghue, the senior clerk, were both in the service here in the earliest days. The old wooden military barracks—where a remnant of the 40th Regiment remained until October, 1857, when that symbol of empire vanished from Ballarat, as it has more recently from Melbourne—has disappeared, and the site is now occupied by more sightly and more permanent buildings.

The present Post Office at the north-east corner of Sturt and Lydiard streets, is the sixth one erected since Ballarat became the resort of the gold-seeker. At first there was a "shanty" on Old Post Office Hill, as the top of Golden Point was named. Then there was a tent near the corner of Sturt and Camp streets. Then a wooden building at the south-west corner of Lydiard and Mair streets, where the Royal George hotel now stands. No street delivery of letters was granted till 1856, and old residents remember still the crowding and quarrelling to get at the old post-office window, the police having sometimes to interfere for the maintenance of the peace. In 1858 the present site was selected and an ugly office erected, which was opened on the 10th of September, 1858, the first night mail to Melbourne having been despatched from Ballarat on the 1st of July in the previous year. In November, 1859, the post-office, opened in September, 1858, was taken down and another built, which in its turn was removed for the erection of the present one in January, 1864. Offices, in continuation of the present post-office, have lately been built adjoining in Lydiard street, the new offices being intended for the treasury and electric telegraph departments of the Government here.

Electric Telegraphic communication was first had between Ballarat

M

and Melbourne on the second anniversary of the Eureka Stockade action.   The *Ballarat Star* of Tuesday, the 4th of December, 1856, contained the following announcement :—

The first telegraphic communication between Ballarat and Melbourne and *vice versa*, took place yesterday afternoon at twenty minutes past three o'clock. Last evening, about eight o'clock, the representatives of the Press on Ballarat were invited by Mr M'Gowan to witness the working of the telegraph.   There being no office accommodation ready at present, the spot selected was the last post near the Unicorn hotel on the Township.   A wire was carried from the post to a small testing machine placed on a stump at its base, and thence, to secure moisture, carried to the stream adjoining, which runs from Bath's claim [now Cobb's corner].   Mr Humffray, who was at the Melbourne station, trans. mitted the following remarks to Mr M'Gowan:—"The establishment of electric telegragh communication between Ballarat and Melbourne is a far more pleasing event to celebrate on the anniversary of the 3rd of December than stockades and massacres."*

At the intersection of Sturt and Lydiard streets is a monument commemorative of the tragical exploration expedition of Burke and Wills in 1861.   Plans for a monument were prepared as early as February, 1862, by Canute Andersen, at the instance of a committee of townsfolk, but the project slept till February, 1863, on the 7th of which month the foundation stone was laid by his Excellency Governor Barkly, with accompaniment of much display of processions of public bodies, benefit societies, parading of volunteers, flags, music, and addresses.   The commemoration was a special duty for this city, for Wills, the ardent and chivalrous youth who was brave Burke's second, had lived in Ballarat, where his father practised medicine for some years.   To do this duty well had been honorable, but with the picturesque celebration of the foundation laying the enthusiasm of the committee and the public died.   The money collected only sufficed to raise a sombre block of bluestone as the base of the projected monument and the unsightly mass lay there, a mark for the gibes of visitors, until March, 1866, when another committee was formed, and the work of discussing ways and means of finishing the structure re-commenced.   Money could not be collected to carry out the first

---

* Intelligence of the bestowal of Knighthood upon Mr Ronalds, the inventor of the telegraph in England, has led to the publication of the fact that the Mr Ronalds referred to was the brother of Mr Ronalds, who once had the Wendouree Nursery, in Ballarat, and who was also a man of considerable attainments.   Several nephews of the inventor are still in the colony.

and better design, and after more than a year's delay the present monument was decided on, the borough council voting money in aid of the work. Mr Andersen again prepared plans, and again gratuitously. The bottle with coins and documents deposited by Governor Barkly was exhumed, the original stonework having been removed, and on the 26th August, 1867, Thomas Davey, mayor of the borough, re-laid the bottle, and the present structure was thereafter erected. The monument now consists of an octangular stone reservoir, with a square pier in the centre, surmounted by a cast-iron basin and a fluted column of iron bearing four gas lamps, and an urn as a finial. Water is laid on from jets above the iron basin whence it flows, as from a huge inverted umbrella, into the stone receptacle beneath. In the masonry rising from the stone basin and supporting the iron superstructure, marble slabs are inlaid, on which are the following inscriptions :—

North side: In memory of the explorers who perished while crossing the Australian continent in the year 1861. East side: Robert O'Hara Burke, leader, died 30th June, 1861 ; William John Wills, second, died 30th June, 1861 ; Ludwig Becker, naturalist, died 29th April, 1861 ; Charles Grey, assistant, died 17th April, 1861. South side: Erected by the inhabitants of Ballarat.

The Caledonian Society was formed in November, 1858, and the first sports were held on New-Year's Day, 1859, on what is now known as the Eastern Oval. Mr Hugh Gray was the first president, and with him as judges on that day were Charles Roy, Donald M'Donald, and Donald Gunn, the pipers being Andrew Wattie and Donald Rowan. There had been two annual gatherings before this, the first being held in the ground at the rear of what is now Farrington and Co.'s Red Lion Brewery, at the south-west corner of Drummond and Webster streets. At this first gathering Edward Dufferin Allison, M.D., presided. The Buninyong Highland Society was formed about this time also. The Copenhagen Grounds, near the Royal Park, were for some years the Ballarat Society's trysting place, and now the gatherings are held in the Recreation Reserve in Eyre street. A wrestling club was formed in 1856, and some accomplished athletes exhibited feats in the Cumberland and Westmorland styles, as well as in the Devon and Cornish kinds of wrestling. These feats were first performed in the Charlie Napier

Theatre, and they afterwards formed a portion of the programme of events at several of the Caledonian Society's New-Year gatherings. Dugald M'Pherson, of Bungeeltap, is now the society's chief, Robert Glover is the president, and Hugh Gray is the secretary.

The Hibernian Society is a benefit society, formed in Ballarat on the 9th July, 1868. The first president was Mark Young; vice-president, Michael O'Grady; secretary, Michael Deegan; treasurer, John Berry. The present president is James N. Healy; vice-president, Michael M'Donald; secretary, Thomas M'Cormack; treasurer, John Berry. There are branches now all over Australia, and the parent society in Ballarat proper numbers 500 members. The members wear green scarves and other decorations, and sometimes give sports or concerts in aid of the public charities.

Since the days when the might of the British Empire was locally represented by a Commissioner in a drugget-lined tent, and a ragged regiment of hangers-on, composed of clerks and constables and cooks, Ballarat has been visited by Governors and a Queen's son. The Prince Alfred made a "joyous entry" on the 9th of December, 1867, when both town and suburbs held high holiday. After two or three days' stay, all full of feasting, dancing, levees, processions, presentations of addresses, laying memorial stones, or doing, or suffering, other things common to royalty and loyalty, His Royal Highness departed. The royal progress never dazzled by magnificence of princely generosity, but it cost the people a good deal of money and hero-worship; and the Prince the exercise of much politeness and patience. It is impossible to strike an accurate balance sheet in relation to events in which sentiment and imagination so largely mingle.

This large city we have now looked at in mere outline, for there is no space here to enumerate further details, or to count up its friendly society lodges, temperance organisations, and other associations for social or benevolent purposes, though we must mention the existence of a Magdalen House in Grant street, and a Ladies' Benevolent Clothing Society, acting partly independently and partly in conjunction with the Benevolent Asylum. The Temperance Society has a wooden hall in Humffray street, and a site in Lydiard street for a permanent building the foundation stone of which was laid on the 11th of December, 1867, by His Royal Highness Prince Alfred, in the presence of John W. Gray, president of the league, the Anglican Dean of Melbourne, the Hon. Thomas Learmonth, the Rev. J. J. Halley, and a large concourse of spectators. It must also be noted that there stands across the Yarrowee, in Grenville street, the Alfred Hall, the largest single room in the city, built of wood, and with great rapidity, at the joint expense of the borough councils of Ballarat West and East for the celebration and in commemoration of the visit of Prince Alfred. Nor must be omitted the railway, one of the best in the world. Its present terminus is in Lydiard street, Ballarat West, the Eastern borough having its station about half a mile from the terminus. The railway was opened on the 11th of April, 1862, and communicates with both Geelong and Melbourne. At the present moment the extension of the railway hence westward and north-westward is under discussion.

The country adjacent to the town of Ballarat is included in the territory governed by the Shire Councils of Ballarat, Buninyong, Grenville, Creswick, and Talbot, and the Road Board of Bungaree The functions of these bodies are analogous to those of borough councils but are rural rather than urban, the making of roads, bridges, and culverts in the rural territories they govern being their chief duties. Their revenues are derived, like those of borough councils, from rates and licenses with government subsidies in addition proportioned to the local revenue. The term "shire" does not mean here what it does in England, but merely indicates the particular rural territory administered by a given rural local body. The Road Board is a similar body with less powers, but it is probable that the boards will gradually disappear in being either absorbed in existing shire councils or in becoming shire councils themselves.

A comparison of Ballarat with Sandhurst and Geelong is desirable, but that we can only glance at. Sandhurst, the only gold-field's rival of this one, was created a municipality in April, 1855, and a borough in October, 1863. Its last year's assessment returned the rateable property at £114,158, and the income at £12,792, the tenements rated numbering 5206, revealing, on the basis of calculation adopted for Ballarat, a population of 23,427. The population and wealth of Geelong are not much superior to those of Sandhurst, and Ballarat ranks indisputably to-day as the second city in the colony.

The great spectacle presented to the eye of the visitor in these days is marked, to the inner eye of the old resident, with many deeply graved lines of toil and trouble.   Many a man has fought on bravely, year after year, against rocks, drifts, floodings, poverty, and almost despair.   Not quite despair, however, for else all had been lost.   There was still hope that at last gold would be reached, and that hope and his own native courage and independence have made to the miner the dry crust, the drink from the often-watered tea-leaves, the narrow cheerless tent, general privations, and sometimes sickness, the experience of long periods.   Such were some of the men, such the pluck that created this city.   Many of them obtained industrial victory, but many more only had " the consciousness of battle, and the resolve to persevere therein while life or faculty is left."   And many fell, as is the miner's too frequent lot, victims to foul air, treacherous earth-slips, water-bursts, personal recklessness, and mine-engendered diseases.*

Any one of the diggers of 1851 or 1852 who looks now upon this city cannot fail to reflect on the contrast of the present and the past.   To those who have remained here during all the intervening years the growth and transformation of the place have seemed less magical than to others, for they have been like those who witness the progress of their children from infancy to youth and manhood. The progress has been seen, but it has been only at special moments that the mind has grasped the fact that the child has disappeared and a man has taken the vacated place.   There has come a day when the mind has, by some quick process of projection upon the past, brought it into line with the present, and then the little child looks out from the larger, soberer, countenance of the man.   It is only for a moment, and then the younger vision disappears, save to the peering sight of memory that follows sadly, and clings lovingly to the fairer and fresher form that will not stay but retreats, with ever increasing velocity, as the new realities and duller cares of the present crowd in upon the mind.   So with the old digger now as he walks about these spacious gas-lit streets, where he no longer needs the candle in the broken bottle as a lantern after dark, but where every thoroughfare is adorned with crowding edifices, and is glittering with the blaze of a more artificial life, and the results of

* See Appendix G.

accumulated wealth. As he looks there come moments when all the scene dissolves into its original elements. Through all the rattle of street strife, over all the display of churches, towers, halls, and noisy warehouses, his eyes see something and his ears hear something invisible and inaudible to others. Over all the array of aggregated civic opulence and beauty, and its dark shadows of want and haggard strife for bread, there steal to him the silence of the beginning, the few white tents among the forest trees that are no more, the half-dozen columns of curling smoke from the camp fires, the round, oval, and square pits of the shallow-ground digger, the scanty patches of newly turned up golden soil ; and the fresh breeze, that came over the old silent odorous bush and its pastoral reaches of grass-land, breathes upon him instead of the noisome exhalations from the gutters and sewers and by-ways of the thickly peopled town. In another moment that scene, too, glides past. He is in an absorbing series of mutations, and the past moves along before him like a panorama in which every scene quickens the vision with the light of familiar sights and the warmth of pleasant memories. Streets of tents and shingle houses now stretch out in sinuous lines. They wind among hillocks of dirt and scant bush, upon the slopes and the flats and the hill-tops. Merry crowds of men work briskly at windlass and cradle and puddling-tub, and others ply the many trades and callings which the increased multitude have demanded with their gold, their fancies, and their necessities. Then night comes with its glittering camp fires, the crashing of felled trees, the discharges of multitudinous firearms, the song from tent and windlass, the laughter of the lucky or the careless, the music from the dancing saloon, the oath of the profane, the ribaldry of the drunken, the solemn, or jubilant, but sacred hymn of those who in that way wor-ship God. As he sits by the lessening light of his fire, with the pungent aroma of the grass-tree and the peppermint in the air about him, the gazer sees still other visions. In such moments, as our Australian Kendall has said—

> The phantom of his youth is apt to come,
> And flit before him as he sits alone,
> And float about him like a fitful dream,
> A sweet sad light amidst the gathering gloom.

He wearies at last and enters his tent. By the flickering light of the decaying embers of the open-air fire he fastens his canvass door, lies down upon his mattrass of gum-leaves, or grass, or straw, and is soon in dreamland.   He wakes to find it was, indeed, but a passing vision of what once was where this wide-reaching city now spreads out its arms and rears its "tower-encircled head."   All is changed, save the "evelasting hills" by day and the eternal procession of the stars by night, and all has come about by the enterprising industry evoked by the unconquerable love of gold.

The same power operates now as in the earlier days.   The working miner, with his pinched, weary, wan visage, his little bundle of food, and his billy of tea, going along the paved streets at midnight, past stately houses of business and luxury, to his dreary dirty labor below ground, and the jovial cigar-smoking well-fed speculator at the Corner in the broad noon-time are aiming at similar ends, though both, by sore stress of changed conditions, are now forced to indulge in less brilliant expectations.   Both men aim at that which every shaft, every engine, every pile of stones or waste of mullock and sludge, as well as every office and shop and field reveals—the desire of domestic comfort, the means of personal gratification, or the ability to give happiness to others.   Amidst all the mutations of the outward and visible the inward and invisible impulse remains the same.   Everything indicates one resistless force and points to one humble pioneer.

It is not our purpose to enquire what might have been the future of this locality, or of the colony, had the quiet and comparative solitude of pastoral settlement not been broken-in upon by the gold discovery with its sequent hordes of population, and all their busy and creative industry.   To those who come after us we shall appear as pioneers.   We, looking back to that which, in the swift evolution of events in this place, seems to us a distant past, think of the still earlier pioneers whom we followed hither.   And as we look we connect what they did with the yet unrevealed future of the colony. The gold-digger's work must ever be a factor in the great sum of Australian history.   It is not all, certainly, and its relative value must decline.   But, across the many-threaded tissue of our young national life, the wealth, and enterprise, and influence of the gold-fields run in a bright broad band of gold ; and, in the far-off future, the historical student, when he searches among the foundation-stones of empire here, will find the base of one of the strongest columns of national greatness inscribed with the names of the golden cities of Victoria, and, first of all, the name of the first and the richest— Ballarat.

In looking at these wide-spreading streets and thickly clustering dwellings, and green and beautiful oases of flowers and trees, and far reaching, well-tilled fertile lands, that lend their ornamentation to the general landscape, the thoughtful spectator naturally asks what it all signifies. Truly it is the outcome of the plodding thought of Esmond as he walked among the sierras of California and remembered the home he had left in Victoria. This three-boroughed city means, reflectively, a reminiscence and a hope lighting up the mind of that quiet gold hunter, and, more remotely, of alcadi Hargreaves also, as he sat in judgment upon delinquent diggers, or peered with questioning eye through the Golden Gate of the Pacific, Australiaward, and saw as in a vision, the golden glory of his late home rising like Aurora, radiant with light and beauty. It is but true that every field of yellow grain, every tree in our orchards that bends beneath its golden fruitage, every flower that waves its odorous beauty in our gardens, every line of grace and elegance in our stately piles of architecture, every demonstration of our civilisation, from the tall temples of religion to the costly shrines of literature and art and the richly stored houses of commerce, from the glittering carriages and the rustling silks of the luxurious rich to the crowding hosts that fight the daily battle of life's hard labor for bread, is but a homage to the enterprise of Esmond of Clunes, and his immediate followers, the discoverers of this the first and the richest of the gold-fields, and the battle ground of the political freedom of Victoria.

APPENDICES.

—⊷⊙⋇⊙⊷—

APPENDIX A.

The recommendation of the Committee of Parliament, prior to the
year 1857, was that £10,000 be divided amongst certain claimants,
and that Hargreaves should have £5000 and Esmond £1000, but
the Parliament reduced Hargreaves' vote to £2500 and Esmond's
to £500; the £10,000 recommended to the batch of claimants
selected being reduced one-half. There appears to have been a
motion carried by Dr. Greeves for a vote of £5000 to Hargreaves,
but that must have been a conditional vote or else a reversal
took place as the final award was only half the sum recommended by the Committee. Humffray, in July, 1857, enquired
in the Assembly why Esmond had not had the £1000; and
subsequently the Parliament did the tardy justice to the Clunes
discoverer of voting him the balance of the £1000 originally recommended. Ten years after Humffray's question as to Esmond,
namely—in July, 1857, Frazer moved in Hargreaves' interest and
asked the Assembly to vote him £2619, the balance of the sum
recommended by the Committee of Parliament. The motion was
refused by the House, but by a narrow majority, nineteen voting
for and twenty-one against the motion. Most people, probably,
will be of opinion that Hargreaves was amply rewarded, whatever
may be thought of the official recognition of Victorian discoverers.
To them the Governments and Parliaments appear to have shown
a rather wayward disposition, and to have distributed votes upon
principles not always very obvious. The persistent refusal of
recognition of Beilby's claim seems to be an instance in point, for
though he could not claim as a producer of gold he gives evidence
of priority as a revealer of its existence, and it is reasonable to pre-
sume that his revelation was one of the impulses that led to

explorations whose results are now before the world. The reward paid to Hiscock for the discovery of a locality which scarcely paid the miner as a gold-field, contrasts also with the non-recognition of Connor's and Merrick's parties who discovered Ballarat itself. If any principle should be held to have guided the Governments of the day, it may be assumed that valuable discovery, not barren discovery, first claimed attention. Yet Hargreaves, who discovered nothing in Victoria, got more than Esmond, and Beilby, who first announced discovery, and Connor's and Merrick's parties, who actually discovered Ballarat, have received nothing. It must be felt that if Hargreaves merited what he received some of the Victorian discoverers and revealers met with scant acknowledgment, and that amongst these last the unfortunate J. Wood Beilby, and the Golden Point discoverers, may be included.

(For Land Sales Appendix see Appendix D.)

APPENDIX B.

REPRESENTATIVES IN PARLIAMENT FOR BALLARAT FROM THE FIRST ELECTION IN 1855 TO THE YEAR 1870.

1855.   BALLARAT.

November 10.   Peter Lalor, John Basson Humffray, nominated to a seat in the old Legislative Council before the Constitution Act came into force.

BALLARAT WEST,

INCLUDED IN NORTH GRENVILLE UNDER THE CONSTITUTION ACT OF 16TH JULY, 1855,

1856.   ONE MEMBER.

October 3....   Peter Lalor returned unopposed.

BALLARAT WEST,

PROCLAIMED AN ELECTORAL DISTRICT IN 1859, WITH TWO MEMBERS TO REPRESENT IT IN THE LEGISLATIVE ASSEMBLY.

1859.   GENERAL ELECTION.

August 26.... John Robinson Bailey	1502
Robert Malachy Serjeant	1341
Duncan Gillies	963
William Frazer	878

1859.

November 5..   J. R. Bailey returned unopposed, having accepted office as Postmaster-General in the Nicholson Ministry.

1860.

November 12 J. R. Bailey	1502
D. Gillies	963

Mr Bailey had changed the office of Postmaster-General for that of Commissioner of Trade and Customs, and was again elected.

1861.		
August 2....	GENERAL ELECTION.	
	D. Gillies	1209
	Wm. Collard Smith.......................................	969
	John Phillips	790
1864.		
February 4 ..	Robert Lewis..	1092
	Wm. M. K. Vale...	952

This was to fill the vacancy created by the retirement of Mr W. C. Smith, January 18, 1864.

1864.	GENERAL ELECTION.	
November 3..	D. Gillies...	1443
	W. M. K. Vale..	1435
	Geo. G. Morton...	929
1865.		
September 11.	W. M. K. Vale..	1450
	James Service	1070

Mr Vale resigned his seat with a view of testing the feeling of the constituency on what was known as " The Constitutional Question," or " The Tack," and was re-elected.

1866.	GENERAL ELECTION.	
January 29..	W. M. K. Vale...	1443
	D. Gillies	1383
	T. Cooper...	1316
1866.		
August 6....	W. M. K. Vale..	1099
	Thos. Carpenter	558

Mr Vale having accepted office in the M'Culloch Ministry as Commissioner of Roads was re-elected.

1868.	GENERAL ELECTION.	
February 20..	W. M. K. Vale..	2251
	D. Gillies	2217
	H. B. Chalmers...	2021
1868.		
May 7.......	Chas. Edwin Jones	2663
	D. Gillies...	2363

Mr Gillies accepted office as Minister of Lands and Survey in the Sladen Ministry, and was defeated on presenting himself for re-election.

1868.		
July 30......	C. E. Jones...	2383
	W. M. K. Vale..	2325
	Joseph Attwood Doane	1750

Messrs Jones and Vale had accepted office in the second M'Culloch Ministry and were re-elected.

1869.		
March 27....	C. E. Jones...	2442
	J. A. Doane...	1082

Mr Jones resigned his seat and his office of Commissioner of Railways, and presented himself for re-election to test the feeling of the constituency on certain public charges which seriously affected his character as a member of Parliament. He was re-elected.

1870.		
May 10......	C. E. Jones...	2605
	W. M. K. Vale..	2046

Mr Jones had been expelled the House of Assembly for "corrupt practices." Mr Vale resigned his office as Commissioner of Customs and his seat in the Assembly, to contest the election with Mr Jones, "in the interests of political honesty," and was defeated.

1870.
May 22......

John James 2368
D. Gillies 2201
James Eddy.. 97

This was a contest for the seat vacated by Mr Vale.

1870.
April 25.....

Archibald Michie elected without opposition.

Mr James resigned to give Mr Michie the chance of a seat in the Assembly, Mr Michie having accepted office as Attorney-General in the third M'Culloch Ministry without having a seat in Parliament.

BALLARAT EAST,

1856.
October 10...

INCLUDED IN NORTH GRANT.

J. B. Humffray (elected) 690
Thos. Loader... 255
George Black 24

BALLARAT EAST,

PROCLAIMED AN ELECTORAL DISTRICT IN 1859, WITH TWO MEMBERS TO REPRESENT IT IN THE LEGISLATIVE ASSEMBLY.

1859.
August 26....

GENERAL ELECTION.

John Cathie 1136
J. B. Humffray... 1112
Richd. Belford... 556

1860.
December 7..

J. B. Humffray returned unopposed.

Mr Humffray had accepted office as Minister of Mines in the Heales Ministry.

1861.
August 2 ....

GENERAL ELECTION.

J. B. Humffray... 1245
Jno. Cathie 851
Andrew Semple 706
J. Christian Lyon 20

1864.
November 3..

GENERAL ELECTION.

C. E. Jones.. 702
Charles Dyte... 521
T. Corcoran 437
J. B. Humffray... 332
A. Semple.. 242
Samuel Deeble.. 107

1866.
January 29 ..

GENERAL ELECTION.

C. E. Jones.. 954
C. Dyte 939
T. Corcoran 670

1868.
February 29..

GENERAL ELECTION.

C. Dyte.. 1042
J. B. Humffray... 836
C. E. Jones.. 826
James Eddy... 777

APPENDIX C.

The physical difficulties in the way of printing were great in the early days of the gold-fields, as in the beginning of all new settlements. Some of these difficulties have been referred to in the text. Mr D. D. Wheeler, who was one of the founders of the *Standard* and *Trumpeter* and a shareholder in the first *Star* co-partnership, writes of the latter journal :—" Its first number was printed and published in the middle of a hurricane and inundation, with the printers nearly up to their middle in water." This was in what is now Bridge street before the levels were raised there. Mr Wheeler hazards the opinion that the *Nation* appeared more times than is stated in the text. He may be literally correct, but the facts are not materially different. As to the *Trumpeter* Mr Wheeler says:— " It was revived by its original proprietor early in January, 1856, and continued for about twelve months, when it lost its ground in competition with the *Star* and *Times*." In August, 1857, a little paper named *The Corn Stalk* was published by Mr J. Oddie, the editor being Mr J. N. Wilson. It continued about two years. The latest addition to newspaper literature here is *The Commonwealth*, a monthly publication, which appeared for the first time in March, 1870. It is edited by Mr W. Clarke, Grand Master of the Orange Lodges in Victoria.

APPENDIX D.

First sale of Ballarat lands, from the *Geelong Advertiser*, 25th August, 1852:—

Government Land Sale.—The first day's sale tooks place yesterday, in Mr. Forrest's room. The attendance was very numerous, and the bidding spirited. Not a single lot was withdrawn, and many allotments, as will be seen, realised very high prices. Lots 2 roods each; upset price, £4 per acre. Lot 6, section 1; Robert Reeves, £80. Lot 7, sec. 1; T. C. Riddle, £80. Lot 8, sec. 1; T. C. Riddle, £82. Lot 9, sec. 1; P. W. Welsh, £170. Lot 10, sec. 1; P. W. Welsh, £155. Lot 6, sec. 2; Fred. Brequet, £86. Lot 7, sec. 2; Benjn. Poulton, £95. Lot 8, sec. 2; Alex. M'Laren, £95. Lot 9, sec. 2; T. C. Riddle, £150. Lot 10, sec. 2; T. C. Riddle, £155. Lot 1, sec. 3; Jas. Austin, £170.

Lot 2, sec. 3; T. C. Riddle, £181. Lot 3, sec. 3; Alex. M'Kenzie, £130. Lot 4, sec. 3; Thos. Wilkins, £105. Lot 5, sec. 3; Fred. Brequet, £90. Lot. 1, sec. 4; P. W. Welsh, £235. Lot 2, sec. 4; T. C. Riddle, £270. Lot 3, sec. 4; Jas. Austin, 115. Lot 4, sec. 4; Wm. Frazer, £140. Lot 5, sec. 4; Arthur M'Leod, £120.

Second sale of Ballarat lands, from the *Geelong Advertiser* of 25th November, 1852:—

Upset price, £8 per acre.—79. Ballarat, 2 roods, county of Grenville, parish of Ballarat, allotment 1 of section 1; bounded on the north by Sturt street, on the east by Lydiard street; T. C. Riddle, £130. 80. Ballarat, 2 r., allot. 2 of sec. 1; bounded on the north by Sturt street, and on the west by Armstrong street; T. C. Riddell, £140. 81. Ballarat, 2 r., allot. 3 of sec. 1; bounded on the west by Armstrong street; James Wilson, £81. 82. Ballarat, 2 r, allot. 4 of sec. 1; bounded on the east by Lydiard street, and on the west by Armstrong street; R. Reeves, £69. 83. Ballarat, 2 r., allot. 5 of sec. 1; bounded on the east by Lydiard street, and on the west by Armstrong street; Thomas Bath, £70. 84. Ballarat, 2 r., allot. 1 of sec. 2; bounded on the north by Sturt street, on the east by Armstrong street; Thomas Powell, £105. 85. Ballarat, 2r., allot. 2 of sec. 2; bounded on the north by Sturt street, and on the west by Doveton street; James Noble, £89. 86. Ballarat, 2 r., allot. 3 of sec. 2; bounded on the east by Armstrong street, and on the west by Doveton street; A. R. W. M'Leod, £78. 87. Ballarat, 2 r., allot. 4 of sec. 2; bounded on the east by Armstrong street, and on the west by Doveton street; Thomas Bath, £60. 88. Ballarat, 2 r., allot 5 of sec. 2; bounded on the east by Armstrong street, and on the west by Doveton street; A. Glenn, £61.

Third sale of Ballarat lands, from the *Geelong Advertiser* of 2nd June, 1853:—

Ballarat, 2 roods.—Allotment 1, section 1; Thomas Bath, £250. Allot. 2, sec. 1; P. W. Welsh, £202. Allot. 4, sec. 1; withdrawn. Allot. 9, sec. 2; P. W. Welsh, £100. Allot. 10, sec. 2; Wm. Burrows, £110. Allot. 2, sec. 3; Wm. Burrows, £190. Allot. 4, sec. 3; Alex. Mackenzie, £105. Allot. 6, sec. 3; Fred. Hitchins, £105. Allot. 4, sec. 4. P. W. Welsh, £135.

Sale of Main road frontages.—We take from the *Ballarat Star* of the dates, generally omitting lots not actually sold. Many lots were temporarily withheld because of disputes or mining requirements:—

First Day.—Monday, 8th December, 1856.
BRIDGE STREET.

Allot. 1 block A, 10 perches ; upset, £65 ; valuation of improvements, £200 ; P. Huddart; withheld. Allot. 2 of A, 9 p.; upset, £58; val., £380; H. J. Bruun, upset. Allot. 3 of A, 21 p.; upset, £142; val., £720; T. Lang and Co., upset. Allot. 1 of B, 10 p.; upset, £65; val., £507; J. B. Humffray, upset. Allot. 3 of B, 4 p.; upset, £26; val., £170; Blackburn and Baird, upset.

Allot. 4 of B, 6 p.; upset, £40; val., £270; G. Jackson, upset.   Allot. 5 of B, 5 p.; upset, £32; val., £200; R. Dennis, upset.   Allot. 6, of B, 6 p.; upset, £45; val., £270; E. Aldrich, upset.   Allot. 7 of B, 5 p.; upset, £42; val., £220; Annie Reed, upset.   Allot. 8 of B, 11 p.; upset, £75; val., £900; R. and A. H. King, upset.   Allot. 9 of B, 8 p.; upset, £52; val., £550; M'Farlane and Smith, upset.   Allot. 7, block C., 8 p.; upset, £53; val., £150; C. E. Tolhurst, £125.   Allot. 11 of C, 9 p.; upset, £62; val., £800; G. Hathorne, upset. Allot. 14 of C, 9 p.; upset, £60; val., £436; Irwin, Wanliss, and Co., upset. Allot. 15, of C, 8 p.; upset, £52; val., £270; C. E. Tolhurst, £100.   Allot. 19 of C, 14 p.; upset, £82; val., £600; Kirtland Hogg, £90.   Allot. 20 of C, 12 p.; upset, £82; val., £1250; Robinson and Wayne, upset.   Allot. 7, block D, 3 p.; upset, £20; val., £30; W. Jeffrey, £41.   Allot. 8 of D, 6 p.; upset, £37; val., £75; J. and B. Ivey, £165.   Allot. 9 of D, 7 p.; upset, £47; val., £130; C. E. Tolhurst, £100.

In the foregoing, all the lots sold were bought by the occupiers, save the three bought by C. E. Tolhurst.

Second Day.—Tuesday, 9th December, 1856.
BRIDGE AND MAIN STREETS.

As on the first day, "the excitement was very intense; whenever a brisk bidding took place the victor was either cheered or hissed, according to the view taken of his conduct in the business." Almost invariably the sales at the upset price were to the occupiers in every day's sale, as at that time the premises were valuable, and the occupiers, as a rule, preferred rather to buy the freeholds than accept the heavy valuations from speculators.

Allot. 17 of D, 8 perches; upset, £52; valuation of improvements, £160; H. Farley, £180.   Allot. 9 of D, 4 p.; upset, £22; val. £70; W. Barham, upset.   Allot. 29 of D, 7 p.; upset, £47; val., £110; H. Farley, £170.   Allot. 30 of D, 6p.; upset, £40; val., £65; H. Farley, £170.   Allot. 3, block E, 15 p.; upsst, £110; val., £1200; Williamson and Hiles, upset.   Allot. 4 of E, 8 p.; upset, £80; val., £900; Gibson and Stewart, upset.   Allot. 5 of E, 17 p.; upset, £130; val., £800; T. and J. Bray, upset.   Allot. 3, block H, 9 p.; upset, £70; val., £1250; M'Cleverty and Leake, upset.   Allot. 4 of H, 7 p.; upset, £50; val., £325; Isaacs and Myers, £110.   Allot. 5 of H, 6 p.; upset, £40; val., £200; C. E. Tolhurst for E. Hunt, £150.   Allots. 8 and 9 of H, 12 p.; upset, £85; val., £800; J. R. Grundy, upset.   Allot. 10 of H, 5 p.; upset, £35; val., £170; J. Keene, upset.   Allot. 11 of H, 13 p.; upset, £100; val., £550; C. E. Tolhurst, £110.   Allot. 12 of H, 8 p.; upset, £60; val., £550; M'Callum, Neil and Co., upset.   Allot. 13 of H, 6 p.; upset, £45; val., £350; Sander Lazarus, upset.   Allot. 14 of H, 5 p.; upset, £35; val., £120; T. Jackson, upset.   Allot. 16 of H, 12 p.; upset, £80; val., £400; J. M'Cafferty, upset.   Allot. 17 of H, 6 p.; upset, £38; val., 230; R. H. Sutton,

£40. Allot. 18, of H, 6 p.; upset, £40; val., £250; Isaac Crawcour, upset. Allot. 19, of H, 6 p.; upset, £42; val., £130; H. Farley, £165. Allot. 20 of H, 5 p.; upset, £32; val., £130; H. Farley, upset.

Third Day.— Wednesday, 10th December, 1856.
MAIN STREET.

Allot. 21 of H, 8 perches; upset, £52; valuation of improvements, £280; H. Farley, upset. Allot. 22 of H; 14 p.; upset, £97; val., £1500; Mitchison Bros., upset. Allot. 23 of H, 17 p.; upset, £100; val., £530; H. Coe, upset. Allot. 24 of H, 7 p.; upset, £45; val., £100; H. Farley, £170. Allot. 25 of H, 5 p.; upset, £35; val., £40; H. Farley, £500. Allot. 2 of block J, 7 p.; upset, £47; val., £160; Atkins and Taylor, upset. Allot. 3 of J, 4 p.; upset, £22; val., £0; Atkins and Taylor, £155. Allot. 5 of J, 14 p. (Yarrowee hotel); upset, £100; val., £425; H. Walters, £250. Allot. 6 of J, 5 p.; upset, £32; val., £220; Price and Thomas, upset. Allot. 7 of J, 23 p.; upset, £155; val., £1250; A. E. and R. Alexander, upset. Allot. 10 of J, 7 p.; upset, £45; val., £250; C. E. Tolhurst, £70. Allot. 11 of J, 8 p,; upset, £52; val., £775; Graham Carrick, upset. Allot. 15 of J, 7 p.; upset, £45; val., £400; J. Webster, upset. Allot. 16 of J, 6 p.; upset, £40; val., £120; Lachlan M'Pherson, £70. Allot. 17 of J, 9 p.; upset, £57; val., 737; Henderson and M'Lean, upset. Allot. 18 of J, 6 p.; upset, £42; val., £240; Davis and Levey, upset. Allot. 20 of J, 7 p.; upset, £47; val., £300; Loyns and Foley, £100. Allot. 21 of J, 7 p.; upset, £47; val., £80; T. Blanchard for Sheppard, £110. Allot. 22 of J, 8 p.; upset, £55; val., £300; Susanna Walker, upset. Allot. 34 of J, 6 p.; upset, £40; val., £120; Ivory and Patchell, upset. Allot. 1 of block K, 5 p.; upset, £33; val., £150; H. Farley, £150. Allot. 2 of K, 6 p.; upset, £37; val., £210; H. Farley, £70. Allot. 3 of K, 6 p.; upset, £40; val., £350; J. Cox, upset. Allot. 4 of K, 7 p.; upset, £40; val., £570; W. Cooper, upset. Allot. 7 of K, 4 p.; upset, £27; val., £240; W. Bridges, upset. Allot. 11 of K, 6 p.; upset, £42; val., £600; H. Carpenter, upset. Allot. 12 of K, 6 p.; upset, £42; val., £350; W. Everett, upset. Allot. 13 of K., 7 p.; upset, £45; val., £150; H. Levey, £90. Allot. 14 of K, 5 p.; upset, £32; val., £150; H. Levey, upset. Allot. 15 of K, 9 p.; upset, £62; val., £620; D. Sweeney, upset. Allot. 16 of K, 13 p.; upset, £84; val., £850; Patrick Kean, upset. Allot. 17 of K, 7 p.; upset, £47; val., £450; J. Howell, £50. Allot. 18, of K, 4 p.; upset, £27; val., £175; D. Oliver, upset. Allot. 10 of K, 13 p.; upset, £89; val., £750; P. De Lorce, £260.

Fourth Day.—Thursday, 11th December' 1856
MAIN STREET.

Allot. 21 of K, 8 perches; upset, £57; valuation of improvements, £285; owner, upset. Allot. 22 of K, 8 p.; upset, £57; val., £140; S. De Young, upset. Allot. 25 of K, 8 p.; upset, £67; val., £175; C. E. Tolhurst, £110. Allot 26 of K, 10 p.; upset, £62; val., £100; H. Farley, £153. Allot. 27 of K, 5 p.; upset, £50; val., £547; Chambers Bros., upset. Allot. 1 of block M, 1 p.; upset, £10; val., £40; Rees, upset. Allot. 2 of M, 4 p.; upset, £42; val., £150; T. Murphy, upset. Allot. 3 of M, 7 p.; upset, £50; val., £400; Eyres and Newman, upset.

N

Allot. 4 of M, 7 p.; upset, £50; val., £85; Eyres and Newman, £190. Allot. 1 of block O, 2 p.; upset, £15; val., £110; Luin Sing, upset. Allot. 2 of O, 8 p.; upset, £52; val., £320; Wittkowski, upset. Allot. 4 of O, 5 p.; upset, £55; val., £200; S. de Crain, upset. Allot. 5 of O, 8 p.; upset, £55; val., £400; Harford, upset. Allot 6 of O, 6 p.; upset, £43; val., £200; J. Furlong, upset. Allot. 7 of O, 5 p.; upset, £36; val., £20; Jackson, £46. Allot. 8 of O, 6 p.; upset, £41; val., £110; A. Malcolm, upset. Allot. 9 of O, 3 p.; upset, £23; val., £200; Mumby, upset. Allot. 10 of O, 11 p.; upset, £75; val., £650; T. Murphy, upset. Allot. 11 of O, 6 p.; upset, £42; val., £350; W. Searle, upset. Allot. 12 of O., 6 p.; upset, £40; val., £350; Brannen and Wrigley, upset. Allot. 13, of O, 24 p.; upset, £165; val., £2270; Cowan, upset. Allot. 15 of O, 7 p.; upset, £50; val., £130; M'Clymont, upset. Allot. 16 of O, 5 p.; upset, £33; val., £60; W. F. Jordan, £80. Allot. 17 of O, 7 p.; upset, £50; val., £100; Davis and Edwards, £650. Allot. 18 of O, 6 p.; upset, £40; val., £650; Pleydell, Williams and Axford, upset. Allot. 22 of O, 6 p.; upset, £38; val., £220; D. Ronaldson, upset. Allot. 23 of O, 4 p.; upset, £28; val., £100; E. Speed, upset. Allot. 24 of O, 7 p.; upset, £45; val., £325; Bignell, upset. Allot. 25 of O, 3 p.; upset, £23; val., £130; Tyree, upset. Allot. 26 of O, 3 p.; upset, £21; val., £180; A. P. Bowes, upset. Allot. 27 of O, 12 p. (Horse Bazaar hotel); upset, £85; val., £750; A. P. Bowes, upset. Allot. 29 of O, 6 p., upset, £38; val., £250; R. B. Gibbs for the Bank of Australasia, upset. Allot. 30, of O, 6 p.; upset, £40; bal., £390; R. B. Gibbs for the Bank of Australasia, upset. Allot. 32 of O, 7 p.; upset, £50; val., £1000; R. and S. Gibbs, upset.

Fifth Day.—Friday, 12th December, 1856.

MAIN STREET.

Allot. 1 of block P, 8 perches; upset, £55; value of improvements, £360; Dowling, upset. Allot. 4, of P, 9 p.; upset, £63; val., £120; J. T. Shaw, £110. Allotment 5 of P, 4 p.; upset, £28; val., £80; J. T. Shaw, £70. Allot. 6, of P, 8 p.; upset, £57; val., £637; Lazarus, upset. Allot. 7 of P, 10p; upset, £70; val., £500; Jackson, upset. Allot. 9 of P, 16 p. (John O'Groat hotel) ; upset, £100; val., £800; Alex. Stewart, upset. Allot. 10 of P, 7 p.; upset, £50; val., £800; Evans and Co.; upset. Allot. 11 of P, 6 p.; upset, £42; val., £220; Sinclair, upset. Allot. 12 of P, 8 p.; upset, £53; val., £500; Samuels, upset. Allot. 13 of P, 8 p. (Devonshire House); upset, £50; val., £400; owner, upset. Allot. 14 of P, 12 p.; upset £84; val., £520; George Whitfield and Co., upset. Allot. 15 of P, 8 p.; upset, £57; val., £592; Bailey and Thomas, upset. Allot. 16 of P, 8 p.; upset, £31; val., £180; S. Alexander, upset. Allot. 17 of P, 14 p.; upset, £95; val., £300; H. Farley, £100. Allot. 20 of P., 7 p.; upset, £50; val., £275; Munro, upset. Allot. 22 of P, 14 p. (Police-court and store); upset, £90; val., £2000; Wm. M'Crea, upset. Allot. 23 of P, 23 p. (Montezuma Theatre); upset, £157; val., £8500; withheld. Allot. 1 of block Q (Royal Mail hotel) 8 p.; upset, £57; val., £1550, withheld. [This is at the corner of Main and Eureka streets, and is one of the few buildings in that part of the town that escaped all the fires of the igneous era.

Allotment 32 of O is the opposite corner, and has been burnt. The re-built premises are now a "marine store." The premises bought by the bank were burnt and only partially restored. No one would now give for the premises half the value in 1856.] Allot. 3 of Q, 27 p.; upset, £182; val., £1700; Rodier and Rowe, upset. Allot. 8 of Q, 9 p.; upset, £62; val., £727; Tuxen and Co., upset. Allot. 9 of 'Q, 9 p.; upset, £82; val., £400; Shepherd, upset. Allot. 10 of Q, 11 p.; upset, £72; val. £415; G. Braham, upset. Allot. 11 of Q, 7 p.; upset, £50; val., £150, H. Farley, £115. Allot. 12 of Q, 6 p.; upset, £42; val., £100; H. Farley, £100. Allot. 13 of Q, 12 p.; upset, £105; val., £650; S. Morwitch, upset. Allot. 14 of Q, 13 p.; upset, £87; val., £600; Montefiore and Co., upset. Allot. 15 of Q, 10 p.; upset, £65; val., £630; Stewart and Gaskin, upset. Allot. 16 of Q, 6p.; upset, £42; val., £150; G. Lesser, upset. Allot. 18 of 'Q, 8 p.; upset, £53; val., £220; W. B. Robinson, £120. Allot. 10, of Q., 9 p.; upset, £55; val., £300; A. M'Nicol, upset. Allot. 20 of Q, 25 p.; upset, £150; val., £3000; Cleve Bros., upset. Allot. 21 of Q, 8 p.; upset, £65; value, £550; Walker, upset. Allot. 22 of Q, 8 p. (Washington hotel); upset, £77; val., £2500; W. Emery, upset. Allot. 23 of Q, 8 p.; upset, £58; val., £420; W. Trewin, upset. Allot. 24 of Q, 7 p.; upset, £45; val., £250; Spencer, upset. Allot. 26 of Q, 8 p.; upset, £52; val., £800; Wittkowski, upset. Allot. 27 of Q, 6 p.; upset, £44; val., 180; Stubbs and Co., £70.

Sixth Day.—Saturday, 13th December, 1856.
MAIN STREET.

This day's sales were of the frontages between what is now Eureka and Durham streets. The miners were busy there then, and many lots were withheld on that account.

Allot. 4 of block R, 7 perches; upset, £46; value of improvements, £550; Cohen, upset. Allot. 7 of R; upset, £45; val., £300; owner, upset. Allot. 9 of R, 9 p.; upset, £58; val., £500; A. Morwitch, upset. Allot. 13 of R, 8 p.; upset, £52; val., £200; Barker, Clare and Co., upset. Allot. 16 of R, 5 p.; upset, £35; val., £90; H. Farley, £90. Allot. 17 of R, 10 p.; upset, £47; val., £630; Hobson and Warner, upset. Allot. 18 of R, 6 p.; upset, £42; val., £170; L. Hyman, upset. Allot. 19 of R, 6 p.; upset, £41; val., £250; C. Hewitt, upset. Allot. 20 of R, 6 p.; upset, £37; val., £250; S. Goodman, upset. Allot. 22 of R, 6 p.; upset, £37; val., £210; A. S. De Young, upset. Allot. 23 of R, 12 p.; upset, £70; val., £750; Harriman and Graham, upset. Allot. 24 of R, 5 p.; upset, £43; val., £450; J. Cantor, upset. Allot. 27 of R, 1 r. 8 p. (Charlie Napier Theatre); upset, £250; val., £5300; withdrawn. Allot. 28 of R, 18 p. (Criterion House); upset, £144; val., £3500; Hemingway and Jones, upset. Allot. 29 of B, 1 r. 21 p. (United States hotel); upset, £320; val., £8000; withdrawn. [The whole of the large and then valuable properties in allotments 27, 28 and 29 were swept off in the fires that so often devastated that part of the town. On the site of the theatre was built one of stone and brick. It is now a brewery. It and all the other two lots would not now realise the valuation on the old wooden United States hotel.] Allot.

N 2

33 of R, 5 p.; upset, £31; val., £170; H. Farley, upset. Allot. 34 of R, 7 p.; upset, £50; val., £200; Nemeceke, £110.

Seventh Day.—Monday, 15th December, 1856.

The frontages in this and the eighth days' sales lay between the Charlie Napier and the Caledonian Bridge. Several lots, including the Red Hill Bakery and Victoria hotel were withdrawn at this sale.

Allot. 35 of R, 7 perches; upset, £60; valuation of improvements, £375; J. Latham, upset. Allot. 36 of R, 10 p.; upset, £82; val., £500; A. Harris, upset. Allot. 37 of R, 6 p.; upset, £51; val., £200; F. Luhning, upset. Allot. 38 of R, 8 p.; upset, £66; val., £330; J. Palmer, upset. Allot. 39 of R., 6p.; upset, £51; val., £350; C. Boyd, upset. Allot 40 of R, 8 p.; upset, £66; val., £150; J. Cowell, upset. Allot. 9, block S, 10 p.; upset, £67; val., £600; Tidmash and O'Reilly, upset. Allot. 20 of S., 8 p.; upset, £52; val., £45; T. West, £90. Allot. 21 of S, 7 p.; upset, £50; val., £170; J. and T. Thomas, upset. Allot. 22 of S, 9 p.; upset, £40; val., £70; Ball, upset. Allot. 23 of S, 5 p.; upset, £30; val., £30; H. Farley, £35. Allot. 6, block T, 5 p.; upset £52; val., £10; H. Farley, upset. Allot. 7 of T, 5 p.; upset, £32; val., £35; H. Farley, £40. Allot. 8 of T, 5 p.; upset, £47; val., £100; W. F. Ellis, upset. Allot. 9 of T, 5 p.; upset, £48; val., £100; Forster, upset. Allot. 10 of T., 8 p.; upset, £52; val., 170; G. Whitty, upset. Allot. 11 of T, 8 p.; upset, £52; value, £250; M. Tartakover, upset. Allot. 12 of T, 7 p.; upset, £50; val., £440; W. Polkenhorne, upset. Allot. 13 of T, 6 p.; upset, £37; val., £90; H. Farley, £40. Allot. 14 of T, 6 p.; upset, £37; val., £160; J. Miller, upset.

Eighth Day.—Tuesday, 16th December, 1856.

Allot. 15 of T, 5 perches; upset, £32; valuation of improvements, £40; P. Hauser, upset. Allot. 16 of T, 3 p.; upset £52; val., £160; E. Beibetz, upset. Allot. 17 of T, 3 p.; upset, £22; val., £50; A. Dusautoy, upset. Allot. 18 of T, 4 p.; upset, £27; val., £15; J. Crawford, upset. Allot. 19 of T, 9 p.; upset, £60; val., £220; T. West, upset. Allot. 20, of T, 15 p.; upset, £102; val., £1500; Wilson Bros. and Co., upset. Allot. 21 of T, 3 p.; upset, £17; no improvements; Wilson Bros. and Co., upset. Allot. 22 of T, 7 p.; upset, £47; val., £120; J. Levey, upset. Allot. 23 of T, 6 p. (A. Arbuthnot); upset, £35; val., £35; no offer. Allot. 24 of T, 5 p.; upset, £28; val., £90; N. Martin, upset. Allot. 25 of T, 8 p.; upset £46.; val., £75; M. Metzendorff, upset. Allot. 26 of T, 7 p.; upset, £30; val., £70; C. R. Thatcher (the well-known singer, familiarly called "the inimitable"), upset. Allot. 27 of T., 6 p.; upset, £55; val., £75; J. Egan, owner; no offer. Allot. 1, block U, 17 p.; upset, £80; val., £560; W. T. Jackson, upset. Allot. 3 of U, 8 p.; upset, £46; val., £325; J. Reid, upset. Allot. 4 of U, 14 p. (Hope restaurant); upset, £78; val., £260; owner, upset. Allot. 5 of U, 6 p.; upset, £32; val., £70; Isaac Johnston; no offer. Allot. 6 of U, 7 p.; upset, £38; val., £150; Shaw and Thomas, upset. Allot. 7 of U, 17 p.; upset, £92; val., £75; A. Oakey, upset.

Tuesday, 8th September, 1857.

On this day were sold lots in the triangular block G, Bakery Hill, bounded by Victoria, Main, and Humffray streets, and lots in blocks I and N, in Victoria and Humffray streets. All but one lot were sold at the upset price. We give a few of the best known sites in this and subsequent days' sales :—

8th September.—Lot 3 of G, 20½ perches (Exhibition Mart); upset, £200; valuation, £4000; Robertson, M'Intosh, and Smith. Lot 14 of G, 7 1-10 p. (London Chartered Bank); upset, £58; val., £800; Bank. Lot 26 of G, 10¾ p. (Six Days' Store); upset, £48; val., £500; Lilley and Miller. Lot 7 of N, 11 2-4 p. (Temperance Hall); upset, £42; val., £600; trustees. Lot 8 of N, 13 4-5 p. (old St. Paul's Church); upset, £51; val., £750; withdrawn. 3rd December.—Allot. 2 of E, 14 4-10 p. (Exchange hotel, Bridge street); upset, £98; val., £1400; P. Yott. Allot 1 of F (North Grant hotel), 9 6-10 p.; upset, £59; val., £2000; Smith and Diggins. Allots. 1 and 2 of H, 11 p.; upset £100; val., £3500; Bradshaw, Salmon, M'Cleverty, and Leake. 10th March, 1858.—Allot. 26 of J (Hope Bakery, corner of Barkly and Main streets), 19 p.; upset, £130; val., £1200 ; P. Mason. Allot. 2 of L, 10½ p. (Beehive House, at opposite corner); upset, £73; val., £1300; Alexander Bros. 3rd March, 1859.—Allot. 29ʙ of R, 24 8-10p. (United States hotel, or Victoria Theatre, Main road); upset, £121; val., £2000; George Hathorne.

The first sales on Soldiers' Hill took place in 1859, and from 1855 downwards sales of lots surrounding the first sales of 1852 in the West, and 1856 in the East, were held. Some of the frontages in the Main road realised prices at the rate of £12,000 per acre. Early in 1855 several sales of frontages in Ballarat West were made by the Government. At the same time lands previously bought changed hands at improved rates. Messrs J. and T. Oddie reported on the 18th December, 1855, the sale of 15 acres (Green's paddock, Webster street,) by S. Irwin for £750, 15½ acres by T. Brown for £967 10s, 2 acres on the Creswick road for £202, ¼-acre in Doveton street for £95, 30 feet in Dana street at £4 per foot, for ¼-acre lots fronting Wendouree Swamp at £58 each, and ¼-acre in Armstrong street, at £264. The auctioneers also reported on that day an improvement in the building business, and " a number of stores and neat gothic-looking houses in course of erection."

APPENDIX E.

In the Legislative Assembly, on the 31st of May, 1870, while the House was discussing a vote for the Nelson, ship, Mr Frazer said " he had been informed that the flag unfurled on board the Nelson was the identical flag that was flying over the Eureka Stockade at the time of the riot. (Laughter.) The flag in question was subsequently stolen from the court, and had never since been found." This is possible, perhaps, but hardly probable. The flag was hauled down by trooper, or policeman, John King, who is now living in or near Warrnambool. King was a native of Mayo, Ireland, and he gave the flag, or what was left of it—for it was much torn, and was also lessened by relic-hunters taking bits of it—to Inspector P. H. Smith, who also was a Mayo man. Smith died in Melbourne, but where the flag is the writer has not been able to learn. The colored title page of this History displays a representation of the insurgent flag as hoisted at the Stockade. It may be stated here that the news of the attack on the Stockade reached Melbourne on the same day while Governor Hotham and Secretary Foster were attending divine service at St. James' Church, in Melbourne. Attorney-General Stawell and others were seen earnestly talking near the church, waiting for the Governor, and when his Excellency came out Foster went his way home, the Attorney-General and other of the Ministers accompanied the Governor to the Government printer, Mr John Ferres, and urged him at once to issue a placard. This placard was printed and posted about the city on the Sunday, although dated as on the previous day. This placard was the one in which the Governor calls on "all British subjects to abstain, not only from identifying themselves" with " evil disposed persons," but "to render support and assistance to the authorities." The placard by the French consul was printed also on the Sunday. At the Governor's special and personal request also, on the 6th of December, a placard was issued with the words in large letters "Sevastopol is taken." This was declared to be a stratagem to divert public attention from a meeting to be held on that day in Melbourne for expression of sympathy with the Ballarat diggers. (*Vide* page 79 of this book.) Many of those who were officially close

to Sir Charles Hotham in those days were warm in his praise.   They
spoke of him as "a splendid fellow," and asserted boldly that he
was misled by bad advisers.   In further reference to the Eureka
business, it may be mentioned that a writer in the Ballarat *Evening
Post* on the 10th June, 1870, says :—

On the 30th of August, 1867, I paid to one of the members of the committee,
who were collecting subscriptions at the time for repairing the Eureka monument, a small sum, which I collected from a few friends, for the purpose of
having the name of William Clifton, of Somersetshire, inscribed on the said
monument ; yet now, after two years and ten months, it has not been done.
William Clifton's name could not be found out at the time, as he passed, and
was generally known, by the name of "Specimen Bill."   He died a day or
two subsequently to Captain Wise, the last victim of that fatal morning that
expired in the hands of the Government.   He was personally known to one of
our present members for Ballarat East, J. B. Humffray, Esq., who visited him
the time he lay wounded at the Camp.

With regard to the attack on the Stockade, the writer has a
letter signed "John Neill, late of the 40th Regiment," and dated
from Devil's Gully on the 7th of February, 1870, or shortly after
the first publication of the preliminary History as a supplement to
the *Ballarat Star* in January, 1870.   Neill thus describes the
approach of the troops and what followed, his grammar only being
amended and redundant matter omitted :—

As a military man, and one who took a most prominent part in all the
military movements of that day, I beg leave to offer a remark upon the statement made by the Government officer of the Camp.   The small force consisted
of detachments of the 12th and 40th Regiments, and a few troopers and
foot police, the whole under the command of Captains Thomas and Wise, and
a Lieutenant of the 12th—I forget his name.   The order to fall-in and be silent
was given, and when Captain Thomas had spoken a few words we were put in
motion, led by Captain Wise.   The party had not advanced three hundred
yards before we were seen by the rebel sentry, who fired, not at our party, but
to warn his party in the Stockade.   He was on Black Hill.   Captain Thomas
turned his head in the direction of the shot, and said—" We are seen.   Forward,
and steady men !   Don't fire ; let the insurgents fire first.   You wait for the
sound of the bugle."   When within a short distance of the Stockade, the insurgents fired.   Captain Wise fell, wounded mortally.   The same volley wounded
the lieutenant of the 12th, already spoken of, and three of his men; two killed
one wounded of the 40th—Privates Michael Roony, Joseph Wall, killed ;
William Juniper, badly wounded.   The Camp officer says the police were the
first to enter the Stockade.   He is wrong.   There was not one policeman killed
or wounded during the whole affair.   When Captain Wise fell the men cheered,
and were over in the Stockade in a second, and then bayonet and pike went to

work. The diggers fought well and fierce, not a word spoken on either side until all was over. The blacksmith who made the pikes was killed by Lieut. Richards, 40th Regiment. Honor to his name: he fought well and died gloriously. It was rumored that at that time the police were cruel to the wounded and prisoners. No such thing. The police did nothing but their duty, and they did it well for men that were not accustomed to scenes of blood or violence. To my knowledge there was only one wounded man despatched, and he kept swinging his pike about his head as he sat on the ground. His two legs were broken, and he had a musket ball in his body. He could not live, and it was best to despatch him. His name was O'Neill, a native of Kilkenny, Ireland. I heard this statement from a sergeant of police, and I know it was correct.

It is but just that it should be stated that, in reply to Raffaello's statement that Kennedy took up the cause of the diggers out of mere regard for Scobie, Kennedy avers, in a letter in the *Ballarat Star* of the 22nd December, 1856, addressed to Raffaello :—

If suffering and loss be a proof that I have something more than talking heroism, or a prejudicial love for my country or countrymen, I am the man that can give that proof. Last year the same Thomas Kennedy sacrificed £1800 for the cause of the diggers alone ; but that is not all, I have sometimes wrought ten hours a day for three days running on bread and water on account of these rows.

Kennedy generally defends himself in his letters against Raffaello's criticisms, and says, as to the license-burning meeting, that he refused to join that movement unless 4000 came forward to join the League. He then says :—

But, Raphaello, I well remember on that day that when you came forward and addressed the public (to use your own phraseology towards other people in page 59th), "such suicidal rant" was used by you that day that I was compelled to take you by the arm and conduct you from the front of the platform to nearly the middle of it, and I believe from that moment your Italian blood was aroused, and in some measure interprets some part of your work.

Most people who knew Raffaello will be ready to say that Kennedy's story is not very improbable.

APPENDIX F.

From the Registrar-General's returns for the year ending 31st March, 1870, we take the following tables, showing the number of holdings, total areas held, areas under tillage, and the produce raised within the territory around Ballarat, that is within the shires of Ballarat, Buninyong, Creswick, Grenville, and Talbot, and the Road Board District of Bungaree. The first table gives in acres the holdings, areas, tilled land, and the areas cropped with wheat, oats, barley, hay, and potatoes. The second table gives the aggregate yield of each grain crop in bushels and of hay and potatoes in tons :—

LOCALITY.	Holdings.	Areas.	Under Tillage.	Wheat.	Oats.	Barley.	Hay.	Potatoes.
Ballaratshire	775	86,376	55,945	16,127	11,296	1,670	14,678	1,693
Buninyongshire	1,078	82,508	17,647	3,137	7,028	467	2,729	2,304
Creswickshire	679	92,045	42,223	21,560	10,064	1,914	3,022	1,533
Grenvilleshire	372	27,007	5,199	627	1,091	72	2,177	369
Talbotshire	359	38,824	11,489	5,776	2,892	140	1,789	55
Bungaree Road Board	451	23,748	7,501	1,502	3,127	235	695	1,003

LOCALITY.	Wheat.	Oats.	Wheat.	Rye and Bere.	Hay.	Potatoes.
Ballaratshire	377,497	285,751	46,183	6,146	23,997	3,617
Buninyongshire	82,426	208,612	14,115	3,151	4,581	6,129
Creswickshire	531,689	278,637	60,566	6,074	4,651	3,204
Grenvilleshire	12,581	29,794	2,208	—	3,744	627
Talbotshire	117,308	69,737	3,398	20	2,857	110
Bungaree Road Board	45,551	106,169	7,504	2,645	1,614	3,372

The returns show that the total area under tillage in all the shires and road districts of Victoria was 797,903 acres, so that over one-sixth of the tilled land of the colony was in the Ballarat district. It is seen, too, that the same district produced over one-fifth of the entire crops of the colony. This will be seen more clearly in the following table wherein are shown in bushels the totals for the whole of the shires and road boards, and those for the six local board districts which go to make up what is generally known as the Ballarat district. The totals for the colony include returns from boroughs and corporate towns but they are so small as not to appreciably affect the comparison, and we shall therefore regard the shire and road board totals as giving the total for the colony :—

LOCALITY.	Wheat.	Oats.	Barley.	Rye and Bere.	Hay.	Potatoes.
Whole Colony	5,580,614	3,667,789	680,872	65,297	210,862	123,441
Ballarat District	1,167,052	978,700	133,974	18,036	41,444	17,059

In further illustration of the magnitude of the consumption of pastoral produce here, the subjoined figures are given:—

Place and Year.	Cattle.	Calves.	Sheep and Lambs.	Swine.
London, 1867	240,650	18,665	1,373,000	25,425
New York, 1868.................	298,480	82,940	1,400,620	976,508
Ballarat, 1869....................	28,613	2,717	588,064	14,000*

The London returns are from " Whittaker's Almanack," and the New York returns from the *New York Tribune.* It is seen that the Ballarat consumption of sheep and lambs is nearly half that of either the English or the American metropolis, but it must be stated that the London consumption is only partly reflected in the above return, since vast quantities of meat in carcase are sent from nearly all parts of the United Kingdom to the London market. Still the enormous relative consumption in Ballarat shows the better condition or larger purchasing power of the people here in relation to what is called " butchers' meat," wages being higher and prices lower here than in England.   This table will be better understood if we say that the number of sheep thus shown to pass through the markets of London, New York, and Ballarat gives the following proportions of annual consumption :—In London, less than half a sheep per head of population; in New York, about $1\frac{1}{2}$ sheep per head ; in Ballarat, over $14\frac{1}{2}$ sheep per head of population annually.   We append market price returns, as published in the *Ballarat Star* of the 17th of June, 1870, in Ballarat, premising that a general depression in mining and commerce exists and has somewhat affected the markets :—

WHOLESALE MARKETS.

Flour and Grain.— Flour, £10 5s to £10 10s per ton; wheat, 4s 4d to to 4s 6d; feed oats, 3s 3d per bushel; bran (20 lb. per bushel), 11d, bags in; pollard, 1s per bushel; maize, 5s 6d.

RETAIL MARKETS.

Fruit and Vegetables.—Fruit was plentiful during the week, as were also vegetables, business, however, being dull.   The following are the prices ruling:—Apples, 4d to 6d per lb.; pears, 3d to 4d per lb.; boquets, 3d to 6d each; turnips, 3d per bunch; carrots, 2d per bunch; parsnips, 2d per bunch; cabbages, 2s to 4s per dozen; onions, 7s to 8s per cwt.; celery, 2d to 4d per head; horse-radish, 3d to 4d per head; herbs, radishes, lettuces, cress, 1d to 2d per bunch; oranges, 9d to 1s 6d per dozen; lemons, 1s 6d per dozen.

---

* 13,479 pigs passed through Messrs O'Farrell and Son's Yards alone in 1869, selling at an average price of 25s 6d each.

Meat Market.—The supply of beef and mutton was good, all being of first-rate quality. Mutton, 2d to 4d per lb.; beef, 3d to 5d per lb.; steak, 4d to 7d per lb.; corn beef, 20s per cwt.; veal, 4d to 6d per lb.; pork, 8 to 9d per lb.

Poultry, Game, and Fish.—Fish and poultry were plentiful during the week, but no game of any description. The prices were:—For young poultry, 3s to 7s per pair; tame turkeys (young), 7s 6d to 20s per pair; geese, 4s to 6s each; ducks (tame), 6s to 8s per pair; wild rabbits, 1s to 1s 6d per pair; flathead, 6d per lb.; whiting, 1s per lb.; pike, 1s to 2s each; ling, 8d per lb,; other fish, from 6d to 9d per lb.; crayfish, 1s to 2s 6d each. Business was very dull during the week.

Dairy Produce.—The quantity forward of good quality was very light. Fresh butter, 1s 4d to 1s 8d per lb.; potted do., 1s to 1s 5d per lb.; eggs, 2s 4d to 2s 6d per dozen; milk, 7d per quart; colonial cheese, 8d to 1s per lb.

Wholesale Fruit Market.—Fruit was plentiful during the week, especially oranges. The prices are as follow:—Apples, 12s to 14s per case; potatoes, £3 to £3 10s per ton for district grown; Warrnambool, £4; onions, £6 10s to £7 10s per ton; lemons, 18s per case; oranges, 9s to 10s per case.

The same journal in its monthly summary for England on the 16th June, 1870, said:—

The following are our quotations for the four weeks:—First week—Best manger hay, £2 15s to £3 5s; chaff do., £2 5s to £2 12s 6d; oaten straw, 25s to 30s; wheaten, 20s to 25s per ton; oats, 3s to 3s 1d; seed, 3s 6d; milling wheat, 4s 3d to 4s 4d; seed, 4s 9d to 5s; English barley, 4s 6d; Cape, 2s 10d to 3s; seed, 3s 6d; rye, 3s to 3s 3d per bushel; potatoes, £2 15s to £3; carrots, £2 5s; flour, £10 5s per ton; bran, 10d; pollard, 11d per bushel. Second week—Hay, best manger, £2 10s to £3; chaff do., £2 2s 6d to £2 10s; straw, 25s per ton; feed oats, 3s 1d to 3s 3d; seed, 4s; milling wheat, 4s 3d to 4s 4d; seed, 5s to 5s 3d; English barley, 4s 6d; Cape, 2s 10d to 3s; seed, 3s 3d; rye, 3s 3d per bushel; potatoes, £2 15s to £3; flour, £10 5s per ton; bran, 11d; pollard, 1s 1d per bushel. Third week—Best manger hay, £2 10s to £2 15s; chaff do., £2 to £2 10s; straw, 20s to 25s per ton; oats, 3s to 3s 3d; seed, 3s 6d to 4s; wheat, 4s 3d to 4s 4d; seed, 5s; English barley, 4s 3d to 4s 6d; Cape, 2s 10d to 3s; rye, 3s to 3s 3d per bushel; potatoes, £2 15s to £3; flour, £10 5s per ton; bran, 11d; pollard, 1s 1d per bushel. Fourth week—Best hay, £2 15s to £3 5s; chaff do., £2 7s 6d to £2 12s 6d; straw, 25s to 30s per ton; wheat, 4s 4d to 4s 5d; seed, 5s to 5s 3d; oats, 3s to 3s 3d; seed, 4s; English barley, 4s 6d; Cape, 3s to 3s 3d per bushel; potatoes, £2 15s to £3; flour, £10 5s to £10 10s per ton; bran, 10d to 11d; pollard, 1s per bushel.

APPENDIX G.

While others have risen to wealth and position on the results of his thought among the sierras of California, and towns and cities

have sprung into existence as creations of the gold discovery,
Esmond is working to-day as a laboring man for wages at the
very spot where he first found gold in Victoria.   A dozen years
ago he asked for a bit of land at Clunes, and it was refused,
though the Ballarat Mining Board supported his request.   On the
3rd of September, 1858, the *Ballarat Star* wrote :—

> With regard to the application of Mr Esmond, we think the Mining Board
> showed a very laudable desire to give to the first finder of gold in Victoria some
> recognition of his valuable services, and the Government would only be acting
> as the exponents of the general opinion of this district if it were either to
> advise the Warden to make the grant, or at once to issue to Mr Esmond a lease
> of the area he seeks to obtain.   Whatever Mr Esmond may have done for
> Victoria—and we have only to look around us, everywhere to perceive the
> magnificent results of his discovery—he has done but little for himself.   He is,
> in a word, a poor, struggling man ; and one, too, approaching the season of
> "the sere and yellow leaf."   Let him, then, for justice's sake—for pity's sake,
> we had almost said—have a reach of the very reef he discovered, and, by dis-
> covering, made a million fortunes for others, while aiding Britain in her wars,
> and Britain's sons in laying the foundation of "an Empire in the South."

APPENDIX H.

The low lands of Ballarat East have always been liable to inundation.   On the 8th of June, 1863, the *Ballarat Star* said :—" Ever
since the diggers of ten years ago pitched their tents along the line
of the squatters' bullock-dray tracks through the Buninyong Gully,
the Main road has been a difficulty.   No end of money and curses
have been expended upon it."   This was said apropos of a flood
then just gone down, which had inundated the Main road and
adjoining localities two or three feet deep.   On the 16th December,
1855, there was a summer flood, for both in summer and winter the
locality has often been thus visited, loss of human life occurring on
several occasions.   In this flood three men and one woman were
drowned at Magpie, the rush there then being near its height.
The last flood took place on Saturday, the 16th October, 1869, and
was one of the most disastrous of a disastrous series, in which many
scores of thousands of pounds worth of property has been destroyed.

Indeed, the elastic recuperativeness of the town, and of the Eastern half especially, has not been shown more emphatically than in the frequent scourges by fire and flood which it has suffered, and from which it has so bravely recovered.

APPENDIX I.

The rush to Magpie in 1855, when the shallower portions of Frenchman's and White Horse were worked, was a stirring episode in local history. A canvas and shingle town, with 4,000 or 5,000 inhabitants, sprang up there, for the ground was rich in many places. One shaft yielded 100 ounces off the bottom; one claim, and the areas then were small, yielded 130 lbs., another 120 lbs.; one tub of dirt off the reef gave 11 lbs. of gold, and the papers of the time say share gambling was then prevalent. As the leads were traced across the valley to Sebastopol Hill the Magpie town disappeared, and not a vestige is now left of all the busy life there fifteen years ago.

APPENDIX J.

In the *Ballarat Star* of the 11th October, 1855, appeared the following obituary notice :—

DIED.—After a long, tedious, and absurd existence, the Local Court of Ballarat breathed its last yesterday morning. The funeral oration to be preached by Signor Carboni Raffaello on the site of the late Eureka Stockade next Sunday. N.B.—The congregation are requested to bring a pinch of snuff for the preacher.

This was in reference to the resignation of Messrs Milligan, Yates, Donald, Wall, and Ryce, because the Government had not supported the court in its battle with the lawyers. The resignations led to the breaking up of the Court, and a vote of thanks to the chairman Daly, opposed, however, by the uncompromising Raffaello.

APPENDIX K.

Vern's courageous eccentricities of a verbal and caligraphic kind have been amply demonstrated. Here are four original letters lying before us now, which we re-print here, with all their underlinings and other original features. They appeared in the *Ballarat Star* at the time of the dates :—

Black Lead, 2 | 10 | 56.

(To the Editor of The Star.)

Sir,—The *Geelong Advertiser* of the 22th of Sept. had inserted in its Ballarat correspondence 4 charges, two of wich reflected severly on the character of Mr. Humffray. I should not have taken any notice of those charges had not, in your issue of yesterday, Mr. Amicus—sive Denovan again reiterated the same. I now feel it my moral duty to contradict those charges, however much I may be blamed for doing so, for, as you well know, Mr. Editor, my motto has always been "Fiat justicia et si pereat mundus," and for that simple reason I can not allow Mr. Humffray's character to be blasted innocently, or allow his opponents to obtain votes under false pretences wich otherwise would tell for Mr. Humffray. The charges to wich I refer are, first—"That Mr. Humffray excited the diggers to rebellion, and afterwards deserted them." The second is—"That Mr. Humffray was sumonsed to appear as witness against the State prisoners." These charges are calculated to influence a great many votes now on Ballarat— namely, the old remnant of the physical-force party. Few people on Ballarat are so thoroughly conversant withe the circumstances out of wich these charges arose then the writer of this article.

In contradiction of the above charges, allow me to state facts, and nothing but facts. It is now universaly known that during the Reform League agitation the leading members of that agitation were Mr. Humffray, Black, Lalor, and Vern. The two latter were stern physical-force advocates. Mr. Black was rather undecided, sometimes voting on one side sometimes on the other; while Mr. Humffray always was, and always has been, a moral-force man. The history of that melancholy affair is to well known to be repeated here ; let it however suffice, Mr. Editor, that at the last moment, when Lalor was organising on Bakery Hill, Mr. Humffray was at his post, ready to address the diggers. He was solicited to do so by Ross and Vern, and, in order to insure him a patient hearing, Ross offered him our standard—the *Southern Cross*, thinking that the sight of our revolutionary emblem would at least make the person of the standard bearer inviolable. However, no sooner was the flag seen in Mr. Humffray's hands then the excited multitude wrested it from him, even threatning to murder him, unless he immediately left the ground ; nor could all Vern's influence have prevented the perpetration of such an atrocity. What Mr. Amicus would have done under such circumstances I do not know, but I believed then, and do so now, that Mr. Humffray was perfectly right in not addressing such an infuriated mob.

The second charge is still more unfounded then the first, but in order to set the matter beyond contradiction at once, allow me to explain how it was that Mr. Humffray's name was on the list of the Crown witnesses for the State trials. It is well known that McGill received a free pardon from the Victorian government, notwithstanding his complicity in that rebellion. The reasons asigned for his pardon were, that he was an American. Humffray, who always was friendly towards Vern, naturaly thought that if one was pardoned the other should be also, and hence he exerted himself strenuously on Vern's behalf, so much so that he introduced in the petition *on behalf of the State Prisoners* a separate clause relating to Vern, and it was during the presentation of *that petition*, and while urging Vern's case before Sir C. Hotham, that Mr. Humffray betrayed such an intimate acquaintance with all the minutias of that unfortunate rebellion, that Mr. Stawell, who was present at the audience, asked Humffray a few questions relating to Vern's case, to one of wich he inadvertently replied, " *that he had heard it so from Vern himself.*" Immediatly on the closing of the audience Mr. Humffray was sumonsed as a Crown witness, but do you know against *whom* he was to appear ? *Against F. Vern.* This Mr. Humffray told me himself. However, Vern had to be captured first before he could be *hung*. Allow me also to say that this incident never caused Vern the least uneasiness, inasmuch as Humffray had proved himself his best and truest friend. I think the strongest proof of this is, that *Mr. Humffray knew Vern's retreat, came daily to see him, and performed for him all those little offices of friendship* wich his unfortunate situation required, and that at a time when *he could have made £500 by betraying Vern.* This constitutes Mr. Humffray's *treason ! What a serious offence !* Surely, after this, Mr. Humffray will be deemed anything but a traitor ! *Humffray, indeed, was the rebel's best and truest friend.* Humffray, also, was the first man that came to the assistance of our lamented friend Ross.

These are facts, and, I think, sufficiently strong to contradict the above foolish reports. Believe me, Mr. Editor, that no party feeling, nothing but *candour*, induced me to write this letter. I remain Your's,

Mr. Editor, F. VERN.

To this letter the Editor of the *Ballarat Star* appended the following note:—"Mr Vern, like but too many more, is rather too fond of exercising his ingenuity in guessing at the names of authors of letters. Mr Denovan had nothing to do with *Amicus.*"

(To the Editor of The Star.)

SIR,—I observe in your issue dated Oct. 4th, a letter signed F. Vern. I have not the honor of acquaintance with that gentleman, but I beg to enclose you a letter I received, marked immediate, from a person of the same name, and I leave your readers to form their own opinions about the consistency of the two productions. I am, Sir, yours faithfully, THOMAS LOADER.

Mr. Loader !

Sir !

Having lately been at Egerton diggings, I took the liberty, though per-
sonaly unacquainted with you, to canvass a little for you. I met with some
success, but time, or rather the want of time, prevented me from following
up the success gained. However, I left Mr. Brown—M.D., at Egerton to
canvass the whole of the district. As it is your intention to visit Egerton
to-morrow, I hope you will comunicate with Mr. Brown—you will probably
have a preliminary comittee organised.   Your's,   F. VERN.

Black lead, 28 | 9 | 56.

(To the Editor of The Star !)

Sir !

Mr. Loader took the liberty to insert in your issue of the 7th inst. a letter
professing to kome from me.

That letter, Sir, is an *unqualified forgery*, and had not Mr. Loader, by his
own flexible preamble and his somewhat plausible excuse " of having received
the same from a person of the same name," put it out of my power of seeking
redress by law, I should have taken immediate steps to prosecute that gentleman.

Mr. Loader knows as well as I do, that there are not two F. Vern's in this
colony ! ! !

I do not deny for one moment that some of Mr. Loader's myrmidon's have
attempted to influence me, and that, too, by means contrary to fair play, in
order to gain me to his side ; but Mr. Loader no doubt know's what my
invariable reply has been, namely, ' that ties of gratitude alone; if nothing else,
would prevent me from entering the field against Mr. Humffray.' But, Mr.
Editor, every reasonable man can see the drift of Mr. Loader's design in
publishing a letter, wich is such a *malicious falshood*, worthy only of a *Baron
Munchhausen or a Gulliver*, that namely, of nullifying any effect wich my
former letter might have produced on Ballarat. My former letter was written
with no party feeling wathsoever, nothing but candour induced me to write
that letter, and it was anything but gentelmanly conduct in trying to nullify
or contradict that letter by such means as Mr. Loader has employed, and that,
too, when that letter did not in the least reflect on the character of Mr. Loader.

In conclusion, Mr. Editor, I deny most emphaticaly that the letter, wich Mr.
Loader pretends of having received, was written by me, and I hope that I may
find out the author of it in order to have him punished according to law. Mr.
Editor, in common justice, I ask you to insert this letter.

Written by

Black lead, 7 | 10 | 56.   no fictitious F. VERN.

To this letter the editor of the *Ballarat Star* appended the
following note, in which the present writer entirely concurs :—
" Some men are badly used. Mr Vern is so. He sends us a letter
referring to Mr Humffray ; we publish that letter knowing it to
be genuine. Mr Loader hands us another which had been sent

to him. This we also believe and know to be genuine and publish it. Again Mr Vern sends us a letter—the present one—disavowing the authorship of the one to Mr Loader. We believe and know it to be genuine and publish it. The public can judge for themselves—*the three letters are from the same pen.* We have shown the letters (which are still in our possession and open to the inspection of the curious) to friends of both Mr Humffray and Mr Loader, and they agree with us that either all the letters are genuine or they are forgeries—take your choice, Mr Vern, of either alternative. Mr Vern's courage has become proverbial, his truthfulness is now deserving of an equally honorable distinction." Vern does not seem to have made any response to this revelation. As has been said, he was intrepid. Just after the Stockade affair he procurred the publication in the Melbourne *Age* of a letter from his pen, purporting to be dated from the Port Phillip Heads, and announcing his eternal farewell to a land where his abilities had been so unappreciated. That letter was written in the *Age* agent's office in the Main road, Ballarat ! But too much has already been said respecting this singular actor in the Ballarat rising.

APPENDIX L.

Besides the Ballarat Cemetery, where the bodies of the diggers and soldiers who fell at the Eureka repose, and the newer cemetery on the northern boundary of Soldiers' Hill, there is a reserve for a cemetery on the south-eastern borders of Ballarat East. This is as yet unused. Where the Eureka Lead crossed what is now Eureka street, there was a bush graveyard, where some of the first diggers were buried. The miners disturbed the bones of the dead when following the lead there. In a hollow south of Golden Point and Grant street, and near the line of Barkly street south, there is a little graveyard where the bodies of Chinese were buried in the earlier days. But in the still earlier days solitary graves were dug about the slopes of the ranges before clergyman or graveyard was thought of, or was available. The digger died and was buried by his mates, or whoever found the body, and the grass-grown mounds may still be found here and there, generally

beneath some drooping branches of fragrant peppermint, and sometimes enclosed with a lichen-sprinkled and mouldering fence of
rude fashioning.

James Vallins, elsewhere mentioned in these appendices, gives the
following graphic picture of "life at the diggings":—

In 1856 one of the shareholders in our claim died, and as he had neither
friends nor money, we resolved to bury him ourselves. A coffin was procured,
and, after sundry nobblers were taken and a bottle provided for the journey,
the coffin was placed upon a cart, one of the mourners undertook to drive,
which he did, with a short pipe in his mouth the whole distance, the remaining
ten walking by the side of the cart, all (except myself, who neither smoked
nor drank) with short pipes in their mouths. Several halts took place for the
purpose of liquoring up until we arrived, when we set to work, in spite of the
remonstrances of the sexton, to dig the grave ourselves. While doing so, the
horse was allowed to graze about the cemetery, dragging the coffin with it. At
every spell the bottle was produced, and drinks round took place. This
occurred so often that, before the grave was half sunk, all (except one) were too
far gone to work, and just in the right trim for talk. The one sober man in
the crowd had to finish the grave himself. The sexton was then sent for, the
coffin after much trouble lowered in the grave, the burial service read—the
men sobbing and hiccoughing audibly the whole time, and it was with
difficulty some of them were prevented from falling into the grave. One
man remained to fill up the grave, while the rest staggered off to complete the
spree commenced at the burial of their mate.

APPENDIX M.

The nature and extent of mining operations in the Ballarat
district, compared with the colony generally, are gathered from
another series of facts. The mining returns for 1869 made the total
outlay in Victoria for timber for mining purposes to be £563,233 5s.
Of this £245,936 18s 8d, or nearly half, was spent in this district,
and of the latter amount £143,001 18s 9d, or nearly half, in
Ballarat proper. In the deep grounds the ancient auriferous drifts
have often given up interesting memorials of primeval times.
Trunks and branches of trees petrified or charged with silicates and
metalliferous accretions have been found, and one notable occurrence in a mine on the Frenchman's Lead was much talked of at
the time. The miners discovered there a kind of water-spout coming
down through the basaltic rock that lay upon the gutter-drift, and

this was found to be the place of the remains of a charred and semi-petrified tree, which had apparently stood by the side of the ancient water-course when the overflow of lava had surrounded the tree and buried the water-course and all the adjoining land.   In one of the mines at Haddon, some fossil fruits or seeds were found, unlike any present vegetable productions in Victoria.   They were like small fossil oranges, with the rind hard and black and the pips dried and rattling when the fossil was shaken.   The inference from these and cognate facts is, of course, that our auriferous alluvial deposits were probably for the most part produced under somewhat similar meteorological conditions to those of the present day, with climatic differences and violent disturbances intervening.   James Vallins, chairman of the Miners' Association, one of the oldest of the Ballarat diggers, writes to us as follows, on the part of John Sawyer, who prospected Sailors' Gully:—

About the middle of 1853 myself and seven others commenced prospecting. We were six sailors out of eight, and were called " the sailors." The gully was called Sailors' Gully after us.   Swift and party, Americans, commenced prospecting Prince Regent's Gully about the same time. We obtained a double claim, 48 ft. by 24 ft., as a prospecting claim. We were the first I could discover to slab the shaft from surface to the bottom, the practice being to sink a round shaft as far as the ground would stand, then square and slab the rest. Our first shaft was lost in the drift at about 70 feet from the surface. This was the first drift with heavy water touched on Ballarat. The second shaft was lost in the drift at 90 feet from the surface.   This caused the whole ground to be rushed both above and below our ground.   Our third shaft we succeeded in bottoming at 107 feet—then the deepest hole on Ballarat—dead on the gutter.   The water was very heavy, and we were obliged to use two buckets, one up and the other down, for the first time on Ballarat.   We had to send to Geelong and get made to order two water-buckets.   The first gold got was a nugget weighing 2½ oz. weight, sent up in the water-bucket.   The largest piece of gold got from the claim was 100 oz.   Hundreds of people came to see us every day, and as we were very hard worked we had to post a notice for them to read, instead of asking questions:—" Notice.—Bottomed at 107 feet.   Large quantity of water.   Got a nugget."

Mr Vallins writes as follows about the "Jewellers' Shops," and other matters—the parentheses are ours:—

The use of frames for suporting shafts instead of hanging them with battens, the present method of puddling water back in shafts, is due to Thomas Bradbury, and the use of wooden air-pipes under ground, were all first used in amalgamated claim Nos. 23 to 27, Frenchman's Lead, Sebastopol, where I was working. (This was in 1856.)   I remember that great curiosity was excited (in 1856, when the diggers were entering on the plateau now known as Sebastopol) by Mr Walsh, the barrister, appearing in a jumping case on Sebastopol, the first time, as far as I could learn, that a lawyer had been seen pleading on a claim. In the Jewellers' Shop claim (Canadian) in which my mate (R. N. Sankey, now in New Zealand) was a shareholder, two Cornishmen were engaged. They worked about six weeks, and were paid eight pounds weight of gold each as wages. The shareholders divided (received) about £1700 each. They were robbed of more than half their ground. The headings (upper portion of the gutter drift) were left four feet high, and would yield half an ounce to the tub. The paddocks (collected washdirt) yielded eight ounces to the tub. The claim yielded twenty ounces of gold to the square foot, or about three hundred pounds weight in all.

APPENDIX N.

The census returns for Tasmania, collected on the 7th of February, 1870, show the total population of that colony to have been then 89,977, or not much more than double the population of Ballarat. By the same returns it is seen that the population of the Tasmanian metropolis was 19,449, and of Launceston, 10,359; so that the population of this city may be set down as greater than that of both Tasmanian towns put together. This comparison shows what the gold discovery has done. And this is seen more conclusively when it is remembered that Victoria was at first colonised from Tasmania. Five-and-twenty years ago Tasmania patronised Victoria, and took note of its sparse population, which then did not equal that of Ballarat to-day. A writer in the Melbourne *Age* some time since said:—

There are many thousand Victorians to whom the marvellous growth of their own colony is comparatively unknown. In an old Tasmanian almanac I find a mile-stone from which it is possible to measure progress. The period is before the gold discovery, and just suggests what might have been our position but for the metallic talisman which attracted population to our shores. The Van Diemen's Land Royal Kalendar of 1848, compiled by J. Wood, and published in that year by Dowling, of Launceston, and Walsh, of Hobart Town, devotes a page and a half out of three hundred pages to some statistics about Port Phillip. The population about Port Phillip (in 1846) was 32,879, of which 20,174 were males, and 12,685 females. Van Diemen's Land at that time contained 60,000 people, and New South Wales 153,000; there were 5198 houses in Port Phillip. The annual imports amounted to £315,571, and the exports, £425,201.

APPENDIX O.

Mr Wainwright, an old colonist, states that Mr Francis was buried at the homestead on the Woodlands run, on the Wimmera. This run is next west of the Decameron run, and is now held by Wilson Bros. Ten years ago the grave was not only fenced and well kept, but a shear-blade, and presumably the one with which the murder was committed, was then sticking in the grave-top. A wooden tablet told the story of the murder. The probability, therefore, is that the event took place on the Woodlands run.—*Vide* page 4, Chapter I.

APPENDIX P.

In the body of this work testimony has been borne to the general character of the early diggers as being highly respectable in the best sense of the phrase. We have cited the opinions of several public men, or men acting in a representative capacity, to show that the mass of the miners were at all times men who loved order as well as freedom. Here is one more witness. In a recent charge to an Otago jury, his Honor Judge Chapman, late of the Victorian bar, thus speaks of the Victorian miners :—

In Victoria I have had considerable experience as to the state of the mining population in most of the important districts there. My professional avocations constantly called me to Ballarat and other places. I was engaged for a considerable time in cases arising out of mining contracts and mining disputes, and that led me to observe the condition of the mining population. I found them industrious and energetic to an extraordinary degree ; persevering often against hope, and amongst them almost a total absence of crime. I believe that the same is the case here. We have persons that come from the mining districts, and we often find them describing themselves as miners ; having been detected in crime in the mining districts they have to give some description of themselves, and they then call themselves miners. They are not miners ; in very rare instances at least are they so.

APPENDIX Q.

There were Chinese in Ballarat before the close of the year 1852. The general body of that people have been orderly and industrious, working as market-gardeners, storekeepers, coach-drivers, and miners. They have lived in settlements of their own mainly, but some occupy houses in the main streets of Ballarat East. Leprosy, filth, opium-smoking, and unmentionable vices have made a portion of the Chinese a moral and physical pest. To that excellent police officer, Serjeant James Larner, the public owes a good deal for his kindly and persistent attention to the miseries, and his energetic opposition to the vices of the Chinese. In a return to the Government last year the sergeant estimated the number of the Chinese population at 1501, and classified them as follows :—266 storekeepers, 550 miners, 120 hawkers, 250 gamblers, 5 publicans, 15 butchers, 100 thieves, 15 brothelkeepers, 150 gardeners, and 30 half-caste Chinese children.

APPENDIX R.

From a return by Charles S. Reeves, official agent for this district for winding-up companies under the Statute, laid before Parliament in June, 1870, it appears that from the 5th of May, 1868, to the 3rd of March, 1870, the winding-up of fifty mining companies was ordered by the Court of Mines, on which the aggregate of debts proved was £30,290 2s 2d ; the amount recovered at date of return, £4962 18s 2d ; official agent's charges, £1074 6s 7d ; law charges, £1526 13s 5d ; distributed to creditors, £2019 18s 1d. This shows that more than half the moneys recovered were swallowed up in expenses.

APPENDIX S.

The following code of rules for the guidance of the diggers *inter se* was drawn up by some humorist or humorists in the early days of Ballarat, and was posted about the diggings for the behoof of all on the field. It lets a little light in upon the modes of thought, the customs, the amusements, and the phrases in vogue then, and which are only partially known to the later comers :—

THE DIGGERS' TEN COMMANDMENTS.

Published expressly for Ballarat : Price 6d.

A MAN spake these words and said :—" I am a digger, who wandered from my native home, and came to sojourn in a strange land and ' see the elephant !' And behold, I saw him, and bear witness, and that from the key of his trunk to the end of his tail his whole body had passed before me ; and I followed until his huge feet stood still before a Clapboard Store ; then, with his trunk extended, he pointed to a candle card tacked upon a shingle, as though he would say *Read*, and I read—.

THE TEN COMMANDMENTS.

I.—Thou shalt have no other claim but one.

II.—Thou shalt not make to thyself any false claim, nor any likeness to a mean man by " jumping " one, whatever thou findest on the top above, or on the rock beneath, or in a crevice underneath the rock, for I am a jealous Dog, and will visit the Commissioner round with my presence to invite him on my side ; and when he decides against thee thou shalt have to take thy pick, thy pan, thy shovel, and thy "swag," and all thou hast, and go "prospecting," both north and south, to seek good diggings—and thou shalt find none. Then, when thou hast returned in sorrow, thou shalt find that thine own claim is worked out and no pile made thee, to hide in the ground, or in an old boot beneath thy bunk, or in buckskin or bottle beneath thy tent, but hast paid all that was in thy purse away, worn out thy boots and thy garments, so that there is nothing good about thee but the pockets, and thy patience be like unto thy garments ; and at last thou shalt hire thy body out to make thy board and save thy bacon.

III.—Thou shalt not go " shepherding " before thy claim is worked out· Thou shalt not take thy money, nor thy gold-dust, nor thy good name to the gaming-table in vain, for Monte, Twenty-one, Roulette, Faro, Lansquenet, and Poker will prove to thee that the more thou puttest down the less thou shalt take up ; and when thou thinkest of thy wife and children thou shalt not hold thyself guiltless but insane.

IV.—Thou shalt not remember what thy friends do at home on the Sabbath day, lest the remembrance may not compare favorably with what thou doest ; six days thou mayest dig or pick all that the body can stand under, but the other day is Sunday when thou shalt wash all thy dirty shirts, darn all thy stockings, tap all thy boots, drink all thy nobblers, mend all thy clothing, chop all thy firewood, make and bake thy bread, and boil thy pork and beans, that thou wait not when thou returnest from thy long tour weary. For in six days' labor only thou canst not work out thy body in two years, but if thou workest hard on Sunday also thou canst do it in six months—and thy son, and thy daughter, thy male friend, and thy female friend, thy morals, and thy conscience be none the better for it, but reproach thee, shouldest thou ever return with thy worn-out body to thy mother's fireside and thou strive to justify thyself because the leaders, jews, and fossikers defy God and civilisation by keeping not the Sabbath day, and wish not for a day's rest, such as a true digger's memory, youth, and home, make hallowed.

V.—Think more of, and how thou canst make it fastest, rather than how thou wilt enjoy it after thou hast ridden rough-shod over thy good old parents' precepts and examples, that thou mayest have something to reproach and sting thee when thou art left alone in the land where thy father's blessings and thy mother's love have sent thee.

VI.—Thou shalt not harm thyself by working in the rain, even though thou shalt make enough (out o' "core") to buy physic and attendance with. Neither shalt thou kill thy neighbor's body by shooting him, except he give thee offence, then, upon the principle of honor, without principle, thou mayest, though by "keeping cool" thou hadst saved his life and thy conscience.

VII.—Thou shalt not grow discouraged and think of going home before thou hast made thy "pile," because thou hast not "struck a lead," nor found a "nugget," nor sunk a hole on a "pocket," or the "gutter;" but in going home thou shalt be deemed a "shicer" and go to work ashamed, and serve thee right, for by staying here thou mightest strike a "lead," and thyself respect, and then go home with enough to make thyself and others happy.

VIII.—Thou shalt not fossick out specimens from thy mates' pan and put them in thy mouth, or in thy purse ; neither shalt thou take from thy sleeping partner, or tent-mate, his gold to add to thine lest he find thee out, and straightway call his fellow diggers together with the "traps" and put thee in limbo vile, or brand thee like a horse-thief with R upon thy cheek, to be known and feared of all men, Ballarat in particular; and if thou steal a shovel, pick, or pan from thy toiling fellow digger, hanging will be too good for thee, and the sooner thou makest thyself scarce the better, and for ever hang down thy head.

IX.—Thou shalt not "blatherskite" about "new rushes" to thy neighbor that thou mayest benefit a storekeeper who hath a store with provisions, tools, swags, &c., he cannot sell, lest, in deceiving thy neighbor, that he may, returning through the bush with nought save his revolver, present thee with the contents thereof, and, like a dog, thou shalt fall down and perish, and die the death of a bushranger.

X.—Thou shalt "shepherd" but one hole at a time, nor covet thy neighbor's gold, nor his claim, nor move his stake, nor wilfully take washing-stuff not thy property, nor wash the tailings from his sluice's mouth, nor in any way molest him in his claim. And if thy neighbor have his family here, and thou love and covet his daughter's hand in marriage, thou shalt loose no time in seeking her affection, and when thou hast obtained it thou shalt "pop" the question like a man, lest another, more manly than thou art, should step in before thee, and thou covet her in vain ; and, in the anguish of disappointment, thou shalt quote the language of the great, and say—"Let her rip," and thy future life be that of a poor, lonely, despised, and comfortless bachelor !

THE END.

Another Little One.—Thou shalt not dig up a public road unless thou canst afford to fix it again as good as before, less thou injurest the drayman to benefit thyself, and he curse thee every time he passeth. Amen !

Last, But Not Least.—Thou shalt be particular not to leave thy swag at thy boarding-house without making satisfactory arrangements with the man whose grub thou hast eaten, for it is better to have a good name than much riches. Amen ! Amen ! !

PRINTED AT "THE BALLARAT STAR" OFFICE, STURT STREET.

GOVERNOR LA TROBE

GOVERNOR SIR CHARLES HOTHAM

SOME
BALLARAT REMINISCENCES

William Bramwell Withers

Some Ballarat Reminiscences.

I AM writing this in the young November. How beautiful this city is in these first early days of the Spring-tide. And all its suburban reaches, too, and farther away. Away and away, over hills, and plains, and wood to where the purple distances of the Pyrenees, and the hills about Ararat to the north west, Mount Emu in the west, and the nearer Divide on the north east and south, with Mounts Warrenheip and Buninyong as homely, familiar, often-climbed landmarks. But then it is the green new birth of the season that glorifies all the landscape as it touches our gardens and lawns with fresh charm of blossom, bud, green blade and swift out-putting of floral color and odour.

It is forty-three Novembers ago, now, since I first came where this city is now, and then was not. A long cry from its spring of '52 to this of '95. The visible change is, indeed, a metamorphosis. And to one who has seen nearly the whole of the transformation there comes at times a suspicion that one has really grown old, and is a stranger once more in the same place which is not the same place. Ah! but the eternal hills are still where they were, and though they, too, have undergone the mutations which civilisation imposes upon most of nature that she approaches, they remain where they were, and their old familiar outlines look like old friends, tried and abiding. Black Hill close at hand, Mounts Warrenheip and Buninyong, and all the ranges and all the level plains have been shorn of most of the indigenous forest growth which made the site of the city and its surroundings " a woody theatre," when its first diggers rushed hither for the gold. "A sylvan scene" it was when I and my mate pitched our first tent near the foot of what was then fitly called Black Hill from its dense growth of gum trees. We pitched on the slope where Humffray-street now winds along, following the bullock-dray track of primæval pastoralists and rushing gold-hunters. All the slope, including the Bakery Hill of the historic days that were to be, was then lightly sprinkled with wattle and honeysuckle and bastard gums. Five and twenty of us had come up from Melbourne, after crossing in the "Hannah" from Natal. Some cockneys had a huge umbrella tent, in which they found good shelter ; but some Scotch fellow-passengers were bent on less fanciful housing. They had a good-sized square tent, and they built a good sod lum, and so had something more like a solid home of civilisation. We were all womanless, of course, and had to do our own cooking, and washing, and mending, and bed-making. But these details of early goldfields' life have been too often described to warrant repetition in these pages.

The invasion of the diggers began eighteen months before my arrival, but other rushes had taken away hosts of the hunters, and Golden Point was almost deserted when I came. Golden Point, Black Hill Flat, the gullies north and south, were already partially invested, and the shallow deposits, which afterwards led the digger on to the famous deep leads of the sixties, seventies, and eighties, were by the end of '52 pretty well all in hand. But the forest was still untouched, so to speak, or was only smitten here and there close at hand, as the diggers swung their axes for fuel or ridge poles, or rude windlasses, or for bark or slabs for an occasional rotten shaft—the firstlings of the deep lead miner's needs of the coming days which cut down whole reaches of forest for timbering the mines that the later days had seen opened. The valleys of the Yarrowee and the water-shed of the glen between the Buninyong hills and the Canadian and Hiscock's ranges were lightly timbered and still picturesque, though the former valley had, by the time of my arrival, been terribly splotched by the debris and the shafts of the digging operations going on there. The dray tracks of the squatters from Geelong and Buninyong to Ercildoune and other stations westward and south-westward trailed their devious lines over range and valley, and across the western plateau, the diggers pitching their tents along the line that led from the glen aforesaid to the western plateau. Soon the storekeepers followed upon the heels of the diggers, and thus the main road, now Mair-street, Ballarat East, came into being. The dray tracks up the plateau, bifurcated in directions where Sturt-street and the Creswick-road of the city now are. But I am anticipating.

When I went to get my first gold-digging license at the Commissioner's Camp in November, 1852, there were some half-dozen or so of tents forming the camp, which lay near the edge of the escarpment of the plateau overlooking the Yarrowee. It was a steepish green slope by which one approached the camp from the valley whence I climbed to the commissioner's tents. The site was between two gullies and dray tracks, the gully on the north being the site of the Mair-street of to-day, that on the south the site of the lower end of the Sturt-street of to-day. A log lock-up and a log hut for the police had been built a few yards to the west of the commissioner's tents, and the late " Paddy Welsh " had a store of logs a little further west. Mr. Meek, the author of caligraphic historiettes of Victoria, may also at that time have had a log hut further on in the line of the present Lydiard-street, but I never saw it. All the plateau then, where the City of Ballarat now is, was forest, lightly timbered for the most part. The Camp-street of to-day connecting Sturt and Mair streets, winds right through the site of the commissioner's tents of 1852. The valleys were pretty generally cleared already of their timber, and both the Yarrowee and its tributary down the valley where Mair-street now runs were changed from the clear brooklets of the year before to muddy streams, whose banks were shoals of gravel thrown out from the tubs and cradles of the diggers. But the creek that ran down where Mair-street is was still clear and drinkable. It carried the overflow from Yuille's Swamp (now Lake Wendouree), and the water which the Gnarr Creek brought from Soldiers' Hill and the ranges that way. I remember gratefully drinking of that " brook by the way " one torrid day at the end of November or the beginning of December, when my mate and I humped our swags to join the first rush to Creswick's Creek, which had just broken out. By that time some of our South African fellow-passengers had become philosophers enough to eschew digging and accept hire as members of the somewhat Falstaffian ragged corps of police on the green camp-mound. Others had taken work in building a rude dam across the Gnarr, so as to intercept the waters coming down, and give a supply for the camp and the diggers thereabouts in the valley. That dam was where the pathway now begins to ascend from Mair-street to the railway station. The creek has long since vanished from view, transformed into a big sewer, culverted and buried beneath buildings and roadways for a quarter mile's distance, reaching from the Yarrowee to the intersection of Webster and Doveton streets. Towards the end of December, one hot day, luckless and mateless, I humped my swag back from Creswick's Creek (now Creswick), a sadder, but, I fear, a not much wiser man. Bunked with my Natal chums in the camp that night, and in the morning breakfasted at the camp cook's *al fresco* kitchen on the slope where Hill-street now runs up from Grenville-street to Camp-street. The cook was old Glover, who had acted as galley doctor on the Hannah. He was baking damper about a foot or so in diameter, and had hot coffee and mutton chops ready. It was open housekeeping in a very literal sense, and I set-to with a fool's appetite, then shouldered my wallet and joined a digger who was passing with his swag, bound, like myself, for Melbourne. Before I reached Warrenheip I was disabled by a rapid dysentery, the man left me as I crawled slowly on, and more dead than alive I reached Melbourne on Xmas Day, after putting up in hotels at Ballan, Bacchus Marsh, and Keilor, being bundled out by the Ballan landlord in the morning, as " no sick men are wanted here," and being robbed between Ballan and Bacchus Marsh by a band of diggers with a dray returning to Melbourne, to whom I had entrusted

my swag for carriage to the hotel at the Marsh. The heat and old
Glover's prog did for me, and at Keilor I had to give my name to a
strange bedroom mate, as it seemed to me the end of my march had
come.   But I rode in a dray on the Xmas morning to Melbourne, and
rest there soon cured me.   Then a sojourn in Canvas Town, where the
slopes of Government House and the military barracks now are, then
pick and shovel work at road-making, merchants' dray-driving, wharf-
clerking, reading for the press, reporting for the press, and by June
1855, I found myself again in Ballarat, where I have been ever since.

This hiatus of two and a half years in my Ballarat life included all the
Eureka Stockade and pre-Stockade periods of turmoil, so that I came
afterwards to the consideration of the history of the place free from the
hot local entanglements of actual participation in the troubles of the
time.   It fell to my lot to become more or less acquainted with all the
leaders in both the moral and physical force reformers of that day,
from Peter Lalor on one side and John Basson Humffray on the other
to the captains of Lalor's insurgent band, and many of the sympathising
on-lookers who kept their skins whole and worked upon safer and more
constitutional lines for the political liberties we have to-day, and whose
advent was accelerated by the brave if hot-headed men who rallied
round Lalor at the Stockade.

Ballarat.   W. B. WITHERS.

Some Ballarat Reminiscences.

II.

IT is the historic Third of December as I resume my pen, but do not be alarmed, Mr. Editor, I am not going to run over the well worn track which the day recalls to memory. In these pages of yours the story has been told in brief by Mr. John Lynch, one of Lalor's captains on that day. Almost entirely I concur in the sketch he gave of the day and its aims and results, and the story has also been told elsewhere. A quarter century has gone by since the " History of Ballarat " was written, and this is the 41st anniversary of the bloodshedding at the Eureka Stockade. Swiftly the years seem to have gone. To-day is as bright and sunny, the sky as blue as then, for Nature does not change with our changing moods and memories. The dawn to-day was as calm and clear, and as balmy with vernal scents as forty-one years ago, when the military and the police stole upon the diggers' Stockade, the sentry's shot was fired, the military returned fire, the Stockade was scaled and the dead and wounded lay about the bloody ground on that now far away Sunday morning. But if there is no change in the eternal procession of the seasons, there is no monotony, but a Divine variety. And man adds by his co-operate labours to that variety. Some phases of it are before me, both in thought and in actual vision, as I write, but of them by-and-bye. Let us on this anniversary of the Stockade encounter say our reverent *requiescant* over the dead. Ah me, how the ghosts of the departed crowd round one as he meditatively strokes his grey beard and calls over the roll of the absent ones. Most of those who were here this day forty-one years a-gone are also gone, for they were not all like John Lynch, that hale Irish evergreen, who is here to-day, upright, lusty, sunburnt, eye as clear, voice as cheery, brain as busy as ever. More power to him, though no more he goes in procession with the garlanders who decked the resting place of the slain diggers, and delivers no more orations to their memory.

For, sooth to say, the hot emotions of the days that followed close on the fatal day have cooled down, and garlands and processions, and orations at the graves are no more. Lalor, who never unbent to such celebrations, is gone, but his bronze statue in Sturt Street keeps his features as in life before us, and helps to keep his memory green. But this *vera effigies* of the commander of the diggers at the Stockade is not true in *that* relation. It does not present to us the

223

handsome athletic Lalor in his early manhood. It gives us the man past middle age, still upright and of manly port as of old, but worn and wrinkled by the passage of the years, and the impress of official cares and of a more artificial life. The pedestal of the monument bears a curious blunder which ought to have been corrected before now. It tells the bewildered stranger who may have read our Constitutional history, that Lalor was elected to the old Legislative Council in 1885, and that he was elected in 1880 Speaker of the Legislative Assembly which was not in existence when he was elected to the Council. The error is in the date 1885 being put on the record instead of 1855. His ardent friend and follower, the fiery, red, little Italian, Carboni Raffaello, who fought with him and wrote his eulogy and wept bitter tears over the tragic outcome of the Eureka camp, is gone. Many a time I watched the glitter of his mobile eyes as he championed the diggers' rights in the long since dead Local Court, which was one of the outcomes of that Stockade defeat that was also a victory. This is no paradox. The times have long since given the proof otherwise. The last time I remember meeting him was one day near the junction of Sturt and Bridge Streets. He was working in a claim not far off in the flat where the lava rock had just been struck, and he shouted out his favourite accost, " Great works !" as he held up a piece of the rock which had in it some bright crystals of, I think, carbonate of lime. It was then a new found curiosity here. Carbonate, Carboni, Carbonari ! Did Raffaello call himself Carboni because he had been of the Carbonari ? I do not know. He was said to have been a follower of Garibaldi in his struggles for Italian freedom, and to join here in the patriotic crusade against " the wolves " of office and their rough insolence came to him as naturally, no doubt, as his red shirt and his drill under Lalor's subalterns. He went hence many years ago, for Rome, it is said, and perhaps he, too, is with the majority. But his scarce little eulogy of Lalor and the diggers' rising is still to be found here and there, with its vivid sketches, its caustic limnings of character, its apt classical citations. For Raffaello had been to school, and he was fired with poetry as well as patriotism.

James William Esmond, too, is gone. He was the first public revealer of the existence of gold in Victoria. He was one of Lalor's officers at the Stockade. He was not a scholar like Raffaello, had no professional status like Lynch, but he had an Irishman's love for a fight against tyranny. Poor Esmond ! He had his foibles and he paid the penalty. Stricken with a wasting incurable disease he lay long in bed, and it was a coincidence that he died on the anniversary of the Stockade day. A few days before he died I asked him if he would not like to see a priest, and he said he would like to have Dr. Delany to visit him. His wish was fulfilled, and it was at Esmond's grave I first met that scholarly and genial clergyman. It is five years ago to-day, Esmond died a little before midnight. I saw him a few hours before, and said, "You remember the day, Esmond?" "Ah yes," he said, "its the twenty-sixth anniversary," meaning, of course, the thirty-sixth. When I had bidden him "good-bye," I strolled over the ranges towards the source of the old Eureka lead, and by me as I write is a yellow immortelle I gathered within sight of the Stockade monument. The day was like the fatal Sunday, like to-day also. From the crest of the range I could see all over the Ballarat field, over the scenes of the old 1854 gatherings, over the Cemetery where lay the dead soldiers and diggers, over the spot where Esmond was living his last short hours. It was a time and an outlook to help point the *sic transit* moral. But the air is thick with ghosts. Not only the accumulated memories of the local dead of more than a generation past, but the ghosts of others whose dust reposes upon other shores!

> Though other friends have died in other days,
> One grave there is where memory sinks and stays.

Now that Esmond is gone I may mention that he was the Stockade officer whose story of the fight is given at page 109 of the second edition of the "History of Ballarat."

I have referred to the cessation of the anniversary mortuary rites in celebration of the memories of the slain diggers of the Stockade. But though those festivals are over now, the dead are not forgotten, and it is probable that as the years go by poetic legends will gather about the day and its deeds and its dead. In this day's *Ballarat Courier* is a full column of verses in very small type. Their heading is "For Freedom at Eureka," and they are dated "Creswick, 1st December, 1895," the signature being "J. Gavan Reilly." They purport to be a narrative by an old greybeard to his grandchildren, telling the story of emigration from Ireland to the gold land, and of the events which led up to the Eureka tragedy. Here is the concluding stanza:

> It was might against right at Eureka;
> Injustice and tyrannous laws;
> We fought but to have the wrongs righted,
> And shed our hearts' blood for the cause,
> And time, the great healer of all things,
> Has righted the wrongs of the past.
> The fight at Eureka for freedom
> Was the first in this land—and the last—

The leader who led the "rebellion"
    Was pardoned by country and Queen ;
He died, all too soon, full of honours,
    But never forgotten, I ween.
In the dim mists of time yet advancing,
    The shrine of the time honoured dead
Shall still be kept sacred and holy,
    For the sake of the heroes who bled.
And children shall ever weave garlands
    On the third of December each year,
To place at the shrine of the heroes,
    To country and memory dear.
United, our sons shall do honour,
    Emulate the illustrious brave,
Who fought for our birthright of freedom
    And found, at Eureka, a grave.

It is not my good fortune to have any knowledge of this poet. He may be of the younger generation who look at the past through the colouring hues of distance, or the very greybeard who sings the song of memory glorified with the halo of the pathetic long-ago. Or he may even be one who felt he was fit to respond to Samuel Irwin's summons to the Creswick diggers a few days before the encounter at the Stockade. Irwin told me he wrote the letter himself, and he dwelt with special unction on the fact that he had deeply underlined the words " or any MAN on Creswick." The letter is cited at page 99 in the second edition of the " History of Ballarat." Alas, Irwin, too, has vanished into the silences. He was a Trin. Col., Dub., man. A capable journalist, modest, genial, slightly Bohemian. He was in all the agitations that led up to the stockade, knew all the leading men, wrote voluminously as a newspaper correspondent, and when all the troubles were over he worked for some years as sub-editor and editor here, and for the most part on the *Ballarat Star*. After a while he declined upon easier lines and became a civil servant in one of the Government departments, the Lands department if my memory serves me rightly, and he was still in the service when cancer in the breast killed him in his yet comparatively young manhood. I see him now with his tall figure, his fair complexion, his merry face, his kindly grip, and I hear him with his North of Ireland accent. Ah, may he, too, rest in peace.

But how many requiems one must utter as he looks back upon the long line of the receding years. And on the long roll of events. How dim the echoes seem now of the boisterous passions, the hot strife, the angry resolves, the proud brave throws of the dice of fortune, the bold fights for redress of wrongs, and the steady labour for a more real and politically articulate liberty.

226

Gone the fires of youth, the follies, furies, curses, passionate tears,
Gone like fires, and floods, and earthquakes of the planet's dawning years.

No, not gone, absolutely, that vigorous mixture of splendid indignation, and stern resolve, and wild and visionary aspirations which
made up the battle cry and action of the insurgents of the Eureka.
Out of it all came somewhat sooner the chartered rights we have
to-day. Even the errors in aim and in action were very real things
then. There was life and movement in them, and they did their
work, and the work remains, though the distance softens the outlines,
deadens the sounds, rectifies proportions.

I have said that Irwin declined from public action as a journalist
and ate the bread of the State. So Humffray, extruded from politics
by the action of developing democracy, declined upon inactive years,
literally hobbling through chronic diseases to the grave, stranded
long before in the shallow eddies of straitened means and enforced
idleness. He was a son of Wales, and ever loyal to the race he
sprang from. Long before him had gone the little firebrand of the
Ballarat Times, whom Lola Montes horsewhipped one day in the
Main Road because he wrote unpleasant things about her. This
English Seekamp, whom she called Scamp, fought in his paper right
valiantly for the diggers, if not always very wisely or coherently.
After the whipping, Lola gave a champagne supper at her hotel in
the old Main Road, distributed cigarettes of her own making, and
made the time very merry for her guests. If Seekamp was valiant,
so also was Manning, one of his Irish journalistic coadjutors, and with
more coherence and point. He, too, is no more. Then there was
Irish Richard Belford, printer, part-proprietor of the *Ballarat Star*,
Colonel of the Volunteers, Mayor of Ballarat East. A black-haired,
ringletted-head, close shaven face, almost priest-like in visage, and
apparently as of Galway, or Spanish blood, or both. The present
Hon. T. D. Wanliss, M.L.C., was his partner in the *Star*. Wanliss
the Scottish, prosaic Protestant, Belford, the warm Celtic Catholic.
An unpropitious conjunction. They fell out, the Irish Dr. Clendining
(now dead) arbitrated, the partnership dissolved, and Belford disappeared, dying, if I mistake not in Queensland, where also Seekamp
was said to have found his quietus.

[In last month's paper were some typographical errors. At page
674 for " now Mair-street " read " now Main-street ;" at page 675
for " valley where Mair-street now runs " read " valley where Main-
street now runs ;" at page 676 for " physical force reformers " read
" physical force reforms."]

Ballarat.   W. B. WITHERS.

Some Ballarat Reminiscences.

III.

W RITING of the day, 30th November, 1854, when Lalor's muster marched from their old trysting place, on Bakery Hill, for the site of the Stockade, in apprehension of a fresh digger hunt by the camp authorities, Raffaello says :—" We were within one thousand in the ranks, with all sorts of arms down to the pick and shovel. We turned by the Catholic Church, and went across the gully. Of this I have perfect recollection : when the "Southern Cross" (flag) reached the wood leading to the Eureka on the opposite hill, the file of two abreast crossing the gully extended backwards up to the hill where the Catholic Church stands." This church was the old St. Alipius, a frame and canvas structure, whose lineaments are engraven in many Catholic memories, and are faithfully represented in a print not long ago issued at the instance of the authorities of the church here. The present St. Alipius Church is on the site of the old one, but covers, of course, a larger area. I mention this, not as a piece of news, but by way of introduction to the remark that all the Christian denominations were very early represented here, clerically, after the diggers began their gold-hunting. It will be no news to many of the *Austral Light* readers to read that Father Dunne was the first priest who officiated here. Much of that interesting story has been told already, I believe, to Catholic readers. How much I do not know, and so I have thought it well to say here that having been unable to ascertain locally the exact spot where the first services were celebrated on this goldfield, I wrote to Father Dunne, now of Albury, N.S.W., and that venerable clergyman favors me, "from memory," with the following narrative in reply :—

"About the beginning of '51 I was appointed by the late Archbishop Goold to the Coburg mission. Before the discovery of gold at Ballarat, Dr. Goold and the late Dr. Fitzpatrick sailed for England, leaving Dr. Geoghegan (afterwards Bishop of Adelaide) in charge of the diocese of Melbourne. The great rush to Ballarat took place in August and September, '51. Nearly all the men of the whole of Victoria went there in quest of gold.   I was requested by Dr. Geoghegan to go to Ballarat in September, '51.   I cannot say the exact date on which I arrived there.   A small case containing the vestments, &c., for the celebration of Mass, and a few articles of clothing, were sent up by a team.   The team did not arrive in time for the first Sunday after my arrival, so we had to be satisfied with the Rosary, and a short sermon.   I got shelter in the tent of Mr. John O'Sullivan, who was a timber merchant in Melbourne, and shared with him the work of making the 'damper,' boiling the 'billy,' and cooking a bit of meat, when we'could get it, on some bent hoop iron, in real bush fashion.   Ballarat was then a rough place to live in, no milk or butter, no eggs, nothing but damper and mutton, no house where you could get a bed or a cooked meal nearer than Buninyong.   The tariff for bed and board was about £1 per day.

"My first Mass at Ballarat was celebrated in Mr. O'Sullivan's tent about the third Sunday of September, '51.   I had a large congregation of men who knelt outside the tent.   The congregation on the following Sunday was still larger, numbering about 500, and continued to increase each Sunday till the rush took place to old Bendigo, and other goldfields which were discovered about the same time.   It would be difficult for me now to point out the spot on which Mr. O'Sullivan's tent was situated.   It was not far from the creek where the alluvial gold was washed.   The whole of Ballarat was then a thick forest of splendid timber, which was ruthlessly destroyed to make room for tents.   I continued at Ballarat till about the end of November, when I was asked to attend a sick call up the Wimmera, near Horsham.   On my return for the next Sunday, Mr. O'Sullivan and his tent were gone, and Ballarat nearly deserted, so I mounted my horse and returned to Pentridge, now Coburg.   The offertory collection I received while at Ballarat was generally given in small nuggets, which I handed over to the Catholic Association Fund, for bringing out priests to Melbourne. I may mention that there were only eight or ten priests then in the whole of Victoria.   After Dr. Goold's return, in '52, the Rev. M. Downing, who died at Geelong, was appointed to Ballarat.   He got up a slab church, a photograph of which I saw with Archdeacon Slattery of Geelong."

I take it that the "slab church" Father Dunne mentions is the St. Alipius Raffaello refers to.   I was within it once or twice, the floor being mother earth.   But Father Dunne's still more primitive surroundings were, as to the congregation, *al fresco*.   An old Catholic here tells me he had to kneel on quartz gravel, and he thinks it was near Brown Hill.   Father Dunne's narrative is a graphic picture of the situation in those days of the Ballarat origins, and all old pioneers will endorse and appreciate the reverend pioneer's story of the time.   The sick call to the Wimmera, and the eight or ten priests for all Victoria, are historic touches of value.   Fancy a sick call over a distance greater than from London to Salisbury in England.   To-day there are more priests on this one goldfield than were in all Victoria when Father Dunne came here to encounter the rude conditions of "the days that are no more."   The offertory nuggets, too, are indeed a golden reminder of the old times.   It reminds me of the sight I once had of showers of nuggets upon the stage of the old Queen's Theatre, in Queen Street, Melbourne, in the early fifties, when G. V. Brooke and other artists were in their first vogue there.   What a metamorphosis of the Ballarat landscape since the days of Fathers Dunne and Downing.   If one strolls down westward from the site of the old "slab church," past the site too, in his way, of Lalor's old Bakery Hill meetings, where the late Tim Hayes used to be chairman, he sees a splendid city where Father Dunne's "thick forest" was.   Perchance Macaulay's couplet may occur to him.

> " From where Cortona lifts to heaven
> Her diadem of towers."

Or, if he walk there by night, the long line of electric lights along Bridge and Sturt Streets may remind him of Bulwer's "alabaster lamps," if the immediate surroundings do not fit in with the " perfumed lights" which the sham Prince of Como associated with his romantic picture.

In my last I hazarded the prophecy that poetic legends will by and by gather about the Eureka Stockade story.   Since then a Mr. J. Neilson has followed Mr. J. G. Reilly's example, and betters his exemplar.   I cull a few lines from his contribution to the *Courier* :—

> " The Slain are buried—are long at rest—
> The weapons are rusted with long disuse ;
> They lie where the great peacemaker, Death,
> Has furled their flag in endless truce.
> It fell to their lot, as it falls to all
> Who strike for freedom and strive in vain
> To set men free, or to wrest the thrall
> From fettered spirit or shackled brain.
> The cross, the scaffold, the knotted thong,
> The world metes out for the good and just ;
> For those who would battle with shame and wrong,
> The rifle-bullet and bayonet thrust.

The bell-bird sings in the drowsy wood
Its springtide song in the fervid noon,
The dark swan glides with her downy brood
Where the bul-rush nods in the cool lagoon ;
High overhead in the azure sky
The eagle soars on his sunlit plumes ;
And wild birds, rainbow-tinted, fly
Where yellow gold of the wattle blooms.
But the dead are deaf to each joyous sound ;
Their eyes are dark to the gladsome light ;
And life flows on in its ceaseless round—
Birth, and bridal, and burial rite.

Still sorrow sighs, and pleasures call,
While laughter, and love, and mourning meet ;
The spires of the Golden City fall
In clear-cut shadows across their feet.
And ever, like ocean's distant boom,
The batt'ries roar and the stampers pound ;
The white fleece twines on the swift steam loom.
And the big trip-hammer shakes the ground.
But still, in the hush of the silent night,
When skyward floats the vapor grey,
Between the dying of the moon
And dawning of the day,
The jewelled points of the South Cross pass
Through trailing mist, and the night winds sigh,
And whisper amid the rustling grass
　　　Where the men of the ' Fifties' lie."

But Mr. Reilly's muse is not exhausted. On the contrary, it is only pluming its wings for other, and it may be, higher flights. He has seen the *Austral Light* in his Creswick home, and he has written to me with permission to make what use I may of his communication. He refers, among bursts of patriotism and poetry, to the lost flag of the diggers at the Stockade, and says :—

To create a patriotic feeling amongst the rising generation, you must have some emblem—and that emblem I believe exists in the flag that was used by the Insurgents in '54. Am I wrong in asserting that some private person at Minyip I forget the name—has that banner of liberty ? Does the possessor know the value of it to Australians, or is he keeping it until it becomes priceless, in order that he may be repaid for keeping it all those long long years ? I have an idea that the name is nobly Celtic, and if it would not be out of the way, I would dare to suggest through the medium of the columns of the *Austral Light* that an appeal be made to the supposed holder of the flag (I am only stating this from what reference I saw made to the whereabouts of the flag in the *Sydney Bulletin* some time back) and I am sure that it would be forthcoming, either as a gift to the National Museum, or to a Society or body of responsible Australians who would take care of it for posterity to see. I would even suggest to the whole-souled priest in that district to wait upon the supposed holder or holders, and get him to hand it over, and thus win undying fame and glory.

I quote the above mainly because of the reference to the "whole-souled priest," as it may chance that the priests generally thereabouts, seeing Mr. Reilly's remarks, may interest themselves in the matter. It is a long time now since I engaged in correspondence anent the flag, my last effort for its recovery being the setting the Old Colonists' Association secretary here in motion. I had hoped that his official status might be more productive of success, but nothing ever came of it. Perhaps Mr. Reilly's guess is right as to the motive of the supposed holder of what, if still existing, is certainly a very interesting relic of the Stockade period.

Mr. Reilly burns, as an Australian born son of a Eureka Stockader, for the day when the Stockade site, "instead of being a deserted spot, bare and scorched with the relentless sun, will be a grove of beauty, carefully tended and watched by the patriot hearts that will assuredly be born with nobler attributes of love than many of my Australian brothers appear to have at present." He longs for an Australian national hymn, duly set to music, and he forthwith strikes his lyre again :—

> O wondrous isle, beneath whose harbor lights
> The white winged fleets of nations sweep between.
> O land of gold, uprisen in the years that live within the memory of
>   our Queen ;
> To thee we sing, and if perchance the sword
> Must be unsheathed to guard our native isle ;
> Let it be as one line of gleaming steel,
> Contesting every inch of Freedom's soil ;
> One flag, one song, triumphant as the sea
> That hems us in with flying wind-swept foam ;
> One bond of love as quenchless as the stars
> That flame and shine in skies above our home.

But Mr. Reilly remembers also with emotion his Melbourne experiences of a decade or so gone. "I owe (he says) all my application to the teachings and good example set by the brilliant intellects that emanated from St. Patrick's College, and gathered together years ago in the old St. Patrick's Hall under the name of the Young Men's Society." Need I add that he also hopes some day to be a contributor to the *Austral Light* otherwise than in this indirect fashion ?

Ballarat.   W. B. WITHERS.

232

Some Ballarat Reminiscences.

IV.

SO much verse writing about the Eureka Stockade, and, since my last, a fresh outburst of interest here over the still somewhat mythical flag, that I feel compelled to add to the details of the Stockade story before I leave it for good and all. It is seven years ago now since I called on Lalor's old friend, Stephen Cuming, at the house on a knoll at the head of Clayton's Gully, where he lived before the fight, and where he still lives, in his 76th year. A sturdy, hale, bronzed, white-bearded, grey-blue eyed, teetotal old Cornishman then, and still the same, barring the wearing of the intervening years. I was collecting details ·for some chronicles of the time, and in reply to my questions, he said: "After the soldiers and police retired, Lalor was put upon Father Smyth's horse, and he rode into the ranges and got shelter in a tent near Warrenheip. In the afternoon of the day of the fight, the woman of the tent told him she had to go into Ballarat, and so left him alone. Lalor, fearing that the woman was going to inform the police of his whereabouts, at once made up his mind to leave the place. I felt, somehow, that he would make for my place before long. I had left him in the Stockade at one o'clock that morning, and told him, should any disaster happen to him, to come to my place, and I said to my wife, 'We must look out for Lalor,' so I was on the look-out, and (his house commands the Stockade site and the ranges towards Warrenheip) towards sundown of the Sunday I saw a strange figure coming across there (pointing across the Buninyong railway line to the ranges east of it), wearing a belltopper—a most unusual thing in those days—and a long-tailed coat. Sure enough it was Peter disguised in Father Smyth's clothes, and I went out and met him. We housed him, gave him refreshments, and dressed his arm, and I told him it would have to come off. I told him we would make room for him if he wished, but that Father Smyth's place would be safer, as the police would hesitate to search the priest's house, but would not scruple to do so at a digger's place. So I went and saw Father Smyth, and he agreed with me, and when it was dark I set out with Lalor, revolver in hand, for Father Smyth's house. We did not meet a soul, and when we got to the priest's place Lalor was put into a bed in a little out-house. The next thing was to get a doctor, and I went for Dr. Doyle, of Golden Point, who said it was a case for amputation. 'All right,' said Lalor, 'let's know the worst.' He was a very brave man, you know, with all his defects. Dr. Gibson and Dr. Stewart and I were there while Dr. Doyle performed the operation. Well, about that time Bishop Gould came up, and he was opposed to his clergy taking any part in the movement, and Lalor was spirited away from Father Smyth's place, and a few days after that a messenger came to me from Lalor. I went and found him in bed in a small tent on Black Hill Flat, where there was only just room for a man to lie down, and we got him shifted to a nice large tent belonging to Michael Hayes at the foot of Black Hill. He stayed there till he got a carter named Carroll and little Tommy Marks to take him to Geelong."

So far for Cuming, and I give his words because they are perfectly trustworthy, and have a certain historical value, as have also some other communications made to me by Catherine Hayes, the widow of Timothy Hayes, the chairman of the Bakery Hill meetings of the diggers before the Stockade affair, by Marks, and by the son of Carroll. Mrs. Hayes is now dead, but Marks and Carroll are still here. When I waited on Mrs. Hayes in 1889 she was in her 71st year, residing with her son, Captain Hayes of the local militia. She was bright and quick in speech, as became the woman who told the police, when they arrested her husband, they should not have so easily had their way were she a man. When I interviewed Mrs. Hayes, Father Smyth's humble presbytery still remained, perhaps does still, as the kitchen of the present presbytery by St. Alipius Church, near Hayes' residence. Mrs. Hayes assisted at the amputation. "Two tables," she said, "were set side by side, and Lalor was laid upon them. Father Smyth was going to hold the basin, but he was nervous, and said to me, 'Can you hold it?' and I said, 'Yes, I can.' Dr. Doyle seemed timid, too, and Lalor cried out, 'Courage, courage, take it off,' and it was done. Lalor, after that, was put in Father Smyth's bed, and three sacks were filled with the blankets, sheets, and things that were soaked with the blood from the arm and the wine given him to drink, and the arm was put in with the clothes, and I saw McGrath and Phelan burying it all down a deep hole. I could show you the very spot now." The hole referred to was one of the old alluvial shafts near what is now the junction of Wills and Princes' streets.

Marks' story and Carroll's confirm Cuming's statement as to the conveyance of Lalor to Geelong. From Marks' narrative I clip the following: "We stuck to the bush as well as we could, Lalor being concealed as well as we could in one of Carroll's covered drays. It was on a Sunday in February, and awful hot, the bush was on fire in some places. We went by the Trial Saw Mills Road, and kept the coach road and Buninyong on our right, and so on till we got to the Separation Inn. There were two old lags there, and they spotted Lalor in the dray, and said, 'That's he, and there's £200 to be got for him.' So what did we do, but we made 'em dead drunk, and left 'em on the floor of the bar, and then the word was 'Harness up and away.' We got safe into Geelong on Tuesday night. We had a cup of tea at Carroll's place, and then Peter and I started for Miss Dunne's. It was a moonlight night, and Peter went along the shady side of the streets and I on the other with the swags." And so Marks left his charge, and went on to Melbourne, whither he had been subpœnaed as a witness in the State trials of the insurgents then pending.

This Eureka Stockade business I will close by some reference to the flag referred to by Mr. Reilly as being at Minyip. The fact is that the flag is in Ballarat, and was there when Mr. Reilly was hoping the "whole-souled priest" at Minyip would interest himself in the matter. But I was ignorant of the fact until a week or two ago, albeit, as mentioned in my last, I had endeavoured a year or two ago to get the flag for the Old Colonists' Association here. There has been founded here an Australian Historical Record Society, and at the first meeting to discuss preliminaries, reference was made to the desirability of also having a museum of old time relics, and I made mention of the Stockade flag, which was said to be somewhere in the country. Mr. James Oddie, the president of the Fine Arts Gallery Association here, at once said, "We have the flag at the Fine Arts Gallery;" and upon that hint I have since then been enacting a kind of commission *de vexillo inquirendo*. For, not to pun of malice afore-thought, I may tell you it is, at the time of this writing, a vexed question whether the Minyip flag is the diggers' flag or no.

[The foregoing has been in type since last February, but was held over at our contributor's request in order that he might complete his inquiry about the flag. Subjoined will be found Mr. Wither's further contribution.]

What flag was it the insurgents had flying in the Stockade on the day of the fight ? What became of that flag ? These are the questions which I have been trying to get answered during the last two months, and I have expended enough postage stamps, shoe leather, oral appeals, to me now innumerable greybeards, and personal and other examinations of newspaper files to entitle me to a minor canonization, if such a thing be possible. "But," it may be retorted, "you yourself stated years ago in print what the flag was." That is true in a sense not by any means exhaustive of the actual issue now raised. The description in the "History of Ballarat" is as follows:—"On a flag-staff was hung the insurgent flag—the Southern Cross. The flag had a blue ground, on which, in silver, the four principal stars of the constellation of the Southern Cross were shown." This description was based on Carboni Raffaello's, in his little pamphlet, corroborated by other descriptions—oral and written, and available at that time. It is obvious that the description is open to cross-examination. Thus—what is meant by "silver?" Mere whiteness of colour as contrasted with the blue, or what? How were the stars arranged? Were they on a church cross, or was there no such cross, but simply the stars of the constellation on a plain blue ground? Such testing for more complete description I never thought of a quarter century or so ago, because the flag was regarded as only a very small accident of the larger matter of insurgency and its tragical outcome. The "History" was written sixteen years after the encounter, and we were fairly close then to the events. But now we are over forty years away. Now we are on the fringe of the time when legend and poetry, and a certain blending of patriotism and veneration in some quarters are, it would seem, beginning to gather about the Stockade and the moving episodes which led up to it ; and so, to embroider,

" With gay enamell'd colors mix'd,"

the plain prose of history. This means, also, that we have now reached the distance where relics begin to have a distinct value. We are entering the period when what had previously seemed, perhaps, to have quite unimportant relation to the historic struggle is acquiring, I will not say a fictitious value, but a quite new relative importance. The age of relics, as has been said, is upon us. Hence the founding of the "Australian Historical Record Society," the mooting of plans for collecting and storing documentary records of the local past, of forming museums of relics of historical interest. And thus it comes about that a greater importance has come to be attached to the flag captured by the attacking force at the Eureka Stockade.

This new interest is essentially inquisitive in its results. It prompts a root inquiry. It at once assumes a cross-examining attitude. If relic-holders have an instinct for assessing values, relic-buyers or collectors, if they have brains, "want to know, you know," about the evidence as to any claim of relic-possession. Well, there is in the Ballarat Art Gallery a tattered flag, which is declared to be the actual flag taken from the insurgent diggers at the Eureka Stockade by the attacking force on the fatal Sunday

morning, forty-two years ago come next December.   For my sins it
is laid upon me now to put the two questions above, and endeavour
to find if satisfactory answers are procurable.   I will not say that
I shall find a verdict, but I will assume that my readers are a kind
of jury, and will say to them, after the manner of law-court officials
—Hearken to the evidence.

The first thing to get at, if possible, is an authentic description
of the flag at the Stockade.   I take it that the descriptions in
Raffaello's book and my " History " are true and valid—so far as
they go.   Raffaello is very precise, too, in one way, for he says in one
place :—" The flag is silk, blue ground with a large silver cross,
similar to the one in our southern firmament ; no device or arms,
but all exceedingly chaste and natural."   But the descriptions do
not go far enough when the validity of a concrete flag, or of the
remains of a flag tendered as a relic of the true and actual flag, is in
issue.   The outline or, so to speak, generic classification given years
ago has now to be made specific and detailed, so that, if possible, a
picture of the actual flag in question may be obtained, whether out
of men's memories or from available sketches of the flag.

And the moment I began to burrow amongst the old Stockaders
and other survivors of the Stockade time, I found myself in a chaos
of contradictory descriptions of the flag.   Dim recollections, con-
fused visions in the memory, positive assertions, and as positive
denials.   Of the score or two of men who had seen the flag *at the
Stockade*, hardly any two would agree on even an outline sketch.
Some thought it was blue, some red, some white, one actually had
seen a black flag.   Some said that the flag bore on it a cross
(ecclesiastical), some said it did not, but only the " Southern Cross,"
meaning the *Crux Australis* of astronomy.   And most of them, if
they ventured something like a positive assertion on the point, would
frankly admit on cross-examination that they " really could not say
now, to be certain, it was so long ago."   And this is, really, quite
natural.   We look at a flag and pass on, but if asked a day or two
after to give a detailed description of it, who of us could do so with
the minute exactness necessary to satisfy the relic-hunter's quest ?
Who has not had doubts sometimes whether a given incident
occurred one day or two days past, and only solved the doubt by
calling up collateral evidence.   Well, suppose forty years have
passed, would not the solution be probably impossible.   And so it
evidently is a matter of prime difficulty now to get a clear description,
orally, of the Stockade flag.   Only a year or two ago, while Lalor
was, in fact, still living, a group of men were disputing as to which
arm he lost at the Stockade, and men who had been accustomed to

see him frequently had to cudgel their memories for a longer or shorter time before they could positively say which arm it was. Some of my most intelligent witnesses were the least positive when questioned about the flag. In the Stockade time there were flags galore all over the diggings. Every store had its flag, every theatre, every hotel, every eating-house. But who of all the hosts that saw the flags flying would have been able to give at request what may be called a scientific description of any one of them ? Well, add to this difficulty—as to a present and visible fact—the lapse into the invisibility of forty years and more, and the chaos of description or no description which I have mentioned will be easily understood. Of all my respondents, during this enquiry, whether orally or by letter, only one has given me a clear and positive, and I believe quite veracious description of a flag in connection with the insurgents. I say *a flag* advisedly, as being a possible differentiation from the actual Stockade flag. The witness in question was Mr. John M'Neil, of 120 Victoria Street, a keen-witted man of evidently exceptional faculty for observation and retention of facts. He says :—" I was at the Bakery Hill meeting when Lalor swore the diggers, and a man named Robert M'Candlish unbuttoned his coat and took out and unfurled a light blue flag with some stars on it, but there was no cross on it." M'Candlish is not here nor his whereabouts known, nor does M'Neil know what became of that flag. M'Neil, when confronted with the flag in the Art Gallery, shook his head, and rejected the flag as one never seen by him before. Others, actual Stockaders some of them, have shaken their heads at it, and others only mutter doubts and confessions of memories barren of exact pictures of the flag flown at the Stockade. If a second M'Neil as to positiveness and precision might have been looked for, it might reasonably have been in the person of Stephen Cuming, Lalor's sheltering friend, who had been about the stockade as well as the Bakery Hill meetings. Here is his evidence :—" I saw the flag (at the gallery), and scrutinised it, and came to the conclusion that possibly it is the very identical flag displayed at the ' Slabaide ' over forty years ago, and in my opinion it may not be. I expected to have seen a little tint of red color on the face ; but through the lapse of time this color might have disappeared. Neither is the blue color very distinct, which was so in the original. I am even now sure nearly anyone might have concocted the banner, and, moreover, my impression is that the flag was more artistic. Anyhow, we might do worse than reject it ; it will be something for posterity to worship. But I am informed that the present owner requires £150 cash down for the relic. Of course, that is a question for the art authorities to decide. Permit me further to remark, the size of the flag seems about the same as the original. Sorry I cannot give a positive yea or nay." I give Mr. Cuming's statement in full, not for its lack of puzzling references to color, but because of his close relations with Lalor at the time, because he is quaint and somewhat iconoclastic, and because he is, I think, incorruptibly veracious.

Now to the flag in the Art Gallery. A few years ago, soon after the close of the Industrial Exhibition here in 1890-1, I learned through Mr. Archibald, curator of the Warrnambool Museum, that " the Stockade flag " was in the possession of a trooper named King, who had pulled it from the staff in the Stockade during the action. King, or his widow, was said to be living in the Wimmera district, and I at once put the president and secretary of the Old Colonists' Association on the quest for the so-called relic of the Stockade, but they failed to get possession of it, and the matter dropped. As soon as I heard that the flag in question was in the Art Gallery here, I began the new quest, and found that Mr. James Oddie, the president of the Fine Arts Association, had heard from a minister in Buninyong that he had seen the flag in the Wimmera country. Mr. Oddie at once took steps to get the flag, and Mr. Powell (the secretary of the association) addressed the holder of the flag, that is the widow of the trooper King. The flag was transmitted to Mr. Powell by post office parcel with the following letter :—

Kingsley, Minyip,

1st October, 1895.

Dear Sir,—In connection with the wish of the president of the Ballarat Fine Arts and Public Gallery for the gift or loan of the flag that floated above the Eureka Stockade, I have much pleasure in offering loan of flag to the above association on condition that I may get it at any time I specify, or on demand by myself or son, Arthur King. The main portion of the flag was torn along the rope that attached it to the staff, but there is still part of it around the rope, so that I suppose it would be best to send the whole of it as it now is. You will also find several holes, that were caused by bullets that were fired at my late husband in his endeavours to seize the flag at that memorable event.—Yours, &c.,

MRS. J. KING (per Arthur King).

The flag sent by the widow King is, or was, as far as one may judge in its tattered condition, twelve feet long by eight feet wide, is of blue bunting, and has sewn upon it, in some whitish material, a cross carrying five stars on its limbs. It is much torn at the ends, and parts are gone, including parts of two of the stars. There are also many holes in the flag, but whether they are bullet-holes, as Mrs. King says, or moth-holes (as Mr. Archibald has submitted to me in a plea for the relic being placed in a glass case) I cannot take it upon me to determine.

This Trooper King flag is, clearly, not the one M'Neil saw and describes so positively. Now, it seems to me that there is nothing wildly improbable in the supposition that more than one flag was flaunted at the meetings of the diggers immediately prior to the Stockade encounter. The point is, now, as to the flag taken at the Stockade, and we will call some further evidence upon that issue. Mr. John Lynch, one of Lalor's band at the Stockade, and already known as a writer upon that episode in Victorian history, has favoured me with several communications on the flag business. But he has not a clear vision of the Stockade flag in his mind's eye, though he inclines to the Raffaello and "History of Ballarat" version. In almost his latest letter to me, he says—"Whilst unable to produce evidence sufficient to silence all objections, I am perfectly satisfied that there was but one flag, and that the *very* one before which we knelt and swore, and which we afterwards saw so rudely treated during the conflict at the Stockade." In a previous letter he says :—"I do not remember having noticed a white cross, if, by that, he meant white stripes connecting the starry points, but would not positively maintain that there was none. I never had the curiosity to examine the flag closely, and a casual look at an object, which, at the time, I did not deem of much importance, might not have been sufficient to afford a full grasp of its accessories, or stir me to note the minutiæ of its settings if tricked out at all." Thus Mr. Lynch corroborates my story as to the chaos of no-descriptions, and illustrates my theory as to the new interest evolved in the passage of the years, for he is enthusiastic as to the necessity of a proper scrutiny into the validity of the claim set up in respect of the King flag. Mr. Lynch says, as to the capture of the flag :—"I have a vague recollection of its being pulled down by the soldiers amidst a chorus of jeers and ribald shoutings. A private of the 40th Regiment told myself and other prisoners that he was one of those who rough-handled it." And he again says :—"At this distance of time I would not take it upon me to identify that flag."

Mr. Lynch points out the apparent discrepancy between his soldier's story in the camp lock-up after the fight, and that of the capture of the flag by trooper King. Point is also given to this conflict of evidence by a statement made to me by Mr. Theophilus Williams, J.P., late mayor of Ballarat East. He tells me that his tent was hard by the Stockade, and he saw the fight, and is prepared to affirm on affidavit that he saw "two red-uniform soldiers haul down the flag." He also remembers that the flag had on it a cross, "something" like that on the flag in the Art Gallery. In a later letter from Mr. Lynch is the following :—"The soldier's reference to the flag was merely incidental, and all that I remember distinctly of his allusion to it was

that he helped to tear it down.   .   .   .   I take it as an established
fact that the reavement of the Standard-pole, flag and all, was the
work of the regular soldiery." At the very start of this inquest I
saw the importance of testing the King claim by inquiry as to the
uniform worn, and Mrs. King writes in reply to my letter to her on
that point :—" I do not know what colour uniform was worn by my
late husband, but he was in the police force at Melbourne at the
time. I suppose the police uniform was worn." Colonel Rede, who
was the chief civil officer in camp here during the trouble with
the diggers, writes me :—" The pensioners were old soldiers sworn in
as police, were dressed as policemen and led by a police officer,
Captain Carter, and were the first in the Stockade, and pulled down
the flag." This tallies with the statement in the "History of
Ballarat," given by another civil camp officer, whose name I
may now give—Mr. Huyghue, clerk to the Commissioners,
and afterwards warden's clerk here. Both Mr. Huyghue
and Colonel Rede, I apprehend, relate what they heard
immediately after the fight, and from what should be the
very best authority, though their evidence is traversed in the
"History," second edition, by a soldier of the 40th. In the same
edition one of Lalor's captains (Esmond) says :—"Captain Wise led
the scouts on foot, who broke into the Stockade, where Lalor was."
M'Combie, in his " History of Victoria," says :—" In a few minutes
the military carried the entrenchment at the point of the bayonet."

The civil and military authorities looked on the insurgents as
mere rioters, and on that basis the flag of the Stockaders would not
be regarded as a trophy to be proud of like a ' color ' taken from an
enemy on an ordinary battlefield, but rather as " an old rag " to be
rent and trampled on contemptuously. Indeed, some of the people
about the Stockade have said that they thought the flag was destroyed
there and then. I put this aspect of the matter to Colonel Rede,
who replies :—" I always thought the flag remained in the possession of the police. I do not remember that there was any importance
attached to the flag." But I also owe to Colonel Rede's courtesy
some evidence of great interest of a concrete sort. He enclosed to me
a fragment of the " Eureka flag, given to Mrs. Clendinning by Dr.
Alfred Carr, who was doing the medical duties of the Camp at that
time." Mrs. Clendinning, whose daughter Colonel Rede married,
was then residing here with her husband, the late Dr. Clendinning,
who thereafter filled for many years the office of coroner for Ballarat
and district. This fragment and a fragment of the King flag I submitted to the expert inspection of Mr. Grainger, the manager of the
Sunnyside woollen mills here, and he thought the two were similar,

but he wished to have a larger fragment for comparison, and Colonel Rede kindly sent me all that Mrs. Clendinning had, a piece two or three inches square. Mr. Grainger was so courteous as to meet Mr. Oddie and me at the Art Gallery, when he minutely compared the Dr. Carr fragment with the King flag, and said the fragment was a part of the flag. That is to say, it was identical in material and construction, the warp in both flag and fragment being cotton and the weft mohair. So we seem thus to have, presumptively, a connection expertly established between the Carr and the King flag, and, if so, a connection of the King flag with the camp after the Stockade action. Mr. Archibald informs me that the flag " passed from King's possession for a short time into that of the late Peter Henry Smith, inspecting superintendent of police, whose wife (widow) and family live at South Yarra. Mr. Smith returned the flag to King, with whose family it has been every since." This, I fear, is not evidence in the forensic sense, albeit it is, presumably, trustworthy in a certain sense. I wrote to the widow of Mr. Smith, but she is the only person who has not replied to my enquiries in this matter. Perhaps she had nothing to say.

The late Marcus Clarke, then Secretary of the Melbourne Public Library, wrote to Lalor on the 13th September, 1877, at Parliament House as follows :—" The bearer, Mr. John King, has brought to the Public Library a flag which purports (sic) to be the original flag flown at the Eureka Stockade. He offers it for sale to the trustees, and I think the institution would be glad to possess such a relic, if we could be sure that it is the original flag. Mr. King says that you would be sure to recognise it. Would you kindly give him a line to say what you think about it." Now, this reference by King to Lalor is, surely, evidence of good faith, and of the validity of the King claim. Marcus Clarke's note to Lalor was transmitted by Lalor to Mr. J. Noble Wilson, who is now managing director of the Ballarat Trustees, Executors, and Agency Company, and he handed it to me to copy, as also Lalor's note accompanying it, undated, but posted in Melbourne on the 21st September, 1877, in which he says :—" King is the man's name who brought the flag to Mr. Clarke. I believe it to be the true flag, although it does not quite agree with the details given in your letter." The details referred to were extracts from the first edition of the " History of Ballarat " relative to the stockade flag. Lalor wrote another undated note to Mr. Wilson, saying :—" Do you think you could find the maker or anyone whose memory would be more accurate than mine." So we have here the man who swore in the diggers by the " Southern Cross," admitting 23 years after the battle that he could not be certain what the flag was like. What wonder, then, if now, after more than 40 years have elapsed, this trail of the serpent of dubiety is over all the evidence available ? A trustee of the Melbourne Public Library informs me that no such flag is in the museum there, whence I conclude Lalor's halting testimony, or some other reason, induced the trustees of the library to consider King's offer as one not to be entertained. Then, we have an exhibition by Mr. Oddie of the Art Gallery flag to Mrs. Morgan and Mrs. Oliver, still of this city, who made a flag ostensibly for the insurgents, but they both say the King flag is not the one they made. The flag they made was made to order, and they say it bore in the centre "The Lone Star of Texas," and they think, but are not sure, " The Stars and Stripes " in one corner. I mention this because it has been largely rumoured here that the diggers' flag was made by those ladies. But all they seem to know is that they made a *flag* to somebody's order in the usual way of their business at that time. Curiously enough, underneath the flag in the gallery is a water-colour sketch by Mr. Huyghue of the action at the Stockade, in which is seen a flag with a cross like, as to outlines, that on the King flag. Mr. Huyghue is dead, or he would be a witness of direct and most pertinent interest. It is presumable that the artist had his hint from the flag Dr. Carr obtained Mrs. Clendenning's fragment from. The flag shown as the digger's flag in the first edition of the " History of Ballarat " was printed from a sketch by Mr. Huyghue, and was a fairly exact likeness of the cross and stars on the King flag.

In conclusion we have to hear some evidence touching the flag, produced as the insurgents' flag at the trial of the Stockade prisoners, before the Supreme Court, in Melbourne, in the first quarter of 1855. This evidence comes from the files of the Melbourne dailies, and has been kindly extracted for me by a Melbourne journalist. It is sad to know, however that the *Ballarat Times* file of the early fifties is lost, and that the file of the *Geelong Advertiser* of the same date has been mutilated. " Spy Goodenough " deposed that— " There was a flag hoisted when the meeting (Bakery Hill) commenced. It was a blue flag with a white cross. I will not swear that the flag produced was the flag, but it was something like it." The reporter *(Age)* added in a parenthesis—" The flag was shown to the witness ; it was that known as the diggers' flag, and bearing the sign of the much talked of Southern Cross. It is a plain white cross on a blue ground." The same journal makes Goldfields Commissioners Amos and Webster depose similarly as to the flag being blue with a white cross, but neither they nor Goodenough say anything about stars on the flag, and the King flag as we have seen, is blue with a white cross carrying five stars in the same white colour and material, three on each limb of the cross, one, of course, serving in the centre for both limbs. Other witnesses similarly described the flag hoisted by the diggers, and the *Herald* reports barrister Chapman, who defended, as recognising the flag produced in court as that of the Anti-Transportation League, and "presented to the League when the deputation from V. D. Land visited the colony, or it was so perfect a copy of the League flag that none could tell the difference between them." The *Herald* reporter had his parenthesis also, and said :—" The flag was here displayed : it bore the Southern Cross on a blue ground." The *Argus* Ballarat correspondent, writing on the fatal Sunday, says :—" The flag of the diggers, the 'Southern Cross,' as well as the Union Jack, which they had to hoist underneath, were captured by the police." He also reported that " Hugh King, constable of police, in his evidence said 'a blue flag with a white cross and five stars was visible in the Stockade.' Hugh King was one of the attacking force." Whether " Hugh King " should be " John King " does not appear. The Geelong correspondent of the *Argus* has a letter in that journal of 5th December, 1854, narrating a tale told to him " by an intelligent gentleman " who was present at the Bakery Hill oath meeting. All that concerns us in this enquiry is the following :—" He found a tall flagstaff erected, on which was floating a blue flag with a white cross upon it. In each corner of the cross and the centre was a blue star, the five stars representing the five Australian colonies." If this " intelligent " witness was not colour blind we have a quite new feature introduced. He is the only deponent who saw blue stars.

But on the 31st May, 1870, the Legislative Assembly, when discussing a vote for the ship Nelson, was startled by Mr. Frazer saying " he had been informed that the flag unfurled on board the Nelson was the identical flag that was flying over the Eureka Stockade at the time of the riot." (Laughter.) This was said in connection with reference to the exhibit at the trial, and Mr. Frazer added—" the flag in question was subsequently stolen from the court, and had never since been found." If this be true the King flag is not likely to be the flag produced at the trial, but then Mr. Frazer might have lighted on a mare's nest.

In face of the absence of clear concurrent evidence as to what the Stockade flag was in detail of make and in kind of material, that is to say of what the writers of the fifties really meant by the " Southern Cross " flag, the relic hunter will naturally want to know what became of the exhibit at the trial of the state prisoners.

For he will as naturally assume that, at any rate, that exhibit was the real flag. To establish the claim of the owners of the Art Gallery flag, then, it seems essential that they should provide evidence of continuity of possession, or of such continuity of possession, as shall satisfy reasonable men that the court exhibit has remained, either actually or potentially, in their keeping from the date of the trials until the present day. Upon the assumption that the court exhibit was not a fraud, the proof of its identity with the King flag would also be proof of all that is wanted to clear all dubiety as to what the Stockade flag was, and would, as it seems to me, be a satisfactory answer to the two questions with which this paper starts. Can the King family supply that necessary evidence? If they can, the Raffaello silk flag and the M'Neil-M'Candish flag both vanish into limbo of the unreal in so far as our problem of the two queries is concerned, though both may have had, upon the hypothesis of several flags having been at one place and time or another displayed at meetings of the diggers, a real existence as "diggers' flags." Our only quest here is for the flag captured at the Stockade by the assaulting force on the 3rd December, 1854. If the Huyghue flag sketched for the first edition of the "History of Ballarat" was also the Carr-Clendinning fragment flag, as is probable, it is also inferrable that the flag was this one seen and handled at the Government camp immediately after the action at the Stockade, was in keeping by some Government officer, and was the flag produced at the State trials. Was King the officer who had the flag at the camp, and did he produce it at the trials, and is the flag in the Art Gallery that flag? Anyone can see that it answers fairly well to the Huyghue sketch.

Ladies and gentlemen,—You have heard the evidence presently available ; consider your verdict.

Ballarat.   W. B. WITHERS.

Some Ballarat Reminiscences.

SOME fluff from the Eureka Stockade flag discussion, some jetsam cast up on the sands, some asides thrown in by correspondents, some aftermath crop since the publication of my last, seem to require clearing out of the way before I can fancy that I have really done with the business for good and all as I promised myself.

On the day the last article appeared, a correspondent from Egerton, signing "George Hartley," wrote to me thus:—"As you are wanting to know about the Eureka flag I will inform you, as I remember it to be a blue flag with white (not silver) stars; it has a 'Southern Cross' on it. I slept under it that night, as it was nailed to 'Tom the blacksmith's shop.' Tom slept in his stretcher, I slept on a slab beside it. Tom was a mate with 'Dutch Harry' (H. Schmedding). He (Tom) was killed in the morning. Yours, &c." I send you this as a sample of the *lucus a non* lucidities of some of those I have had to deal with in this enquiry. Mr. Hartley's note has, however, brought forth other fruit. I enclosed it in an envelope to our old friend, John Lynch, and he writes:

"Tom was the blacksmith who made the pikes, slept in the Stockade, and was killed in the morning. Poor fellow, he fared worse than did Johnny Cope in the morning. I have here with me at present a visitor who was then about 13 years of age, and saw Tom in his dying moments. He had known Tom for some time, and the agonies of the dying man left a lasting impression on his mind. He says that Tom died some hours after the conflict was over. My guest takes a great interest in the discussion of the flag affair, so that he went purposely to see and examine it in the Art Gallery. He is not quite sure, but leans to the side of scepticism. He thinks it likely to be one of the many sign-flags bearing the same device, the same blue color, and the same texture that used to be flaunted over the stores. I go a little further in my scepticism, being incited thereto by the closing sentence of Mrs. King's letter. If the "several holes that were caused by bullets fired" at her husband be the effect of the cause assigned, then her husband must have been the luckiest man that ever escaped from danger with a whole skin : or the firing squad must have been the most blundering marksmen that ever handled a firelock. And be it remembered that the firing at this critical juncture must have been done by the military, for the flag was despoiled long after resistance on the diggers' side had ceased, Was it likely that the military would fire upon one of their comrades, or is it to be said that they tried to do so

246

but failed to hit him ?   Homer's deities used sometimes to rescue their favourites,
but if Mrs. King's story be true, the divine partiality in favour of Trooper King
has far exceeded any such manifestation heard of before."

Mr. Lynch's criticism is so obviously provoked by the whole
premises that he will not be surprised to know that similar remarks
—barring the classical reference—occurred to one or two persons
here during the late inquiry.   A Mr. Howard, in a note enclosed
to me by Mr. Lynch, says : " I do not remember a trooper being
inside the Stockade at the time.   They all kept scout outside the
Stockade, running down all the people they could."   I do not give
much value to this, as it is not positive evidence, but, contrasted
with Colonel Rede's statement, is evidence of variety.   Under date
7th May, I have a note from " Robert Dengan," an alderman of
Ashfield, in New South Wales, who says : " I will be pleased to
forward you some particulars re the storming of the Stockade.
Now, I saw the flag on that memorable Sunday morning, and will
also give you the name of the man who had the flag in his
possession just after the battle."   Had I not encountered so great
a host of people who " knew all about it," and who turned out to be
absolute duffers on examination, this Ashfield alderman's promise
would quite excite me.   As it is, I await his promised communication with philosophic quiet, even though he closes his note thus :
" In the meantime don't lose sight of the King flag."   The Art
Gallery authorities here, who have the flag, seem to have made up
their minds, evidence or no evidence to the contrary, that the King
flag is the real article.   Before the lately published pros and cons saw
the light, the said authorities had found their verdict, or had
accepted the King flag as valid.   They pinned to the flag in the
Gallery, and still keep there the following statement : " Flag hoisted
during the engagement between the diggers and Queen's troops at
the Eureka Stockade on 3rd Decr., 1854, and taken down by
trooper Arthur (sic) King towards the close of the action."   So now
we have a John, a Hugh, and an Arthur King implicated in the
business, and the confusion still more confounded.

Among Lalor's closest acquaintances, both before and after the
Stockade days, was Mr. Wanliss, now the Hon. T. D. Wanliss,
M.L.C.   He came up from Melbourne on the Saturday before the
fight, at Lalor's request, but, when he went to the Stockade, Lalor
was asleep, and he left without disturbing him.   Now, Mr. Wanliss
is a pretty shrewd man, and he saw the flag, but when I tested his
memory I found it a blank, or rather it seemed to be something like
a photographer's picture in the dark developing room.   He only
remembered stars at first, but, as I mentioned Huyghue's picture

247

and the King flag, he began to fancy he saw the outlines of a cross dimly appearing. So you see all sorts of witnesses contribute to the dubiety of the business. Raffaello, generally so clear, is graphic in the following bit from his 56th chapter, but adds no corroboration of the trooper claim. He says: " The old command ' charge ' was distinctly heard, and the red-coats rushed with fixed bayonets to storm the stockade . . . A wild ' hurrah ' burst out, and the ' Southern Cross ' was torn down, I should say, among their laughter, such as if it had been a prize from a maypole." Mr. Lynch corroborates Raffaello incidentally in one of his notes to me before my last article appeared. He says: " Colonel Rede's account is liable to objection. The place of honour he assigns to the pensioners is a new ingredient, and is not in accord with the order in which the military moved. The movement being in echelon, which requires a formation of successive charges, would be incompatible with the occupancy of a certain fixed place by any portion of the advancing force. The truth is that the Stockade was stormed by the soldiers, and that they were supported in flank by the cavalry, who occupied the place which Colonel Rede assigns to the pensioners."

I may mention the fact that other " relics " of the Stockade have been about at various times. An Irishwoman at one time claimed to have the sword worn by Captain Wise at the fight, and divers very enquiring visitors waited upon her and saw the sword, but nobody seemed to be satisfied that Captain Wise's sword had fallen to so very improbable custody, and so that business ended. Pike heads and old-fashioned pistols are extant here with more or less of valid claims to authenticity, but they are of inferior fascination to that which would belong to the real flag or even to Captain Wise's sword.

How high-handed were some of the proceedings of the Camp officials in the Stockade time everybody knows, who knows of the history of the license agitation. One or two of the persons I approached during the flag enquiry gave me bits of their experience. Mr. W. B. Rodier, J.P. now of Hawthorn, one of the oldest Ballarat pioneers and the first chairman of the Municipal Council in Ballarat East, chanced to be here on a visit and I asked him if he remembered the flag. He did not, but he remembered that just after the Stockade affair the camp authorities posted on his store in the main road a placard offering £400 reward for Lalor. He did not like the camp people and declined to have his store made use of in this way, so forthwith tore down the notice about the rebel chief. Webster, the Commissioner, had him arrested forthwith, and he was hauled off in his shirt sleeves to the " lousy logs." The arrest was, of course, unjustifiable, and the camp people were puzzled how to deal with the prisoner. One asked what the charge was. "Oh sedition," Rodier replied, "for I said 'Joe' was not dead when I pulled down the notice." This was a retort upon the cry of the troopers in the hour of triumph at the Stockade for they had then shouted that "Joe"— the outraged diggers' mocking epithet applied to the license-hunting police—"is dead now." Rodier was put in the logs in contact with lice and unmentionable filth and then "discharged" after a few hours' detention. He had no redress, for a shield of "indemnity" was thrown over all the camp blunders of the time. Mr. R. M. Sergeant, J.P. told me of two little matters of the time. One day during the time of the Bakery Hill meetings before the Stockade tragedy he saw Col. Rede have a narrow escape from diggers' wrath. The Commissioner was riding on his horse among the holes, and two or three diggers noticed him. One of them said "Let's put the —— down a hole." The Commissioner seemed to have heard the threat and his hand moved towards his breast as if, as Mr. Sergeant concluded, to draw his revolver. But he rode quietly on and the menaced assault did not take place. On another day Mr. Sergeant was going along Lydiard and Mair streets, to get letters at the Post Office, which was then at the south west corner of Lydiard and Mair streets. It was a day when troopers were scouring the thoroughfares near the camp to keep them clear of loiterers, and one trooper rode in among the crowd at the Post Office and smashed his own head against the verandah, but the head being hard or the verandah soft no great damage was done to either. Another little episode was told to me by Mr. Goddard, father of the present President of one of the local A.N.A. Lodges. He lived on Bakery Hill close by the old trysting place of the diggers during the license agitation, and as he was standing at his doorway one day a trooper rode along and ordered him to clear off. Naturally enough he demurred, and the trooper's response was a sabre cut across the wrist. "There's the mark, you see," he said as he showed me a scar on his wrist. Such yarns as these might be told galore of those days, and all of them true—if your yarner be not a liar. If you knew your man you could, of course, duly appraise the value of his story, and the Rodier and Sergeant and Goddard stories may be accepted as authentic touches illustrative of the times just before and after the storming of what Stephen Cuming called the "Slabaide."

Apropos of Cuming, that shaggy-bearded old pioneer lives where the old and the new are both about him. As I have said before, he lives to-day where he lived in the days before the Stockade. When I called to see him about the flag, we stood, two old grey beards, on the mound where his home is. It is a bit of the primitive bush subdued by the rude home-making of forty years and more. On one side, eastward, the modern in the shape of the railway to Buninyong was seen. Beyond, in that midsummer drought, stretched dry, brown, burnt-grass-strewn paddocks and ranges. On the Western side lay dreary reaches of long deserted worked-out diggings. Through the russet and green of some apple trees, as we talked, one saw north-eastward the grey monolith and the gums which mark the spot where the insurgent diggers fell on the bloody Sunday morning. The tough old man lives on, proud in the spirit of independence which animated the men of the early fifties, honest, law-abiding, but resolutely defiant of misrule. He is not the only one left to tell of the old times, and the old grievances. A good few survive here and there, strong, sturdy, proud representatives of a race of pioneers whose real worth and spirit the rulers of the pre-constitutional period utterly failed to comprehend or appreciate. This much I may say without being understood to applaud all the men, or all the aims of the men who took up arms against the misrule of "the days that are no more."

One of the old pioneers, whom I interviewed during the flag inquest, had some stories of the immediately past-stockade days. He is now an accountant and commission agent, but was then a young fellow attached in some clerical capacity to the old Charlie Napier Hotel and Theatre. At the time referred to the diggers were in full blast upon the rich alluvial deposits of the Red Hill and Red Streak, and the whole flat traversed by the Main Road was riddled with shafts at the close quarters of those days of small claims. The Charlie Napier people had a bar at the rear as well as at the front, so that the diggers on every side might have easy access to the potables they hankered after. But the shafts were so close that ingress and egress was a matter of utmost difficulty, mullock and water and tailings pressing and flowing here, there and everywhere. The gold was there, and every foot of ground was rushed. A shaft was even put down in the pit of the Victoria Theatre next door, and dramatic and concert hall business went on in conjunction with the diggers' work in the shaft. At that time, Thatcher, the topical song-maker and singer, was engaged at the Victoria or the Charlie, and he worked in the pit-shaft episode with one of his rough and ready creations. The thinnest jokes and the grittiest of doggerel went down in those days when everybody was young, gold as well as grog was plentiful, and hope's iris tints irradiated the ugliest material surroundings. In those times too came the little sensation caused by horsewhipping, which Lola Montes administered to poor little Seekamp of the *Ballarat Times*, because he wrote unpleasant things about her in his paper. But my accountant friend reminded me of another whipping in which Lola was the whippee not the whipper. The wife of one of the actors at the Victoria, where Lola was playing, had discovered, or thought she had discovered, a treason between her husband and the Bavarian Countess, and the jealous wife did what she could to literally whip the devil out of the versatile Lola. It was only a forty-eight hours' wonder, and things went on thereafter as usual. Of the value of the wife's suspicions I know nothing. They belong now to the dead past. Let them lie there without more disturbing.

Occasional gleams of humour have relieved the dull dreary encounters I have had in the quest for the truth about the Stockade flag. Here is a happy burst of mingled fun, and fancy, and fact, whose graphic lines are luminous with accurate description as well as hot with not absolutely unwarranted satire. It is a communication from one of the oldest pressmen in Victoria, a gentleman who has both a provincial and a metropolitan reputation as one of the ablest of the host of "recording angels" in this colony. He now rests from his labours and smokes the pipe of peace in well-earned retirement.

"DEAR ANCIENT,—You ask me did I "ever *see* the diggers' flag which they had at their Bakery Hill meetings, and at the Stockade ?"—meaning, of course, the banner of which a simulacrum appears in the title page of your *History of Ballarat (Editio princeps, 1870)*. No, I never did. I was not there, not there my child. My luck kept my wandering feet from Ballarat until some four months after the Eureka episode, which was just then rather in contempt than otherwise. So many, you know, had peeped behind the scenes. What I laughed at most was the stories in vogue of the 'too previous' storekeepers and others, including a certain sawn-timber-yard firm, who had managed (having a sweet forecast of Government compensation) to get their dead stock 'seized' by the 'rioters.' I would almost take oath that the Stockade itself was actually built with the short-sized, sawn slabs of which the local dealers had such a heavy supply, but which, when the Gravel Pits lead ran deep, were knocked out of demand. But I am lapsing into scandal, and had far better keep to your question.

"True, absence of body prevented my ever seeing the Eureka flag, in all its native silk and tinsel, but I well recollect that the fac-simile in your book struck me with surprise. Because I had up to then always trusted in the account so often given me of the soldier of the 40th who, when the 'unpleasantness' was over, calmly hauled down the gaudy streamer, and put it in his pocket, to be never again heard of even in the form of handkerchief. I don't imagine that for some time there were many inquiries on the subject. The idea of exploiting it had not arisen. Having had a hand in or sympathised with the Stockade movement was a boast not yet invented. At the very first start, perhaps, and especially in distant Melbourne, the flow of feeling was different. For example, some ten or twelve days after the fatal Sunday, I was at a concert at the

251

Melbourne Theatre Royal vestibule (the theatre itself was built next year). When the late Ebenezer Syme came in with a rough looking companion whom he introduced to me as Frederick Vern, for whose apprehension £500 was on offer. In fact we made a party—I think the late J. J. Ham was one—to look at the placard outside the City Police Court, from whence we adjourned to the Duke of Cornwall hotel and quoted 'battle-axe.' Not a little proud were we all at the time, but the glow dwindled as we knew more of Vern, and realised that nine-tenths of those concerned in the outbreak were fresh from the land of Smith O'Brien. Many months elapsed before so many discovered that they had all along been on the side of the 'rioters,' and entitled to take credit *pro ratâ.* Not for two years (Dec. 1856) were the first honours paid to the fallen, when began the era of tall talk and exaggeration which I am not sure has ended. Playing it low down was never a favourite game on dear old Ballarat. Oh for the old days there! I shut my eyes and am in fancy again at one of the local public meetings of the period—the still early fifties. There is the old 'hall,' with its walls of scantling and roof of calico. There is the Chairman, and round him grouped the expectant speakers, each (like us reporters at the adjoining trestle table) smoking his hardest; while Weekes, or A. A. O'Connor, or Kennedy, or that wonderful Highlandman from Buninyong, 'poured his throat' in fiery appeals, or scathing epithets. How the frail erection rang with the sympathetic roaring, the clapping. the stamping, and the ramping.

" To come back to the Flag once more, What I wonder is that you have not now extant a dozen such, if not more, each as authentic as the other ? This is no time for mock modesty."

I trust that now, so far as your columns are concerned, I may take leave for ever of this Eureka Flag story.

Ballarat.   W. B. WITHERS.

Some Ballarat Reminiscences.

FIRST let me correct two typographical errors in my last paper. The "monolith and gums" of the Stockade site should be "monolith and guns," for the Victorian Government, in its generosity, made us a present of four old guns, to serve, I suppose, as a kind of cynical reminder of the inherent defenceless-ness of the original Stockade. The other error was "immediately past-Stockade days," instead of "immediately post-Stockade days."

In connection with ecclesiastical origins here, it may be mentioned that of all the ministerial pioneers to this place, Father Dunne, and the Presbyterian minister of Buninyong, the Rev. Thomas Hastie, are the only survivors. Both, I suppose, are for the most part out of the fight now. The Presbyterian is, and Father Dunne's great age will also probably compel more or less of retirement from active warfare. Mr. Hastie is the Nestor of them all, for he came to his charge in this district, in 1847. He saw the pastoral life before the gold discovery; saw all the hurly-burly of the diggings rush; saw the evolution of this great city from the primitive bush, or the bush torn and rent and splotched by the gold-hunters; saw hosts of sub-pioneers vanish into the silences, and, literally deafened with the long trail of the years, and all the tumult of the battle, now sits apart waiting for the end. He is well on in his ninth decade.

How much shorter was the earthly term allotted to Father Shiel, once Archdeacon of Ballarat, and then Bishop of Adelaide. His active spirit was, perchance, too much for its small frail tene-ment. How he was loved here, how respected by all the churches, save the very narrowest! He did good church-building work here. Under his pastorate the nave and aisles of St. Patrick's, were built, and the handsome iron railing of to-day, made to supersede the old post and rails of the primitive days. Father Shiel was contemporary with the late Rev. William Henderson, of St. Andrews, opposite to St. Patrick's. They were good friends, indeed, and had their occasional jokes. Mr. Henderson's first church was of wood, then one of stone was begun, and a blast of wind blew down the green wall one day. The Irishman slily joked the Scot about the "Prince of the powers of the air," and pointed to the prostrate west wall. "Ah," retorted

253

the ready Scot, as his eye twinkled with the fun, " he hasn't the same grudge against you, perhaps." How often did I see the spare, ascetic, but merry-eyed little priest pacing to and fro in the St. Patrick's reserve, with his cap and gown, and breviary, whose perusal would be ever and anon accompanied by an exhilarating pinch of snuff. He lent me Newman's *Apologia* to read, and one was irresistibly fascinated, but, alas, not converted. The Archdeacon's elevation to the episcopate, refted him from glad but sorrowful friends here, most of whom " saw him no more."

The Presbyterian, too, has joined the majority. He also was a merry soul. Fresh still in my memory is a night under canvas I spent with him and Major W. C. Smith, and Captain Campbell, of the Ballarat Rangers. The night was the night of the wind and rain storm of the "Wet Werribee" encampment in the sixties. Henderson was Chaplain-Captain, I was " war-correspondent." The Major lay on a mattress, the rest of us in straw and water, holding on by turns to the ridge pole of the tent, as the storm howled round us. The Chaplain-Captain led the merriment with Horatian, and other citations, and we were as jolly as possible under the circumstances. What is more, we saved our tent, and when day broke we saw whole lines of wrecked canvas, and soaked and wearied soldiers falling in for a speedy march off the field of meteoric discomfiture. Alas, of all our tent party of that now far-off night, your humble servant is the sole survivor.

But to return to early clerical services here. Father Smythe preceded the Archdeacon, and his pastorate was more of the east than the west of Ballarat, for in his day the west had not emerged. Father Smythe was removed hence to Castlemaine, in 1856, but his congregation loved him so much, that all that was possible was done to retain him here. The *Star* of that time referred to his " scholarly attainments and gentlemanly bearing," and went on to say : " It is now over two years since Father Smythe was appointed to Ballarat ; he has passed through trying times the meanwhile, in a manner which not only gained for him the love and gratitude of his own communicants, but earned for himself the respect and esteem of those of all creeds." As the priest was here during the licence trouble, and sheltered Lalor in his hour of need, it is no wonder that he came under the frowns of the secular rulers of the time, but the general conscience of the people here regarded him as both a good priest and a good hater of despotism.

As to the later developments of Catholicism here, the creation of the diocese, the life and death of the first bishop, the consecration of the present bishop, the dedication of St. Patrick's Cathedral, and other matters of Catholic interest, your readers as readers, probably, of other publications, have had at the hands of better informed recorders, ampler details than I can furnish. Ballarat has been a very *nidus* of bishops, Catholic and Anglican. Drs. Shiel, Moore, and Delany, of the Catholic Church, and Drs. Julius, Green, Stretch, and Cooper, of the Anglican Church, attest the prolific quality of the soil. In the matter of church buildings, the Anglicans seem to have come off, in some sense, worse than all the rest of the denominations. The Wesleyans and the Presbyterians have, like the Catholics, what may pass for cathedral edifices, but the fatal effort of the Anglicans, during the late tragic boom period, to build a more splendid church than all besides, left only a heap of unfinished arches, walls, and foundations, that present now a desolate aspect of weather-stained ruins.

Before closing these church matters, however, it may be allowable to mention the large work done already during Dr. Moore's episcopate. His predecessor had not time to do much more than lay the foundations of some additions to the church and school furnishing of the diocese, but how much of fruitful suggestion he may have left to his successor, is unknown to this writer. Certain it is that the present bishop has led the way in embellishing the city with many costly piles, or has purchased and added to buildings previously existing, the bulk of these undertakings being in aid of Catholic education and charity. It is sufficient to name the Convent school of St. Mary's Mount, the Convent school in Victoria Street, Nazareth House, and the Monastery at Wendouree, to show what has been done in that way, whilst St. Patrick's College, Sturt Street, the original Holy Ghost College, is another example of the liberal provision made for the supply of that education which alone can satisfy the Catholic conscience. In these projects I take it that Bishop Moore has written his name ineffaceably upon the annals of the diocese.

Before I leave my memories of St. Patrick's some mention must be made of the late Father Power. He was one of the pioneers of what I may term applied sacred music in Ballarat. Father Power was one of Archdeacon Shiel's priests in the Ballarat mission, and when the Archdeacon was elevated to the see of Adelaide, the curate was transferred to Geelong, where he died of lung disease in 1869, at the early age of forty-two years.

> Who would not sing for Lycidas,
> He knew himself to sing,

if not in the Miltonic sense, in a melodious way, for this Lycidas of mine had a sweet tenor voice. And something more than that, he had an exquisite taste in music and a passionate fondness for it. When he first came to St. Patrick's there was no choir, no instrument, no pretence of an efficient production of the lyrical portion of the services; but he set himself to work and soon had a harmonium and a few drilled choristers, and divine service was thenceforth freighted with something of the higher graces of sacred song. Father Power was a composer, too, in a small way, and several of his compositions are still held in memory by some of the old pioneers, who had the privilege of his more intimate acquaintanceship. His face is before me as I write, more vividly visible than those of some of my living acquaintances, and I peruse the placid features now with singular facility. It is the face of a mildly-rapt religious, serenely at rest within the harbour where no disturbing questions are asked, and where there is no cavil with the soul-searching mysteries of "all this unintelligible world." One might fancy there mingled beneath the long, lank hair, and overspread all the clean-shaven face expressions of the blended piety and poetry of his ancient, ancestral faith, so "rich with the spoils of time," and of the seraphic joy which comes from constant tuneful communion with St. Cecilia. Out of the far-off look of his eyes would come gleams of humor or of ecstasy, piously sensuous, as an innocent mirth, or a gust of melody or harmony moved his soul at intervals. But there was nothing sensual in the sensuous, and this, one might easily believe, soon rose to the purely spiritual, wafted on the wings of reverent faith as the sounds of music lifted the pious soul above all earthly things. There be priests and priests, verily, and, oh, what measureless differences. But Father Power was one, if I do not wofully misjudge him, of the sort John Banim had in his mind when he sang :—

> Who, in the winter's night,
>   Soggarth aroon !
> When the cold blast did bite,
>   Soggarth aroon !
> Came to my cabin door,
> And on my earthen floor,
> Knelt by me, sick and poor,
>   Soggarth aroon !

Rest, then, in peace thou sweet, priestly singer of the earlier time and early doom, and with thee all who have served and loved as faithfully as thou, Soggarth aroon ! I do not mourn—why should I ?

> He has moved a little nearer
> To the Master of all music,
> To the Master of all singing

This reference to Father Power brings before me again some other of my memoranda of the old days. Catherine Hayes visited Ballarat in the early fifties. Then Madame Onn, a star of much smaller magnitude. But Madame Onn was the first professional artist to assist in the Catholic services here. When the first St. Alipius Church, of canvass and weatherboards, was the chief Catholic temple here, Madame Onn and the still extant ever-green, John Lake, sang there, a harmonium having been specially provided for the occasion. That was in Father Smyth's time.

My memoranda slide from the sacred to the secular, and one declines upon operas and concerts, theatres and music halls. A mere mention of leading names of musical visitors is an alarum to the memory and of love to the lover of old days, the old songs, the old and vanished singers. What a brilliant roll of the long-gone performers is spread out from Anna Bishop, and Laglaise, and Coulon, and Seide, and Loder, our first stars in opera, down through Lyster galaxies of Italian artists to such brilliant, wandering, single lights as Ilma de Murska, Carlotta Patti, the Halle's, the Wilhelmj. And if one were to adventure upon even a skeleton draft only, of the old days, and deeds, and doers of the drama in Ballarat, it would out-stretch in length, if not surpass in mortuary horrors, the fearful file of ghosts that scared Macbeth from his propriety. Indeed, to me, there is a trail of death over so much of this reminiscent vision of old Ballarat that it seems ungracious, some-times, to obtrude such sad memories upon the present, and before so many who " Knew not Joseph," and, perhaps, care less about all this withered, dead and buried past.

Ballarat.   W. B. WITHERS

Some Ballarat Reminiscences.

ONE is not to get clear yet of the old dramatic memories. Just now the *Australasian* publishes a claim on behalf of that journal's Tasmanian correspondent that he "discovered Jefferson," the creator of the Rip Van Winkle of the stage. The correspondent in question is one "Notos," and if I do not blunder, he was in the old days a reporter on the Ballarat press, one of the first Local Court, and afterwards an editor of the *Star*. This will be near enough to enable old pioneers to identify him. As to the claim of Jefferson's "discovery," it is quite possible that the Ballarat press was first to praise him, "and that highly," and in such sort as to stamp him with special mark as an actor of large original histrionic faculty, and "Notos" was a gentleman of such shrewd observant powers as enabled him to judge well and appraise with just regard to the facts. Whether "Notos" wrote his own claim in the *Australasian,* or somebody did it on his behalf, the following is the claim, and I am of opinion that in the main it is fairly correct:—

"Mr. Jefferson came to Victoria early in the sixties—I forget the exact year— and he played Rip Van Winkle in Melbourne without causing any particular sensation. He then went to Ballarat, at that time a great theatrical centre, and rather famous for its appreciation of good acting, where in a short time he was recognised as a great actor in a great part. He went back to Melbourne, and then had a warm welcome as Rip Van Winkle and even in some other parts—such a welcome as carried him eventually to London. Now, the person who wrote up Jefferson in Ballarat, who proclaimed that a great actor had appeared, was no less a person than "Notos," your Tasmanian correspondent, who took so much trouble in the matter that he succeeded in making the whole of Ballarat, and, apparently, the Melbourne people, see something which they had not seen very clearly before. For, certain it is, that after his return from Ballarat, where he played at the old Theatre Royal in Sturt Street, now no more, he had a long run in Melbourne, where he became famous. "Notos" never spoke to Mr. Jefferson, as he found it prudent to avoid the friendship of actors, as most critics have who do their duty, but several persons who have seen Mr. Jefferson in America have said that he always admits that he got his big start in Ballarat. I make this statement for the honor and glory of Ballarat, which in the early days—the days that are no more—had a considerable reputation for its theatrical judgment, so much so that many actors have said that if they succeeded in Ballarat they were secure of the rest of the colony. In truth, the Ballarat audiences of those days were good judges, but very lavish of their praise when they approved."

Aye, "are no more," indeed. There was a time when the Royal

was the home of the best dramatic art here, and "Notos," or
"Notos'" friend's claim for Ballarat eminence as an appraiser of
acting values seems to have had some sort of endorsement from
"Orion" Horne, unless, by the bye, his endorsement was only
"biz." In 1862 Horne appeared on the Royal stage, and recited a
prologue he had written to his adaptation of Beaumont and Fletcher's
"The Honest Man's Fortune." Horne and his prologue were rap-
turously greeted. I give one bit from his lines:

> Beaumont and Fletcher—in that noble age
> Before "burlesque" usurped the British stage,
> Scoffed down the Drama with its punning rhymes,
> Till sense and feeling almost look like crimes,
> Made tricks with words thought clever if not jinglish,
> Tinselled Tomfools destroying the Queen's English.
> Those men we named, like warriors with drawn swords,
> Meant *something* by their scenes, in deeds and forthright words,
> Wrote earnest-hearted plays, with rational ends;
> Were true in smiles and tears, and William Shakspear's friends.
> And therefore, in Ballarat here to-night,
> Stand we in garb of Queen Bess' time bedight,
> And now commit—a trust most fit and due—
> The fortunes of an *Honest* man to you.

The Royal was built by a joint stock company, and G. V. Brooke
laid the foundation stone on the 20th January, 1858, and W. Hoskins
opened it with Jerrold's "Time Works Wonders" on 27th December
of the same year. Time worked very unpleasant wonders with the
company of owners. They paid £500 a week in salaries at one
time, and finally landed in the Sheriff's hands. After the wreck,
some years afterwards, the survivors met at Craig's Hotel, and E.
C. Moore, the company's secretary, had the only morsel of salvage
available, to wit, the auctioneer's cheque for £8 balance, which had
lain *perdu* all the intervening time in the minute-book. *Mirabile
dictu*, the cheque was honored. It is notable that no fewer than four
of the men who had to do with the founding of the Royal perished
even more tragically than the company's venture. Moore, the secretary, pistolled himself at Prahran; Carver, the valuator, one night
lay in bed reading a novel, put the book down, and then pistolled
himself as he lay in the bed; Salmon, the auctioneer, poisoned himself in his house in Sturt Street; Brooke perished in the wreck of
London in the Bay of Biscay.

The Royal was bought by Rowlands & Lewis, the cordial
makers, and they sold it to the Ballarat Temperance League in
October, 1864. The League bought in a fine frenzy of desire to
"dish" the alcoholists, but were scared by a statement that

Bouchier, the original holder of the site, had a contract by which all proprietors of the theatre were bound to keep it open as a theatre. Bouchier living then next door, and being a publican, the meaning of the contract was obvious.   The League backed out, and the late Walter Craig bought the theatre for less than £3,000, and sold it on the 10th August, 1868, to R. S. Mitchell for £5,500.   Mitchell still holds the site, and the Bouchier site also.   He built a fine three-story block, of which the Royal became the westermost end.   He had many severe fights with various fates, and in 1873 he took down the Corinthian façade of the theatre and turned a part of the vestibule into shops.   The last performance in the theatre was by Rockfeller's Minstrel Company, who closed on 17th July, 1878, and after that the house altogether was given over to shopkeepers.   Thus, in the place where Brooke, Cathcart, Jefferson, Kean, Montgomery, Celeste, Matthews, Ellen Tree, Fanny Lockhart, the Gougenheims, the Dons, Hoskins, and others had played—where the glories of opera had flashed so often, where pantomime, farce and burlesque had made the place echo a thousand bursts of laughter, and where the more serious drama had drawn many a sob and tear, one saw all its histrionic and lyrical triumphs become mere silent memories, buried, too, beneath the heaped-up wares of tailors, drapers, and other shopkeepers.

"Notos," or his *Australasian* friend, must bear the cost of this revival of the old Royal times.   The older East was rich also in its theatrical histories, but they shall not now be exhumed, nor of the modern Academy of Music will I say any more than that in my last the names of Ristori and the Majeronis were inadvertently omitted from the brief list of "star" lights that appeared there.

The world, we are told now-a-day, is very small, and, in faith, the "globe-trotter," and steam, and wire, and cable have done a good deal towards making the statement true in one sense.   So did the gold discovery years before the globe-trotter proper had been evolved from the whirl of modern science and adventure.   One 'Xmas Eve, in the middle fifties I was sitting in my tent at the Red Hill, when a horseman rode up to a tent a few yards off, and shouted: "Hello, Hagan; have you got a fat goose?"   Hagan's apparent avocations were hawking fish and fowl, wife-beating, and anti-Father Mathewism, and the hawking part of the business accounted for the 'Xmas Eve visit of the horseman whose voice fell upon my ear as the awakening of an old world echo.   Looking out of my tent I saw that my ear had not deceived me, and that the horseman was Joseph Charles Byrne, a big, strong-voiced Irishman, with whom I had in the first half of the last of the forties, drunk some very fair sherry in his office in Pall Mall, London. The wine was poured out as a libation to fortune over my payment for 300 acres of land which I was then and there entitled to select in the colony of Natal. Byrne was at that time an emigration agent for the British Government, and he had in Natal one Moreland as his appropriately named agent for the oversight of the selections chosen. Mine was near to the capital, Pietermaritzburg, and when I left Natal on hearing of the Australian gold discovery, I sold it to Mr. Shepstone, the Secretary for the natives, afterwards the Sir Theophilus Shepstone, of much honorable fame in various public affairs in South-Eastern Africa. What Byrne's business was in Ballarat I do not remember, save that he dealt occasionally, in various stores. He was a man of great enterprise, and some of his critics said he was not sensitively scrupulous, but I must speak as I found, and to me he was an honest man. Whilst in Ballarat there was what our American cousins call "a difficulty" one day between Byrne and the late Judge Trench, at the George Hotel, touching some lady, but the affair does not seem to have been a very serious one. Anyhow, it soon blew over, and Byrne finally disappeared, and the last I heard of him previous to his death was his being on friendly terms with Louis Napoleon, President or Emperor, for whom he was said to be acting in his old capacity as emigration agent. What form that could take with a French Government I hardly know, and Byrne never made history probably in that relation.

Byrne's enterprise once led to a rather comic episode here. Amongst his belongings was a tiger which used to be exhibited at the Montizuma Hotel and Theatre. The tiger's keeper ran up a long bill with Lynch, the landlord, who refused to give up the beast until the keeper's debt was settled. Byrne's plan of campaign did not include so direct a method of getting possession as that, He sued Lynch in the County Court, and got a verdict for £250, reducible to a shilling on payment of costs and surrender of the tiger. William Tweedie, the bailiff of the court, and hailing from Byrne's own land, was in due course armed with the necessary warrant for seizure of the tiger or enforcement of the verdict. Lynch was from the United States, and having seen life there and here was not easily scared. He said to Tweedie, "I'll give you the tiger, and here is the shilling and the costs." Byrne and the bailiff were led round to the rear, where the tiger was in his cage, and Lynch said, "There's the tiger, Mr. Tweedie; take it." Tweedie turned to Byrne, and said, "There's the tiger, Mr. Byrne; you can take it." Byrne said, "Oh, but you must fetch it into the Main Road;" but Tweedie, as severely exact as Shylock, retorted, "There's nothing about that in the warrant," and so left to the owner the task of all further disposal of the *corpus* of the County Court suit.   Men were hired to get the caged beast on to a dray for removal to the western township.   This was a heavy piece of business, but it was successfully done so far as getting the beast on the dray, but in going through the Main Road bogs of that time the dray was capsized near the intersection of Humffray Street, the cage burst open, and the tiger bolted into the store of a man named Hopkins near by.   Byrne, perplexed more than ever, offered £50 to anybody who would catch the runaway. The job was not a nice or a pleasant one to accomplish, but a dare-devil sailor-digger took it in hand.   The tiger lay crouched under a rude bush table, and the sailor, or one Lanty Ryan, got on the table and began to prod the beast, the cage having been placed alongside, and the tiger being roused from his position, had the good sense to at once walk into the cage, and was thereafter taken to Byrne's quarters in the West.   The thing was soon over, and it was said that Byrne got out of paying all the £50.   Thatcher, the ballad-maker and singer, of course made some doggerel out of the fun, and sang it for some nights to screaming diggers at the Charlie Napier.   Here drops the pall.   Byrne is dead; Thatcher, the idol of the diggers of the fifties, is dead; Wrixon, the judge who found the £250 verdict, is dead; Francis Greene, the clerk of the court, is dead; Tweedie, the bailiff, is dead; and how many more of the actors in the scene this deponent knoweth not.

Ballarat.   W. B. Withers.

Some Ballarat Reminiscences.

THOUGHTS, memories, are the swiftest globe-trotters after all, and their warp and woof make a web that touches many shores and binds them all together in a more or less substantial mesh. Byrne's Xmas Eve quest for a goose in Ballarat caught me up and whirled me off to Byrne's office in London, thence to Natal, touching divers people in the process. Hagan's Anti-Father Mathewism was mentioned, the great temperance Apostle being at the same time in my mind's eye as I saw him a few months before my meeting with Byrne in Pall Mall. It chanced that when in London I used to quarter at Hart's Temperance Hotel in Aldersgate Street, and at the time in question Father Mathew was also staying at the same place. It was when, now fifty years gone, that good priest was trying to convert the intemperate Londoners to total abstinence. About the middle height, in his sixth decade, but robust and ruddy, his whole person seemed to be brimming over with energy and kindliness. Many a morning on descending the stairs to the entrance of the hotel I had to pass between a host of men, women, and children waiting to see Father Mathew. They were mostly Irish, and probably were some of the fruits of his zealous Apostolate, for he worked very hard, held immense gatherings on Kennington Common and elsewhere, and his pledged followers counted by the thousand. It was during his temperance mission in England that Walter Savage Landor flung at him that good-humored bit of rhyming :

"O, Father Mathew,
Whatever path you
In life pursue;
God grant your reverence
May brush off never hence
Our mountain dew."

Surely these two men were, in some respects, the veriest antithesis of one another. One devoting himself body and soul to the consuming labors of a temperance crusade for the salvation of the souls and bodies of the victims of vice ; the other sunning and shading himself at Fiesole amidst its flowers and vines, and purple Appenines, while spicing all that febrile life with the stimulants imbibed from his scholarly intimacy with the classics of two milleniums. There he was, within touch of the Brownings and other British Florentines, and within sight, so to say, of the immortal Duomo which led Michael Angelo to the larger immortality of St. Peter's in Rome. So, too, he was, as it were, in an atmosphere of Catholicism, this doubly-steeped classicist, this man with impulses of tenderness, of wild passions, of leonine courage upon occasions. But if he fell upon those mediæval Catholic surroundings he had also fled from other mediæval Catholic memories in Wales. His home at Llanthony Abbey was not happy, for he could not get on with the Welsh, and he fled away, shooting this Parthian arrow : " The earth contains no race of human beings so totally vile and worthless as the Welsh." This burst almost justifies Dickens' parody in his Bleak House (Boy-thorn). Landor was not orthodox in faith, I fear, but he reverenced the author of Christianity. There is a tender pathos in his words—I quote from memory : " There is but one Guide. We know him by the gentleness of His voice, by the serenity of His countenance, by the wounded in spirit who are clinging to His knees, by the little children whom He hath called unto Him, and by the disciples in whose poverty He shared."

But what has this to do with Ballarat ? Nothing, save that it comes somehow to be a bit of the web of circumstances and recollec-tions already mentioned. That web touched Natal, as we have seen. Let us look at a loose thread or two more, touching that African shore or that, and this Australian one as well. When I was about to start one time from sea port Durban to the fifty miles inland capital Peitermaritzburg, a young Irishman named Murphy, whose acquaintance I had made, asked leave to be my fellow-traveller, and of course had it instantly. In those days there were no coaches or omnibuses, much less railways, and as neither Murphy nor I belonged to the local equestrian order, we had to do the journey on shank's pony. I had performed the operation once or twice before, and knew the ropes, including the solitary plank which then served as the only bridge across the Bushmans River on the eastern side of Peiter-maritzburg. But rain had come on and had delayed our march, and so night fell, and with it heavier rain, before we reached the river. We could not find the plank, and to attempt to ford the stream would have been mere madness. There was nothing for it but to camp out for the night, and as we had no shelter, nor tent, nor tree, nor umbrella, and were both weary with the march, we fairly caved in and lay down in the rain upon the closely cropped herbage. Poor little Murphy ! Heaven save him, he was smaller

than my little self.   He had had, no doubt, a more delicate handling
than I ; was, perhaps, less suited to the rough initials of emigrant
life.   Anyhow, he had been chanting in distressingly minor tones
for the few last miles of our journey, and he fairly broke into a sub-
tearful whine when he found that there was nothing for it but to take
our repose as stated.   We lay down exhausted, my big Newfound-
land dog, a co-emigrant himself from our native Wessex, lying
benevolently close to me on the weather side, Murphy by me on the
lee.   Still, as the rain kept pattering down, my friend on the lee
maintained his doleful tearful complaints.   He was " soaked, aching,
dying," and the remorseless patter kept on.   At length, in hope of
silencing Murphy's wailing, I bade him, as I lay abdomen to grass,
get on my back, and he actually did so.   This lasted for a while,
but not for long, for my time had come for complaint, and Murphy
had to shift.   Dawn found us footsore, bone sore, soaked and dirty,
but we were soon across the river, and into kindly old Yorkshireman
Hardman's primitive boarding house in Long Market Street.   Some
time after that I was blessed with the sight of Murphy stalking down
the street where the Government Offices were.   He was in *grande
tenue*, as became a recently appointed civil servant.   It was a
resurrection, a metamorphosis.   The dull, dimmed, sodden chrysalis
of the Bushmans River bank had burst out in butterfly radiance.
His dress was of the exquisite order, and in one hand he bore a big
nosegay; in the other, grasped ancient palmer-wise, a stick longer
than himself.   One could hardly say :

> " And the great Lord of Luna
> Comes with his stately stride."

For, soothly speaking, Murphy looked neither great nor lordly, but
he strode down the slope from Fort Napier towards the public
offices as if he was the happiest man alive.   And that happy vision
was the last I had of him.   We never met again.

To have done with the Natal threads of the web, let me say that
I was roofing in my little house in Church Street, Peitermaritzburg,
and about to rush off to Australia and Ballarat as the Anglicans
were laying down the foundation stone of a new church exactly
opposite to my place.   The building afterwards became the Anglican
Cathedral, with Dr. Colenso as the first bishop.   There was no
Bishop Colenso then.   He and his conversion to Kaffir arithmetic,
in whole or in part, touching the book of Genesis or other Bible
problems, were yet to come upon the Natal field of funny things.
Before I left Peitermaritzburg a journalistic acquaintance, who had
come out from England to see his brother, the managing man of the
Natal Witness, used to drop in at my place now and then and, prone

on my bed, spout Shakespearian or Goldsmithian passages more or less in harmony with his moody, if not cynical, humor. He had held a Government office in Adelaide, and was on sick leave in England, when his brother advised him to bring out type and so forth as there was room for a new paper in the Natal capital. This was done, and failed. One day, in 1853, I was sipping coffee in a hostelry in Bourke Street, Melbourne, and as I lifted my coffee cup I saw a pair of eyes glittering upon me. My friend had done as I had: washed his hands of Natal and come to Melbourne. We were both on the *Argus* for awhile after that, then he gave up journalism and had office under the Victorian Government, which he vacated under stress of results of certain eccentricities. For awhile his course was devious. He came to my early Ballarat home once or twice, vanished again, revisited South Australia, had presently £1,000 left him by a relative in the old country, and that was a fatal gift. His eccentricities became acuter, and some of his post-legacy exploits in Melbourne were striking but inexpressibly sad. Poor fellow! he ran through every shilling; and at last came to grief in South Australia. *On retourne toujours à ses premiers amours.* Poor —— had strayed, weary, heart-sore, mind-shaken, back to his first colonial home, fallen upon the terriblest shallows. He is long since gone to the majority. May he rest in peace.

Talking of my Natal Australian friend leads me out of that circumbendibus straight back to Ballarat early old memories in connection with the law courts here. For my friend was Supreme Court reporter for the *Argus*, and thus I fall upon some forensic matters in the Ballarat early days. My first reporting in Ballarat was for the now dead *Ballarat Times* with Lola Montes' whipped "Scamp" (Seekamp) as proprietor and editor. The court house was a wooden building in the Camp, and stood nearly opposite to what is now the Masonic Hall in Camp Street. Mr. Turner was the police magistrate, and he had as court clerk Robert Le Poer Trench, who died not long since as pensioned ex-Judge Trench. The clerk had doffed his Irish wig and gown for the clerkship, but soon resumed his barristerial status, made much money, spent it bravely, touched liberal politics at an official tangent during Graham Berry's reign, and at last landed upon the County Court bench. Turner, P.M., vanished after a few years, as did the late Captain Hepburn, J.P., one of the old squatter magistrates who sat with Turner, I remember, the first day I attended there as Seekamp's representative. It was a coincidence that in the still earlier days another Turner had something to do with the second court of the district, the primæval court having been at what is now called

Chepstowe, near Carngham, on the late Phillip Russell's station. This Turner had squatted at the end of the forties or beginning of the fifties upon land at Buninyong, or Boninyong, as it was then called, that place being the centre of local justice before Ballarat came to be the greater place.   Turner gave leave to a cobbler to occupy a hut on the land close to what became the site of the present Buninyong police court, and when the gold rush made the curial change from Chepstowe necessary the gold commissioner bought the hut and right of occupation for £50, and the first courts for Boninyong-Ballarat were held in the hut.   When Judge Wrixon came afterwards with the larger duties and dignities of General Sessions and County Court, the hut was not big enough, and the little wooden kirk of the Rev. Thomas Hastie was used as a court house until the Ballarat Camp became the Government head quarters.   Then after came another coincidence, *au rebours*, so to.speak.   The Buninyong kirk was used as a court house, and the Ballarat court house I reported in was used as a church by the Anglicans.   Judge Wrixon, with his Irish clerk Greene, came on to Ballarat in December, 1853. One of the outcomes of the post Stockade reforms was the appointment of new territorial justices.   I am officially informed by the courtesy of the present solicitor general, that the first batch of magistrates appointed within the Ballarat district after the year 1854 comprised, William Bradshaw, Samuel Irwin and John Victor, of Ballarat, appointed as " territorial magistrates of Victoria," on the 25th June, 1855, and Somerville Learmonth, of Burrumbeet, on the 12th November, 1855, Samuel de Vignolles being appointed stipendiary magistrate of Ballarat on the 15th November, 1855. Irwin, an Irishman, was a Trin. Col., Dub. man, and so was Victor a Cornishman, and David Fitzpatrick, another Irishman, was appointed to the territorial magistracy about the same time, though his name is not in the list officially supplied to me.   He is still here, and of seemingly evergreen vigour ; but Irwin is in the shades, and Victor and Bradshaw have left for other woods and fields, as did Learmonth also some years ago.   Poor old serio-comic de Vignolles also soon vanished, and is, I think, with the ever-increasing majority.   After him came Clissold as P.M., son of an Anglican clergyman.   Clissold was a muscular sailor and cricketer of great enthusiasm.   He gloried in the glorious game, and at the farewell luncheon given to him at the Eastern Oval testified to the hold the game had upon Englishmen, quoting Horace's *Cœlum non animum*, as meaning that wherever an Englishman travels he carries with him his cricketing outfit.   He was one of the best magistrates we ever had here.   The last I heard of him he was yachting in the

Mediterranean. The present judge Gaunt was also one of our P.M.'s but he fell a victim to Graham Berry's reign of terror over the "curled darlings" of the civil service, and fell back upon his barristerial status, and so won eventually a judgeship. Others of mediocre fame filled the bench chair at intervals. Mr. Leader, the present P.M., is the only one who has had the unwelcome distinction of being made to invoke the law for libel or slander against a practitioner in his court. But that matter is still pending as I write, so no more of it now.

W. B. WITHERS.

Some Ballarat Reminiscences.

THE first sitting of a Supreme Court judge in Ballarat was in 1856, the late Mr. Justice Williams, father of Sir Hartley Williams, having opened the first Assize Court here on the 12th December of that year. The court was held in the old police court at the Camp already mentioned, the place being in part glorified for the occasion by the laying down of some bits of carpet. There were no javelin men, nor aught of the mediæval pomp of English assize progresses when the judge made his entry into Ballarat. The judge came in by the Buninyong road on his way from Geelong, escorted by the sheriff (Rogers) of the day, the police superintendent (Foster), some troopers and a few leading citizens. But the procession had a comic interpretation amongst the diggers. The *Star* of that time reported :—" It was somewhat laughable to find that his Honor, being so escorted, was taken by several of our miners to be a desperate bushranger lately captured and conveyed to durance vile by a strong police force." Mr. Chapman, who afterwards was Attorney-General in Victoria, and on several occasions an acting judge of County courts and sessions, and a judge in New Zealand, was the Crown Prosecutor at this first assize. That ponderous person, the late Crown Solicitor Gurner, was also present as adviser in the proceedings.

As became the historic dignity of the occasion, the judge delivered an address on the opening of the court, and said :—" No previous description, no imaginary picture had led me to anticipate the magnitude of the town which I yesterday entered for the first time. What a change from the first rude tents and huts of the transitory digger to the closely packed and substantially erected stores and dwellings of the populous and prosperous community in the midst of which this court is now about, for the first time, to lend its aid in the public administration of justice." His Honor alluded to the Stockade affair, and held that those troubles " owed their origin to feelings of a far different kind from disaffection to the law or disloyalty to the sovereign." He also gave a text for teetotal use in declaring that " at least one-half of the cases for trial have had

their origin directly or indirectly in the abuse of spirituous drinks."
The learned judge was probably a little out in his reckoning there,
and we may discount a little his ascription of loyalty to the
Stockaders. Yet he was right in essence, perhaps, as to the bulk of
them, for all that the bulk wanted was just rule and political freedom,
not caring one cent who ruled in England in comparison with the
desire for good law fairly administered here, and for freemen's participation in the parliamentary government of the colony. Mr.
Justice Williams' glowing description of the Ballarat of forty years
ago needs retouching now that tent life is almost entirely unknown
in this centre, and the " transitory digger " has, for the most part,
managed to house himself in fairly comfortable civilised conditions.
But he is " transitory," all the same, as all new " rushes "
demonstrate. This, too, is of the race. The old world sent
originally, and still sends, its " transitory " adventurers to the four
winds of heaven in quest of gold or adventure, the but founding of
colonies, of cities, of homes galore, is the splendid racial result.

I do not think we were a specially drunken lot of people in those
first assize court days. Brothel robberies, other robberies, and
attempted robberies under arms, larcenies, burglaries, assaults,
made up the list set before the court, but it did not appear that drink
was specially prominent in the list of crimes. Some big purloinings
were done in those days. One, Andrew Hislop, a carter, camping
near Buninyong on his way up from the seaboard, had had stolen
from his drays during the night 400 lbs. flour, five bags of rice, a
case of eggs, two casks of butter, two bags of sugar, two tins of con-
fectionery, and two cases of porter. That case came before the court,
but a bigger haul, made about the same time, never did. This latter
was a performance in Ballarat itself. Messrs. Clegg and Bailey (who
are still here) had a store at Poverty Point, and one night, in the
absence of one partner, and in the presence of the other serenely
sleeping, some theives cut open the canvas side of the store and
carried off fifty bags of flour, some bales of canvas, and a large
selection of boots. The flour was worth £12 a bag at the time, and
the loot totted up to about £600. All this, however, only goes to
show that similar conditions produce like possibilities and results.
Where there are aggregations of men and carcases of wealth there
the vultures of crime will gather, too. Ballarat was not different
from Melbourne or any other place, and is not to-day, and Mr.
Justice Williams' moralising on the drink question had no more
pertinence then than similar deliverances have at the present
moment.

Mr. Justice Williams' opening address drew journalistic attention

to the address of Chief Justice A'Beckett at the opening 'of the first assize court at Geelong in 1851 or 1852. That address was remarkable, in that it treated gold digging as a disreputable pursuit, and the people who followed it as not worthy of sympathy, let their troubles be what they would.   Sir William, I suppose, did not lack ordinary power of penetration, and he came of a family not a little famous in some modern forms of notability.   I wonder if they clomb back in their genealogical tree to the more famous St. Thomas of Canterbury.   If they did how great the contrast between that Beckett and this one.   He yonder, in time and space, of stately presence and a Catholic of high dignity and fighting power : this one, a cripple, little in bodily size, weak, puny, and a Unitarian, like the late Higinbotham, C.J.   Truly the " ringing groove of change " in the succession of Victorian Chief Justices presents some notable incidents.   We have had four altogether, and of the four, three have been Irishmen.   First came the English Unitarian, then an Irish Anglican, then An Irish Unitarian, and now the Irish Catholic. But all this is by way of parenthesis.   Sir William A'Beckett's Geelong address seemed to show that he was shocked by the rude concussions given to official and social use and wont by the gold rushes.   They were new then, and all the old and relatively settled pastoral, mercantile and official comings and goings were upset, so the Chief Justice bore down upon the diggings, life of the time with a sort of *nolumus leges Angliæ mutare* temper, lawyer and conservative as he was.   He pointed his finger at the first rush and said :—
" This state of things is still existing, and unless some measures can be devised for putting an end to its cause, is likely to continue." Alas, Sir William, and they did continue, as the cause did.   Yet see what your learned junior said at the Ballarat opening assizes, how he praised the diggers, and how he was impressed by the dwellings of the " populous and prosperous community."   But the Chief Justice had sympathies with quieter and staid economies.   He had felt the unwelcome change, " what is daily and hourly taking place around us to our own cost, socially and pecuniarily."   Yet Providence was kind to the wicked disturbing gold diggers " in a country where the elements of civilisation have been for some time in full operation : and notwithstanding the enormous amount of indirect taxation which the non-digging population pay as the price of their adherence to other pursuits—the difficulties which the Government *have* had to contend with in keeping at work *its* official machinery, and in maintaining any degree of order and security amidst an increasing population and a diminishing police—in spite of the disheartening drag which hangs upon the efforts of all who

271

attempt to counteract or check the spread of the gold mania—there is yet unimpaired among us the basis of a moral and social fabric whose preservation and security are of infinitely more importance to the colony than that of the ore-diggers' tent or the ore-diggers' gold." O dear! Sir William, but did not the tent, and the gold and their owners belong to the social fabric? No doubt His Honor was troubled by the rude disruptions caused by the gold discovery. Like Mr. Latrobe, the perturbed Governor of the time, he forgot his syntax in the heat of the argument, as italicised above. He felt so strong the shock to society, and its effect upon the wage-paying class, that he lost sight of other phases of the possible result—at least in a measure. " I fear," he said, " that until this concentration of mass after mass upon the locality of the goldfields that is now going on be checked or discountenanced," no change for the better is likely, wherefore " little anxious am I to see the crowds assembling thus surrounded with more facilities for pursuing their labor than the exigencies of their positions, so far as peace and order are concerned, absolutely demand. The call for sympathy, I confess, falls dead upon my ear from persons who have voluntarily hazarded, for the mere sake of lucre, the dangers to which they are exposed."

Some allowance must be made for the state of mind of a delicate, crippled, nervous man, horrified by the social overturn which had touched his pocket as well as his nerves, but his address was hardly becoming the judicial bench even then; and looking at it in the light of later facts, it seems sadly in want alike of insight and of the policy of justice. The address reads as the deliverance of an exasperated man, and to such a frame of mind the warning was natural " that they who swell the mass must not only not expect immunity from its perils, but should remember that they are in a colony whose Government has other interests to protect and other expenses to meet than those to which the fatal facility of gold digging has so suddenly given rise." It was a logical sequence to such sermonising that the address should wind up with a denunciation of some lynching cases that had then recently happened at Fryers Creek.

In the process of time the miner has evolved from the digger, his incorporated companies with long share lists from the simple co-operative mateships of the earlier days and the shallower auriferous deposits, but still the gold hunter was a nuisance to the bench if a prolific source of income to the bar. The intricate and long winded mining suits of a decade or two ago, if they worried the judges, and especially the judges of the lower courts, helped to build up the fame of that great equity judge of the Supreme Court, the late Mr. Justice Molesworth, in his function as Chief Judge of the Courts of Mines. Judge Rogers, of the Ballarat Court of Mines, had a severe fight of afflictions in connection with our heavier mining litigation period, for the intricacies, the novelties, the wonderful conflicts of evidence, the seeming uncertainties of mathematics and science in the hurly burly of opposing surveyors, were a trial to a judge so painstaking and so loftily, and sometimes testily conscientious as he. The huge maps, often conflicting as the oral evidence, the Statute or the local regulations, the puzzles of industrial terminology, the adaptation of old equity maxims to new conditions, the wearisome procession of witnesses with their involving crosslights or shadows, and the long winded harangues of opposing counsel were enough to exasperate any common human being with only A'Beckett tolerance of inconveniences. Judge Rogers was always a valiant defender of the proprieties, and I remember his chastisement of a slovenly solicitor one hot day for appearing in court attired in a not over clean holland blouse. Propriety in speech, too, was another of the judge's demands. " A ' bob,' sir, what do you mean ?" was one day his mode of bringing a witness to book for thus offending with the slang synonym for a shilling. A witness on another occasion entered the box wearing no coat, his naked shirt sleeves proclaiming at once mild weather, and a horrible ignorance of the judge's ideas of the fitness of things, so the judge lectured him severely for the want of decent regard to the dignity of the court. The judge's sense of propriety had other impulses. It was touched to finer issues. He invariably showed his sense of immorality in either parties or witnesses by refusing or reducing costs or payment of expenses when such a course was practicable, and to the one time common plea of debtors that they had lost by speculations in mining, the judge had the uniform retort that they had no right to adventure with other people's money. The bar, too, was sometimes chastised by his honor's moral birch. A litigant who had retained a barrister found himself alone when his case was called. This was in 1861, before the amalgamation of the two branches of the profession, the act of counsel was bad, and Mr. Rogers spoke like an indignant seer, forecasting events to come. He said : " An attorney appeared for the barrister, and the client is deserted by both attorney and barrister, who had, however, first denuded the unhappy client, not only of the fees, but of his papers. There is no bar in the colony, and the sooner the legislature settles the exact rights of the profession, and makes barristers equally liable with attorneys for neglect the better." I have dwelt upon Judge Rogers'

273

sayings and doings because he was our first and longest resident judge, because he bore the weight of the heavy litigation of the great mining suits' period, because he consistently championed high dutifulness in lawyer, client and witness, and was ever an example of painstaking devotion to duty himself.

Looking back, one cannot help, in spite of the possible taunt of being *laudator temporis acti*, feeling that the old days were better in some respects than to-day. I looked in at the assize court the other day when barrister-attorney Tuthill was being tried for uttering a "scandalous libel" against police magistrate Leader, and of which charge Tuthill was very promptly acquitted of legal malice, and so went free. On the bench was Sir Hartley Williams, son of the judge who opened the first assize court here. Sir Hartley was very grey haired, and his son acted as associate. *Sic transeunt.* All was new. There was a fresh race of reporters, and they had risen to the height of the era of "amalgamation." They had arrived where the vanished ones had not. They, too, had become officers of the court, and they arose, as did the bar, when the judge entered upon the bench. All new ? No, not all. There was one old barrister present, unretained in the case, bent with age, almost toothless, robeless, glancing about with curious looks of *quasi* isolation, lips moving with the soliloquising garrulity of stranded age. A generation agone he had been busy in the same court before other judges, in other cases, a leading counsel, and with others of greater eminence now no more. Where can we now find the brilliant array of forensic talent that marked the fifties, the sixties and the seventies ? Those were the days when Court of Mines and Circuit Court were attended upon occasion by all the best men at bar. Let me spy back alphabetically. They were the days of Aspinall, Atkyns, Billing, Bunny, Dawson, Dunne, Fellowes, Higinbotham, Holroyd, Ireland, Michie, McDermott, Sitwell, Wilberforce Stephens, Trench, Wright, Walsh, Webb, Wood. Those were the days when Joseph Henry Dunne was made a crown prosecutor, and pervaded the Circuit Courts with his portly presence, his magnificent deportment—less severely classic than Sir Redmond Barry, but more ponderous—the perfumes of his bottle of Eau de Cologne, which carefully placed upon the bar table, served for the occasional baptism of a spotless handkerchief, and helped to mitigate the profane odors of the common people. I see him now with his Dan O'Connell like presence, his black locks, his dark hazel eyes. I see, too, the sharp, pungent Wright ; the mild grey quickly intelligent eyes of the occasionally caustic Dawson ; the broad jaw and forehead, the restless, fun-lit, grimacing, sometimes severe face of

Richard Davies Ireland; the too Bardolphian and ever witty Aspinall; the deprecatory, quiet Billing, in his tentative plunges in a knotty mining point all new to his practice; the heavy, homely, accurate, laconic Fellowes; the mediæval-looking Atkyns, with his quiet humor, his ample pinches of snuff, his kerchief as big as a modest towel, and generally of a ruddy amber color. All those and more are now dead. Peace to their shades. Billing was, I think, a Londoner. Was he, I wonder, a descendant of that Lady Billing, wife of Edward the Fourth's Lord Chief Justice, who plunged thrice into matrimony, and caused to be set up in St. Margaret's, by the Abbey of Westminster, a memorial to her three husbands?

Lawyers sometimes have felt the powers of the world to come. Sir Thomas More did. I will close this discursive paper with a borrowing from the same London writer who tells me of Lady Billing and her three husbands. He is writing of " Typical Churches," and in connection with Chelsea Old Church he says:— " The south aisle, called, ' the More Chapel,' was built by ' Blessed Thomas More ' in 1528. More loved his church. Though he was Chancellor of England, whenever there was a procession the crucifer was Thomas More. The Duke of Northumberland found him on one occasion vested in a surplice, and singing in the choir. ' God's body,' said he, ' my Lord Chancellor, what, a parish clerk; you dishonour the King and his office.' To which More replied: ' Nay, you may not think your master and mine will be offended with me for serving God, his master, or thereby count his office dishonoured.' Sir Thomas was not, however, all ' butter and honey,' as may be seen from his epitaph, which he wrote before his death, and which is on his tomb in the church. In this there is a curious gap. More describes himself as follows: ' *Neque Nobilibus esset invisus—nec injucundus populo—furibus autem et homicidis, hereticisque molestus,*' which, being rendered in the vernacular, signifies that he believed himself liked by the ' classes,' popular with the ' masses,' but a person to be dreaded by thieves, murderers and heretics. Erasmus, it is said, objected to this coupling of heretics with thieves and murderers, and, figuratively, drew his pen through ' hereticisque.' "

This is all, in forensic phrase, im-pertinent as coming under my heading of " Ballarat Reminiscences," but " it is all along o' them lawyers," and is dragged in on their much involving skirts. And now the further hearing of these reminiscences may be adjourned *sine die.*

Ballarat.   W. B. Withers.

A

A'Beckett, Lady; 27
A1 Lead; 131
Abbot, C.A.; 43
Aboriginal names; 1
Aborigines 1, 7, 8, 9, 48
  Borhoneyghurk; 9;
  food gathering; 10;
  King Billy; 9; King
  Jonothan, 9; religion;
  40; of the Murray; 9;
Adams Store, Golden
  Point; 37
Adelaide; 266
Adelphi Theatre; 43, 63
Adeney, W.H.; 162
Agricultural and Pastoral
  Society; 174, 175
Airey, George; 5
Aitken J.; 2
Akehurst, Arthur; 87
Albion; 135, 136, 139,
  147
Albury; 228
Aldrich, E.; 192
Alexander Bros.; 197
Alexander, R.; 193
Alexander, S.; 194
Alfred Hall; 120, 154,
  170, 174, 181
Alfred Memorial; 159
Alfredton; 151
Allison, Edward; 179
Alluvial gold mining;
  127, 144
Alphabetical Foster; 116
Americal Consul,
  Tarlton; 60
Amicus; 206, 207
Amos; 56, 76, 78, 243
Anderson's Creek, 27
Anderson's homestead; 3
Anderson, Andrew; 168,
  170, 176
Anderson, Canute; 178,
  179

Anderson, Henry; 2, 3
Anglican services; 40
Anti-Transportation; 244
Apples; 202
Ararat; 144; 219
Arbuthnot, A.; 196
Archibald; 3; 239; 242
Architect - Caselli; 161;
  Cuthbert; 155, 159;
  Doane; 153, 157, 160,
  165, 170, 188;
  Dowden; 163; Jones;
  159; Porter; 160;
  Robertson; 159; Shaw;
  163; Terry; 162;
Armstrong, D.; 19, 30
Asches Lead; 131
Ashfield, 247
Aspinall, B.C.; 101; 274,
  275
Asylums; 37
Atkins; 193, 274
Auctioneers; 197
Austin, James; 190, 191
Australasian Hotel; 113
Axford; 194

B

Bacchus Marsh; 36
Bacchus, W.H. ; v, 6,
  20, 21, 174
Backhouse & Reynolds;
  161, 169, 170
Bacon price; 31
Bacon, Mr; 127, 130
Bagge, C.H.O.; 157
Bailey; 117, 118, 187,
  194, 270
Baillie; 4
Baird, J.; 174, 175
Baird, Samuel; 153
Baker, James; 121, 141
Bakery Hill; 120, 206,
  219, 228, 230, 234,
  249
Bakery Hill Lead -
  goldfield; 35

Bakery Hill Meetings,
  26, 42, 45, 58, 62, 66-
  8, 91; 92, 98, 105, 238,
  243, 244, 249, 251
Ballaarat surveyor; 153
Ballan; 6, 221
Ballarat:
  .Agricultural & Pastoral
  Society; 174, 175;
  Ballarat Banking Co.;
  176; Banks; 144;
  Benevolent Asylum;
  160; Cattleyards; 175;
  Cemetery; 208;
  Chamber of Commerce;
  169; Churches; 152
  College; 163, 167
  Courier; 43; Cricket
  Club; 168; Flat; 46;
  Fine Art; Gallery; 235,
  236, 238, 239, 242,
  245, 246, 247; Fire
  Brigade; 168, 171;
  Library; 156; 168;
  Goldfield; 3, 24. 228,
  Hospital; 159;
  Horticultural Society;
  173; Hotels; 152;
  Industrial Institute;
  141; Land Sales; 190;
  Local Court; 121, 122,
  127; Police Court; 98;
  Population; 32;
  Mayors; 153; Mining
  Board; 204; Mining
  Exchange; 133 Naming
  of; 10; Nuggets; 148;
  Philharmonic Society;
  170; Population; 152;
  Proclaimation of; 35;
  Rangers; 171, 254;
  Town Hall; 152;
  Trustees; 242
Ballarat East 3, 72, 111,
  134, 155; 204:220. 240
  Churches; 156;
  Footpaths; 156; Hotels;

156; Basin; 130; dwellings; 156; Town Hall; 41, 111, 156
Ballarat Leader; 42
Ballarat Punch; 42, 43 172
Ballarat Reform League; 52, 59, 60, 62, 63, 68, 70; 200
Ballarat Standard; 42
Ballarat Star; vii, 42, 43, 67, 72, 86, 89, 103, 112, 114, 117, 123, 124, 130, 226, 254
Ballarat Temperence League; 170
Ballarat Times; 41-42, 43, 44, 68, 98, 100, 227, 243
Ballarat Town Clerk; 153
Ballarat Trumpeter; 42
Ballarat Volunteer Rifle Regiment; 171
Ballarat West; 3, 8, 46, 135; Fire Brigade; 171
Ballarat, Borough of; 8
Ballarat, East, Borough ; 8
Balliang; 4
Band of Hope Co.; 129, 135, 137, 139, 147
Banim, John; 256
Banks; 176; of Australasia; 176, 194; Ballarat; 144
Baptist church; 166
Barham, W.; 192
Barker; 153
Barker, Clare & Co.; 195
Barkly, Gov.; 178, 179
Barley; 175, 201
Barnes, 176
Barry, Redmond; 142, 169
Barter of goods; 37
Barwon; 4
Basaltic plateau; 46
Bateman; 43
Batesford; 36
Batesford Hill; 22
Bath's Hotel; 35, 90, 100, 171, 173

Bath, Mrs Thomas; 38
Bath, Thomas; 25, 35, 174, 178,191
Bathurst digger; 16
Batman's Hill; 5, 40
Batten, W.H.; 168
Batteries; 133
Batty, James; 22
Batty, T.; 24
Beale's Dam; 158
Beattie, James; 100
Beazely, Rev.; 7
Bedford; 172
Bedwell; 7
Beef; 203
Beibetz, E.; 196
Beilby; 19, 45, 187
Belcher; 134
Belford, Richard; 155, 157, 160, 168, 171, 172, 189, 227
Bell, John; 30
Bendigo; 6, 36, 229
Bendigo anti-licence agitation; 51
Benson; 50, 51
Benson, William; 49
Bentley; 53; 58
Bentley's Hotel; 54; 55, 58, 59, 90, 94
Berrima; 15, 17
Berry, Graham; 266, 268
Berry, John; 180
Beverin, F.F.; 156
Bible Christians; 166
Bickett; 141
Bickford, J.; 160
Biddle's Saw-mill; 36
Bignell; 194
Billing; 274, 275
Bilton; 174
Binks, Rev. W.; 165
Binney Rankin, Alex.; 153
Binsted, F.; 172, 173
Birch's Creek; 5
Birch, Arthur; 5
Birch, Cecil; 5
Bishop, Anna; 44, 257
Bishop, Matron; 160

Black, Alfred; 70
Black, George; 63, 73, 189
Black; 58, 59, 62, 67, 70, 84, 86, 90, 104, 206
Black Hill; vi, 22, 25, 57, 199: Flat 35, 234; Goldfield; 33; Lead; 35; Quartz Mining Co; 150: Black Lead riot; 104
Black Lead; 104, 131
Blackburn and Baird; 191
Blacksmith; 83; James, John; 39; McLachlan; 7; at Eureka; 200
Blackwood; 121, 133
Blair; 80, 92
Blakeney; 5
Blakeney's Creek; 8
Blanchard, T.; 193
Bland, Henry Rivet; 142
Boilers; 133
Bolger, Patrick; 153
Bolingbroke; ix
Boninyong Gazette & Mining Journal; 41
Bonshaw; 3, 6; 152
Boquets; 202
Borhineyghurk; 9
Botanical Gardens; 161, 167
Boughen; 160
Boulton, A.J.; 172
Bowes, A.P.; 194
Bowker; 121
Bowman; 4
Bouchier, 260
Boyd, C.; 196
Bradshaw; 70, 110, 197 267
Brady; 63
Braham; 195
Braidwood; 17
Brameon; 160
Bran; 202
Brannon; 194
Bray, J.; 192
Bray, Kate; 163
Bray, T.; 192
Bread price; 31

Brecon Hills; 110
Brentani; Carlo; 20
Brequet, Fred.; 190, 191
Brewery; 156, 195
Bridges, W.; 193
British Parliament; 109
Brooke, G. ; 170, 230
Brooke; 44, 260
Brough Smyth; v, vii, 101, 148
Brown Hill; 3, 33, 230; Goldfield; 35; Hotel; 8; Slaty Creek; 6;
Brown, 21, 23
Brown, Dr; 207
Brown, James; 83
Brown, T.; 197
Bruhn, Dr.; 18' 170
Budden; 73
Bullarook; 3, 1157, 74
Bullocks 7, 8, 17, 26, 156
Bulwer; 230
Bungaree; 201
Bungaree Road Board; 181
Bungeeltap; 180
Buninyong; 3, 21, 22, 35, 87, 121, 133, 174, 201, 220, 235, 250, 252, 253, 267:Gold Mining Co.; 3; goldfield; 3; Gully; 204, Highland Society; 179, Hotel; 7; Magistrate; 44, newspapers; 43; naming of ; 10; Railway; 233
Bunny, 274
Burke; 58
Burke, Robert O'Hara; 91, 178, 179
Burnbank; 20, 38
Burra Burra Co.; 132
Burrows; 159
Burrows, William; 191
Burrumbeet; 2, 10, 175, 267
Burrumbeetup Run; 6

Butchart, G.; 159, 174
Butcher, William; 121
Butter price; 31
Byrne, Joseph; 260-2
Byrne, M.G.; 42

C

Cabbages; 202
Caledonian's Society's New Year Gatherings; 180
Caledonian Bridge; 196
Caledonian Lead; 131
Caledonian Society; 179
California; 126: gold; 14
Callanan, Patrick; 83
Callanan, Thomas; 83
Cameron, Donald; 20
Camp Hill; 177
Camp officials; 52, 92
Campaspe; 11
Campbell; 135; 254
Campbell, D.S.; 7
Campbell, James Macfie; 100
Campbell, John; 155
Campbell, Matthew; 153
Campbell, William; 18, 20
Campbellfield; 7
Canadian; 32, 138, 151; Monster nugget; 44; Gutter; 135
Canadians, 45
Candle manufactory; 156
Cantor, J.; 195
Carboni, Raffaello; 62, 66-68, 70, 80, 83, 87, 98-100, 102, 104, 120, 123, 124, 200, 205, 224, 229, 236, 240, 245, 248
Carmichael, A.;54
Carngham; 4, 133
Carpenter, H.; 193
Carpenter, Thomas; 188

Carr, Dr Alfred; 58, 241, 245
Carrick, Graham; 193
Carroll, Patrick; 234
Carrots; 202
Carver, John Smith; 153
Caselli, Henry R.; 161, 164, 168
Cashell; 222
Castlemaine, 40, 254, 272
Cathcart, 260
Cathie; 80, 111, 113, 114, 117, 168, 189
Catholic Chapel, Bakery Hill; 51, 228
Cattle; 175
Cattle Station Hill; 5
Cavanagh; 25
Cazaly, Peter; 160
Celery; 202
Celeste; 44, 260
Cemetery; 208
Ceres Farm, 35
Chalmers, H.B.; 170, 188
Chamber Bros.; 193
Chambers, Lucy; 44
Chancery Lane (renamed Eureka St);
Chapman, Judge; 20, 213, 244, 269
Charles, Mrs; 170
Charlie Napier Hotel & Theatre; 43, 71, 120, 173, 179, 195, 250, 262
Chartism; 68, 112
Chidlow, Thomas; 120, 123
Chilian Mills; 46
Chilwell, 22
Chinaman's Gully; 46
Chinese; 214: Burials; 209; Doctor; 22
Choral Society; 171
Christchurch; 41, 161, 173
Christmas; 221, 222, 260
Christie, L.S.; 170

Churches; 39, 161-167
Clarke; 43
Clarke, Alfred; 21, 37, 41
Clarke, Rev. W.B.; 16, 18
Clarke, W.; 3, 19, 190
Clayton's Gully; 233
Clegg; 270
Clendinning, Dr George; 155, 227, 247, 241, 245
Clendinning, Martha; 241, 242
Clerical Managers; 133
Cleve Bros.; 195
Clifton, William; 199
Clissold, 267
Clunes, 20, 25, 27, 35, 133, 144, 172, 204: Naming; 20; Company; 128; Newspaper; 43; Reefs; 46
Clyde Company; 3
Clyde Inn; 3
Cobb's Corner; 35
Cobblers; 130
Cobbler's Gully; 46
Cobbler's Lead; 131, 137
Coburg Mission, 228, 229
Cockneys, 219
Coe, H.; 193
Coffee, 221
Coghill's Creek; 4, 5
Coghill, David; v, 4, 5, 11
Cohen; 195
Colac; 38
Coleman; 171
Coleman, George; 6
Coleman, J.F.; 57, 91
Colenso, Dr; 265
Collins, C.W.; 164
Colonial Bank; 140, 176
Comb, Joseph; 153
Commercial Bank; 140, 176
Common School; 167
Communism; 112
Company shares; 137
Congregational church; 166
Connor; 21, 22, 23, 25, 187

Constitution; 116
Cooking, 220
Cooper, Dr; 255
Cooper, T.; 188
Cooper, W.; 42, 168, 171, 193
Copenhagen Grounds; 179
Corcoran, T.; 189
Corio Bay; 1
Corkhill, W.; 54
Corn Exchange; 174
Corn Stalk; 190
Corn; v
Cornish; 179, 233
Coulon; 257
Council Chambers; 174
County Court, 44
Court House; 142, 177
Court of Mines; 143, 214
Courtis; 173
Cowan; 153, 174, 194
Cowell, J.; 196
Cowland; 153
Cox, J.; 193
Coxhead, Frederick; 84
Courts; 269-271
Cradle; 132
Craig's Hotel; 9, 36, 100, 171, 176
Craig, Walter; 170, 260
Crain, S. de ; 194
Crane; 160
Crawcour, Isaac, 193
Crawford, J.; 196
Creswick; 4, 46, 80, 121, 131, 133, 172, 181, 201: 225, 231;Goldfield; 35; Diggers; 67, 79; Goldrush; 33, 149; Newspaper; 43
Creswick Chronicle; 42
Cricket; 167, 267
Critchley, Robert; 121
Criterion House; 195
Croke; 222
Crowe; 83
Crown Lands alienation ; 60

Cuming, Stephen; 233, 238, 239, 249
Cummins, J.; 159
Cummins, M.J.; 160, 172
Cummins, Rev. R.T.; 162
Curtain; 81
Curtin; 70
Cuthbert, C.D.; 153, 155, 159, 163
Cuthbert, Henry; 159, 168

𝒟

D'Arcy; 1
Dairy Produce; 203
Dalton's Flat; 46
Daly, James; 121, 141, 159, 171, 172, 205
Damper; 221
Dana, Capt. H.E.; 19, 30
Darling, Sir Charles; 118
Darlot; 4
Davey, Thomas; 153, 170
David Jones and Co.; 49
Davidson; 130
Davidson, R.; 160
Davies; 171
Davies, A.; 160, 171
Davies, H.; 161
Davis; 193, 194
Dawson, 274
Dead Horse 9, 35, 46, 131
Decameron Run; 213
Deeble, Samuel; 189
Deegan, Michael; 180
Deep workings; 126
Defiance Lead; 137
Delany, Dr; 30, 255
Dengan, Robert; 247
Denney; 163
Dennis, R.; 192
Denovan; 42, 207
Denver; 16
Derwent Co., Tasmania; 1
Derwent, Constable; 50
Devonshire Lead; 131
Devil's Gully; 199
Devonshire House; 194
Dewar, A.; 160

Dewes, Police Magistrate; 53, 55, 58, 59; 95
Diamond, John; 83
Dickinson, Thomas; 156
Dickson, R.; 174
Digger's Advocate; 59
Digger -hunting; 53, 66, 72
Diggers Ten Command-ments; 215
Dignam, Thomas; 100
Dilke; 16
Dimant, A.; 160
Dimelow, James; 167
Dimsey, W.; 160
Dingo; 8
Discovery of gold - Golden Point; 21
Dispenser - Garrard; 159
Dixie, J.; 159
Dixon; 16
Doane, Joseph.A.; 153, 157, 160, 165, 170, 188
Doctors: Chinese; 22; Clendinining; 155; Embling; 79, 80; Green; 255; Greeves; 18, 186; Hillas, T; 159, 172; Kenworthy; 69, 70, 173; Kupperberg; 170; McFarlane; 160; Otway; 46, 60, 61; Owen; 159; Power; 7; Richardson; 173; Shiel; 163; Stewart, J.; 153, 168, 172; Wills; 178; Brown; 207;
Dodds, J.; 160, 168
Dolly's Creek; 21
Don, Lady; 44, 260
Donaghey, George; 83
Donald; 91, 92, 123, 205
Donald, Robert; 120, 123
Donnelly, S.; 160
Douglas, J.A.; 159
Doveton, 25, 30
Dowling Forest; 3, 4, 9
Dowling; 194
Downes, F.C.; 170
Downing, Fr M.; 63, 229, 230

Doyle, Dr T.; 159;234
Dragoon; 81
Draper, 176; David Jones; 49
Draper, Rev. D.; 165
Drury, A.; 159
Dunn, G, 24
Dunn, Thomas; 21, 22, 23
Dunne, Alicia; 84; 235
Dunne, Father; 40, 228, 229, 230, 253
Dunne, John H; 160, 274
Durham Lead; 131
Dusautoy, A.; 196
Dushesne; 20
Dutch Harry, 246
Dyte, Charles; 91, 118, 155, 158, 168, 189

E

Ebden, C.H.; 2
Ebenezer; 163
Eddington; 176
Eddy, James; 189
Edwards; 194
Edwards, C.H.; 159, 169
Edwards, John; 156
Egan, J.; 196
Egerton; 133, 207
Eistedfod; 167
Elbertfeldt; 83
Elder; 135
Election (post -Eureka); 128
Electoral Act; 112
Elliot, M.; 159
Elliott, W.; 173, 196
Ellis; 157
Embling, Dr.; 79; 80
Emery, W.; 195
Emu; 8 9
Engine drivers; 133
Engineers, 133: Bagge, C.; 157; Jones; 172
Engines; 132, 133
Ercildoune;1, 2, 174, 220
Escort trooper; 49
Escorts; 146

Esmond, James William; vi, 15, 18, 21, 25, 46, 70, ,71, 76, 86, 105, 145 186, 204, 224
Esmond's Diggings; 23
Esmond's Lead; 71, 131
Essex Lead; 131
Eureka; 45, 66, 138, 173: Attack; 62, 67, 78: Stockade; vii, 47, 62, 66, 72-7, 92, 98, 108, 199, 209, 222, 223, 228, 239, 248, 250: Creswick contingent; 67: Deaths; 66, 74, 82,83, 84, 225, 246: Drilling; 66, 72: Naming of; 33; Military; 73, 239: Monument; 106, 199, 232; Prisoners, 240, 243, 244, 248, Rewards; 84; Swearing allegiance; 66, 67: Weapons; 69, 74: Wounded; 159
Eureka Anniversay; 223, 225, 237, 252, 253,
Eureka Flag; 32, 62, 66, 67, 69, 74, 81, 198, 228, 231, 233, 235-250
Eureka Gutter; 135
Eureka Hotel; 53, 94
Eureka Lead; 33, 35, 60, 72, 209
Eureka St.; 21
Evans; 42, 153
Evans & Barker; 160, 176
Evans & Co.; 194
Evening Mail; 43
Evening Post; 43
Everett, W.; 193
Exchange Hotel; 197
Exhibitions; 141
Explorers; 11
Eyre, Magistrate; 44
Eyres; 30, 193, 194

F

Fairburn; 6
Farley, H.; 192, 193, 195, 196

Farr, Rev.; 164
Farrington's and Co.; 179
Fawkner, 60, 80, 92, 93, 116
Fawkner, John Pascoe; 100
Fellmongers; 158
Fellows, 274
Fennelly, Rev. R.; 163
Fenton; 83
Ferres, John; vii, 198
Figgis; 172
Finlay, John; 127, 161
Fire Brigades; 171
First store; 6
Fish; 203
Fisher, David; 1, 3
Fisken, Arch.; v, 3, 174
Fitzgerald, C.; 24
Fitzherbert; 169
Fitzpatrick, Dr; 228
Fitzroy, A; 15
Flagging; 152
Fletcher, Thomas; 42. 57, 58, 59
Flour; 31, 202, 270
Flour mill; 1, 5
Flude; 167
Foley; 193
Food price; 31, 270
Foot police; 49
Foreigners; 51, 96
Forest Creek - see Castlemaine
Forests; 3, 219, 220, 229
Fossils; 211
Foster; 89, 269
Foster, Col-Sec.; 58, 60, 61, 116, 172
Foster, Henry; 159
Francis; 3
Francis, J.; 160
Franklin Lead; 131
Franz; 170
Fraser; 63
Frazer; 118, 198, 244
Frazer, William; 118, 121, 160, 168, 186, 187, 191
Free-traders; 116
French consul; 198

Frenchman's Gully; 46
Frenchman's Lead; 130, 131, 210, 205
Frenchman; 80, 135
Fruit; 202
Fulton; 80
Furlong, J.; 194
Furnell; 78
Fussel, John; 155

G

Gab, George; 6
Gab, Mrs; 6
Gambling; 139
Game; 203
Gaol; 176
Gardner; 6
Gardyne, Lt; 78
Garibaldi, Giuseppe; 224
Garrard, J.; 159
Garrard, Mrs; 159
Gas Co.; 172, 173
Gas lighting; 136
Gaskin; 195
Gates; 170
Gaunt, Judge; 268
Geelong; 1, 7, 23, 86, 181, 229, 234, 255, 271
Geelong Adverstiser; 41, 71, 80, 82, 88, 190, 190, 243
Geelong Mutual Mining Assoc.; 21
Gell, F.; 160
Geoghegan, Dr; 228, 229
George Hotel; 261
Germans; 171
Gerrard, Charles; 22
Gibbs; 169
Gibbs, John; 155, 172, 173
Gibbs, R.B.; 159, 161, 169, 194
Gibson, Dr; 45, 234
Gilbert, Duncan; 153
Gilchrist; 174
Gillespie; 118
Gillespie, R.; 117
Gillies, Duncan; 118, 121,

142, 187, 188, 189
Gingellac Run; 5
Gipps, Sir G.; 5
Gittens, Patrick; 83
Glendaruel; 87
Glenn, A.; 191
Glover; 221, 222
Glover and Co.; 155
Glover, Robert; 180
Gnarr Creek; 157, 21
Goddard, 249
Gold - Gold Aggregate; 143, 144
Gold & Aborigines; 15
Gold: Assay, 1851; 17: Ballarat; 147: Companies; 135: Cradle; 22: Diggers; 26, 220: Discovery; 18,186: Ballarat; 7, 14-24; Esmond; 21; Hargraves; 21: Exports; 146: Leads 128-131
Gold Commissioners 23; Dana: 19, Wright; 19:
Gold Licence, 23, 48, 220: Agitation; vii, 64
Gold nuggets: Ballarat; 148, 230; Black Hill; 148; Buninyong; 148; Canadian Gully; 148; Dalton's Flat; 148; Eureka; 148; Koh-i-Noor; 148; "Never Too Late to Mend"; 17; Union Jack Gully; 148; Webbville; 148;
Gold origin of; 14, 148
Gold Price, Ballarat; 135
Gold tax; 15, 32, 48
Gold yield; 143, 144, 149
Gold-broker; 6
Gold-field Reformers; 112

Gold-fields of Victoria; 131, 148
Golden Point, 8, 21, 23, 26, 27, 35, 39, 45, 49, 126, 131, 132, 135, 220, 234

Golden Point Range; 46
Goldfields agitation -
  Bendigo; 51
Goldseekers Lead; 131
Gong Gong; 8
Goodenough, Henry; 243
Goodman, S.; 195
Goold, Bishop; 163, 228,
  229, 234
Gordon; 133
Gougenheim, 260
Government Camp; 39, 37,
  66, 75, 76, 157, 220,
  245, 266, 269: Ballarat,
  64; Creswick; 62
Government House; 222
Government Gazette; 87
Government Surveyor; 18
Government Printer; vii,
  198
Graham; 195
Grain; 174
Grainger, 241-242
Grampians; 2
Grange; 19
Grant; 80, 54, 116
Gravel Pits; 33, 35, 43, 45,
  57; 66, 131, 138
Gray, Hugh; 179, 180
Gray, John W.; 54, 181
Gray, Wilson; 113
Great Dividing Range; 219
Great North-West Co.; 138
Green, Dr; 255
Green, Francis; 44, 262
Green, Samuel; 83
Green, William; 120,
Greenfield, A.M.; 172
Greenwood; 22
Greeves, Dr.; 18, 186
Gregorius; 51
Gregory - see Gregorius; 51
Greig; 49
Grenville; 118, 181, 201
Grenville College; 167
Grey, Earl; 15, 26, 28, 33,
  40
Gripe; 160
Grog-sellers; 38

Grundy, J.R.; 192
Gualter Soares, Rev; 163
Gulliver; 207
Gum Tree Flat, 45, 131,
  134
Gunn, Donald; 179
Gurner, 269
Gymnastic Reserve; 168

𝓗

Hackett, Acting Police
  Magistrate; 60
Haddon; 131, 133, 211
Hafele, John; 83
Hagan; 260
Haines; 18, 90, 93, 116
Hall, Lt; 78
Halles; 257
Halley, Rev. J.; 181
Ham, J.J.; 42
Hambrook; 105
Hamilton; 7
Hanafin, Patrick; 83
Hand-in-Hand Co.; 136
Hanly, Michael; 83
Hanmer, Mrs; 43, 85
Haphazed Lead; 131
Happy Jack; 83
Harford; 194
Hargreaves; 15, 18, 21, 32,
  186
Harmonium; 257
Harriman; 195
Harrington; 121
Harris, A.; 196
Harris, H.; 169
Harris, Sgt; 81
Harrison; 41, 43
Hart's Temperance
  Hotel, 363
Hartley, George; 246
Harvie, W.; 173
Hasleham; 42, 83, 87
Hastie, Rev. Thomas; v,
  7, 9, 10, 40
Hathorne, G.; 192
Hatter; 130
Hauser, P.; 196

Hawthorn. 248
Haverfield; 5, 6
Hay; 201
Haydon, M.D.; 174
Hayes, Captain; 234
Hayes, Catherine; 44, 234
Hayes, Timothy; 58, 98,
  100, 230, 234
Heales Ministry; 117
Heales, Richard; 117
Healy, James; 180
Hebrew Synagogue; 166
Heifer Station Creek; 19
Hell Fling Mob; 135
Hemingway and Jones; 195
Henderson; 193
Henderson, Rev. W.; 163,
  172, 253
Henty' S.G.; 19
Hepburn; 175
Hepburn, B.; 173
Hepburn, John.; 4, 5, 85,
  172, 266
Herbs; 202
Hewitt; 195
Hibernian Society; 180
Higenbotham, C.J.; 271,
  274
Hiles; 192
Hilfling; 49
Hillas, T.; 159, 172
Hiscock; 18, 21
Hiscock's; 21,23, 27, 35,
  220
Hislop. Andrew; 270
History of Victoria; 12, 40
Hitchens, Fred.; 191
Hobson, R.J.; 159
Hobson & Warner; 195
Hogart, W.; 30
Hogg, Kirtland; 192
Holloway; 5, 6
Holmes & Salter; 35
Holy Ghost College; 255
Holy Trinity, Sebastopol;
  162
Holyoake, Henry; 58, 62
Holyroyd; 274
Homan, Rev. P.; 162

Hope Bakery; 197
Hope Restaurant; 196
Hope, J.; 160
Hopkins River; 3
Horse Bazaar Hotel; 194
Horses; 17
Horsham; 229
Horticultural Society; 173
Hoskins; 260
Hospitals; 37
Hotels - first in Ballarat;
  35, 35
Hotham, Lady; 46, 52
Hotham, Sir Charles; 46,
  52, 54, 57, 58, 60, 79,
  85, 88, 90, 92, 94, 96,
  97, 106, 107, 116, 198,
  199, 207
Howe, George; 25
Howell, J.; 193
Howell, William; 40
Huddart, P.; 191
Humffray, John; 53. 58, 58,
  59, 63, 64, 68, 73, 91,
  92, 101, 102, 110, 111,
  112, 114, 115, 116, 117,
  118, 157, 162, 168, 169,
  173, 178, 186, 187, 189,
  191, 199, 206, 207, 222,
  227
Hunt, E.; 192
Hutton, Capt.; 1
Huyghue; vii, 177, 243,
  245, 247
Hyde Park Corner; 151
Hyman, L.; 195
Hynes, John; 83

I

Imigration; 32, 48
Inglis, Peter; 6
Ingram; 91
Inkermann; 130, 131
Innes, George; 6
Irish; 222
Irvine, Rev.; 5
Irving; 155, 170

Irwin, Samuel; 54, 56, 89,
  110, 159, 226-227
Irwin; 38, 60, 61, 68,
  82. 192
Isaacs; 192
Italians, 138, 224, 257:
  Carboni; 102: Claims;
  45: Design; 176:
Ivey. B.; 192
Ivey, J.; 172, 192
Ivory; 193

J

Jackson; 194
Jackson, G.; 192
Jackson, T.; 192
Jackson, W.T.; 196
James, E.; 161
James. John; 39, 120, 189
Jamieson's Hotel; 6
Jamieson's, Buninyong; 36
Jeanes; 21, 23
Jefferson; 44
Jeffrey, W. ; 192
Jessup, B.; 172
Jewellers; 45; Brentani; 20
Jewellers Shops; 135, 138,
  211, 212
Jewish Synagogue; 166
Jim Crow Ranges; 11
John O'Groat Hotel; 194
Johnston, Commissioner;
  51, 55, 59
Johnston, Isaac; 196
Johnston, J.; 172
Jones; 40, 118, 172
Jones, Charles E.; 188, 189
Jones, David; 49
Jones, Edwin; 118
Jones, J.H.; 159, 168
Jones, Joseph; 170
Jordan, W.F. ;194
Josephs, John; 100
Julien, Robert; 83
Junipar, William; 199
Just, Mr; 172

K

Kangaroo; 8
Kean, Patrick; 193
Keatch, P.; 172
Keeley's Hotel; 113
Keen; 44
Keene, J.; 192
Kelly, A.; 172
Kennedy, Thomas ; 58. 59.
  62, 64, 67, 68, 86
Kenworthy, Dr; C.J.; 69,
  70, 159, 173
Kerr; 17
King Billy*; 9
King Jonathon*; 9
King of the Splitters; 6
King, A.J.; 192
King, John; 198
King, R.; 192
King, William iv; 1
Kinnear, C.; 128
Kirk; 157
Kirk's dam; 158
Knight, J.G.; 146
Koh-i-Noor Company; 135
Kupperberg, Dr; 170

L

La Trobe, Gov. 26, 132
Labor office, Bakery Hill;
  49
Lady Barkly Lead; 131
Lake: Burrumbeet; 1, 2, 4
  Wendouree; 3, 157, 170;
  Lal Lal; 3, 4, 5, 8, 27,
  174; Creek; 6; Station ; 6
Lalor's stump; 120
Lalor, Peter; 8, 53, 62, 63,
  70, 76, 78, 83, 66, 67,
  69, 73, 4, 84, 86, 87, 90,
  99, 101, 102, 103, 104-5,
  110, 112, 114, 116, 117,
  118, 187
Lamb, Robert; 121
Land Bill; 114
Land Convention,
  Melbourne; 113

Land Legislation; 113
Land Production, 201
Land Sales; 35, 187, 191
Lang and Co.; 169
Lang, T.; 173, 191
Langlands; 92
Langlands, Henry; 79
Langley; 78
Larner, Sgt James; 214
Latham, J.; 196
Latrobe, Gov. Charles; 15, 19, 26, 33, 41, 52
Launceston; 212
Law and order of the gold fields; 29
Lazarus; 194
Lazurus, Sander; 192
Le Gould, L.; 172
Leake; 70, 192, 197
Learmonth; 174
Learmonth Brothers; v, 2, 7, 9; 10, Somerville; 3, 9, 142; Thomas; 1, 3, 68, 181
Lederderg; 20
Leggat, James; 106
Legislative Assembly; 53, 93, 101, 109, 113, 114, 116, 198
Legislative Council; 18, 27, 79, 89, 90, 94, 99, 187
Leigh; 3
Leigh Goldfield; 33
Leigh River; 27
Leonard, 175
Lesser, G.; 195
Lessmann; 70, 73, 105
Lettuces; 202
Levey, H.; 193
Levey, J.; 196
Levitt; 5
Levy, W.; 91
Lewis, Rev.; 39
Lewis, Robert; 153, 159, 160, 168, 188
Lewis, T.; 164
Lexton, 35
Library; 156
Licence burning; 64

License hunt; 50
License tax; 15
Liederkranz Society;
Lilley and Miller; 197
Lindsay; 23
Linton; 131, 133
Lister, Cornelius; 170
Little Bendigo, 35, 45
Little River; 4
Loader; 207, 208
Loader, Thomas; 113, 189
Local Court; 120, 121-124, 124, 125, 141, 205, 258
Lockhart, Fanny; 160, 260
Loder; 257
Loddon; 2
Logan; 44
London; 230; Chartered Bank; 8, 176, 197; Exchange; 133; Exhibition, 1862; 146
Lone Star of Texas; 243
Longerenong; 3
Lord; 51
Lorenz; 153
Lydiard, 30
Lynch, John; 76, 105, 240, 223, 224, 246, 247, 248
Lynn; Adam, L.;44, 159
Lynn, R.; 159
Lyon, J. Christian; 189
Lyons; 193
Lyster; 257

M

Macarthur, Col.; 70
Macarthur, Deputy Adjutant-General; 106
Macgregor, John; 120
Mackay, G.G.; 160, 168
Mackenzie,Alex.; 191
Macpherson, J.A.; 119, 120
Macrae, Donald; 168
Madden, Rev. P.; 160, 163
Magdalen House; 180
Magistrates; 44
Magpie; 204
Magpie rush (1855-6); vi

Mair, William; 30
Maize; 202
Majeroni; 260
Malakoff Lead; 131
Malcom, A.; 194
Manhood suffrage; 112
Manning, John; 69, 98 00
Markets; 202
Marks, Tommy; 234, 235
Martial Law; 91
Martin; 121, 160, 196
Masonic Hall; 266
Mathews, Charles; 44, 170
Matthews; 260
Mayors; 155
McCafferty, J.; 192
McCallum; 192
McCandlish,R.; 238, 245
McCarty, Hugh; 70
McCleverty; 192, 197
McClymont; 194
McCombie; 5, 12, 20, 40, 77, 80
McCoy, Prof.; 142
McCoy, R.O.; 163
McCrea, William; 59, 155
McCulloch Ministry; 118
McCulloch, Sir James; 117, 120, 142, 161
McDermott; 274
McDonald,Donald; 179
McDowall, James; 153, 168, 174
McFarlane & Smith; 192
McFarlane, Dr; 160
McGill, James; 70, 73 76, 85, 103, 104, 207
McGlyn, Edward; 83
McGowan; 178
McGrath; 234
McIntosh, J.; 175, 197
McIntyre, Andrew ; 56, 57, 58, 59
McIvor; 160
McKenzie, Alexander; 191
McLachlan; 7
McLaren, Alexander; 190
McLean; 193
McLeod; 175, 191

McMurdoch; 128
McNeil, John; 238, 245
McNicol, A.; 195
McPherson, Dugald; 180
McPherson, Lachlan; 193
Mears; 154
Meat price; 31
Mechanics' Institute; 168,
    169
Medwell, J.; 175
Meek; 220
Melbourne; 1, 5, 19; Gaol;
    124; *Herald*; 42, 67, 77
Mercer, Major: 3
Meredith; 36
Merri Creek; 152
Merrick; 187
Merrick; vi, 21, 22, 24
Mia-mias; 8, 39
Michie; 120, 274, 274
Michie, Archibald; 189
Miles, Richard; 156
Military troops; 65, 66:
    12th Regiment; 3, 61,
    199: 40th Regiment;
    61, 78, 93, 177, 199, 240
Milkmaid's Lead; 131
Miller; 93, 169
Milligan; 205
Milligan, Edward; 120
Milligan, Robert D. 123
Milne, Sgt-Maj.; 54
Milne; 58, 95
Mine Managers; 133
Mineralogical surveyor; 18
Miners' Association; 141
Miners Right Lead; 131
Miners; 133, 221
Mining: Ararat; 143, 144:
    ...Ballarat; 143, 144:
    Beechworth; 143, 144:
    Castlemaine; 143, 144:
    Gippsland; 143, 144:
    Maryborough; 143, 144:
    Sandhurst; 143, 144

Mining: Accident Prevent-
    ion; 141; Board; 142;
    Mining Claims; 128;

Companies; 133;
Exchange; 133, 176;
Institute; 141; Reform
Association; 141, 142;
Mining regulations; 126
Minister of Mines; 157
Miners' Exchange; 170
Minyip; 231, 235, 239
Miskelly; 121, 141
Mitchell; 18, 168, 170, 260
Mitchell, Sir Thomas; 4
Mitchison Bros; 193
Molesworth; 125, 273
Moliagul; 45
Mollison; 2
Molloy, William; 100
Monster Meeting: Bakery
    Hill; 58, 62; (1862);
    111
Montefiore, S.; 195
Montez, Lola; 44, 101;
    227, 250-257, 266
Montezuma Hotel &
    Theatre; 43, 169, 170,
    194, 261
Montgomery; 44, 260
Moore; 175, 255
Moore, E.C.; 42, 172
Moore, George; 160
Moore, Thaddeus; 82, 83
Moore, W.; 159
Moran; 71
Morgan, Mrs M.; 165, 243
Moorabool; 3, 6
Morris, D.; 160
Morrison's Station; 11
Morrison, Michael, 83
Morrison, Simon; 175
Morrison's Diggings; 23
Mortlake; 7
Morton, George; 175, 188
Morwitch, A.; 195
Morwitch, S.; 195
Mosterd; 92
Mount Misery; 86
Mount Pleasant Lead; 131
Mount, J.H.; 172
Mounted troopers; 49, 71,
    78

Mt Alexander; 2, 4
    Diggings; 28, 30, 31:
    Population; 32
Mountains: Aitkin; 1, 2;
    Blowhard; 11;
    Buninyong; 1, 2, 6, 9,
    10, 36, 219; Emu; 219
    Gambier; 19; Mercer; 3;
    Misery; 2; Pisgah; 11;
    Pleasant; 168; Rowan;
    11; Warrenheip; 10, 219
Mtezendorff; 196
Muir, Robert; 153, 159,
    169, 174
Mullins; 83
Mumby; 194
Munchhausen, 207
Munro; 194
Murchison, Roderick; 18
Murder: By Aborigines; 10;
    James Scobie; 53; Hut-
    keeper; 9, 10;
Murdering Valley; 10
Murnane; 64, 71
Murphy; 264, 265
Murphy, T.; 193, 194
Murray River; 4
Murska, Ilma de; 257
Musgrove, R.W.; 172
Music and theatre; 170
Mutton; 203, 221
Myer; 192

$\mathcal{N}$

Napier, Charlie; 120
Napoleon; 102
Narmbool run; 3
National Bank; 140, 176
National Grain Show; 175
Native Police; 19, 30, 49
Native Youth Lead; 131
Navarre; 19
Neil; 192
Neill, John; 199
Neilson, J.; 230
Nelson Shaft; 130
Neville; 3
New Chum Gully; 35, 46

New North Clunes Co.; 145, 146
New South Wales Bank; 140
New Years Day; 180
New York Wall St.; 133
Newman; 193, 194
Newspapers; 41-43
Nicholls, F.; 160
Nicholls, Henry R.; 120, 123, 128, 141, 158
Nicholls, R.U.; 173
Nicholson; 117
Nicholson, G.; 172
Nickle, Sir Robert; 70, 74, 80, 85, 90
Nightingale Lead; 131
Niquet; 160
North Grant Hotel; 197
North Grenville Mercury; 42

O

O'Brien, Smith; 252
O'Connor; 114
O'Connor, Alfred Arthur; 113, 118, 121, 129
O'Connor, D.; 168
O'Farrell, 175
O'Grady, Michael; 180
O'Groat, John; 194
O'Meara, J.; 159
O'Neil, Michael; 83
O'Neil, Thomas; 83, 200
O'Reilly; 196
O'Shanassy; 100, 117
O'Sullivan; 229
Oakden; 153
Oakey, A.; 196
Oats,; 201
Ocock, R.; 44, 160, 171, 173
Oddie, James; 23, 25, 40, 153, 159, 160, 173, 190, 197, 235, 239, 243
Oddie, T.; 197
Old Ballaarat Cemetery; 106

Old Colonists' Association; .232, 235
Old Post-office Hill; 37, 41, 177
Oliver, Mrs; 243
Oliver, A.; 170
Oliver, D.; 159, 168, 170, 193
One-Eye Gully; 131
Onions; 202
Onn, Madame; 257
Opera; 257
Opossums; 6
Orange Lodges; 190
Oranges; 202
Orphan Asylum; 161
Orton, Rev.; 40
Otway, Dr.; 46, 60, 61
Overlanders ; 4
Owen, Dr; 159
Owens; 80

P

Paddy's & Crawfish Leads; 131
Paddy's Gully; 132
Palmer, Sir J. 27, 196
Palmer; 158
Papenhagen's Store; 170
Paper scarcity; 37
Paris Bourse; 133
Park, A.S.; 160
Parliamentary representatives; 111, 187
Parrot ; 10
Pasley, Capt.; 78, 92
Pastoral settlement; 12
Pastoral times; 5
Patchell; 193
Patit, Carlotta; 257
Paul, Lt; 78, 78
Pears; 202
Pennyweight Flat, 45, 131
Perewur Station; 6
Perry, George; 170
Pettet; v, 3, 4
Pettett's Look-Out ; 11
Phelan, John; 100, 234

Phelps; 128
Phillips, John; 18, 188
Pigs; 5
Pikeman; 69, 72, 84
Pikeman's dog; 82
Pikes; 200, 248
Pincott's Dam; 158
Pinkerton and Co's; 41
Pleydell; 194
Plough; 5
Police; 88, 233, 244, 249, 250
Police Court, 41, 57, 153, 194: Buninyong; 7
Police reinforcements; 61
Polkenhorne; 196
Poole, Rev.; 167
Pope, M.M; 118
Poppet-heads; 133
Population; 212
Port Phillip; 12
Port Phillip Bay; 85, 152
Port Phillip exploration; 4
Port Phillip Heads; 209
Port Phillip Quartz Co.; 145, 146
Porter, Christopher; 160
Portland Guardian; 42
Portland; 19
Post Office; 8, 177
Post Office Hill; 177
Postmaster; 37
Potatoes; 10, 31,175, 201
Potter, J.; 160
Potter, Rev. John; 162
Potts, Capt.; 103
Poulton, Benjamin; 190
Poultry; 203
Poverty Point; 270
Powell; 239
Powell, Thomas; 191
Power, Dr; 7
Power; 255-257
Powlett, F.A.; 59
Prendergast; 114
Prentice; 4
Presbyterian church; 164
Presbyterian; 41
Price; 193

Prices in Ballarat, 1852; 31
Primrose, Mrs; 22
Prince Albert Hotel; 57
Prince Alfred; 180, 181
Prince of Wales Lead; 137
Prince Regent's Gully; 35, 46, 50, 211
Private Property Law; 35
Protectionists; 116
Public Library; 169
Puck; 84
Pyrenees; 2, 12, 15, 19, 219
Pyrites; 149

Q

Quartz: 16: Mining; 144; Claim area; 129
Queen Victoria; 1, 159
Quendo, Capt.; 78
Quin, Edward; 83
Quinlan, William; 83
Quinn; 63

R

Railway; 157, 181
Randall, T; 118
Rankin, A.B.; 159
Reade, Charles; 17
Red Hill, 35, 45, 49, 72, 135, 250, 260
Red Hill Bakery; 196
Red Jacket Co.; 137
Red Lion Brewery; 179
Red Streak, 45, 131, 250
Redan; 130, 131, 136
Redan racecourse; 136
Rede, Resident. Commissioner; 55, 59, 60, 66, 92, 100, 241, 242, 248, 249
Reed, Annie; 192
Reed, Joseph; 121
Rees; 193
Reeves, Robert; 35, 190, 19
Reid, J.; 196
Reilly, J. Gavin; 30, 230, 231, 232, 235
Reinforcements - police; 61

Religion; 7, 33-4, 39
Republicanism; 112
Reservoir; 157
Revenue; 140, 175
Reynolds; 63
Richards, Ellis; 156, 164
Richards, Lieut.; 98, 200
Richardson, Dr; 173
Richfould, William; 19
Richmond; 152
Riddle, T.C.; 190, 191
Ringrove; 153
Riot Act; 64, 91
Ristori, Adelaide; 260
Road 3; 36
Robertson, John; 83, 159
Robertson; 175, 197
Robinson's Store; 37, 38
Robinson Bailey, John; 153
Robinson, George C.; 156
Robinson, William B.; 91, 155, 159, 169, 192, 195
Robson, J.; 170
Rockfeller; 260
Rock mining 131
Rodier, W.B.; 155, 159, 169, 171, 172, 195, 248
Rogers, Judge; 121, 142, 269
Roman Catholic priests; 63
Ronaldson, D.; 194
Roony, Michael; 199
Rosenblum, 169
Ross' Creek; 3
Ross, Capt.; 3, 64, 69,73, 76 80, 83, 85, 103, 175, 206
Rotten Gully; 33
Round Water Holes; 6
Rowe; 195
Rowlands; 156, 170
Roy, Charles; 179
Royal Commission; 101
Royal George Hotel; 177
Royal Mail Hotel; 194
Royal Park; 179
Rush to Browns; 131
Rush to Carngham; 131
Russell, George; 3, 4

Russell, Rev. J.G.; 162
Russell, Phillip; 267
Ryce; 205
Ryce, James; 120, 123

S

Sabbath observances; 33
Sabbath; 142
Sadlier - Davies; 161
Sailor's Gully; 35; 46, 211
Sailor's Hill - renamed Wesley Hill; 41
Salisbury; 230
Salmon; 197
Samuels; 194
Sanctified Mob; 135
Sanderson, J.; 39
Sandhurst; 181
Sandhurst banks; 147
Sankey, R.N.; 212
Sawyers; 6
Sawyer, John; 211
Sayers; 170
Scarsdale Lead; 131
Schmedding; 4, 246
School of Mines; 141
Schools; 7, 41, 167
Schoolteacher- Bedwell; 8
Scobie, James; 53, 106, 200
Scotchman's; 35, 46, 131
Scott, Andrew; 4
Scott, Mrs; 4
Scott, W.; 155, 160, 161
Scottish; 219
Searle, W.; 194
Sebastopol; 3; 8; 74, 130, 134, 205; Fire Brigade; 171
Seekamp, Henry; 42, 86, 100, 101, 105; 227, 251, 266
Seide; 257
Sellick's Buninyong; 36
Semple, Andrew; 189
Separation Inn; 36, 235
Serjeant; 50, 117, 118, 139, 187, 235

Service, James; 188
Settlers; 30
Seven Hills; 5
Shaft sinking; 127
Shaw; 196
Shaw & Dowden; 163
Shaw, J.T.; 194
Sheehan, Luke; 83
Sheep; 17, 175
Shepherding; 127, 130
Shepherds; 7, 9, 19, 130, 193, 195
Sherard, C.W.; 120, 121
Shiel, Dr; 163
Ships: *Hannah;* 221; *Nelson;* 244
Shuter's Hill; 11
Sim, W.; 174
Simson; 4
Sinclair's Hill; 26
Sing, Luin; 194
Sitwell; 274
Six Days' Store; 197
Slattery, Archdeacon; 229
Sleep, J.T.; 172
Sleuth, Commissioner; 50
Smallpox; 9
Smeaton; 4, 5, 85, 174
Smith & Diggins; 197
Smith, A.R.; 173
Smith, H.; 170
Smith, John; 153
Smith J. T.; 35, 118
Smith, P.H.; 198
Smith, R.; 160
Smith, William C.; 15; 21; 118, 153, 158, 159, 160; 168, 170, 172, 188
Smyth; 148
Smyth, Fr Patrick; 51, 63, 68, 73, 92
Smythe's Creek; 4
Smythesdale; 9, 121, 133
Smythesdale goldfield; 33
Smythesdale Lead; 131
Smythesdale newspaper; 43
Sodawater Lead; 131
Soldiers; 61, 233

Soldier's Hill; 36, 61, 75, 197, 209, 221
Soranson, Jacob; 100
Southern Cross Flag; 62, 236, 242, 243, 246
Speciman Gully; 50, 76
Specimen Hill, 26, 199
Speed, E.; 194
Spencer; 195
Spencer St Railway; 151
Splitters; 6
Springs; 85
Squatters; 1, 11-12, 26, 30; 111
St Alipius; 51, 228, 229
St Andrew's; 163, 164, 253
St George Co. No. 2; 137
St George United Co.; 137
St James', Melbourne; 198
St John's; 162
St Mary's Mount; 255
St Patrick's Cathedral, Ballarat; 253, 254, 256
St Patrick's Cathedral, Melbourne; 154
St Patrick's College; 255
St Patrick's Day; 160
St Paul's Church; 79, 162, 197
Stainbank; 154
Standard & Trumpeter; 190
Star Hotel; 67, 104, 105
Star; 190
Stars and Stripes; 243
State prisoners; (*see Eureka)* 85, 100-101, 206
Station Peak; 10
Shaw; 196
Stawell, Attorney-General; 60, 94, 198
Steam machinery; 131, 132
Steam driven batteries; 133
Steinfeld, E.; 155, 170
Stephen, George Milner; 46
Stephen, Sir George; 114
Stephans; Wilberforce; 274

Stewart, Alex.; 194
Stewart, Donald; 6
Stewart, Dr J.; 153, 159, 168, 172, 174, 195
Stieglitz; 121, 133
Stirling's Hawking Dray; 37
Stock trading; 133
Stock-rider; 6
Stock; 140
Stoddart; 170
Stone Flagging; 152
Stone Quarry Lead; 131
Storekeepers; 220: Barkers & Evans; 160, 176; Campbell, D.S.; 7; Clegg & Bailey; 270; Shannahan, 70
Stower; 170
Strachan; 18, 100, 175
Strathloddon Station; 20
Straw; 175
Streets: Albert; 152, 164; Aldergate; 265; Armstrong; 41, 152, 162, 164, 166; Ascot; 160; Barkly; 49, 165, 166; Beverin:165; Bridge; 8, 131, 152, 156, 224, 230; Burnbank; 164; Camp; 44, 72, 221; Chancery Ln; 21; Creswick Rd; 9, 20; Dana; 35, 41, 165, 167; Dawson; 166, 167; Doveton; 221; Durham; 43; Drummond; 159; Dyte's Pd; 167; East; 63, 167; Esmond; 43; Eureka; 21, 45, 53, 72, 105; Eyre; 165; Flinder's Ln; 79; Grant; 166; Grenville; 221; Hill; 221; Humffray; 42, 44, 45, 63, 156, 162, 164, 166, 167; 219; Lydiard; 9, 35, 41, 46, 220, 249; Lyons; 165; Macarthur; 164; Main Rd; 8, 41, 43, 57, 66, 70, 71, 74, 104, 105,

152, 156, 166, 220, 227;
Mair; 220, 221, 222,
249; Market Sq; 41; Mile
End Rd; 152, 154, 159,
161, 164, 165; Peel; 131;
Pleasant; 166; Queen; 72;
Skipton; 152, 166;
Spencer; 151; Stawell;
72; Raglan; 21, 234;
Sturt; 8, 9, 46, 72, 141,
152, 154, 156, 159, 162,
166, 167, 221, 224, 230,
258; Swanston; 89; Vic-
toria; 42, 45, 63, 156,
161, 238; Webster; 221;
Wills; 234
Stretch, Dr; 255
Strongman, J.; 160
Strzelecki, Count; 18
Stubbs & Co.; 195
Sturt, E.P.; 59
Sugar price; 31
Sulky; 46
Surveyors- 1, 153: David-
son; 130; Wall; 156
Sunnyside Woollen Mills;
241
Sutton, Rev. W.; 166
Swag; 221, 222
Swamp Lead; 131
Sweeney, Daniel; 155, 168,
172, 193
Swindells, Herbert; 23, 25
Syme, Ebenezer; 60
Symmons, Frank; 83

T

Tait, George; 156
Talbot; 118, 181, 201
Talbot, Mr; 131, 160
Tarleton; 60
Tartakover, M.; 196
Tarte, A.A.; 160
Tasmania; 19; 212
Taylor; 157, 193
Taylor, Commissioner; 62
Taylor, James; 177
Taylor, Rev. T.; 41

Taylor, W.; 3
Tea price; 31
Telegraph; 177
Temperance; 49, 263
Tent; 219
Terrible Gully; 46, 130,
131
Terry, L.; 162
Thakery, Rev.J.R.; 161
Thatcher, C; 196, 250, 262
The Camp; 66
The Herald; 84, 90, 96
Theatres; 43, 156: Charlie
Napier; 173; Royal; 170
Thomas; 193, 194, 196
Thomas, Capt.; 78, 199
Thomas, J.; 164, 196
Thomas, T.; 196
Thompson, Dr; 1
Thompson, W.; 158
Thomson, J.R.; 53
Thonen, E.; 81, 82, 83
Thornton; 21, 23
Tidmarsh; 196
Tillage; 201
Timbering; 220
Tolhurst, C.E.; 192, 193
Tom the Blacksmith; 246
Tontine Theatre; 43-44
Towle, E.; 170
Town Boundaries; 152
Trade and Customs; 187
Trading Companies
Statute; 43
Train G.F.; 85
Tramways; 132, 133
Traps; 50
Treason Trials; 100
Tree, Ellen; 44
Trench, Judge Robery; 261,
266
Trewin, W.; 195
Tristram; 160
Troopers - mounted; 49
Troopers Arms Hotel; 35
Troops - reinforcements; 60
Tulloch, William; 153
Tunbridge, C.; 173
Tuohy, Michael; 100

Turner; 266
Turner of Golden Point; vi
Turner, Richard; 21, 22,
24, 25
Turnips; 202
Turpie, D.; 170
Tuthill; 274
Tuxen & Co.; 195
Tweedie, W. ; 261, 262
Twentyman, J.; 160
Tyree; 194

U

Unicorn Hotel; 178
Union Bank; 176
United Hand-in-Hand Co.;
29, 132
United States Hotel; 195,
197

V

Vale, William 118, 119,
167, 188
Valiant, Lt-Col.; 70
Vallins, James; 210
Vallins; 211
Vegetables; 211, 202
Vennik, Jan; 100
Vern, Frederick; 58, 63, 68,
69, 73, 76, 78, 81, 84,
85, 88, 90, 90, 99, 102,
103, 104, 206, 207, 208;
252
Verner; 5
Vickers, Isaac; 156
Victor, John; 110, 167; 267
Victoria: Bank; 140; Hotel;
196; Lead; 131; Separa-
tion; 5, 47; Theatre; 43,
114, 197; 250
Victorian Constitution; 109
Victorian Land League;
113
Vignolles, Samuel de; 267
'Vinegar Hill'; 73
Volunter Corps; 171

W

Wainwright; 213
Waldie; v; 3, 4, 9
Walker; 195
Walker, J.; 170
Walker, R.T.; 164
Walker, Susanna; 193
Wall; 205
Wall, John; 120, 123, 156
Wall, Joseph; 199
Wallace, Major; 171, 172
Walsh, 212, 274
Walters, H.; 193
Wanliss, T.D.; 53, 192;
227, 247
Wardens Office; 177
Warner, James; 83
Warrenheip; 3, 4, 5, 6, 10,
62, 81, 174, 233
Warrnambool; 198, 233
Washdirt; 136
Washing; 220
Washington Hotel; 195
Watchmaker : Logan; 44;
Water Committee; 158
Water supply; 158
Waterfall; 6
Waterholes; 8
Watson, Meredith; 36
Watson, W.R.; 161
Waugh, Rev. W.; 165
Waverley Park; 3
Wayne; 192
Webb; 274
Webster, J.; 193, 243, 248
Weekes; 63, 252
Welcome Nugget; 45, 145,
176
Welcome Stranger; 45
Wellington Shaft; 130
Welsh; 5, 6, 167, 227
Welsh Company; 132
Welsh, Paddy; 220
Welsh, P.W.; 35, 190, 191
Welshman's Lead; 131
Wendouree; 8, 197
Were, J.H.; 133
Werribee; 10
Wesley Church; 142, 173
Wesley Hill; 41

Wesleyans; 39; Sailor's
Hill; 41; Ministers -
Lewis; 39; Orton; ; 40
West, T.; 196
Westerby; 58, 59
Westgarth; 13, 27, 100,
101, 147
Westminster Bridge; 151
Whatley; 63
Wheat; 1, 5, 175, 201, 202
Wheeldon; 139, 160
Wheeler, D.D.; 42, 190
Whim; 132
Whip; 132
Whitcombe, W.P.; 172
White Flat; 32, 35, 9, 46,
128, 130, 131, 205
White Flat Company; 128
White Horse; 46, 130, 131,
205
Whitechapel; 154
Whitfield, George; 194
Whittaker; 156
Whitty, G.; 196
Wilhelmj, 257
Wilkens, Thomas; 191
Wilkes; 171
Willern; 91
Williams; 194
Williams & Young; 177
Williams, Justice; 44, 269,
270, 271
Williams, Theophpilus;
240
Williams, Thomas; 91, 92
Williamson; 192
Wills, Dr; 91, 178
Wills, William John; 178,
179
Wilson Bros.; 196
Wilson, George; 21, 23, 24
Wilson, James; 190-1; 242
Wilson, John; vii
Wimmera; 3, 213, 229,
230, 239
Windermere; 176
Windlass; 220
Windsor Hotel; 43

Winter's Flat; 3, 22, 39,
132
Winter, John; 3
Wise, Capt.; 74, 76, 78, 85,
106, 199, 248
Wittkowski; 194, 195
Woady Yaloak; 11
Wombat; 8
Women; 34, 37, 38, 40;
220
Wood Beilby, J.; 18
Wood, Harrie, ;vii, 121,
129, 141, 142, 160
Wood, Mr; 131, 134, 142
Woodlands Run; 213
Woodward, W.; 21-23
Wool; 12, 174
Wooley; 7
Woolshed Lead; 131
Wrestling; 179
Wright; 100, 274
Wrigley; 194
Wrixon, Judge; 44, 90 ,
121, 262, 267
Wye; 110
Wyndholm; 4
Wynne, E.A.; 172

Y

Yaldwin; 2
Yarrowee; vi, 8, 25, 26
Yarowee Creek; 57, 220
Yarra River; 152
Yarrowee Hotel; 193
Yates; 114, 205
Yates, John; 113, 120, 121
Yott, P.; 197
You-Yangs; 10
De Young, A.S.;193, 195
Young, F.; 168
Young, Frederick; 155, 169
Young, Mark; 180
Yuille's station; v, 3, 6
Yuille's Swamp; 3, 24,
157, 197, 221
Yuille, William C.; 2